LANGUAGES OF LAW

LAW IN CONTEXT

Editors: Robert Stevens (University of California, Santa Cruz),
William Twining (University College, London) and Christopher
McCrudden (Lincoln College, Oxford)

ALREADY PUBLISHED

Atiyah's Accidents, Compensation and the Law (Fourth Edition), Peter Cane
Company Law and Capitalism (Second Edition), Tom Hadden
Karl Llewellyn and the Realist Movement (reissue), William Twining
Cases and Materials on the English Legal System (Fifth Edition), Michael
    Zander
Computers and the Law, Colin Tapper
Tribunals and Government, J. A. Farmer
Government and Law (Second Edition), T. C. Hartley and J. A. G. Griffith
Land, Law and Planning, Patrick McAuslan
Landlord and Tenant (Second Edition), Martin Partington
How to do Things with Rules (Second Edition), William Twining and
    David Miers
Evidence, Proof and Probability (Second Edition), Richard Eggleston
Family Law and Social Policy (Second edition), John Eekelaar
Consumers and the Law (Second Edition), Ross Cranston
Law and Politics, Robert Stevens
Obscenity, Geoffrey Robertson
Labour Law (Second Edition), Paul Davies and Mark Freedland
Charities, Trusts and Social Welfare, Michael Chesterman
The Law-Making Process (Second Edition), Michael Zander
An Introduction to Law (Third Edition), Phil Harris
Sentencing and Penal Policy, Andrew Ashworth
Law and Administration, Carol Harlow and Richard Rawlings
Legal Foundations of the Welfare State, Ross Cranston
British Government and the Constitution, Colin Turpin
Sexual Divisions in Law, Katherine O'Donovan
The Law of Contract, Hugh Collins
Regulation and Public Law, Robert Baldwin and Christopher
    McCrudden
Freedom of Information, Patrick Birkinshaw
Remedies in Contract and Tort, Donald Harris
Trusts Law, Graham Moffat and Michael Chesterman
Courts and Administrators, M. J. Detmold
Consumer Protection, Iain Ramsay
Subjects, Citizens, Aliens and Others, Ann Dummett and Andrew Nicol
New Directions in European Community Law, Francis Snyder
Reconstructing Criminal Law, Nicola Lacey, Celia Wells and Dirk
    Meure

Languages of Law

From Logics of Memory to Nomadic Masks

PETER GOODRICH

Senior Lecturer in Law at the University of Lancaster

WEIDENFELD AND NICOLSON
London

George Weidenfeld and Nicolson Ltd
91 Clapham High Street, London SW4 7TA

ISBN 0 297 82009 5 cased
ISBN 0 297 82024 9 paperback

Photoset by Deltatype Ltd, Ellesmere Port
Printed in Great Britain by
Butler & Tanner Ltd, Frome & London

CONTENTS

PREFACE

The common law has presented itself historically as a system of memories: the law is tradition and it is precedent but more than that it is immemorial usage; it is practice reverting to 'time out of mind', custom that language alone remembers. If the authority of law is predicated upon the repetition of practices that exceed the memory of man, those practices have the status of law by virtue of the form of their custody, by virtue that is of the institutional language of tradition. It is for that reason that the language of law has always been presented as being more than mere language and other than the simple vernacular. It is, in doctrinal terms, the language of tradition as such, a veridical language that not only carries a store of ideal meanings but is also itself a model for all other forms of language. The language of law is depicted as a language of record, a perfect language that harbours true reference, that corresponds to real events, that is itself a monument, a memorial, a vestige or a relic of previous wisdom and prior judgment. The inhabitants of the legal institution are thus custodians not only of a tradition of rules and of texts but also of linguistic forms and of techniques of interpretation that will unlock the memories of legal language. Within the language of tradition the lawyer is supposed to uncover the forms of life and of ethical practice that the institution was established to record and repeat. The institution was not only to reproduce the memorials of an authorised life, the reliquary of which legal language was the register, but it was also, as a lived and living tradition, to produce, to create new forms.

The argument of this book is that the common law tradition has failed to understand itself as a language and imagery of transmission, of the transmission of a mode of institutional life and of all that the institution implies. It implies the affective attachment of the individual to the order of institutional existence. It implies also the continued creativity, the continued life and productive power of that order, of that plan, of the 'law of the persistence of the plan'. If we begin, however, to piece together an intellectual history of the common law it is apparent above all else that the common law has repressed the productive power of the plan; it has failed to understand or transmit an understanding of the memorial language as a code, as an index of lived existence, of historical forms that cannot be emulated but must be transformed, reinterpreted, repeated in the genuine sense of the practice of tradition, which is to say taken up as an object both of conversation and conversion. The narrative that this study takes up is the narrative of an insular tradition, a history in which the common law denied any authoritative place to scholarly commentary or intellectual interpretation of the tradition. There is no place in the common law institution for a jurisprudence that genuinely interprets as opposed to merely systematises the tradition. In that sense the tradition is one of decay: it exists not as an historical form but as the decaying sense of the institution, a mute pattern of emulation and of imitation. The memories and techniques of the common law abolish the distance necessary to interpretation, and through denying any institutional place to an intellectual discourse of commentary the tradition comes to treat memory as pure surface: as a collection of images without depth or reference, as virtual forms of life, monuments, models, mementoes.

The surface of a tradition is its language and that language is only ever an index, a ruin of a structure, of a lived past and of the order appropriate to it. In denying any place to scholarship and to history the common law tradition closes the possibility of dialogue with the past and ironically uses memory as the means of forgetting: the memorial or monumental language is precisely a language outside of lived time and its material sites, detached from the possibility of any critical account of the fealties of things to their place. The common law does not represent or remember the past; it repeats it by living it, it suppresses it through the immobile memory of the mirror, through duplication. The order of rules becomes the order of things but it is an order that is superimposed upon the living so as to render it homogeneous, a reproduction, an image in the glass. The present study endeavours to understand the religious life of the law, of the institution, as an historical ruin, as the legible surface or marked text of a lived world. The structures of positive law are mobile structures; they exist to be deconstructed, to be reinhabited, to be read and so to be changed.

P.G.   28.9.89   Edinburgh

ACKNOWLEDGEMENTS

How much did it cost? In immediate terms I am grateful to the British Academy, the Nuffield Foundation and Newcastle University Small Research Grants Committee for funding diverse aspects of this research. I am also indebted to the Economic and Social Research Committee for funding a year's release from teaching.

While researching and writing the book I have tried out versions of several chapters at a variety of institutions and seminars. My thanks to Pertti Ahonen and the Department of Politics, University of Helsinki; to Bob Benson and Loyola Law School, Los Angeles; to Lester Mazor and Hampshire College, Amherst; to Fiona Cownie and the Faculty of Law, University of Leicester; to Chuck Yablon and faculty at Cardozo Law School; to Bobbie Kevelson and the Center for Semiotic Research, Pennsylvania State University; and to Tom Gibbons, Anthony Ogus and the Faculty of Law, University of Manchester.

In more personal terms, I owe thanks to John Brigham, Raymond Coulon, Sarah Cracknell, David Galbraith, Anne Griffiths, Christine Harrington, Bernard Jackson, Bobbie Kevelson, Eric Landowski, Ewan Maclean, Bob Moles, Peter Rush and Ronnie Warrington for valuable comments on and criticisms of aspects of this work and its author. My especial thanks to Tony Carty, Costas Douzinas, Neil Duxbury, Susie Gibson, Alexander Goodrich, Yifat Hachamovitch, Tim Murphy and David Walliker for extensive encouragement and for moving me on. In many instances I no longer remember the source of the specific ideas discussed and later transcribed. David Walliker's exhibition, '*Pro Persona Mori*' provides the images that form the basis of the final chapter and discussion with the artist formed the strategies of the accompanying text. Yifat read the whole text many times and greatly improved its health, for which my thanks again, as ever.

P.G.

I

Introduction

The more radical tendency of contemporary critical legal studies has been one of a movement away from grand theory and from the more abstract forms of jurisprudence. The old theories, the sullenly descriptive theories of 'law in general', the political jurisprudence that would offer programmes, maps of how legal studies should be conducted, in short the jaded pedagogy of theory:[1] the patronising

---

1   The didactic conception of theory is distinctive for its externalisation of the question of theory: theory relates to the other, to the research of others, the teaching of others. Theory, for the didact, relates to the social, the political, the legal as external identities, unities which, precisely by virtue of being unities, can be acted upon externally. Their direction can be changed, their harbingers – their representatives – can be educated, their future improved. It is never clear upon what scale of the good or indeed in which territory of progress this improvement takes place. For recent examples we may cite D. N. MacCormick, 'The Democratic Intellect and Law' (1985) 5 *Legal Studies* 172; see also D. N. MacCormick and W. Twining, 'Theory in the Law Curriculum' in W. Twining (ed.), *Legal Theory and Common Law* (1986, Oxford), especially pages 241–2 where, under the title of 'theorizing as abstraction', we learn that 'one can [look] on theorizing as nothing more than the business of asking and tackling general or abstract questions. Typically such questions have somehow or other come to be matters of interest or concern at a more or less particular or concrete level . . .' Such a defensive (and indolent) view of theory is not confined to liberal jurisprudence. Equally didactic in tone and purpose is A. Hunt, 'The Critique of Law; What is Critical about Critical Legal Theory' (1987) 14 *Journal of Law and Society* 5. 'To return to the issue of whether the critical *school* should pursue the project of developing a theory is to pose the choice between theory and conversation' (p. 9). In other words, back at the *schola*, in the classroom, at school, we learn that we can either have a theory or not, we can choose, one commodity amongst many: maybe something political this week? Hunt's own preferred option: 'I have urged that the critical school cannot avoid the challenge of elaborating a distinctive theory of law' (p. 18). See further A. Hunt, 'Juris-prudence, Philosophy of Legal Education: A Response to Neil MacCormick' in

dogmas of the truth, of what ought to be taught, have given way to critical theories of the particular. Critical legal theory might well come eventually to be defined as the theory of particular laws,[1] its concern being to read and re-read what Foucault (following Kant) termed the 'conditions of possibility' of particular texts, legal texts, and here the texts of the common law. In this form, theory is not concerned with the classical but intrinsically uninteresting questions of what law in general is, or with how one can acquire an objective knowledge of law, but rather with the historical and ontological issue of how law is lived, what are its habitual forms, what is the deep structure that allows its repetition in ever different forms.

If it is anything 'in general', Western law is tradition, the tradition of inescapable institutions and of institutional life. It has a history but much more it has memories: narratives of an habitual past being of the essence of legal justificatory argument as a discourse of precedent. The logic of law could well be presented as a structure of memory, while a rhetoric of the immemorial and of the remembered is the stylistic key to the authority of legal texts. The first part of the present work, 'Memory, Precedent and Writing Systems of Law', is concerned with the forms that legal memory takes: with its repetition, its inscription, its representation. To the abstract memories of the archive we have therefore to add the oral memories of lived law, the insignia of repetition as the law relentlessly inhabits everyday institutional existence. The theory of legal memory has to take account not simply of the opposition between the oral and the scriptural as law, but equally of the structure of memory, of how the body remembers, of how the emotional body is made subject to law. That is a question of mnemonics and of the aesthetics of law, a question of the oral and of the visual quite as much as it is of the text and the abstract authority of a scripture. The first part of the work thus examines the nature of a particular tradition, that of the common law, and analyses the practical and material forms that this tradition has taken: what are its rituals, its repetitions, its texts, its symbols, its

(1986) 6 *Legal Studies* 292. Mark Kelman, *A Guide to Critical Legal Studies* (1987, Cambridge Mass.).

1   In addition to R. M. Unger, *The Critical Legal Studies Movement* (1987, Cambridge Mass.), the first major theoretical study of this scope – that is, which has the vision and will to theorise the particular as the particular – is C. Douzinas, S. McVeigh and R. Warrington, *Postmodern Jurisprudence* (1990, London). There is also A. Carty (ed.), *Postmodern Law* (1990, Edinburgh).

icons, its other media of circulation and inscription? These are questions which Derrida has linked to the question of writing in general, that of grammatology or the history and science of all forms of graphic inscription.[1] In grammatological terms the legal tradition, as we have inherited it, is a product of the technology of print. For that reason the historical materials examined in the course of Part One of this study concentrate on the sixteenth and early seventeenth centuries, on the legal literature and curricula manuals, the first printed materials, the first widely available and visible (though less often legible) textual artefacts of the common law world.

An analysis of the material forms through which English law has been memorised, and more significantly 'presenced', necessarily entails an analysis of language. It is language in the end which remembers, it is language which bears tradition and it is through language, through the dense prose of the text, or through the phonic rhythm of the oral history that we remember not simply the appearance of the past but also its discourse, namely that which must have been lived for that appearance and that speech to be possible. In discourse we read language to recollect not simply what was said but the context of what was said, a copious linguistic context that incorporates the memories and the lives, the routines and the emotions, the successes and the failures that are harboured in any discourse, in any act of transmission. They form the history of the present and it is precisely that history which is encountered not only in the speech of the law, in its liturgical annunciation in court or through the media, but also in the physical presence of law, in these words, those books, that building or alternatively in this dock, before

---

1 Grammatology studies the history of systems of inscription: 'if "writing" signifies inscription and especially the durable institution of a sign (and that is the only irreducible kernel of the concept of writing), writing in general covers the entire field of linguistic signs' (J. Derrida, *Of Grammatology* (1976, Baltimore), p. 44). Grammatology allows us to question the significance of the fact that law is written, that in being written it shares the qualities of writing in general: it mixes genres, it is carried by language, it is rhetorically organised, it develops systems of reference and of self-reference and more. We might note also that history and law were the earliest uses of writing and that in consequence either a history or a science of writing is somewhat ironic: 'the science of writing should . . . look for its object at the roots of scientificity. The history of writing should turn back toward the origin of historicity. A science of the possibility of science? A science of science which would no longer have the form of *logic* but that of *grammatics*? A history of the possibility of history . . . ?' (Ibid., pp. 27–8.)

this judge and subject to this mode of address. Thus how was it when you first appeared before the law? Not only what did you wear, how did you speak, what time was it, whose time was it, but also where were you, before which tradition of the law, in front of which bench, in view of which insignia and what icons of legal presence? What century is this, what present?

The question of language, which must now be taken to include all the other systems of signs – of architecture, dress, geography, ceremony, aura and technology – that accompany legal tradition, that prejudge the text as a legal text, the spoken word as the word of the law, that question of language is the question of the institution. To ask what tradition is this, is to ask what institution, what form of life, what road to death? These are again questions of memory, the issue is that of how does one come to know a tradition, an institution, a particular law? The most general thesis presented in this study approaches that issue of tradition on two levels. At the everyday level of tradition as a form of life, the legal tradition is a secular version of Christian morality, a tradition of rules that has been well depicted by Nietzsche as being at base a systematic attack upon the senses, upon bodily pleasures and upon hedonism in all its material forms.[1] At the level of structure, our account of the theological character of the legal tradition takes the form of the argument that the moralistic nature of common law, its antipathy towards desire, is necessarily linked to its forms of memory, its imaginary histories, its particular quality of traditionalism. In the *Philebus* Plato links desire to memory and to the representation of pleasure. Foucault, in his commentary on the *Philebus*, depicts Plato as concluding that 'the appetite . . . can be aroused only by the representation, the image or the memory of the thing that gives pleasure; he concludes that there can be no desire except in the soul . . . it is the soul and only the soul that can, through

1 The principal texts are: F. Nietzsche, *Beyond Good and Evil* (1923, Edinburgh), ch. 5; idem, *The Genealogy of Morals* (1910, Edinburgh), essay 2; idem, *The Will to Power*, I (1909, Edinburgh); idem, *The Twilight of the Idols and The Antichrist* (1915, Edinburgh). From the last mentioned, to take one example: discussing morality as the enemy of nature and arguing that the Church has always endeavoured to annihilate its enemies, the passions and the desires: 'Inasmuch as it says "God sees into the heart of man", it says No to the profoundest and most superior desires of life and takes God as the enemy of life. The saint in whom God is well pleased, is the ideal eunuch. Life terminates where the "Kingdom of God" begins' (p. 30). The point is discussed in N. Simmonds, *The Decline of Juridical Reason* (1984, Manchester), pp. 38–9.

memory, make present the thing that is to be desired and thereby arouse the *epithumia* [desire]'.[1] The links suggested between desire and memory and between memory and representation or image are crucial. The argument to be pursued can be rehearsed quite briefly. In attacking the legitimacy of desire and particularly in circumscribing the domains and occasions of bodily pleasure, the common law embarked upon a rigorous and unrelenting attack upon the history of everyday life. The evident aversion of the lawyer, of the moralist, to the sensuality of material existence, to the history of the body, to philosophical hedonism in all its forms – as semantic play, as the pleasure of the text, as the theatre of lived history – is eventually to be understood, can only be understood, as an escape from memory, a flight from the past as it was spoken and lived, an exodus from history if by history we mean the memory of what was lived, recuperated through material structures, through the body and through discourse.[2]

The argument pursued in Part One of this study is comparative and historical; precisely in being comparative and historical it is critical. It begins with an ironic analysis, an allegory, of failure. In Chapter Two we examine in detail a specific text and a specific failure. Through an extended reading of Abraham Fraunce's radical and polemic study of the (absent) logic of the common law, the *Lawiers Logike*, first published in 1588, it is possible to trace through Fraunce's failure, through the demise of his text unacknowledged by his contemporaries and unread by the profession, the failure to establish any tradition of critical commentary or scholarly interpretation within the English legal institution and curriculum as it emerged in the second half of the sixteenth century. Fraunce's failure to establish a comparative and historical scholarship of English law, his failure to challenge successfully the narrow professionalism and intellectual insularity of the common law, its myth of immemorial reason and of a distinctive and mysterious logic peculiar to English law, was, it will be argued, a symptomatic failure. Fraunce's exclusion from the professional curriculum and reading of law is at one and the same time a social and an institutional question. At a

---

1 M. Foucault, *The Uses of Pleasure* (1985, New York), p. 45.
2 The classic example of such a history is of course F. Braudel, *The Mediterranean and the Mediterranean World* (1972, New York). For synoptic essays, see J. Le Goff (ed.), *La Nouvelle Histoire* (1988, Paris); also J. Le Goff, *Histoire et mémoire* (1988, Paris).

social level he was not part of the establishment; he was 'a university man', a scholar, an intruder upon the Inns of Court and the mystic knowledges of England's (self-proclaimed) 'third university'. At a deeper level his failure to fit in was an institutional question, a failure that left its mark on the tradition that developed in the early seventeenth century. Fraunce could not succeed because the English profession had no institutional site or role for a discourse of scholarship and of interpretation of the law. There was no jurisprudence in the continental sense, no scholars of the common law whose labour could be put to use in the legal system itself. The tradition that developed over the disappearance of Fraunce's work is marked precisely by the absence of any place, any site or institutional role, for scholarship and interpretation in its stronger senses. It is not a tradition that encourages thought, let alone comparative, historical or critical thought: it polices the references, the texts, the memories of the profession and guards them against the outside world. The tradition that emerges upon the back of the anti-intellectualism of Coke and of Davies is a borrowed tradition, a tradition that lacks imagination but has great wealth in terms of the rigour of its institutional effects. The English tradition examined in detail in Chapter Three, draws its language, its method and its institutional power from the ruins of the monasteries and the Roman Church.[1] It is an Anglican tradition, an Engish catholicism, a legal theology of the eternal presence, the establishment of law that takes the place of Fraunce's rather plebeian and puritanical concern with a logic of our knowledge and memory of law.

The divine presence of law is not a novel idea in either the common law or the civilian traditions. Its role, however, is always a specific one. In the common law tradition there was never any successful political revolution to challenge the place of Coke's 'spirit of the law' and its sacral texts. The Anglican legal tradition came to embody both the divine and the secular laws; the common law effectively absorbed the other jurisdiction in the same manner that the Crown – the hieroglyph of all our laws[2] – absorbed the Church. In political terms, that pre-revolutionary tradition was and is vested in the monarch and in Parliament, in the forced institutional union of the

---

1 The classic formulation is R. Hooker, *Of the Laws of Ecclesiastical Polity*; (1969, London); for Book VIII there is now ibid. (1989, Cambridge).

2 For commentary on this point see E. Kantorowicz, *The King's Two Bodies* (1957, New Jersey), ch. 1. See also T. Nairn, *The Enchanted Glass* (1988, London).

temporal, spiritual and legal peerage, of the lords and the commons. It is a *de facto* union, something that happened and continues to happen, an unwritten constitution, a constitution undisturbed by any formal constraint or requirement of justificatory discourse that will measure up to constitutional rules of reason or rational debate. In that sense it is purely English, a tacit form of law, a tradition of manners, a tyrannically repressed jurisdiction. In Chapter Four we examine the only available evidence of an English legal constitution, namely the writing systems and textual forms of law that were made explicit with the advent of print. What were the rules of composition, of circulation, of sending and of receipt of these texts; what theory of language unified them and made them into the memories, the monuments of common law? What explicit or implicit fealties of meaning, what textual fidelities have marked the law in the absence of any constitution, in the absence of any tradition of commentary or jurisprudence of interpretation, in the absence of any institutionally empowered legal scholarship, in the presence of a law predicated upon pure practice?[1]

The question of meaning has always been a question of law, a question of the legitimacy of reference, of faith in the linguistic encoding of reality, faith in the capacity of words to act as the notation of things. The faith attributed to and necessary for the working of any existent language system is a question of its legitimacy; the lawfulness not only of its reference but also of its use is predicated upon its source, its institutional provenance, its badge or other insignia of office. In Chapter Five we move to question that legitimacy, to deconstruct its narrative of unremitting and successful custody and transmission in the postmodern terminology of the fragmentation of tradition and the supersession of the unity of language and of law. The legal tradition founds the legitimacy of social speech; it institutes an order of lawful discourse and prohibits those heterodoxies of speech or writing that are deemed to threaten the security of legal meaning or the order of

---

1 For one recent example, see *D and F Estates* v. *Church Commissioners* [1989] WLR 627, per Lord Bridge (discussing the much litigated question of the recoverability of economic loss in tort): 'My Lords, I do not intend to embark upon the daunting task of reviewing the wealth of . . . authority which bears, directly or indirectly, on the question . . . My abstention may seem pusillanimous, but it stems from a recognition that the authorities, as it seems to me, speak with such an uncertain voice that, no matter how searching the analysis to which they are subject, they yield no clear and conclusive answer.'

legal and political reason. Making use of the example of the contractual basis of all social forms and so of all communication, an example dear to Hooker and the Anglican tradition, we move to deconstruct that unifying myth of an agreed sociality, a contracted meaning and law. Making use of the most sophisticated of the proponents of social contract theory, namely Jean Jacques Rousseau, it is possible to trace within the contract and its theory of origin and transmission a residual linguistic theology, a contractarian semantics which at one of its roots posits a law prior to language, an order of contract which precedes the agreement of reference that is noted in words, a covenant that is prior to both speech and writing, an absolute law. The law continues to haunt the languages of contemporaneity, that contract still holds us; it is the institution we inhabit, the mask we wear.

Part Two, 'Language, Image, Sign and Common Law', moves from a specific history, that of the narrative memory of common law, to particular texts. The movement is one from theory as an analysis of the possibilities of perception (*theorein*) to its specific usages in the reconstruction of historical texts. The postmodern thesis that we are less contracting subjects of law than contracted relics, spectral forms of an Enlightenment project that history has overtaken and overturned, requires a remapping of the entire process of reading tradition. The contract, which we still inhabit – for how else could we speak, write or prepare?[1] – frames both the times and places of our discourse. It is that mordant sense of being contracted by the very geography of our lives, by the institutional site of discourse, by a built environment through which our language must always pass, that is the underside to the specific analyses of Part Two of this study. In Chapter Six it is argued in relation to the analysis of a series of transcripts that a linguistics of courtroom speech must begin with an account of the liturgical site of legal speech and ask specifically what it is that must have been lived for this speech to occur: what has the subject experienced to become subject to this confused sounding of an inescapable speech, that of law? The question of the institutional site of annunciation, of speech, of texts and of images recurs in relation to each of the forms of transmission that is analysed in Part Two. Might it not in the end be argued that it is the background that is more

1   See Derrida, *Writing and Difference* (1978, London), pp. 284–92, well discussed in W. T. Murphy, 'Memorising Politics of Ancient History' (1987) 50 *Modern Law Review* 384.

important than the image, the statement, the archive itself? It is the frame, the distances, the absences, the designation of inside and outside that the frame implies that has to be understood in the text itself.

The question is therefore one of presupposition. What is brought to this text, prior to its reading, in advance of – or, better, in excess of – its literal language? What constituting past has singled out this place, this site, this language as being a specific object, a specific law? So also, in everyday terms, what has been suffered for the subject to look like this, to feel like this, to have this sense and sensibility? Chapter Seven approaches this question in a most detailed analysis of the tradition that precedes a common law text. The tradition is, in its most explicit form, that of English law, and to rest with that single simple observation allows us to look for signs of Englishness in the pretexts, the presuppositions, of our reading of the common law. What are its signs, its icons, its images? We could do worse than begin from the outside, by looking at the insular tradition through foreign eyes. Think of Nietzsche's description, in *Beyond Good and Evil*, in a discussion of respectability and the English vice of anti-intellectualism: 'In the end, they all want *English* morality to be recognised as authoritative, inasmuch as mankind, or the "general utility", or "the greatest happiness of the greatest number", – no! the happiness of *England*, will be best served thereby. They would like, by all means, to convince themselves that the striving after *English* happiness, I mean after *comfort* and *fashion* and in the highest instance, a seat in Parliament, is at the same time the true path of virtue; in fact, that in so far as there has been virtue in the world hitherto, it has just consisted in such striving'[1] – in the rusticity, honesty and manners that form the unwritten creed, the tacit image, of English gentility. That hidden Englishness, that backgame, that Anglican nature is the focus of a lengthy reading through the text and judgment of a peculiarly English case.

If law binds, it binds deceptively, it binds unconsciously and it binds affectively – through acceptance, through the identities of speech and the masks of personality rather than explicitly through any paramilitary invasion of everyday life. The path of the law is that of experience, in the words of one American judge. Could we not take that to mean that we live the law, that what is interesting and at the

---

1 F. Nietzsche, *Beyond Good and Evil*, op. cit., pp. 174–5.

same time frightening about the law is precisely that it is integral to experience, that it is everywhere present, not as command or facile rule but rather as an architecture of daily life, a law of the street, an insidious imaginary. In terms of any phenomenology of the law in its forms of daily life, we would need to study the images of possibility, the imagery, the emotive and affective bonds that tie the legal subject quite willingly, though not necessarily happily, to the limits of law: to this biography, to this persona, to this body and these organs. In Chapter Eight the question of the aesthetics of law, the question of emotive adhesion to law, to all that law implies, is approached through the work of the French classicist and historian of medieval law, Pierre Legendre. His theory encompasses a politics of the images of law, an account of the forms of montage through which the law is presenced in social life. The issue is one of the assemblage of images through which we live our faith in the social and political bond, our fidelity to the legality of social speech, and to all the discourses through which a technologically advanced society carpenters and reproduces an everyday life. The analysis of Legendre's concept of an aesthetics of law provides the background and terminology through which, in the concluding chapter, we analyse a series of contemporary images of lived law.

The detailed attention given to Legendre's aesthetics of law reflects the novelty of the task ahead. The notion of taking the 'art of law' seriously as an art, as a system of representations and visual symbols, is quite foreign to modern jurisprudence. While English jurisprudence has in the distant past paid considerable attention to visual dimensions of legal texts and more particularly of legal proof, that is not a tradition which survived the transition from the ocular to the optic, from a scribal culture of illuminated and glossed texts, of the book as a metaphor for heavenly decree, to the logistics of the moveable typeface and the printed text. The antique tradition of common law that is invoked by Fortescue and Coke is frequently a visually dramatic discipline as well as being violent in its evidentiary and verbal forms. Its texts were 'mirrors' of the law; its forms of proof acted out or recollected the acting out of earlier demonstrations of ownership through testamentary signs and icons of title. The various forms of religious trial by ordeal, of proof through divination, profoundly influenced common law procedures, not simply in the trial of witches or in proof of contested honour but more extensively in the very use of documentation as an iconic form of proof.[1] The tactical quality of legal aesthetics, the continuing and pervasive visual symbolism of the law in its broadest sense, the law as *nomos* or norm and limit of the socially possible, remains to be studied in its contemporary or historical forms.

Building upon the work of Legendre, the final chapter presents a detailed analysis of the work of one artist. Its thesis is that, in the wake of the break-up of earlier modernist and contractarian notions of society and law, of meaning and of rule, jurisprudence would do well to return to the study of the art of law; the representations of legality – of legitimacy – have become the reality, the only reality, of postmodern culture. To pursue that argument requires that we 'look' at specific images and trace not simply the law of our vision[2] but equally the presuppositions of the images themselves. They are images of a law that has broken down, that has fragmented, but in ever more powerful and arbitrary forms: it is a law of masks, of nomadic moveable signs that terroristically invade the intensive zones of everyday life. The law of the image, where the sign plays the law, where the sign organises the very content of daily life – that I suspect is the future of law. Government in such a context, in such a culture, is a matter of moving the signs, of controlling the avenues of circulation of images, of intercepting the hallucinated messages of the microchip age. Its law is the law of the image, the law of the sign. It is a moveable law, a collapsible structure, its hermeneutic that of simple survival. In the place of the logics of memory we now find, we now glimpse, the intimations of another law, a pragmatically nomadic law that fixes itself to the momentary apparitions of the various screens, the televisual apparatuses of post-contractarian communications.

1   See M. T. Clanchy, *From Memory to Written Record* (1979, London) and H-J. Martin, *Histoire et pouvoirs de l'écrit* (1988, Paris).

2   M. F. Plissart and J. Derrida, *Droits de regards* (1985, Paris), translated as 'Right of Inspection' (1989), 32 *Art and Text* 20–98. For commentary, see D. Wills, 'Supreme Court' (1988) 18 *Diacritics* 20.

Part One

MEMORY, PRECEDENT AND WRITING SYSTEMS OF LAW

A Short History of Failure: Law and Criticism 1580–1620

'We are beginning to know. How it beats. How. The Heart of the stranger.'[1]

Failure and the Positive Unconscious of a Science: Abraham Fraunce

I will begin with the history of a failure. It is the history of a discipline that did not come into being. It is a history that did not occur, or at least that has yet to happen. If I therefore invoke an imaginary past, a fictional lineage or, better, a tradition that was never transmitted, it is for good reasons. In the first place there is the romanticism of failure, the attraction of loss, even of nemesis, to the melancholic spirit of a postmodern age. Why study success, in other words, when the realm of possibilities is infinitely more vast, more varied and arguably more enticing? Which possible disciplines of law fell by the wayside, outside of their destiny, beyond the custody of institutional transmission? Who interpreted them out of existence, and why?

In a deeper, structural sense the last question can be posed in a more specific way. If a particularly interdisciplinary conception of law as a discipline[2] never saw the light of institutional acceptance, if it

---

1 C. Peri Rossi, *The Ship of Fools* (1989, London), p. 2.

2 The concept of a discipline is here used in its classical sense: a discipline studies a specific subdivision of knowledge within the scholastic order of knowledges. It is, according to the sixteenth-century proponents of dialectic, predicated upon a series of known, established truths and is in consequence knowledge that simply exists to be schematised according to the requirements of memory and then taught. See P. Ramus, *The Logike* (1574, London), ch. 3.

was never incorporated into the common law tradition despite being written and published in the Inns of Court, then it is inevitable that it at least left marks or traces, that it was not accepted for reasons that lived on. Those criteria of exclusion, of exile or banishment, live on as the positive unconscious[1] of law as a science in at least two senses. Firstly, a discipline is a language, a discourse, a mode of transmission, and it is built upon a series of presuppositions as regards the nature of its object and more specifically the tradition of its recollection and sending-on. The language of law, conceived of as a language of transmission, inevitably incorporates a positive model or representation of the legal discipline as a curriculum, and as an order, but it also presupposes that which method (teaching) and order have excluded, a repressed subject matter, a failed content or form. The language of law carries with it all that is unsaid, that has been driven within, hidden from view: it carries its failures within as an indelible past, as the memory of battle, as litigation. In a broader sense, the materiality of language is always excessive; it carries with it far more than is expressed in any science of law, it betrays the discipline in the very act of conveying or keeping it as knowledge. The language of law speaks into the face of the science that was born in the late sixteenth century because language is always specific; it is attached to the material world, to the lives and contexts of those that have spoken it. Just as the rhythms, the conflicts and uncertainties of those lives cannot be forgotten or eradicated from the life itself, nor from its discourse, so too the language of a tradition is a material culture; it cannot expunge the failures, the repressed histories or the lost causes that accompanied its birth. The lives of those who failed are equally real, equally lived – perhaps they were lived better, but at all events it cannot be denied that they were there.

There is finally a tactical consideration to bear in mind when it

---

1   M. Foucault, *The Order of Things* (1970, London), Foreword; the historian of science must also endeavour to retrace and restore that which eluded scientific consciousness: 'the influences that affected it, the implicit philosophies that were subjacent to it, the unformulated thematics, the unseen obstacles ... the unconscious of science. This unconscious is always the negative side of science – that which resists it, deflects it, or disturbs it. What I would like to do, however, is to reveal a positive unconscious of knowledge: a level that eludes the scientist and yet is part of scientific discourse ...' (p. xi).

comes to lost causes in relation to law. To trace the underside of a discipline – to ask what it cost – is to recuperate the specific motive fears that underlie the form of life, the weaknesses that border any science conceived as truth, the excluded lives, the solitary figures, the ashes of those who were burnt in the name of law. It is not just that myth or irrationality are the necessary boundaries, the limits, of a science, but also that the underside, the failures, the other history of a discipline, provides a ground for reinterpretation. A tradition is a form or language of transmission; it sends on and its surface is in that sense a temporal one: through techniques of repetition, recycling and reinterpretation it establishes sites of temporal recurrence, cycles of recognition, places on a map of the law's progression. The pattern of such development, of the common law as tradition, is most usually presented as one of linear emergence: the law is a route, a path across time and across experience; it is simply the way or schedule by which time is lived. We will return on many occasions to the nomadic temporal quality of the common law tradition. At the moment we would simply observe that the existence of a path or route is, in cartographic terms, a matter of projection, of perspective across a landscape or of a route across the seas. The failed history maps another path, a cross wind on the trade route, a possibility. In this text, however, it will be followed as a possible site of criticism, as an outside that is within the law as a mark, a trace element, a break in the road. To appreciate the alternative that such a history, such a reading of the law as language, allows, consider the nature of the tradition itself. As a science, the discipline of law exists to constrain the use, the possibilities, of language, including the language of the body: it is an arcane, initiate or esoteric language that destroys the play of meanings in the act of establishing literal or artistic legal terms. It is consequently an insider knowledge, a language of shibboleths, of coded terms. To criticise that language will therefore involve having access to it; it will involve being within its circle and bound to its purpose, at least in the grammatical sense of understanding it as a language and of being familiar with its usages. To criticise the law if one lives through the law is a circular and unproductive activity; it is always likely that one does not so much escape it as return to it. The value of failure, of the non-occurring history, is thus precisely the value of the outside within: it provides, perhaps it alone provides, the possibility of a criticism that inhabits a place both outside the law and yet internal to its terms, its causes, its rules. In short, it can mix genres, lead us away or bring us back, but always on our own terms, from a perspective that is free of specific institutional co-option, that is not yet complicit, not yet quite legal prose.

The figure of failure to be followed in this chapter is that of Abraham Fraunce, a rhetorician trained at Cambridge University, a poet, logician and secular iconographer as well; a Renaissance man who moved in the early 1580s to Lincoln's Inn and studied the law, Littleton's *Tenures*, the breviaries, the Year Books, the forensic rhetorical manuals, in short the curriculum – such as it was – at the Inns of Court in the second half of the sixteenth century. The forgotten history or decayed memory is that of his single and reluctantly published analysis and criticism of the common law and its representatives, the history – the oblivion – of his work the *Lawier's Logike*, published in 1588. The history also, the fate, of a specific critique of the common law and its method, in which history can be read *in nuce* the exemplary historical destiny of an attempt to introduce to the common law an historical and comparative dimension of criticism, an attempt to link law to knowledge, to contemporary philosophy, to a non-dogmatic reason or dialectic. In both intellectual and political terms, Fraunce's project was a complex and ambitious one. In intellectual terms, he presented the first systematisation of English law that took account of disciplines and traditions other than that of common law, which was cognisant of the history of other legal systems and that was well versed in both English and continental theoretical traditions. His references range from the Greek and Roman orators to Aristotle and the various medieval versions of scholasticism. His examples are drawn from the law reports and the institutions and opinions of English lawyers, but also from the continental civilian commentators, from Hotman, Cujas and Budé, the historians, the linguists and the poets of European literature. His style is similarly extensive; it draws upon the techniques of forensic rhetoric as then current in the Inns of Court, but it also travels much further to embody elements of Ramist logic, historical philology, arcadian lyricism and vernacular humour. It is a critical and eclectic style appropriate, one might argue, to the founding of a new discipline. In political or institutional terms, Fraunce was also ambitious. His critique of the legal knowledge of his day must be understood as an attack upon a 'dark' and secret professional tradition;[1] it is, possibly implausibly, a critique from the outside of an institution that dogmatically denies that there is any external access to the esoteric truth of law. It is an attempt finally to open a knowledge that is distinctive precisely by virtue of being presented – and lived – as closed, as final and axiomatic, a matter of custody and not of critique, of mystery and not of knowledge. In both respects, both intellectually and politically, it is unsurprising that Fraunce fails, in the sense at least that he is ignored by lawyers, that his logic continued to be ignored, that he remained outside the closure of legal knowledge, shunned by the institution, ignored and still ignored by its historians, its panegyrists, its eulogists.[2]

The question that this chapter poses is what can be learned from this discontinuous history, this shadowy life? It is there, it remains to be read, it will be read as a means of reading the ascendant tradition against itself as a tradition of misinterpretation, of bastard histories and often of flagrant deceit. It will be read so as to smell in the study of law, the 'stench of law',[3] what is elsewhere termed its 'loathsome savour',[4] and so to question the (olfactory) stupor of its reason, the dead density of its prose and the materiality of its 'addictive' body.[5] It

1   Dr John Cowell, *The Interpreter, Or Booke Containing the Signification of Words* (1607, Cambridge), fol. 3a: 'I have both gathered here at home, and brought from abroad some ornaments for the better embellishing of our English laws . . . The civilians of other nations, have by their mutual industries raised this kind of work in their profession, to an unexpected excellency . . . And by this example would I gladly incite the learned in our common laws and antiquities of England, yet to lend their advice, to the gaining of some comfortable lights and prospects towards the beautifying of this ancient palace . . . yet but dark and melancholy.'

2   There is no mention of Fraunce at all in A. W. B. Simpson (ed.), *Biographical Dictionary of the Common Law* (1984, London). The now standard histories are W. S. Howell, *Logic and Rhetoric in England, 1500–1700 (1956, New Jersey)* and W. Ong, *Ramus: Method and the Decay of Dialogue* (1958, Harvard). For a more recent polemic, see B. Vickers, *In Defence of Rhetoric* (1988, Oxford). None provide any detailed discussion of Fraunce.

3   F. Hotman, *AntiTribonian ou discours d'un grand et renommé iurisconsulte de nostre temps* (1567, Paris), p. 111: [on glosses and commentaries] 'such is the state of poverty that one has seen as a result of 260 years of these scholastic doctors, who rendered [the laws] so odious that in the end one has been forced to see them not as great and weighty intellects, but as sophists and wranglers, abusers and imposters of justice . . . what man of sense and judgment can read one page of what they have written on the terms and questions of practice, without laughing at their word play (badinage), or without suffering weariness of heart as at a foul stench.'

4   A. Fraunce, *Lawiers Logike* (1588, London), fol. 3a.

5   W. Fulbecke, *Direction or Preparative to the Study of the Law; wherein it is shewed what things ought to be observed and used of them that are addicted to the study of law . . .* (1599, London).

will be read as pure memory, as an imagined body that remains to be witnessed, a project yet to be projected, to be seen within an enduring tradition of closure and of dismal resistance to both history and comparative criticism. Who, even now, dares criticise or is heard to criticise the law in its most embedded forms, as language, as method and as reason itself? Our reading will thus follow a negative order. It will follow firstly the distinctive terms of Fraunce's critique of common law reason, and second, the terms of its rejection, both implicit and explicit, by the 'sages of the common law'. What happens, in other words, to a critic of the English law?

Criticism and the Logic of Law

In subsequent chapters we will look in detail at the paradigm of English law, the curriculum and method that emerged from the Inns of Court as a response to printing, to the Reformation and to the Renaissance vernacularisation of the disciplines and the sciences. The *Lawier's Logike* is an aspect of its pre-history; it attempts at the time of inception of a discipline to challenge the paradigm that is being established and to draw legal reason towards a different episteme. Its very failure allows us a certain freedom: in attacking the shallow and haphazard insularity of the common law, its base memory of 'almost infinite particulars',[1] Fraunce inevitably follows themes that are common to the ascendant tradition, even if they are reworked so as to attack it. In some considerable measure the themes of his book are the themes of his life and our narrative will conflate the two: what is lived – what is spoken – and what is written.

We can begin then by observing that Fraunce went to Cambridge to study literature, attending the lectures of Gabriel Harvey and being fellow student and colleague of Dudley Fenner, respectively the authors of the first English commentary on Ramus' *Rhetoric* and the first translation of his work on dialectic, the *Logike*. In the early 1580s Fraunce composed the *Shepherd's Logike*, an English Ramistic logic 'setting out the praise and right use of logic'[2] and providing a rendering and comparison of Ramus' *Logike* with that of Aristotle, while still at the university. Soon after the publication of that work he moved to Lincoln's Inn, abandoning the university, but not its

1   Sir E. Coke, *Reports* (1777 edn, London), vol. II, A5a.
2   A. Fraunce, *Shepherd's Logike* (1585/1969, Menston), p. 3.

rigours or method, in favour of law. That his concern with law was scholarly rather than venal or professional is of some considerable significance. It defined Fraunce as an outsider; it made him live as a stranger within the initiate Inn that he had joined. Indeed most of what Fraunce wrote while at the Inns of Court was not about law: with comparative safety he published a rhetoric,[1] a work on symbols, hieroglyphs and arms, a translation of Latin poetry, panegyric poetry of his own and much else.[2] That specific background deserves attention since it is inaugural of both Fraunce's work and his life: 'for myself, I must needs confess I was an university man eight years together, and for every day of those eight years, I do not repent that I was an university man'.[3] That such a defensive statement was necessary in the preface to the *Lawier's Logike* tells its own story. The profession certainly had its share of antiquarians, philologists and scholars of the arcana of law,[4] but their influence was peripheral and largely limited to antiquities; the general depiction of the Inns of Court of the age was of a mendacious, corrupt, unscholarly[5] and even 'ungentle'[6] profession. There is at the heart of the *Lawier's Logike* an explicit and consistent opposition between scholarship and the profession's mercantile interests, its pursuit of lucre or unmerited

1   A. Fraunce, *The Arcadian Rhetorike* (1588/1950, Oxford).

2   A. Fraunce, *Insignium Armorum, Emblematum, Hieroglyphicum et Symbolorum* (1588, London).

3   Fraunce, *Lawiers Logike*, at 2b.

4   As for example Sir Henry Spelman, as well as the more esoteric authors such as Thomas Wilson, George Puttenham or Sir John Ferne. For general information, see R. Shoeck, 'The Libraries of Common Lawyers in Renaissance England' (1962) 6 *Manuscripta* 155.; idem, 'The Elizabethan Society of Antiquaries and Men of Law' (1954) 1 *Notes and Queries* 417; W. Prest, *The Rise of the Barristers: A Social History of the English Bar 1590–1640* (1986, Oxford).

5   Typical examples can be found in Sir T. Elyot, *The Boke Named the Governour* (1531/1907, London), pp. 62–9; Dr John Cowell, op. cit.; Thomas Wilson, *The State of England, Anno Domini 1600* (1601/1936, Camden Misc.); Thomas Powell, *The Attourney's Academy* (1610, London).

6   Sir John Ferne, *The Blazon of Gentrie* (1586, London), pp. 92–3, deploring the fraudulent assumption of gentility and coats of arms by ignoble entrants to the Inns of Court – 'ungentle legists' – and arguing that they should be 'weeded out'. See also Sir G. Buc; *The Third Universitie of England* (1612/1615 edn), London, pp. 968–9: 'it is an error to think that the sons of Graziers, farmers, merchants, tradesmen, & artificers can be made gentlemen by their attendance or matriculation . . . (at) an Inne of Court, for no man can be made a gentleman but by his father . . . because it is a matter of race, and of blood and of discent.'

profit. The lawyers hated the 'fine university men'; they explicitly denied that a good scholar could ever make a good lawyer or, even more irrationally, that an historian could ever understand the history of law or that a philologist could lay bare its languages. In a thinly veiled reference to his own life's work, Fraunce cites the legal scorn of university men who, in the opinion of those wise in the law, 'can better make new found verses of Amyntas' death, and popular discourses of ensigns, armoury, emblems, hieroglyphs and Italian impresses, than apply their heads to the study of law which is hard, harsh, unpleasant, unsavoury, rude and barbarous'. There is, in other words, no room or place either for an independent scholarship of law or for a man like Fraunce himself. Throughout the book a thematic depiction of a particularistic legal anti-intellectualism forces Fraunce again and again to harangue the emptiness of legal education, the spuriousness of legal learning, the greedy and foolish sophistry of the average lawyer: lawyers 'had no light' or method, and they lacked any of the ethics that learning would bring to counter the law of the market place, where the 'upstart *rabulae forenses*' practised their trade:

> [U]nder a pretence of law, they became almost lawless, to the continual molestation of ignorant men, and the general overcharging of the country, with an overflowing multitude of seditious cavillers; who, when their fathers have made some lewd bargain in the country, run immediately to the Inns of Court, and having in seven years space met with six French words, now they ride like brave Magnificoes, and dash their neighbours's children quite out of countenance, with villen in gros, villen regardant, and Tenant per le courtesie.[1]

The profound basis for Fraunce's criticism of the 'lewd bargain' that propels the law, without learning, without mediation, into the market place as a semblance of knowledge or mystery is philosophic. From the scholastic perspective that Fraunce adopts, that of a radically reformed Aristotelianism, a law that is uninformed by philosophy and that systematically and wilfully ignores scholarship is both unethical and a danger to the lives lived in it or subject to it. An ethics in the Aristotelian sense, of which Ramist logic or dialectic is a distant branch, does not exist to teach mere rules, norms or mores. It

---

1   *Lawiers Logike*, preface. See also Sir Henry Spelman, *The Original of the Four Law Terms of the Year* (1614/1723, London), p. 99, discussing common lawyers: '[they] are for profit and *lucrando pano*, taking what [they] find at market, without enquiring whence it came.' A similar criticism can be found in Powell, op. cit., fol. Gg3a.

is not simply a morality, it is habitual and comprehensive: through the law men should learn to desire, through repetition and through learning, to do the right thing in the right place at the right time; they should come to desire justice and as lawyers their lives should embody a true law, a lived law, authentic justice pragmatically located in a specific place and time, England in the last quarter of the fifteenth century, the England of tenures and fealties, of villeinage and socage, of deodand, advowson and frankalmoign. It was precisely customary law, the tradition of habitual bodies and habitual lives, that would be lost if 'ungentle' and ignorant lawyers were allowed to continue to peddle mere rules, norms that simply existed in writing, mores that had no inner or lived content. The time had come, in other words, to take account of the modern world and its episteme, to recognise the possibilities of knowledge, of Renaissance learning, and to discard an opaque law that was in danger of propounding little more than historical archaisms, the mores of forgotten times and abandoned places, a dead 'Norman' law, an abstract justice unbound to any specific time or place, unbound to any particular life. It is the commonality of common law that Fraunce saw as being most visibly and immediately threatened, and by implication it is the *socius*, the relationships that make up a shared habitual world, a life, that were in danger of being destroyed. Behind Fraunce's critique of what could be termed an official or state-run black economy in misunderstood legal terms is a concern to reinstate the time and place of English law as a modern, national discipline, a discipline bound to England.

If we move to ask what the university or scholarship had to offer to law, the question is necessarily particular to the brand of scholarship then current and to the *Lawier's Logike* as an embodiment or development of that currency. Two themes were for present purposes intrinsic to Fraunce's work and intertextual in the *Logike*: the need to develop a national language adequate to the new disciplines; and the need to re-read and rework the classics, Aristotle and Cicero, so as to Anglicise the Hellenistic or scholastic tradition while also incorporating contemporary and international theoretical discourses. As regards the former concern, that of developing English as a national language of the new disciplines, of the disciplines made legible by print, Fraunce adopts but does not greatly extend a much more general concern that preoccupied all of the arts of his day. His contemporary at Cambridge, Dudley Fenner, provides one example of a similar project in the form of a translation and annotation of

Ramus' *Logike* and Talon's *Rhetorike: The Artes of Logike and Rhetorike plainly set forth in the English tongue, easie to be learned and practised* . . .[1] His work was one of many which strove to create a context in which it was possible to assume the desirability of a specifically English and frequently nationalistic presentation of continental traditions of scholarship. It was a movement that, according to Fenner in the preface to his *Logike*, had 'already brought all the arts into French, Dutch and almost into English, and that by the hand of the most cunningest workmen'.[2]

The most extreme, though not atypical example of such cunning workmanship must undoubtedly have been Ralph Lever's *The Arte of Reason, Rightly Termed Witcraft, Teaching a Perfect Way to Argue and Dispute*, published in 1573 and devoted to 'proving that the art of reason can be taught in English'. He further observes in the Forespeache (i.e. preface) that 'for devising of new terms, and compounding of words, our tongue hath a special grace, wherein it excelleth many other, and is comparable with the best. The cause is for that the most part of English words are short and stand on one syllable a piece.'[3] Lever proceeded to devise an entire vocabulary of English neologisms, a complete vernacular lexicon of logical terms, free of any rude, foreign or 'inkhorne' terms. The result is linguistic-ally remarkable mainly for its inelegance. Aristotle's definition of substance and accident becomes, to take one example: 'substance is an inholder, the very groundwork, stay and upholder of quantities, qualities and other inheers'. It is sufficient to note that Lever's specific project failed in the sense that the artificial language of inheers (accidents), inholders (subjects), endsays (conclusions) and the like did not gain philosophical acceptance. His broader championship of English, however, was a commonplace theme of his day and it is one that Fraunce specifically takes up and extends not only in presenting an English language logic of law but also in expanding and critically revising the continental tradition being so presented. Fraunce's project thus did not stop, as did Fenner's, with the relatively limited though none the less important notion of a literal translation of continental dialectic into an English logic. The translation has also to

1   Dudley Fenner, *The Artes of Logike and Rhetorike* (1584, Middleburg).
2   Ibid., at A2a.
3   Ralph Lever, *The Arte of Reason, Rightly termed Witcraft, Teaching a Perfect way to Argue and Dispute* (1573, London) at fol. Ya–b. See also R. Verstegan, *A Restitution of Decayed Intelligence in Antiquities* (1605, Amsterdam).

be critical and conceptual: it was not to be assumed that an inherited post-classical vocabulary should take precedence over critical consideration of the etymology of artistic or technical terms; it was not to be assumed that the contemporary continental logic with which Fenner, Fraunce and others were concerned was free of mistakes or interpolations. In an exactly similar sense, the comparative use that Fraunce makes of civilian law does not assume any priority of method, elegance or order to either one of the systems. In just such a vein he observes:

> [S]ome will say that the civil is more constant and philosophic than, and also by Justinian more methodically, and by later writers more eloquently put down. Yet: they have plebiscita, senatus consulta, principium placita, magistratum edicta, responsa prudentum: we have cases, maxims and principles, customs and usages both general and special; and lastly, continual reforms of new abused statutes and Acts of Parliament. As for Justinian's method, it does not so content the civilians, but that they daily contend with new innovations and continual printing of fresh method, to bring it to better order.

His conclusion is appropriately damning of the rudeness of style of both the professions: 'while one can easily observe that both styles and methods are bad, it is hard to judge which is worse'.[1]

The translation of continental logic and the devising of a properly English logic is thus aimed to draw the law towards a body of knowledge that it had previously eschewed; it was to equip the lawyers with technical philosophical (or, more properly, argumentative) tools and thereby to recognise England as a part of the European tradition, to accept, in Fulbecke's words, that 'the common law cannot be divided from the civil and canon laws [any more] than the flower from the root and stalk'.[2] The inception of a logic of common law, an English jurisprudence, cannot be understood for Fraunce in terms of an insular nationalism: the new discipline is rather to be comprehended as a national genre of a European species, a federal enterprise within the legal philosophic tradition and the *ius commune*, the common law of Europe. So too, for Fraunce, English scholarship could exist only by relating the particularities of an existent discipline, the writings and reports of Bracton, Brookes, Brytton,

---

1   *Lawiers Logike*, preface, pp. x–xi.
2   W. Fulbecke, *A Parallele or Conference of the Civil Law, the Canon Law, and the Common Law of this Realme of England* (1602, London), fol. 2a.

Choke, Crompton, Fitzherbert, Littleton, Lambard, Perkins, Plowden, Stamford and all the rest, together with the language of gard, villein, mortmain, wapentakes and gavelkind, to a method of reasoning and to comparable institutional literatures. As regards the philosophic tradition and specifically that of logic, Fraunce's references span the classics, Aristotle, Plato, Cicero, Laertius and their reception in Renaissance Europe in the work of Valla, Talon, Philip Sydney and most particularly Ramus. For specific comparisons with the legal literature of the civilian reception the references are equally expansive and inclusive, particularly of Hotman, Cujas and Budé, the leading legal philologists and scholars of his era. As to the use to which his breadth of learning, of reading, was put it is necessary first to comment briefly upon the English intellectual context (or intertextuality) that plays in the background, that is the backgame of Fraunce's work. Of the lawyers and the limited tradition of rhetorical and formulary scholarship that accompanied the essentially oral learning process at the Bar more will be said in the next chapter.[1]

The inception of a specifically English tradition of scholarship and of the individual disciplines was initially a linguistic movement. Specifically in relation to law this meant that a general movement towards an English rhetoric for the disciplines[2] had to be accommodated in the form of a reworking of the forensic or legal rhetorical tradition and specifically of its classification and arrangement – properly invention and distribution – of the subject matter and arguments, or in Lever's terms storehouses, of law. Conceived in a critical vein by scholars such as Ascham, Cox, Elyot, Wilson, Puttenham and others, a properly English rhetoric had first to be constructed upon the ground of English usage, a usage free particularly of the inappropriate use of dark, borrowed and elliptic terms rudely taken from other languages, free, as they themselves put it, from the inkpen and hotchpot terms that lived on in the disciplines

---

1   See Ong, op. cit., Howell, op. cit., and more generally J. J. Murphy (ed.), *Renaissance Eloquence* (1983, California). Walter Ong in particular is inaccurate in his account of the English Ramists; one cannot attribute the European tendencies – which Ong studies so well – unmediated to English intellectual life.

2   Consider particularly R. Sherry, *A Treatise of Schemes and Tropes very profytable for the better understanding of good authors, gathered out of the best Grammarians and Orators* (1550, London) and Richard Rainholde, *A Booke called the Foundacion of Rhetorike,*

from their Latin and French past. In law in particular the problem was extreme by virtue of its multilingual and archaic forms, by virtue of its Saxon, Nordic, Norman, Latin and middle English vocabularies. More than that, however, the suspicion existed that in law as in other disciplines, though perhaps less manifestly so, foreign terminologies exclude method and logic in favour of a purely stylistic usage, a rhetoric devoid of content and inappropriate in form, a rhetoric of pure though dark persuasion beautifully denounced by John Jewell in 1548: 'Why fill the forum with cries, vociferations and tears? Why call down the Gods from Heaven? Why raise the shades from the underworld? Why have buildings, temples, columns, tombs, and stones cry out? What do they want of such faces? Why that thrashing about of the body?'[1] Not all rhetoric looks the same in the light of reason, nor do the classical proponents of the discipline necessarily deserve to be transposed into English without criticism or amendment.

The stirring of critical life within the rhetorical tradition and the attempt to introduce elements of a scholastic logic into the Ciceronian tradition find an exemplary expression in the conversion of Fraunce's teacher, Gabriel Harvey, from a purely custodial praise of Cicero to a critical philology in the *Ciceronianus*. It was an enlightenment depicted in strongly personal terms as an awakening, an improvement in the quality of life, the advent indeed of a purer love, a love of a discipline and not merely of a man, Cicero and his Latinity: 'at any rate I virtually preferred to be elected to the company of Ciceronians rather than to the saints . . . I vained words more than content, language more than thought, the art of speaking more than the thousand subjects of knowledge; I preferred the mere style of Marcus Tully to all the postulates of the philosophers and mathematicians.'[2] In the place of a blind Latinity or purely emulative classicism, Harvey moved towards two critical postulates. The first was common to the general Renaissance move towards re-reading the classics. The classical tradition and its sacred authors were to be re-read so as to discover within the text its historicity, to find something more, 'something greater than Cicero in Cicero himself'. To look to

---

because all other parts are founded thereupon (1563, London). The earliest example is Leonard Cox, *The Arte or Crafte of Rhetoryke* (1530/1899, Chicago).

1 John Jewell, *Oratorio Contra Rhetoricem* 1548/1928; *Quarterly Journal of Speech*, vol. xiv, 374.

2 G. Harvey, *Ciceronianus* (1577/1945, Nebraska), at p. 69.

the genesis of Cicero's text, to read and re-read Terence, Virgil, Plautus, Caesar, Sallust, Livy and Pliny, would both expose the weaknesses, 'the warts . . . the ulcers, the scars of diction', in the Ciceronian text, upon the body of the remembered man, and also lay to rest a philology which had become no more than imitation. The second invention proposed by Harvey was more radical in political or topical terms: the history of rhetoric did not merely outdate Cicero, it postdated him as well. There was a history to his reception throughout Europe, the development and amendment of his texts by the 'Germans, the French and British.'[1] Contemporary continental scholarship, in other words, was to be looked upon seriously, favourably, in the persons of Erasmus, Ramus, Longolius, Sturmius, Fregius and the Englishmen Smith and Cheke: 'these men we may not only compare but even prefer to any number of Italians . . . After all, the true, genuine, most ancient mimesis is a tradition given us by the profound judgment of the Cisalpines.'[2] It was to the contemporary scholarship of Ramus and Erasmus in particular that the discipline of rhetoric should move: 'merely pointing out, as some have done, the ornaments of tropes and the embellishment of figures, without indicating the stores of arguments, the quantities of proofs, and the structural framework, seems to me tantamount to displaying a body that is surprisingly beautiful and lovely but deprived of sense and life'.[3] In the place of the study of weightless or winged figures, exposition should, for Harvey, turn to the figures of logic, to the examination of the enthymeme, the rhetorical syllogism, and to 'all the epicheiremata that occupy the intellect'.[4]

Consider then the possibility of a logic of law, a jurisprudence or scholarship, which applied Harvey's two general tenets of method to the legal curriculum. It would be, as it was in Fraunce's hands, a scholarship quite unlike anything that we have come to accept or at least to tolerate in the common law world. It would apply method to rhetoric, and other branches of learning to the study of law. It would read the classics but it would also read contemporary theoretical discourse. It would study the common law but it would study it comparatively: that is, in relation to other disciplines, in relation to

1   Ibid., pp. 80–1.
2   Ibid., p. 82.
3   Ibid., p. 87.
4   Ibid., p. 85.

history and in relation to other legal traditions. It would, in short, draw law into the order of disciplines and, in more brutal terms, into scholarship. In terms of the common law it would attempt to save the law from its insularity and equally to spare jurisprudence the endless repetition or vacuous mimicking of an exclusively legal identity. It would be a critical discipline, a scholarship which moved between different disciplines and across temporalities, one which transgressed merely national boundaries and invoked a definition of law itself as an embodiment of life, as something lived and not merely suffered as the rules of an institution. The law, for Fraunce, is precisely to be understood as a way of living and, more profoundly, as the structure of a life; it is both memory and method in the sense of habit, regularity, rhythm or way of life, a mode or *modus vivendi*. Method is the tensor; it is surface and extension as well being the more familiar order or, in prosaic terms, the systematic form of instruction or *methodus* in the particular sense developed by Ramus and his followers. The observation of the different meanings of method as law is essential in that – unrecognised and uncommented though it may be[1] – at the centre of Fraunce's logic of law lies the precept that law is already a discipline, a memory, a nascent method for every genera-tion. It is – as are all disciplines – a subject matter that had been worked and reworked, ordered and re-ordered, read and re-read in its own peculiar and generally silent way. What that means is that Fraunce comes to law in full recognition of history; he endeavours to apply logic to that specific history and those particular texts rather than to use philosophy to annul history. Even more significantly, he comes to law as an existent rhetoric and not as mere fact: that law is a rhetoric means that it embodies a history of language and of citizenship; it forms lives and repeats memories of how to live, of how one has lived in the past. Far from wishing to abolish the rhetorical dimension of law, as argument and as discourse, as an institution that deals with life – that is, with things which Aristotle deemed probable rather than necessary[2] – Fraunce is concerned with a much more visceral and ambitious project, that of bringing to the civil assembly 'a more easy and elegant kind of disputation, joining rhetoric to logic, and referring that precise straightness to philosophical exercises'.[3]

1   Although there is of course the excellent general discussion of Ramism and memory in F. Yates, *The Art of Memory* (1966, London).
2   Aristotle, *Rhetoric*, II, xxv, 8–11.
3   *Lawiers Logike*, 120a.

This injunction is primary to a practical philosophy or to a rhetoric of the real, a rhetoric which takes up Vico's project of setting down the skills of citizenship, the art of civil discourse as a human form of life with all its passions, its friendships, its silences, its loyalties and its betrayals. These are precisely the terms of memory and the costs of living.

It is certainly true that Fraunce attacks specious rhetoric, and those legal 'orators, as referring all to persuasion and victory, omit orderly distribution; obscure things purposely; amplify; change; and turn all things upside down, placing the best arguments first and last: leaving the worst, in the middle of the speech altogether'. So too, we may note, he attacks the 'custom . . . among grand little mootmen, who cast case upon case, as carters do billets, and for every collateral trifle, run over all the six hundred and thirty three titles of Brookes' abridgement'.[1] The reason for such criticism is twofold. From any perspective of a proper rhetoric such argument or discourse as described is impertinent, digressive, repugnant and sordid; it occupies the mind and the memory with irrelevances, it forms subjects of no value and a polity that is based upon confusion if not directly upon deceit and falsehood: 'as in the universities as in the Inns of Court, the greedy desire of a superficial show in unnecessary trifles makes us want the true substance: they for haste to get a prebend by a degree, make light work and run over two or three epitomes; and we by a moote book and a Brookes abridgement climb to the bar and bar ourselves utterly of the substance of the common law'.[2] Let it be here repeated, however, that it is not rhetoric that was attacked by Fraunce but rather a particular, uneducated and unscholarly use of it. In a material sense it was a lack of ethics that was impugned; these forensic orators did not read the history of their discipline. Bracton and Brytton were no longer in print. These lawyers, in other words, did not know where they were, they did not know what institutional time it was, they acted upon rote and they relied upon an undigested knowledge culled from epitomes, upon an easy display of verbal sophistry and upon an inauthentic life, a decayed tradition, a dead word, a usurious politics. At the level of scholarship, Fraunce simply adverts to the absence of any method, to the lack of dialectic and the absence of any theory of law.

In addition to the requirement that lawyers read, learn and

1   Ibid., 89b–90a.
2   Ibid., 61b–62a.

embody their own tradition as a living tradition, as a living word, the memory and history that Fraunce so copiously annotates for their benefit in his examples from all of the 'authors' of the common law and from its named and anonymous reports, are the novel injunctions that rhetoric be rationalised as a part of civil life and that memory become a history, an order of the tradition understood in conceptual terms. For Fraunce, Ramist method was the instrument that could save the law from the lawyers and return it to the halls, the *scholae*, of scholarship. That point speaks to the fact that law is the essential art of the polis, of politics, and cannot be abandoned to ignorance. It also draws it towards method as the art of arts and the science of sciences (*scientia scientiarum*):

> [A]n art is a methodical disposition of true and coherent precepts, for the more easy perceiving and better remembering of the same: and this methodical or orderly disposition of divers precepts is taught in logic, as pertaining essentially thereunto. So that logic was deservedly called the Art of Arts, the instrument of instruments, the hand of philosophy.[1]

Logic, however, is rhetorical in both substance and form. In terms of form, Fraunce's logic follows Ramus' and divides into invention and judgment with memory as the third division. In formal terms the logic thus follows the classical rhetorical schema with the simple exclusion of style as a fundamental category. In substantive terms logic reasons so as to dispute, to differentiate, to teach and to analyse: 'it is not tied to any one thing, but apt for anything, free from all, yet fit for all, framing orderly, proving strongly, expounding plainly, persuading forcibly, any Art, any cause, any question, any man whatsoever'.[2] It is rhetorical then in the sense that it bends, moves and persuades to action, and Fraunce later specifies admirably:

> I will never think him worthy of the title and name of a logician, that never put his general contemplation of logical precepts in particular practice . . . what precepts soever the common rhetoricians put down for ordering of exordiums and framing and disposing of the whole cause of their speech fitly and according to cause, auditors, time, place, and such like; all those I say are altogether logical, not in any respect pertaining to rhetoric, but as a rhetor may be directed by logical precepts of judgement and disposition.[3]

1 Ibid., 1a–b.
2 Ibid., 3b–4a.
3 Ibid., 115b.

While logic may constitute a higher order of classification and arrangement of a discipline than does the rhetorical art, it is not essentially distinct from rhetoric and it is Fraunce's originality to maintain consistently that logic and rhetoric should be joined as disciplines: 'one logic suffices to dispute all things, necessary or contingent or whatsoever . . . all logic is general, and applicable as well to things imagined, as things that be extant in truth: and therefore to words also, as words have causes, effects, subjects, adjuncts and other arguments to be considered'.[1] The same science of logic applies, in other words, to matters that are certain and to matters of opinion, to the necessary and to the probable, the speculative and the practical, the convincing and the persuasive: the law of reason is a formal law which allows the argument, of syllogistic reason, that 'the conclusion itself does follow necessarily, by force of the form of the syllogism; but yet, of itself, it is but a contingent axiom, although the deduction of it from premises, be, as I said, necessary, by reason of the lawful framing of the syllogism'.[2] Though the subject matter of common law is vast, its reports and its spoken remains distantly scattered, its practices frequently opaque, its languages rude and borrowed, although it is in its content contingent and frequently strange, it can none the less, for Fraunce, be joined to logic and its rhetorical organisation and presentation can similarly be made methodical and straight by recourse to the reasoning of probabilities.

Memory and the Fascination of Law

Rhetoric gives logic a body; logic gives rhetoric a soul. It gives rhetoric a memory that will last, a structure of discourse that exceeds the immediacy of language, that somehow binds the figures, the faces, the masks of its enunciation to a history and to an institution. In organising legal discourse according to the principles of dialectic, of a Ramistic logic which proceeds from the invention of arguments to their disposition in discourse, Fraunce joins logic to rhetoric in a further way. Before we look at the substance of the logic, it is interesting to consider that the motive for introducing method to law is the generic one of presenting a discourse so as to make it amenable

1   Ibid., 5a–6b, 59b.
2   Ibid., 19a.

to memory: the limbs and branches, the particularities and fragments of the common law, are schematised so as to be remembered; they are cut up and put back together (re-membered), for 'method is the chiefest help of memory, [and] instructions for memory, if they belong to any art, must needs be logical'.[1] It is the logic of disposition – that is, the orderly and rational arrangement of a subject matter, of its places or *loci* – that will classically allow easy recall of arguments, though significantly Fraunce also adds advice on diet and exercise as mnemonic aids. The irony of the play involved in such a statement is again that it mixes genres, for memory, the art of *memoria* invented by Simonides, is a rhetorical art which works through the body and through images. Thomas Wilson, to take an example from a contemporary of Fraunce's, adopts the classical fourth division of rhetoric, memory, as the conclusion to his curricula manual, *The Arte of Rhetorique*, published in 1553. Memory is essential to any oral art; it thus has a central place in rhetoric for 'the same is memory to the mind, that life is to the body'.[2] It is interesting then that memory is inscribed in the body, that it requires that one 'keep a diet, eschew surfeits, sleep moderately, accompany with women rarely, and last of all . . . exercise the wit with cunning of memory things without Book'.[3] The order of the sentence indicates that it is the body, the organic memory, that is first or structural; its instances or manifestations in wit or reason or cunning are secondary, accessory. If we think of how memory is to be inscribed in wit also, it requires learning to have places (rooms) and to digest images in them accordingly 'and even as in wax we make a print with a seal, so we have places where lively pictures must be set' – such are the places of memory, an architecture of images that the rhetor will inhabit during the course of speech. The architecture of such imagery, the symbolic rooms of memory as sign, can be understood quite literally. For Cicero, to take one further example, the rhetor should memorise by placing his thoughts in connection with the forum, the building, in which he speaks. Those gargoyles, that balcony and the furniture of the auditorium in which he speaks are the physical host to memories both past and present, both necessary and accidental. Just as individual memory comes through the body, just as it is an embodiment, a re-

1   Ibid., 116b.
2   Wilson, *The Arte of Rhetorique* (1553/1982), p. 420. Classically, see Aristotle, *On Memory* (1972, ed. Sorabji).
3   Ibid., p. 421.

membering of sites of both pleasure and pain, the habitual actions, so in terms of genre or institutions memory is in a specific place; it is attached to these walls, those gargoyles, that stairwell, those tables – why else do they take the form that they do? The institution gathers its memory through its material body, its buildings, its furniture, its windows, its others texts. Memory is the inner discourse of the body – the lesion that will not go, the trauma that even the most vigorous repression simply buries further within or exiles to the memory of the sleeping body, to dream. Memory is simultaneously the inner speech of the institution. It is the institution's soul in the sense that without memory there would be no body, no surface, no skin, neither pleasure nor pain. Without memory, there would be no speech, no institution, neither power nor love, neither desire nor fear. Consider, indeed, law as an institution and specifically as a form of memory, as a history, and as a body of tradition or *corpus iuris*: that is, as precedent, as time immemorial or temporal usage.

The rhetorical issue that underlies and structures the *Lawier's Logike* is precisely that of the nature, the body and the building of an institutional memory: what are its places, what is its structure, what are the images by which we remember it as lawyers and it us as subjects? More specifically in relation to English law, how are we to comprehend a tradition that defines itself not simply as memory but further as memory 'out of mind' or beyond memory, as immemorial usage, as that which exceeds 'living memory' and so incorporates an habitual life, a material structure, a soul if you will that is not the prisoner of any living body? How are we to understand a soul – the spirit of law – that makes the body a prisoner of its own: that is, a prisoner of the images and institutions of material life, of a sedentary and repetitive cycle of being, of memories and maps that were England, the Royal Peace, inveterate practice in the eternal present of myth? Put another way, lived memory is linked more closely to the imagination than to history; it is unconscious, a pure substance, residuous to the techniques, the movements and the mechanics of the body and of all that the body passes through.

At its most profound level the *Lawier's Logike* can be equally well read as a rhetoric of law, as a theory of legal argumentation understood in a topical and figurative sense, as it can be understood as a logic in any stricter or more necessary and demonstrative sense. At the level of inaugural motive, Fraunce's concern is to institute a logic of legal memory, a legal ethics that will embody the patterns and

habits, the law of the uncounted lives and the innumerable generations of a polity, a commonwealth or social body. In a very simple
sense, such a project is in rhetorical terms entirely appropriate; the
path of the law is precisely memory and so the most relevant and
practical science of law will be a theory of memory, of the specific
memories of law, a theory of the mnemonic ground of precedent and
of material life, of the significance of repetition as custom. The art of
memory which Fraunce spells out in terms of a putative logic of law
concentrates on two principal aspects of legal memory: firstly,
language, which carries with it its own memory of meaning, its
morphology as well as its etymologies or notations, the historical
accumulation of lived usage that can be unearthed in the substance of
a language itself; secondly, reason, which is to be understood in terms
of perception or perspicuity, for 'those things we keep best in our
minds which we know by sight and have worked with our eyes'.[1]
Underpinning both categories of legal memory is the argument that
through order an art may reduce the apparently diverse to recognisable schemata; the dismembered or torn[2] body of our law may be
remembered and reformed to the extent that its subject matter, which
is particular and continuously changing, will allow. It is precisely the
'appearance' of reason, the mode of presentation of argument
according to the best available legal topics or invented places of
argument, that guarantees such memorisation as is possible in law:

> [P]rima regula excludes all false and lame precepts, which if it were
> observed in our law, then all repugnant dreams of sergeants and
> counsellors that serve the time and speak for money should not run so
> current for law: nay every judgment given either without reason, or with
> partiality, should not stand for justice: every semble, should not pass for
> a sentence, nor every dictum fuit for a dictator's constitution.[3]

If we turn briefly to the substantive details of the *Lawier's Logike*,
memory governs law not as a series of established particularities,
precedents that will always differ from circumstance to infinite
circumstance, but as 'essential law', as a method of handling, defining
and dividing a system of argument and of sentential (proving) figures.
Memory establishes legal institutions and not the banal specificity of
individual cases: 'so that a man shall by one chapter of [Bracton or]

1 Ibid., p. 430.
2 *Lawiers Logike*, pp. 119a–120b.
3 Ibid., 89a.

Brytton more plainly *perceive* the nature of Garde, Villen and etcetera than by turning and tossing of forty incoherent cases in year books, which do not expound the nature of Garde, Villen, and etcetera, and do presuppose a general *notice* of them'.[1] We remember, in short, through a perception of rational connection, through a conceptual recognition of general relationships, and not through the particular save in so far as the specific image or particular place will call to recollection a relevant pattern or habit or argument: the particular case can provide no 'true definition or explication of the nature and essence of any thing in our law, these singlesowld lawyers and golden asses' who resort to such strategies of precedent give no 'special light' to the issues in hand but rather confuse memory and darken reason.[2] The particular case is indeed prone to destroy memory through digression: 'a man takes upon himself to read from the statute of Fines, and he thrummeth in fifty scattered and undigested cases of estate tail in possession, and as many of the same in reversion, with a cluster of sophistical and incoherent points . . . and makes a well meaning statute the cloak of two hundred ambiguities'.[3] In a more radical definition drawn from Plowden, if the argument appears reasonable then it appears as law.[4] The structure of law must thus be conceived in terms of reason, but it is a rhetorical and mnemonic reason and it is as such, as reasoning that covers ends as diverse as teaching, analysis, disputation and differentation, that the *Lawier's Logike* systematises common law.

The law institutes life as memory through its language and its texts. The legal institution is in its most general sense precisely an inscription of the past in the present; it creates legal personality and subjectivity as a reflection of textual time and of a written imagination. In a very specific sense it establishes a moveable mask, a fictional reason or nomadic body, a body which moves, that is bound and so acts according to the narrative of law. To develop an adequate theory of legal memory is to develop an account of the narrative, the history, through which the law institutes a past – both immediate and immemorial – as text and as progression. Memory is narrational and the law maps that narrative in a story of origins or of the sources from which the law comes, precedent being nothing other than the

1   Ibid., 61a.
2   Ibid., 62a.
3   Ibid., 119a.
4   Ibid., 72a, citing Plowden: 'semblable reason semblable ley'.

cartography of that elastic temporal expanse between the beginning and end of a story, between the exergue and the conclusion, between the exordium and the peroration. The literary scholarship which Fraunce brought from the university is in many senses an ideal discipline for providing the tools which will map the narrative memories of law according to a logic of textual action, a logic of placement which will allow the student of law, the notary, advocate or judge to inscribe a particular circumstance, a case or cause, in the relevant legal narrative and according to the appropriate forms. The first division of legal logic is that of invention. It studies and explicates 'the various divers kinds, characters, affections, relations, and properties of several arguments'.[1] Narrative, in other words, begins with a proposition as to time and place and at the level of legal argument that means that a general head of argument, a category or 'categoreme' – a canon, maxim or rule of consequence – is to be selected as appropriate to the genre or institutional circumstance; it forms the topic, the place or seat or spring of the subsequent narrative action in which the law will institute social being in the mask of legal personality.

The principle of narrative memory as it relates to law is one predicated upon a conception of causes, both logical and legal. In terms of the Ramistic logic which Fraunce follows, at least in a schematic sense, the order of causes is theistic: there is no history without a cause, there is no narrative without origin and that origin is in its most exemplary form the unitary and unifying person of the divinity: 'God is the first and principal cause of all things. All other causes whatsoever are secondary and subject to his eternal direction.'[2] We remember, in other words, by tracing a structure of narrative actions which moves a first principle or *principium*, sovereign or author or God as the case may be, to its consequent or conclusion. Using a variety of examples from the common law, Fraunce proceeds to elaborate the variety of possible causes according to their degree of primacy, the causes of logical narrative being efficient, material, formal and final.[3] The properties of logical narration according to

1 Ibid., 6b.
2 Ibid., 18h
3 See Dudley Fenner, *The Artes*, op. cit., fol. Bib: 'a cause is that which gives some necessary force for the very being of the thing caused'. P. Ramus, *Logike*, op. cit., p. 18: 'the cause is that by whose force the thing is: and therefore this first

types of cause are then set out in terms of aids to specification of the character and content of the narrative: the thing caused must be analysed, the general separated from the special, the thing itself divided into subject and object, the adjuncts of the subject traced. The general schema is commonplace to its epoch and is easily understood. To take some examples: the subject is exercised through its adjuncts, called its object or subject matter as in 'colours be the object of seeing'; or, in terms of the requisite adjuncts to 'presentment' before Justices of the Peace, as set out in Lambard, it is requisite to set out '(i) the name, surname and additions of the party indicted, (ii) the year, day and place in which the offence was done . . . (iv) the manner of the fact, and the nature of the offence as the manner of the treason, felony or trespass'.[1] Once subject, object and further adjuncts pertaining to them have been specified it is necessary to distribute or divide the parts of the argument and to bring them to agreement or to opposition. The best division is from cause and effect, to which Fraunce adds that 'this is a lamentable want in our law, I mean exact division, in place whereof we have nothing else, but either ABC method without coherence or primo notandum, two not three, not four, not five and so on until he come to decimotertio notandum, like dunces in schools and silly babblers in pulpits: that a man were far better to make a new speech than remember this waste and confused schediasmata'.[2] The memory of law, in other words, would sink without trace, were it not for the strategy of logical connection which divides and arranges according to a relation of cause to effect, of subject to object, of general to particular and of definition to thing defined. Along the path of that relation the logician will distribute adjuncts. To take a further example, this time from Stamford on the royal prerogative, the structure of the sentence can be set out in terms of cause and effect, and the relation of (syntactic) progression between them is such that the subject is exercised in the powers of the prerogative and these powers have attached to them certain memorable adjuncts:

> for which cause the laws do attribute to him [the king] all honour,
> dignity, prerogative and preeminence, which prerogative doth not only

place of invention is the fountain of all sciences: for that matter is known perfectly whose cause is understood.'

1   *Lawiers Logike*, 43b–44a, citing Lambard, *Institutions*, bk 2, c5.
2   Ibid., 57b.

extend to his own person, but also to all other his possessions, goods and cattels. As, that his person shall be subject to no man's suit, his possessions cannot be taken from him by violence or wrongful decision: his goods and his cattels are under no tribute, toll or custom, nor otherwise distrainable.[1]

The king rules alone, through a body which is untouchable, inhuman, not his own, a supreme harijan.

The first book of the logic ends with a discussion of places and degree and an exemplification by Fraunce of the way in which any concept can be dragged through all of the topics of invention and distribution and an argument compiled which will prove as much as the subject matter will allow. If we push our reading further, the authority and appeal of the logic resides not simply in the manner in which it aids memory through a reasoned narrative but rather in the relationship it posits between presence and memory, between *logos* and logic. The logic draws argument through the rooms, the places, the corridors, if you will, of memory schematised and imaged so as to be as perspicuous and as straight as possible. The connective principle, already adverted to, is not, however, simply one of visual recollection or remembering. It is more than that; it relies upon a first cause, an origin whose presence is to be traced throughout the argument. It is not only that a legal cause is specific, that it is of a time and place and person, of actions, but also that the construction of legal narrative is dependent upon a transmitted history of prior speech, of the speech of law frozen in the textual history of written usage. The logic establishes the path of legal narrative; it sets up a sorting house, a mail room in which the legal records of past presence can be pigeon-holed as the memory of the common law. These litigants, that body, these properties or words, had fallen to law and here is their monument; this is where they fell; this, as history, was their destiny, their afterlife in law. A logic that classifies and orders a history is not, however, the sum of Fraunce's teaching. The process whereby a logic of law sends on the history of causes, of the originals of the law or at least the legal past, is not the entire narrative. In its rhetorical dimension it requires not simply remembrance but a return to speech, a movement from *logos* to *logos*, from presence to presence: via the avenue of logic, narrative is bestowed a second, rhetorical presence. Fraunce makes an extraordinary point when he distinguishes the

1   Ibid., 6ob.

borrowed – written – argument from the presence of reason: 'arguments borrowed' are properly called witness or testimony and are 'fit only for proof or confirmation'. They take the form of famous sayings, aphorisms, proverbs or natural or written laws, but 'those who use the authority of others instead of argument of their own – are fools ... in these borrowed arguments there is no reason or persuasion, but rather violence and compulsion ... consider not who speaks but how true that which is spoken'.[1] Interesting that a lawyer, or commentator on law, should have the wit to doubt the rational value of common law precedent or what Blackstone called 'establishment' in and of itself. A system of mere rules, something that is no more than a morality, is of little instrumentality: the letter killeth but the spirit, the rhetor, gives life, through speech, through the presence of narrative, through the presence of reason as law and not through the mere invocation of an extinct prose or dry textual dust.

Logic relays the tradition in a particular form; it sends it on and in doing so is forced, in so far as the tradition remains alive, to address it to an audience, to invent recipients, either subjects or those that Karl Kraus termed hallucinations with names and addresses. The specific form of legal presence will be the subject matter of the next chapter; it is predicated upon a narrational constitution, a standing together in the same story. For the moment let us simply report Fraunce's use of the second part of logic, judgment or disposition of arguments, as the method of the habitual or formal presence of law:

> [D]isposition in logic does artificially place, settle, and dispose single arguments one with another, and that first axiomatically, in several axioms: then, proceeding to a syllogism and method, as occasion shall serve. This second part of logic is also called judgment, of the use, commodity and end thereof. For that, by a certain direction, rule and prescription of disposition, arises judgment of the truth or untruth of any axiom; the consequence or inconsequence of any syllogism; and the perspicuity or confused obscurity of any method of proceeding.'[2]

Disposition, in short, coheres the text by ordering the sequence of argument both at the level of the sentence (*gnome*) and at that of units of discourse above the level of the sentence (dianoetical). In each case the subjects of such ordering are axioms, quite literally the bonds of the law (*axioma*) from the Greek, signifying worth of, fit for, dignity or

1   Ibid., 65b, 66b–6;
2   Ibid., 86a.

authority: 'the logicians it would seem, took it for any thing spoken, pronounced, told, as it were, with authority'.[1] The discourse of logic, its use as the vehicle of tradition, is predicated upon a rhetorical desire to order or methodise discourse, to make it appear authoritative, to lend it the stature of teaching or the gravity of law. However such a method is formulated, it is worth observing that law as discourse has no unique claim to authority: 'historiographers, poets, orators and such other speakers and writers, are not bound so strictly to observe this perfection of the first method: but may, according to their matter, meaning, purpose, time, place, persons wisely observe the best of their intent'.[2] Observe also that the authority of legal discourse is a limited and contingent one: the syllogism as a way of formulating arguments may achieve a certain necessity but it is internal to its statement, to the specific linguistic association or 'bond' being made; its subject matter was not in any necessary or consistent sense conceived as being of a demonstrable or non-contingent status. Legal logic simply orders a subject matter of (memorable) axioms of varying degrees of generality and certain only to the extent that they remain tied to the contingency of a past, to a place and circumstance: certainty appertains to 'things past and present'; uncertainty to 'things to come'.[3] All precepts of an art should seek to start from a rule of truth; this ought to be 'necessarily and always true without exception . . . but besides this, they must also be rules of justice, as it were, and also of wisdom, or discretion, or compendious brevity'.[4] We are left to conclude, in other words, that the form of a discourse carried with it the symptoms of its content and it is therefore because legal discourse is future orientated, because the criminal injunction is directed at behaviour yet to come, because the contract determines the potential significance of future events, because a will or a trust or a covenant passes property on to generations to come, to those born and those not yet born, that it will never allow of any greater certainty or necessity than the teaching of method or the resources of memory can provide. In philosophical terms, the logic of law should strive to achieve the status of an ethics, of an habitual and embodied behaviour, a memory inscribed upon the flesh, and not the purely

---

1   Ibid., 87a.
2   Ibid., 113a–114b.
3   Ibid., 87b.
4   Ibid., 88a.

cerebral and subjectifying formalism, the empty monotony, of a morality of rules.

The desire for an ethics can be reformulated in terms of tradition and transmission. Consider that the law begins as an ethics, as an oral way of life, a custody that is spoken through a lived memory, one which makes the body walk upon a particular path. What is important in the concept of an oral tradition is also, however, the fact that an unwritten memory is an unconscious or residual form of life: its writing is organic; it is to be understood both as a fate pronounced as the judgment of the wise and also as an inner speech. In Nietzsche's terms the first writing was an inscription upon the body.[1] The second writing was inscription upon other bodies, upon the text, the vellum made from the skin of deer or the wethers made from sheep. The material form that carries tradition as text – the *textus* is after all a weaving, a wool, something that would go well with wethers – is not insignificant. The text carries a message, an address, a life that grows cyclically, a life that is reproduced in specific forms: something which we hope for although we cannot know with any certainty that it will return as the same. All that we have to hold on to a culture with, or to reproduce or change it, are the uncertain marks, the material lines, of a remembered past now uncertainly present in its future. Alternatively, we are left with no more (and no less) than language as the vehicle of the past in the present. Where legal memory is genuinely a question of time out of mind or of time immemorial, it is language which is exemplary of the unwritten inscription of things and thereby stands for or symbolises the origin of things: 'notation or etymology is

---

1   Nietzsche, *The Genealogy of Morals* (1910, Edinburgh), pp. 65–6: 'How is a memory to be made . . . ? How is an impression to be so deeply fixed upon this ephemeral understanding . . . upon this incarnate forgetfulness, that it will be permanently present? As one may imagine, this primeval problem was not solved by exactly gentle answers and gentle means; perhaps there is nothing more awful and more sinister in the early history of man than his *system of mnemonics*. Something is burnt in so as to remain in his memory: only that which never stops *hurting* remains in his memory.' See also A. Lingis, *Excesses, Eros and Culture* (1983, New York), ch. 2, for a brilliant development of this theme. At p. 23: 'what we are dealing with is inscription. Where writing, graphics, is not inscription on clay tablets, bark or papyrus, but in flesh and blood, and also where it is not historical, narrative. Where it is not significant, not a matter of marks whose role is to signify, to efface themselves before the meaning, or ideality, or logos. For here the signs count: they hurt. Before they make sense to the reader, they give pain to the living substrate.'

the interpretation of a word. For words be notes of things, and of all words either derivative or compound, you may yield some reason made [fet] from the first arguments, if the notation be well made. It is called *Originatio, quod originem verborum explicet; et etymologia, id est, veriloquium.*[1] Where the reason is unknown or the word is obscure then, for Fraunce, the subsequent argument is dangerous. To understand the words of a profession such as law is to understand that which they note, a history, a tradition, the passage of time and of lives. They form the frame through which a body is perceived, they mark, they map, they constitute both the polity and the polity of the soul. If being human is to be a 'speaking being', the forgotten frame of that speech is the discourse of law. In the strongest of terms, at the level of structure, language has its own logic, language frames speech and manipulates discourse; it speaks the Law in advance of the lawyer for, as Fraunce notes, 'words also, as words, have causes, effects, subjects, adjuncts and other arguments to be considered'. It is interesting to think that words have causes and adjuncts, subjects and effects, that language has memories but also its own system, its own logic: we use it as lawyers for the purpose of exchange but what if we were exchanged by language, by legal language, by a system of texts that as individuals we had no power to change.

Of Law and Forgetting

As the author of the *Lawier's Logike*, Fraunce, like his text, was forgotten. He had 'moved the patience' of the lawyers, those whom he 'most desired to be patient', and they responded as he feared: grudgingly, recalcitrantly, they refused to be better scholars, resisted the claims of the *Logike* and ignored the system that it presented. If we read Fraunce now, it is as a transplant, as a thing forgotten by law, as the work of an outsider who remained an outsider for four centuries, perhaps for longer. If we return to our starting point, however, we may suspect that even here the oppositions between inside and outside, between success and failure, us and them, are less hermetic than is often apparent.[2] We argued that there are always

---

1 *Lawiers Logike*, 51a.

2 Nietzsche, *Genealogy of Morals*, op. cit., p. 61: 'Forgetfulness is no mere *vis inertiae*, as the superficial believe, rather it is a power of obstruction, active and, in the strictest sense of the word, positive – a power responsible for the fact that

elements of the outside within, that there is a little pain in our pleasure, that there are traces of failure in every success, while the text itself – even, or especially, when unread – carries with it the lives and practices that surrounded it, that formed its culture. A text is never simply a thing; its materiality is embedded, and whether it was read or remained unread matters little in terms of its essential textuality, its existence as discourse within a formation of discourse or the inception of a science. That a text is forgotten does not and cannot mean that it thereby loses its history; its history is precisely contained in the modes of its disappearance. No text, let us repeat, vanishes objectively, without residue, without trace. Let us say that a disappearance has its own aesthetics; it is never final. In that sense the desire to re-read Fraunce's *Logike* is coincident with the desire to understand legal science from a different frame, from a perspective that has been tilted by non-reception, by the strategies of forgetting that accompany any tradition, that create its underside, its positive unconscious: 'that level of knowledge that eludes the scientist and yet is part of scientific discourse'.

It remains to trace that positive unconscious, that negative structure of legal science, and to specify in this particular instance, in relation to this one text, what it might mean both then and now, in terms of criticism and law, in terms of the institution and of the lives that it institutes. We will trace, in other words, the trajectory of success to read the failures left in its wake; we will trace success precisely in terms of, and from the perspective of, its failures, a tradition understood in terms not of its monuments but of its ruins. In that Fraunce already provides a reading of his own text in terms of its probable failure, its non-reception, our task is made easier: it is at precisely these points that Fraunce saw his contribution as most positive, that it was always likely to fail to gain recognition. These were its points of crisis; these were the arguments that would disappear and that continue to disappear before our eyes. They will be grouped here around three issues or sets of questions. Firstly, at the level of legal culture, how was a relationship to be instituted between the guild mentality of the profession – and the esoteric mysteries that constituted its peculiar knowledge – and the other disciplines and institutions of a rapidly changing polity, a sociality whose techno-

what we have lived, experienced, taken into ourselves, no more enters into consciousness . . .'

logical base was changing dramatically? Secondly, in a more particular sense, if law was a scholarly discipline, or at least as a learned language and as an inherited system of classically dogmatic procedures was to be systematised again in the light of the Renaissance rediscovery of the classics, from where was this rewriting to take place? The philosophy that Fraunce appropriated and worked with was 'modern', but it was also continental. How would these characteristics relate to an insular tradition and an essentially conservative method? Finally, the *Lawier's Logike* presented a positive reclassification of the common law in terms, as we have seen, of a logic of memory: it was concerned to present a theory of legal memory based upon the transmission of historical residues, the memory of what was lived and of the language that recorded those lives. It was in that sense concerned with a secular or essentially profane reading of law in the face of a tradition that was far from secular and which responded to criticism by ever more arbitrarily and vehemently reasserting its own version of a mythic narrative or imagined history in which law was a sacrosanct 'presence', a presence to be called down from its immemorial territory outside of the materiality of any merely lived memory, and beyond the reach of any secular logic or temporally based narrative of institutional languages and institutional acts.

If we are to understand the failed science for which Fraunce stood, if we are to understand the disappearance of his text and to map the place where he fell, it is as well to begin with an account of the concept of criticism for which he and the 'moderns' or Ramists stood. At a general level the notion of a critical reformation of the vernacular disciplines was a simple one. The disciplines were dogmatic in the literal sense of being 'unthinking' or merely learned. In that sense a discipline such as rhetoric or logic, theology or poetry, consisted of little more than a list of learned truths or axioms borrowed from a classical text.[1] As a discipline it thus had no order or method of its own but was based rather upon a singular principle of emulation or imitation; it was to be learned by rote, memorised and passed on. The only history to which a discipline could thus aspire was an internal one, a narcissistic history of its own development: an eternal present of its own peculiar or specific but isolated truths. An internal history also, of course, precludes the possibility of comparison, as between

---

1 *Lawiers Logike*, 7a.

disciplines or as between authors and traditions. It escapes the lifeworld and equally evades placement within any concept of knowledge. Thus, to follow the example used earlier, Gabriel Harvey's attempt to rework the discipline of rhetoric is based precisely upon a desire to re-appropriate and rethink a formulaic tradition. He endeavours to compare Cicero to other authors so as 'to gauge his excellence'.[1] Harvey's purpose was to come to terms with the fact that Cicero, however venerable, was not without fault. How was one to understand what it meant to be a Ciceronian if not by comparing Cicero to other authors and other lives? Thus he comments crucially: 'I began forthwith to understand how dangerous it is for one enslaved to prejudiced opinions to take shelter in the authority of this or that group of men; it is tantamount to entering a slave-dungeon – I saw that I must return to the old masters'.[2] The error of the Italians and of their modern followers was essentially that of developing a method based entirely upon imitation and so free of the possibility of detecting blemishes or faults in the classic texts and free also of any aspiration to develop or translate Cicero across the boundaries of historical eras. Cicero was to be 'presenced' by the techniques of dogma; it was not any part of that method to question or debate Cicero in relation to contemporary knowledges.

For Fraunce, a critical science of law could also begin by questioning the internal history of the discipline and so by challenging the dogmatic quality of legal method: 'they prate of method who never knew order'.[3] Indeed it was not simply that lawyers knew nothing of philosophic method; their discipline was actively hostile to the comparative and interdisciplinary questions that philosophic method brought with it: 'you would love the law but *sine rivali* [without rivals]; you would reign, but alone, *hinc illae lachrymae* [hence those tears]'.[4] It was for precisely this reason that Fraunce turned, at the level of philosophic method, to a critical re-reading of Aristotle and to the development of a modern order for the discipline of law based upon a reworked conception of dialectic. He wished to break down the insular internal history of the common law and its worship of Littleton in favour of a science that could be written into an historically conceived episteme or order of knowledge. He wished to

1 Gabriel Harvey, *Ciceronianus*, op. cit., p. 57.
2 Ibid., p. 71.
3 *Lawiers Logike*, preface, vi.
4 Ibid., vii.

break down the formulae of a system of esoteric and 'hotchpot' writs and uncounted concepts in favour of a science of disputation and judgment with a basis in a philosophic order rather than in a purely contingent accumulation of details and particularities. If the history of legal practice were to be read philosophically, it could be seen not as the arbitrary piling up of coincidences but as the development of categories of argument relating to concepts of property, tenure, servitude, obligation and the like which were the product of an existent lifeworld, the residues of practices, the effluvia of everyday life. At the level of legal knowledge, Fraunce also intended to break down the insularity of the common law by reference to and comparison with other systems of legal classification and practice. It was to the historical school of legal method developed on the continent and to the writings of the civilians that he turned to clarify both the history of European law and the narrative of its geographical passage, its translation and transplantation, across the boundaries of the European states. To understand the failure of those two ambitions, to understand how they were excluded from the science that was subsequently developed, is to understand one part of the positive unconscious of common law method, the fear of materiality, the horror of an historically conceived lifeworld, upon which a dogmatic science is founded. In material terms Fraunce also indicates certain elements of motive underlying those fears. The law, conceived as a market for legal services, would always be most effective and most highly valued if, even in the face of the printing presses and the vernacularisation of the sciences, it could maintain the mentality and closure of an esoteric guild whose mysteries were to remain hidden in a foreign language, whose concepts were to continue to be insular and defined in artistic terms and whose method was to remain inacessible to the order of reason. It was in such a manner that lawyers could maintain the high value of legal knowledge and the financial gentility of the profession. While the desire to continue the market viability of the profession is understandable, it was no part of the scholarship of law to affirm timidly the principles of obscurity upon which that market had hitherto been based. To sell and to understand were for Fraunce two different spheres of exchange even if both were subject to considerations of value. A theory of law such as Fraunce proposed had its value – if it had any – in the order of knowledges and not in that of commodities; its gold was to be the dust of reason and not the immediate coinage of the realm.

The second aspect of Fraunce's failure was of an equally contemporary relevance. To democratise or simply to open up the discipline of law entailed a move away from little England, its insular tradition, its myth of separateness. It required also that the continental basis of that tradition in the Hellenic and Latin classics, the history of their transplantation and translation, be recognised and rethought, that the faces of English scholarship turn again to those particular sources of their inspiration. Even if one were to understand law in purely market terms, the market was placed on a route between London and the continent, historically between Bologna, Montpellier, Paris and London – and what merchant would ignore his suppliers? Consider the two key features of Fraunce's attack on the insularity of English legal knowledge. It required that the newly formed science come to terms both with modernity – the age of the Renaissance – and with the cosmopolitan basis of Renaissance knowledges. These two orientations are connected in the sense that both have their origin on the continent: both modernity and knowledge came, in this instance, from abroad and they came as hotly disputed terms. In invoking these outside causes Fraunce was concerned not simply to recognise but also to translate and rewrite the foreign terms. In an ironic self-parody Fraunce writes: 'Good God what a world is this? What an age do we live in? A sophister of times past was a title of credit, and a word of commendation, now what more odious? Aristotle then the father of philosophy, now who less favoured? . . . Antiquity is [now] nothing but dunsicality, and one's fore fathers' inventions unprofitable trumpery.' Such was the iconoclastic character of the modern age: it challenged the inherited forms, it questioned the wisdom of the classics, it sought to rewrite the dogma of an elliptical and veiled past by drawing it towards the contemporary and, in the case of English law, towards the continent as well.

The institutional and specifically the legal professions' response to the 'moderns', to an intellectual movement concerned to open the law to the possibilities of intellectual history and comparative criticism, is curiously familiar to contemporary ears. The profession had its own procedures, its own method and its own history; it was indeed the best, most perfect and most ancient of all the professions and of all the systems of law. To challenge these internal features of the institution would be to participate in a nihilistic or at least straightforwardly and pointlessly destructive fragmentation of genteel tradition and venerable usage; it would destroy unnecessarily the grand narrative of legal progress and tear down the honoured forms, the separateness, the security, the difference of the profession. More than that, if law was not revered as a practice unto itself, social order would be likely to, indeed undoubtedly would, decay and the polity would eventually be torn limb from limb: its language, its consensual forms of co-existence, its harmonies and hierarchies would all be shattered.[1] And all this for no practical purpose; the critics were philosophers and not lawyers, educators and not practitioners. What could they possibly know of the dreadful particularities, the intricate procedures and the significant forms of a law that was as much a matter of folk memory, of ethnic *geist* or at least of an oral tradition and *communis opinio iuris*, of a tacit knowledge, as it was of explicit textual rules? And again, how could a comparative criticism based upon continental philosophy and civilian law have any relevance to the insular tradition, to the specific usages of our common law, our England? Had not Fortescue already dismissed the continentals and their obsessive sophistry, their casuistry based upon Justinian's imperial law with its absurd principle of *principium placita*? The polemic that Fraunce attempted to inaugurate was thus one which touched the nerves, the economic and political patience, of the established and growing profession; it raised questions in which the stakes were high; it 'in fact concerned the interpretation and control over the philosophical (and hence religious) canon, over the minds of contemporaries and youth, and so ultimately, over a major form of social and political power, at least within the educational institutions of Europe'.[2] In a culture in which it is bad manners, ungentle and perhaps dishonourable to talk politics outside of the specific institutional sites of political discourse, it is surprising that Fraunce here met with silence: why talk to those who lack professional knowledge and worse still probably lack breeding as well? In Coke's unequivocal formulation, 'alas our books of law seem to them to be dark and obscure; but no wise will impute to the laws, but to their ignorance, who by their sole and superficial reading of them cannot understand the depth of them. I will not sharpen the nib of my pen against them, for that I pity the persons, and wish they had

1 As, for example, Thomas Wilson, *The Arte of Rhetorique*, op. cit., pp. 92–3: 'Take away the law, and take away our lives, for nothing maintains our wealth, our health, and the safeguard of our bodies, but the law of the Realm, whereby the wicked are condemned, and the Godly are defended.'

2 D. Kelley, 'Horizons of Intellectual History' (1987) xlviii *Journal of the History of Ideas* 143 at 145.

more discretion'.[1] The tradition, in other words, precisely as tradition, is perfect; it has to be understood, it exists to be understood and there is no place for criticism in that custodial task of exposition of a law too rich and too deep to be fully comprehended in any one body in any one lifetime. The law is always greater, in other words, than its servants, its practitioners: any apparent faults or contradictions are the errors of men and not of the law, for *in hominis vitium non professionis*.[2]

The latter statement brings us to our final considerations of Fraunce's failure, of the terms and conditions that instituted a failure quite literally too profound for words, too profound at least to merit refutation. Where did he fall if he fell outside the law while living with it? Where did he fall if he fell beyond the boundaries of this new science of an age-old and hallowed tradition? Where did he fall if legal history signally failed to record his demise, if he went unread and unremembered? What place was this in the geography of the discipline, a site of non-memory specifically circumscribed for a theory of legal memory? What species of science was it that established itself upon so complete and successful a repression: one which in Heidegger's terms had forgotten that it had forgotten this figure, this text, this memory, this man? Let us put it slightly differently: if legal science established itself upon the negative basis of a refusal of philosophy and modernity, if it refused comparison with other continental thought and with continental law, then it was left with no stronger theoretical basis for its method than memory alone, a memory cut off from reason and lost to contemporaneity. Such a practice of memory refused even to contemplate the possibility of a theory of memory not because it lacked a past but because its memories were not the memories of man, of the lifeworld or of lived history and language, but rather they were those of a sacred presence or of an eternal and mythic continuity of the spirit, the breath and voice of divine reason and natural law. It was *traditio*, which is to say authoritative clericist tradition, sclerotic sacral wisdom, that was recollected in the most excellent and antique of all laws. Its memories were, for Coke, simply and directly the recollection of *vetustatis et veritatis vestigia*,[3] the memories of an age-old truth which was only comprehensible as being the same for all people at all times and in all

1   Coke, *Reports*, Pt X, Aa1b.
2   Ibid., II, 6a–b.
3   Ibid., VIII, L3a–b.

places, legal gold with a value that can only increase, a perfection that cannot know the blemishes or the blandishments of time. The procedures or methods of access to a truth which is conceived as external to the lifeworld and so to the contingency of human relations are the precise antithesis of the procedures of any critical reason or comparative history. Memory in the hands of the legal tradition is not an historical method but rather a technique of faith: through the recollection of previous instances of legal presence, through establishment or precedent, the law continuously rediscovers itself; it is made present to itself as *logos* or the word incarnate. Memory within such a rigorously internal history of a discipline is simply the witness of presence, the testimony of authority, the repetition of externally given truths. In the next chapter we will examine the specific methods and forms of presence that this truth took in the hands of the science of law; we will trace the relationship between memory and *logos* within the tradition that was actually established, our tradition, in which memory is always accompanied by forgetfulness, the *logos* by its shadows.

In conclusion we should note the crucial consequence of Fraunces's failure not simply in terms of the struggle for power within an educational institution but much more profoundly in terms of the character of the English legal tradition. What fell with Fraunce was not only the possibility of a scholarly tradition within the common law but also the possibility of a system of commentary or jurisprudence in the continental sense of a conversation with the past, a rewriting of the law in each act of judgment. Any tradition is based upon memory and upon repetition as the means whereby interpretation in a strong sense is possible. Repetition is never simply repetition. It informs the past, it adds to it, it brings it into the present through conversation, through the oral modes of the lifeworld. Interpretation is the essential scholarly activity for it is commentary that makes texts live, that differentiates the present from the past and recuperates that which must have been lived for a discourse to take the form that it does. The common law tradition excluded Fraunce's account of the logic of memory; it also thereby excluded 'university men' or scholars as active participants in the institution. It was to remain to the present an internally defined and self-perpetuating professional body in which the guild setting of the Inns of Court and of the Colleges of Law were to be the educational and professional establishments, the institutions of a profession in which the scholar or the university had neither authority nor any active role to play. The university was left to emulate the profession and either to imitate its internal procedures of reasoning or to suffer irrelevance. We can go further. It is commentary which makes a theory of memory possible; it is interpretation which relates memory to the lifeworld and tradition to that which is lived. Without commentary, both as method and as institutional place, tradition lacks life; it remains an external and spectral presence, a faith that calls down an absent source to remedy through spiritual presence an otherwise disinvested life. It is memory as initiate hallucination, as hollow form, as uninhabited space. That is the fate of the common law and the significance of Fraunce's failure. That is where he fell and where the common law rose in his place. When the dues are paid, however, is it not more likely that any critical form of legal scholarship in the common law world will judge Fraunce's fall as more heroic and more potent, as more significant and more memorable, than the idle passion or dance of death that took his place? To lose a battle is not to lose the war: *logos* throws many shadows, memory harbours (as repression) that which was forgotten, the common law still awaits its scholars and a history that exceeds the merely antiquarian, a memory that goes beyond the dormant immobility of the display case or the curio shop, a tradition in short that finally steps out of the museum of precedent.

3

The Eucharist and English Law: A Genealogy of Legal Presence in the Common Law Tradition

'At supper . . . Not where he eats but where he is eaten.'[1]

Memory is always the memory of presence. To understand a tradition, to understand a law based upon precedent, one therefore needs to understand not simply the order of its memories but the theory of presence that those memories imply. For the common law tradition, for the science of jurisprudence that blossomed on the soil that had been barren for Abraham Fraunce's theory of historical memory, the theory of presence returns us to the Anglican tradition. It is in the debates between Sir Thomas More and Tyndale over the proper translation of the Bible, over the meaning of the sacraments and so also over the meaning of '*ecclesia*'; between Sir Thomas More and Saint German over methods of interpretation and the correct language of the law; in the oath of supremacy; in Richard Hooker's defence of the old English order[2] and in Coke's attack on the historians, on Hotman in particular, that we can piece together the elements that make up the English tradition and its constitution, that of the common law. The legal tradition had its basis, its foundation, in a notion of tradition and of polity that was borrowed directly from the Anglican Church. While there is nothing suprising in the translation of theology, of religious concepts, into secular law, the details of that process of translation have been sufficiently ignored by the antiquarians who pass for historians of the common law to justify a close analysis of the Eucharist and its meaning for English law.

---

1 *Hamlet*, IV, iii.
2 The expression is taken from D. Little, *Religion, Order and Law* (1970, Oxford), ch. 5. Hooker's *Of the Laws of Ecclesiastical Polity*, Books 1–5 are available in a 1907 edition, edited by C. Morris (London); for books 6–8, J. Keble (ed.) *Works* (1888, London).

Supper at Emmaus

At Emmaus the resurrected Christ was recognised not by face or image, nor by speech or body, but in the simple act of eating. It was, according to Luke (24: 30–1), when the apostles saw Christ breaking bread in the evening at Emmaus that they recognised him as the Son of man: 'their eyes were opened and they knew him; and he vanished out of their sight'. The breaking of bread was the sign of divine presence pre-ordained at the last supper. Emmaus was proof, if you will, of what Christ had said at the last supper prior to his betrayal and sacrifice. Emmaus signified that what dies can live on, that what passes can be remembered, that what is present is always potentially a reference to some other order of being or to some other text. For the sake of simplicity we will examine the last supper itself as the referent of the bread broken or the body betrayed at Emmaus. We will analyse the order of reference established at the last supper while always bearing in mind that at Emmaus Christ's Eucharistic presence was acted out again.

This was no ordinary supper. The Lord ate bread and drank wine for the last time. Here flesh and blood became spirit through an act of Communion. Here man received the first sign of the law through an act of sacrifice. 'That the Lord Jesus the same night in which he was betrayed took bread: and when he had given thanks, he brake it, and said, Take, eat: this is my body, which is broken for you: this do in remembrance of me . . . for as often as ye eat this bread, and drink this cup, ye do shew the Lord's death till he come' (1 Corinthians 12). The Eucharist, the repetition of the Last Supper at every Mass in every church, is the exemplary sign of the Christian faith; it is the sacrament, the appearance of grace, the continuing presence of Christ. It is also the original ritual of authority, the source of power of the Church, in that it is for Catholicism only through the consecration of the bread and wine that they can become substance: that is, the flesh and blood of the Lord.

The significance of the Eucharist to the Church needs little reiteration. It was over the Eucharist that the Church went to war with itself in the Reformation and the Counter-Reformation, a dispute triggered by divergences of interpretation of the nature of Christ's presence in the bread and wine of the sacrament: was the holy presence transubstantial or consubstantial? Was the presence simply 'there', as the reformers claimed, in the text, in the words, in the anaphoric 'this' of 'this is my body', or was the presence more complex, as the Romans claimed, a production of the Church itself by means of interpretation and consecration? Innumerable lives were lost at the stake over the question of how the faithful should interpret the signs of the Lord's presence. What were its proper forms of representation, of re-presencing? The theological debates, however, also have a real political and legal significance, one which is less well known and in need of recuperation.

At one level, the theory of the Eucharist is a theory of signification as such.[1] It is a theory of the sign and of how the sign relates to presence, to an existent or 'experiential' thing, to an object, the body of Christ. It is also a theory of interpretation: behind these words, behind these material objects – bread and wine – is hidden the body of the Lord. Only through commentary, through authoritative interpretation, can we have access to that substance, that body and that blood. Finally, however, we need to observe a more specific historical relation between the theory of meaning, of divine truth, that the Eucharist represents and the development of the common law tradition, a tradition also based upon a theory of signs of truth, of law, and the modes of their interpretation. We may note first that the law comes from God and that the nature of God and of God's presence in the flesh is always going to be an essential question of law. Not only is God the source (*causa causans*) of law, but God is also the arbiter of truth, of meaning and of judgment; it is he who is the judge on the day of the Last Judgment. The conceptual apparatus of the Church, the theology of presence in the Eucharist, becomes in law the question of the 'spirit of law', of the 'living voice of law', of the presence of law as it is disinterred or resurrected through tradition as well as through the legal text, through equity, through the *ecclesia* of the court, through the wisdom of the judges, the sages or holy men (*sacerdotes*) of the common law. Let it not be forgotten also that in merry England in 1532 the Crown annexed the Church and through the Act of Supremacy Henry

---

1   On the thesis of a movement from theology to law, see L. Marin, *Portrait of the King* (1988, London), pp. 3–15; idem, *La Parole mangée et autres essais théologico-politiques* (1986, Paris), ch. 1. Also E. Kantorowicz, *The King's Two Bodies: A Study in Medieval Political Theology* (1956, New Jersey); idem, *Selected Studies* (1965, New York); M. Gauchet, *Le Désenchantement de monde: une histoire politique de la religion* (1988, Paris), especially pp. 292–302; G. Post, *Studies in Medieval Legal Thought* (1964, New Jersey), especially chs. VIII and X. For a psychoanalytic account, see A. Lingis, *Excesses: Eros and Culture* (1983, New York), ch. 5.

VIII, who already had the title of *Fidei Defensor* (Defender of the Faith), became head of both Church and State, of the Lords spiritual and temporal, of the law natural and positive.

How the Anglican Church resolved the question of Eucharistic presence became, by virtue of the Reformation in England, a question of state, a secular and legal question as well as a matter of strict theology. For the purposes of understanding the legal tradition that emerges from that century, for the purposes of understanding our tradition and our law, we need to understand that law as having a source which combines both spiritual and temporal authority. We also need to understand the tradition that emerges most explicitly in the writings of Sir Edward Coke and Sir John Davies, as being an authoritative tradition, a tradition drawn from and backed by the Church. To understand the theory of sources and of memory and interpretation that the lawyers put forward we need to understand interpretatation as such, interpretation as being governed by the theory of *logos*, the theory of the Eucharistic presence as well as of the incarnate word which St John places at the beginning, as source and as light and truth (John 1:1). We will begin with a description of the elements of Eucharistic theory, and then move to examine the parallel discourse of lawyers, the founding documents of the common law curriculum as it established itself at the 'third university', the Inns of Court.[1] Our account will be both conceptual and historical: we begin with a conceptual model and interpretation of certain aspects of the Eucharistic tradition and then relate that model to the particular history of an Anglican common law.

The Eucharist

The narrative of the Eucharist is a foundational one. It is not only that, as Freud discusses at length in *Totem and Taboo*,[2] the story of a

1   See Sir E. Coke, *Reports* (1777 edn, London), C5a; Sir George Buc, *The Third Universitie of England* (1612/1615, London), p. 966: 'But admit that this city had no other colleges in it; but the Inns of Court, nor other sciences studied and professed in it, but the laws, yet might London (as Justice Fortescue well observed and held) be as worthily styled a university as either Angers or Orleans in France, or as Pavia or Perugia in Italy, wherein the study of civil law, is only professed.'

2   S. Freud, *Totem and Taboo* (1939, London), ch. 4, pp. 153–4: 'thus through the ages we see the identity of the totem feast with the animal sacrifice, the theanthropic human sacrifice, and the Christian eucharist, and in all these solemn

sacrifice lies at the basis of all religious and legal traditions, but rather that the particular character of that sacrifice will determine, in metaphysical terms, the forms of sociality, the nature of the community and of its law. It will do so precisely because the Last Supper is an account of the founding of community, of the establishment of an order of memory and of the authority of that memory, its law. It is through the ceremony of Communion, through the ritual of the Eucharist, that the divine is made human, that the word becomes flesh, that authority is made present.

First, the notion of presence itself. Throughout any account of the Eucharist there runs a theme of presence: the ritual of the Eucharist is one of representation; it 're-presences' through the imagery of the Communion, through the bread and the wine and through the words that accompany them, a presence that is absent, a past presence; the signs used in the Communion provide a substitute or duplicate of a presence that is not present in either the time or the place of ritual enactment. The Eucharistic presence is in a literal sense a simulation. In a spiritual sense, however, the presence that is represented is more real than the real; it is the presence of the Spirit, of grace, of the sacred; it is presence in the strong sense of *prae-sens*,[1] that is, of something both before and in advance of the senses, something continuous with but in excess of an object, an anticipation and an imminence that negates, suspends, both time and space by virtue of the power of the event, of a sacrament that 'is a reality complete unto itself, that has an independent existence . . . we must recall that the sacramental is altogether *sui generis*'.[2] If we list the specific attributes of the

occasions we recognize the after-effects of that crime which so oppressed men, but of which they must have been proud. At bottom, however, the Christian communion is a new setting aside of the father, a repetition of the crime that must be expiated.'

1 On the etymology of presence see E. Benveniste, *Problémes de linguistique générale* (1964, Paris), pp. 132–9. On the impossibility of understanding presence except as a unity of diverse elements, as an image that embodies a history and a future, see L. Marin (1986), op. cit., pp. 210–11, 213–16. For a comparable point made in criticism of the Catholic Church, see A. Schmemman, *L'Eucharistie* (1985, Paris). On the general history of eucharist thinking, see Y. Brilioth, *Eucharistic Faith and Practice: Evangelical and Catholic* (1930, London).

2 Schmemman, op. cit., pp. 24–5. Marin (1986), op. cit., makes a similar point in arguing that the image of the king is irreducible, its presence is a unity of elements that do not exist outside of their unity, outside of their representation in the totality of the image, the icon.

Eucharistic presence, we may start precisely with this quality of otherness that presence implies.

Of the Body and of its Sacrifice

The first words of divine presence and equally of the ritual recollection of that presence concern the body: 'this is my body' (*hoc est corpus meum*). However, it is not clear, linguistically, what 'this' refers to, whether the bread or the body. 'This' has a general and confused reference to a presence, to something present, a body, but it transpires that it is an invisible body of which 'this' is no more than symptom. 'This' does not refer directly to any single or particular material body; it refers to a complex sign of presence and more specifically to a sacrifice which will constitute a particular species of body and of presence. Ironically, the breaking of the bread is indicative of a sacrifice, a crucifixion, the destruction of a body so as to cleanse or remit or simply to make a new body. The question of what this body is, which body, remains disputable. In the Catholic tradition the bread represents a hidden body, the body of Christ 'which was given for you', a body which it transpires was in fact sacrified so as to save the order of believers. It is thus the sacrificial body with which we are concerned: the body, this body, has to be read, to be seen through the act of sacrifice: 'for as often as ye eat this bread, and drink this cup ye do shew the Lord's death till he come' (I Corinthians 11: 26).

It is an act of betrayal that establishes an order of belief; it is the destruction of a body that founds the social body and translates a visible presence into the immanent presence, the intimacy of the divine or the *corpus mysticum* of the state. Sacrifice is the exemplary religious act: through destruction, through death or through some other symbolisation of disappearance, of the chance and irrationality of the imaginary, it draws its participants, its witnesses, away from the material world, the world of utility and of things, towards an invisible realm, one of foundations, of sovereignty, of the divine, a realm of myth. That sacrifice is necessary is a matter of ensuring obedience to the gods, but then also to knowledge, to an inaugural legitimacy or space of foundation: 'the greatest negation of the real order is the one most favourable to the appearance of the mythical order'.[1] It is from that space, that mythical order of invisible presence, that the law must speak:

> [I]t is from this perspective, one in which the symbolic sacrifice necessarily accompanies the creation of a foundational [social] space, that the question of [law] must be re-examined. At the bottom of such an interrogation, we can see without difficulty the essential and inescapable political questions that face hyper-industrial societies. What are the forms of sacrifice in such societies?[2]

This is also to ask not only what are the forms of immolation (of consumption) but also what are the forms of betrayal, complicity and guilt that lead the participants back to the site of destruction, the symbolic place of sacrifice?

Intimacy and Authority

In secularised legal terms, the sacrifice founds the authority of law; it establishes the state as the social body, the invisible or mystic continuance that was the Crown and became the sovereignty of Parliament. In terms of positive law, the sacrifice is symbolic: prosaically, it simply denotes the subjection of the individual to law, of the singular body to the social body, of the physical to the spiritual. The constitution, the invisible and unwritten law of laws that founds the English state, can only properly be said to exist in the realm of legal fiction; it is this body, this law, this *corpus iuris* of which the citizen is a subject by virtue of the sacrifice of a portion of reality, a sacrifice traditionally symbolised in jurisprudence by a social contract in which the individual relinquishes a series of natural rights and powers to Leviathan or a sovereign body so as to become a member of that order or continuance that the social body represents. The sacrifice engenders a community based upon the intimacy of having given something up, of having let something go; the complicity of assassins is also the intimacy of community for 'what is intimate, in [a] strong sense, is what has the passion of an absence of individuality'.[3]

---

1 G. Bataille, *Theory of Religion*; (1989, New York), p. 45; see also idem, *The Accursed Share* (1988, New York), p. 55: 'sacrifice restores to the sacred world that which servile use has degraded, rendered profane.'

2 P. Legendre, *L'Inestimable Objet de la transmission* (1985, Paris), p. 67.

3 Bataille (1989), op. cit., p. 50. Note also Freud, op. cit., at p. 138: 'The holy mystery of the sacrificial death was justified in that only in this way could the holy

In psychoanalytic terms, the sacrifice and its repetition in sacrificial rituals, in Communion but also in punishment, binds the law to the power of the symbolic. The sacrifice is an original act of force; the community founds itself through the killing of the father, through an act of foundational violence which comes subsequently to be repeated in purely symbolic forms; the original violence lies in wait, its threat founds an order of law, of obedience to rules, of behavioural normality:

> The father that founds the human social community is the internalised, spiritual father. And this forces us to see that the socialisation does not bind through a persistence in memory of the image of the real threat of aggression from a more powerful other outside, but through the eucharist by which the paternal reality, now vanquished and abolished, is constituted as an internal imperative that makes the libido speak, that is, address itself as the demand of the other.[1]

The acceptance, the internalisation, of authority in the Eucharist can thus be understood as a re-enactment of the sacrifice and of that which the sacrifice most immediately stood for: in giving his body and shedding his blood, Christ submitted to his Father's will, he died that others might be redeemed, but more, he died for his Father – literally, *pro patria mori*. Christ's 'self-oblation to death'[2] is mimicked in each Communion service; the communicant, in remembering the Last Supper, remembers also that he must be prepared to die, to offer himself, if the need arise, if God wills, to be sacrificed. The presence that is duplicated in the Eucharist is a presence of self-oblation, of submission.

Memory, Memorial and Law

The Eucharist represents a sacrifice and it should be remembered that it is one function and indeed one meaning of sacrifice that it introduces the sacred, the *sacra*.[3] How then can one understand the

bond be established which united the participants with each other and with their god.'

1   Lingis, op. cit., p. 98.

2   Brilioth, op. cit., p. 56. Also H. De Lubac, *'Corpus Mysticum': L'Eucharistie et l'eglise au Moyen Age* (1949, Paris).

3   On the etymologies, see Benveniste, *Le Vocabulaire des institutions Indo-Européennes* (1969, Paris), pp. 187–92. See also G. Bataille, *Erotism, Death and Sensuality* (1986, San Francisco), pp. 81–94.

Eucharist other than as a constant reminder, an endlessly repeated memory of the sacred, of its existence, of its presence? The Communion commemorates, it recollects, it is done 'in remembrance of me', and each time that it is done it proclaims a faith by way of living memory, by way of repetition. What is crucial is that such a sacrificial rite of memory constitutes that which is remembered as a memorial, as something more than simple or mere memory; it is, through bread and wine and consecratory words, a return to an origin, an allegory of its continuance and an institutionalisation of an unimpeachable and authoritative presence. The signs of the Eucharist are more than simple references, as Bataille argues: their sacrificial quality returns servile objects to the sacred world. It also turns an act of recollection into a monument of the past, a memory of presence into a sacral assembly, a mystery, a church (*ecclesia*).

Two aspects of the form of Eucharistic memory deserve a degree of emphasis. There is first the quality of a memory that does not simply recollect a past presence, in symbolic or iconic or imaginary form: through the sacraments, the memory of the Church is one which reproduces that presence, which changes the reality of the participants by means of a transubstantiation. The bread and wine becomes flesh and blood, a simple assembly becomes a church and the visible world slips through the veil of things into the presence of the invisible. Such is the power of sacrificial memory that we can go further and briefly redefine the presence that such memory invokes as being more than simple presence; it is, indeed, the presence of the immemorial, of the beginning, an originary presence which is of crucial importance because what such presence signifies is the continuity of the origin: presence can here only be understood as carrying the entire panoply of the past with it. Presence is not what is before the eyes, it is not what is directly experienced; presence is indexical, it is *prae-sens*, in advance of the senses, in excess of the immediate, imminent, the bearer of a history, a predefined alchemical being.[1] It is also the law, not simply because it is that presence, that genealogy, that parental power of the origin that is ingested by each communicant, but more that the sacrificial memory draws us back to the continuity of the sacred, to a truth that unites the living Church against all threats of discontinuity.

1 See Marin (1986), op. cit.: 'if being present (*prae-sens*) does not signify being there, to be in front of [*devant*], but to be before [*avant*], ahead of, at the tip of, in anticipation or excess, without any apparent continuity between behind and before . . . being there [comes to] signify an imminent temporality . . .' (p. 210).

Again with reference to Bataille, 'this sacramental element is the revelation of continuity through the death of a discontinuous being . . . divine continuity is linked with the transgression of the law on which the order of discontinuous beings is built'.[1] Translated into the terms of the common law, the continuity of presence is exemplified precisely through the removal of the discontinuous, through the expulsion – either literal or symbolic – of the transgressor, in each act of judgment, in each affirmation of the law, in each 'discovery' or presencing of the immemorial rules. The presence of the law, its memory of itself, its ritual of identification is one of repetition: it is monumental because presence is never simply presence, and repetition too is always more than the return of the same.

Sign, Text, Word

Finally, and not insignificantly, consider the relation of the sacrament, and of memory, to the text. The Reformation was amongst other things a dispute over the nature of a particular sign or set of signs. In the first instance, Catholicism can be defined as a defence of the difficulty, the opacity of the sign and so also of the scriptures. The Eucharistic sign, 'this' thing here present, indicated for Catholicism a thing, bread, which, in its material form, hid the body of Christ. The bread is in that sense symbolic. Its presence is indexical. Behind it will be discovered its history, the allegory of its origin, and thereby its meaning will be revealed: that which this thing, this bread, symbolises will have been disclosed. The absence which underlies, and surrounds, all presence will have been represented, the 'truth' of the object laid bare to the eyes of grace. The scriptures bear the authority of 'God that speaks it',[2] 'they are they which testify of me' (John 5: 39) and their meaning is for Sir Thomas More in consequence a complex combination of levels of sense. The text is both literal and allegorical, metaphorical and anagogic; its sense is spiritual for:

> [S]ometime he wrote it, and our saviour himself sometimes spoke his words in such wise, that the letter had none other sense than mysteries and allegories . . . which sense God that composed the letter, did when he made it foresee, and more did set thereby than by the sense that

1   Bataille (1986), op. cit., p. 82.
2   Sir Thomas More, *Apologye* (1533, London), fol. 31b.

immediately rises upon the letter, which letters his high wisdom so tempered for the express purpose . . . that such other sense might be perceived therein and drawn out thereof, by such as himself had determined to have the grace to find it.[1]

In linguistic terms, the theory of the sacramental sign is indissociable from the theory of the text. The Catholic concept of the Eucharist was reductionist in the sense that it took the elements of the Eucharist separately. In particular it distrusted the immediate sign, and so where language was the object of analysis the meaning of the text was to be viewed as external to the text itself. The text, scripture, was formally incomplete; it required interpretation, exegesis and, in a full sense, tradition to complete it. Just as the sacrament required the consecratory words of the priest to change its substance, so the scriptures required the consecratory application of tradition, the authority of the cleric, of the priest as interpreter, to complete its meaning. It is precisely that precedence of the Church over the scriptures to which Tyndale and the reformers most objected: 'Judge therefore reader whether the pope with his Church, whether their authority be above the scripture: whether all they teach without scriptures be equal with the scripture, whether they have erred . . . and against the mist of their sophistry take the examples that are passed down in the old testament . . . judge them in all things.'[2] It is to the issue of the text within the Anglican tradition, to the hermeneutic question of the proper manner of establishing and interpreting the textual object, the material thing, the sign as well as the meaning, the apparent as well as the spiritual presence, that our analysis of the development of a common law hermeneutic or English jurisprudence will be devoted.

A Genealogy of the Ancient Constitution: Scripture and Law

Genealogy is grey, meticulous, and patiently documentary. It operates on a field of entangled and confused parchments, on documents that have been scratched over and recopied many times.[3]

---

1 More, *The Confutacyon of Tyndale's Answere*, in *Collected Works* (1973, New Haven), p. 635; see also at p. 750, 'it is the known Catholic Church that discerns the words of God from the words of men'.

2 W. Tyndale, *An Answer unto Thomas Mores Dialogue* (1530; London), fol. iva.

3 M. Foucault, *Language, Memory, Counter-Practice* (1977, Ithaca), p. 138.

The thesis is easy. So too is proving it. It is in the language and it is not a surprising argument. There is a clearly discernible parallel, at the level of structure, at the level of argument and of language as well, between Sir Thomas More's defence of the faith and Sir Edward Coke's defence of the law. There is, indeed, a conceptual descent, from More through Richard Hooker to Coke and Davies in which the Eucharistic apparatus of presence – of authority, of law – moves from theology to jurisprudence, from the Church to the State, from the sacrifice of Christ to the sacrifice of nature and of desire that founds the social contract. In the place of the last supper and its exemplary repetition at Emmaus there is the originary contract, no less of a sacrifice, no less of a constitutional act, one which makes the people present as living members, as membrane of the social body: 'the Parliament of England is that whereupon the very essence of all government within this kingdom doth depend; it is even the body of the whole realm: it consisteth of the king, and of all that within the land are subject to him: *for they are all there present*, either in person or by such as they voluntarily have derived their very personal right unto'.[1] What is done by the social body is done by each and every one of its members. In the words of Sir Thomas Smith in *De Republica Anglorum*, Parliament is where 'everie Englishman is entended to bee there present . . . And the consent of the Parliament is taken to be everie mans consent'.[2] There is the spirit and there is the soul of the law, but it is one which needs to be administered in the same way that the sacraments must be prepared and presented by the clergy. It is administered as scripture by those wise in the law, by those who have possession of the immemorial and unwritten tradition, who can tell, in More's phrase, 'the holy scripture of God from the unholy writing of men'. In terms of the positive law, its context is quite simply that of the most ancient of all traditions. For Coke and for Davies it returns – unchanged – 'good, approved and ancient' to the dawn of time (*bonae et approbatae antiquae regni leges*), a law based upon 'ancient usages

---

1   Hooker (1888), op. cit., pp. 408–9.
2   Sir Thomas Smith, *De Republica Anglorum* (1583/1906, Cambridge), p. 78. Note also Kantorowicz (1965), op. cit., pp. 320–1, arguing that once the *corpus mysticum* has become identified with the *corpus morale et politicum* of the people and synonymous with death for the 'fatherland', *pro patria mori*, the mystical body corporate regains its nobility, 'it is a sacrifice'. The state becomes a secularised *corpus mysticum*, a juristic person that has finally achieved religious status; it

warranted by holy scripture', and tended from generation to generation by tradition.[1]

Following the order of analysis of the Eucharistic enactment of
presence, the transition from theology to jurisprudence can be traced
in relation to comparable concepts. The defence of the Catholic faith
and the Latin language of the Church by Thomas More, and the
defence of tradition and the old order of law by Hooker, both provide
an essentially conservative conceptual language of social and legal
order that find their terminus in Coke and Davies and the tradition
which they establish. By way of introduction, the following points
may be observed. Firstly, in terms of the source of law, all our authors
are agreed that it belongs ultimately to the divine order of the Lord,
an order both established and recollected or made present through
the Eucharist. In Hooker's words, 'whatsover hath necessary being,
the Son of God doth cause it to be . . . a thing of so great use as
government amongst men, and human dominion in government,
cannot choose but be originally from him'.[2] Secondly, the authority of
that law, its social body or continuance, is established in the society of
law as our law, our tradition, God's presence amongst the English.
The space of authority within the common law tradition is one which
rests upon the conjunction of the material and the spiritual, between
tradition and necessity, reason and nature: the unwritten constitution, Hooker's 'threefold cable',[3] Coke's most ancient and excellent
laws of England, our birthright, our inheritance, our sacred judgement, our treasure.[4] Of memory, it hardly need be emphasised that
Coke's version of legal history is a sacramental one; it is a memory
internal to the law, a memory of 'inward grace', of an institution

becomes a people, a prosopopoeia that will not die because the people do not die
(*quia populus non moritur*).

1 Coke, op. cit., Pt IX, A3b. See also Davies, *Primer Reports* (1615, Dublin).
See also Hooker (1969), op. cit., p.232, on tradition as the ultimate ground of the
authority of the crown: 'of law there can be no less acknowledged, than her seat is
the bosom of God, her voice the harmony of the world.' An interesting further
example and comparison can be taken from J-B Bossuet, *Politique tirée des propres
paroles de l'écriture sainte* (1709, Paris), title 10: 'true religion has antiquity as its
manifest mark . . . when one looks at religion one looks at one's ancestors, at
established ways (*bornes posées*) – and at a beaten track'. For analysis of the point
see M. Gauchet, *Le Désenchantement*, op. cit., pp. 12–25.
2 Hooker (1888), op. cit., p. 380.
3 Hooker (1969), op. cit., p. 272.
4 Coke, *Institutes III* (1648; London), L, iii a.

which, like More's Church, regards the visible only insofar as it is a veil of the invisible: 'the outward sensible signs in all the sacraments and holy ceremonies of Christ's Church, by one general and common signification of them all, bytoken and does signify . . . an inward secret gift and inspiration of grace'.[1] Finally to interpret the law is the task of the priesthood, for these are no ordinary signs, no ordinary words, no common texts. For More and for Coke they remain in the Latin and the French to protect the ignorant and to preserve the truth.[2]

The Time and Place of an English Jurisprudence

The emergence of an English jurisprudential literature, a legal dogmatics, may be traced with some precision to a genre of legal writing that first appeared in the closing decades of the sixteenth century. In a superficial sense, this new genre was exclusively concerned with questions of method and was based upon a series of reversals. While earlier jurisprudential literature had accepted the civilian definition of law as 'true philosophy', it had not developed as a distinctive discipline or science. For the bulk of the fifteenth and sixteenth centuries, studies of the philosophy and method of law were to be found in surprisingly disparate dialogues and tracts. Advice on the sources of law and the forms of legal interpretation was to be found in religious polemics,[3] in rhetorical manuals,[4] in notarial handbooks

---

1   More, *Confutacyon* in *Works*, op. cit., p. 78.

2   For analysis of the linguistic point, see my 'Literacy and the Languages of the Early Common Law' (1987) 14 *Journal of Law and Society* 422. For Thomas More, the best examples come from this polemic against St German and will be referred to subsequently. Generally, see Mellinkoff, *The Language of the Law* (1963, Boston).

3   Most well known is Saint German, *Doctor and Student* (1528/1974 edn., London); more polemical are his *A Treatise Concerning the Division between the Spirituality and Temporality* (1534, London), *Salem and Bizance* (1533, London), and *The Addicions of Salem and Bizance* (1534, London). Sir Thomas More responded to those works in *The Apology of Sir Thomas More* (1533, London) and in *The Debellacyon of Salem and Bizance* (1533, London). Sir John Fortescue's earlier *De Laudibus Legum Angliae* (1737 edn, London) also takes the form of an apologia; T. Starkey, *A Dialogue Between Reginald Pole and Thomas Lupset* (1535/1945 edn, London) and Aylmer, *An Harborowe for Faithfull and Trewe Subjectes* (1559, Strasborowe) contain further polemical material.

4   The first curricular rhetorical manual was Leonard Cox, *The Arte or Crafte of Rhetoryke* (1530/1899 edn, Chicago). More widely used in the Inns of Court was

of the *ars dictandi*,[1] in dissertations on education,[2] grammar,[3] legal terms,[4] politics[5] and indeed poetry.[6] The authors of such works were correspondingly diverse and ranged from scholarly printers such as John Rastell to theologians, civilian and canon lawyers,

Thomas Wilson, *The Arte of Rhetorique* (1533/1982 edn, London). Later relevant works include Richard Sherry, *A Treatise of Schemes and Tropes* (1550, London); R. Rainolde, *A Booke Called the Foundacion of Rhetorike* (1563/1945 edn, London); Henry Peacham, *The Garden of Eloquence* (1577/1593 edn, London); Anthony Munday, *A Defence of Contraries* (1593/1969 edn, Amsterdam).

1   The literature on the *ars dictandi* is well covered in J. J. Murphy (ed.), *Renaissance Eloquence* (1983, California), ch. 1; P. O. Kristeller, *Renaissance Thought and its Sources* (1979, New York), pp. 24–59, 312–27; G. A. Kennedy, *Classical Rhetoric and its Christian and Secular Tradition* (1980, London), pp. 173–94. The most substantial evidence of a specifically legal notarial tradition is William West's symbolaeography, *The first part of Symbolaeography, which may be termed the art, or description of instruments and presidents . . . The Scrivener or Notary* (1590/1603 edn, London).

2   Most famously Sir Thomas Elyot, *The Boke Named the Governour* (1531/1907 edn, London). See also D. S. Bland, 'Rhetoric and the Law Student in Sixteenth-Century England' (1957) 54 *Studies in Philology* 498.

3   Richard Mulcaster, *The Firt Part of the Elementary* (1582/1970 edn, Menston); see also C. Grayson, 'The Growth of Linguistic National Consciousness in England' in *The Fairest Flower* (1985, Firenze). As will be discussed later, the vices of legal language were a significant theme of grammatical works and particularly of the polemical literature advocating the vernacular.

4   John Rastell, *The Expocisions of the Terms of the Laws of England* (1566/1567 edn, London); Dr John Cowell, *The Interpreter; or Book Containing the Signification of Words* (1610 edn, London). See also H. J. Graham, 'The Rastells and the Printed English Law Book of the Renaissance' (1954) 47 *Law Library Journal* 58.

5   The political literature, especially that concerned with constitutionalism, is well dealt with by Q. Skinner, *The Foundations of Modern Political Thought* (1979, Cambridge), vol. II, pp. 50–64, 123–35. It includes the work of the civilian Sir Thomas Smith, *De Republica Anglorum* (1583/1906 edn, Cambridge), as well as a lively literature of petitions and pamphlets, some of which are referenced in J. H. Baker (ed.), *The Reports of John Spelman* (1978, London), vol. II, pp. 23–30, and in W. R. Prest, *The Rise of the Barrister: A Social History of the English Bar 1590–1640* (1986, Oxford), pp. 234–52, 287–92. The *Harleian Miscellany* (1810 edn, London) contains John Hare, 'St. Edward's Ghost, or anti-Normanism' (1642), vol. 6; John Warr, 'The Corruption and Deficiency of the Laws of England, Soberly Discussed' (1649, vol. 6); Walter Carey, 'The Present State of England' (1627, vol. 3). Thomas Wilson, 'The State of England A. D. 1600' is in *Camden Miscellany* (1936, London), vol. xvi.

6   Most notably the work of a member of Middle Temple, George Puttenham, *The Arte of English Poesie* (1589, London). See, for biographical details, R. J. Schoeck, 'Lawyers and Rhetoric in Sixteenth-Century England' in J. J. Murphy (ed.), *Eloquence*, op. cit., p. 274.

political theorists, grammarians and rhetoricians. By the first decades of the seventeenth century, that order of precedence and of disciplines had been reversed. A distinctive jurisprudential literature now emanated virtually exclusively from the Inns of Court, and its explicit object of study was no longer a branch of some other discipline – of theology, rhetoric or poetics – but rather a discrete concern with a specifically English legal method and exclusively juridical forms of study and of argumentation.

The most immediate context of the new discourse was that of a response to the importation of continental theory and specifically that brand of scholasticism associated with Petrus Ramus and Omar Talon.[1] It was to a dogmatic and largely uncritical version of Ramism and to the alluring slogans of a nascent modernity that the systematisers of common law turned in their occasional efforts to justify a dogmatic science that would ideally both reflect the glories of the English tradition and equally stand comparison with the philological or scientific exactitude of the continental lawyers and the glossatorial transmission of *ratio scripta*. Initially intended as little more than a gloss upon, or re-ordering of, the traditional poetic and rhetorical divisions and figures, the new literature on the study and method of law was associated with scholars as diverse and idiosyncratic as Cowell,[2] Doderidge,[3] Fern,[4] Finch,[5] Fraunce,[6] Fulbecke,[7] and others, scholars (including Fraunce) whom the profession would endeavour either to ignore or to read as turning to scholastic logic and

1 As regards the English versions of their work, the principal translated editions of Ramus' *Dialectique* were: P. Ramus Matyr, *The Logike* (1574, London) and Dudley Fenner, *The Artes of Logike and Rhetorike, Plainly set forth in the English Tongue* (1584, Middleburg). For the rhetoric, the first translation was Dudley Fenner, op. cit.; A. Fraunce, *The Arcadian Rhetorike* (1588, London), with extensive additional exemplifications and annotations. Earlier interpretative accounts are to be found in Gabriel Harvey, *Ciceronianus* (1577/1945 edn, Nebraska). A huge secondary literature on Ramism can be referred to by way of W. S. Howell, *Logic and Rhetoric in England, 1500–1700* (1956, New Jersey); Walter Ong, *Ramus, Method and the decay of Dialogue* (1958, Harvard); and most recently B. Vickers, *A Defence of Rhetoric* (1988, Oxford).

2 John Cowell, *The Institutes of the Laws of England, Digested into the Method of the Civil or Imperial Institutions* (1605/1651 edn, London); *The Interpreter*, op. cit. Cowell was Regius Professor of Civil Law at Cambridge and provides interesting insights into the eclecticism of the developing jurisprudence as well as of a new concern, taken up directly by Sir Henry Spelman, *The Original of the Four Law Terms of the Year* (1614/1684 edn, London), pp. 13ff., with scholarship and method.

3 Sir John Doderidge, *The English Lawyer* (1631 edn, London).

its tropes of certitude and truth to present a discrete apologetic and pedagogical account of the method of English law. The subjection of common law to the principles of scholastic method enabled the new jurisprudential literature to present a properly doctrinal account of the disparate strands of the legal tradition. The common law became in their texts a unitary discourse, a professional *écriture*, a unique discursive logic, and ultimately an empire of truth supported by a veridical language or orthodoxy that was peculiar to the law alone. In short, the imported and translated scholastic philology enabled the doctrinal systematisers to establish a common law hermeneutic or, by its classical name, a science of interpretation (*scientia interpretationis*). True to its name, the function of such a hermeneutic was to herald or to announce the truths of legal discourse in a didactic and oracular way. The truths in question were drawn from elsewhere, from time immemorial or from divine law, and only doctrine or the peculiar hermeneutic of the common law could safely extract them from their textual custody in the appropriately foreign languages of the ancient tradition.

In genealogical terms,[43] the above historical fiction combines two questions of extreme interest to the inhabitants of an era and discourse which has challenged the verdical language, the truths and

---

4 Sir John Ferne, *The Blazon of Gentrie* (1586, London).

5 Henry Finch, *Nomotechnia* (1613/1636 edn, London); also *Law or a Discourse Thereof* (1627, London). See W. R. Prest, 'The Dialectical Origins of Finch's Laws' (1977) 36 *Cambridge Law Journal* 326, for bibliographical details.

6 Abraham Fraunce, *The Shepherd's Logic* (1585/1969 edn, Menston); *The Lawier's Logike, Exemplifying the Precepts of Logic by the Practice of the Common Law* (1588, London). He was also the author of works of rhetoric, heraldry, Latin verse and of a translation of Thomas Wilson's *Amyntas*. See Fraunce, *The Arcadian Rhetorike* (1588, London); idem, *Insignium Armorum, Emblematum, Hieroglyphicum et Symbolorum* (1588/1979 edn, London); *The Countesse of Pembroke's Yuchurch* (1591, London).

7 William Fulbecke, *Directive or Preparative to the Study of the Law wherein is showed what things ought to be observed and used of them that are addicted to the study of the law* (1599/1829 edn, London); also by Fulbecke, *A Parallele or Conference of the Civil Law, the Canon Law, and the Common Law of the Realm of England* (1602/1618 edn, London) in 2 vols; *The Pandects of the Law of Nations* (1602, London).

1 The concept of genealogy is here used in opposition to the classical philological conception of history In endeavouring to abandon the metaphysical terms of history, in particular those of origin, objectivity and legal proof of precedent facts, genealogy simply traces the contingent descent, the chance affiliations and alien forms from which specific, singular, objects of discourse were

the certainties of doctrinal transmission. The first question concerns the impetus or motive of closure. The earliest accounts of a systematic jurisprudence and accompanying hermeneutic present the common law tradition as being radically separate – in geographical, historical, linguistic and institutional terms – from all other contemporary discourses. Either it is, as Coke saw it, an antidote to other discourses – an immunisation against foreign influences – or it is to be understood more simply as prior discourse, preceding and in consequence also defining and structuring those other discourses with which it comes into contact. The properly genealogical question which the impetus towards closure raises is that of the hidden filiations of an exclusory discourse. The legal hermeneutic is one of annunciation and it is consequently unaccountable in its immediate forms of presentation. The genealogical reconstruction of doctrine, however, interestingly implicates legal doctrine in a series of other discourses. It will be argued in historical detail that, far from being a technical and internal development, the new jurisprudence responded to and was moulded by a series of discourses external to law. Jurisprudence was marked by external discourses and desires, and its subsequent reformulations still carry those marks even though the historians of law prefer to recycle the juridical fiction of a true discourse and its authoritative judgments.

The initial task of a genealogy of English jurisprudence is simply the supplementary one of tracing the repressed discursive affiliations of doctrine or, as discussed earlier, what Foucault termed the 'unconscious' of a science.[1] In the first section of the ensuing argument I will trace the polemical context of legal doctrine. The printing press, the popular indictment of a massively expanding profession, the translation of the Bible, the perceived threat of continental philosophy and the nationalistic advocacy of vernacular languages all played a significant role in forcing the profession to produce an apologetic or defensive literature that would serve both to authenticate the credentials of lawyers and to exclude any non-professional participation in the discourse of law. The underside, perhaps eventually the backgame, of that polemical defence of law and of the mythology of an English *ius commune* buried in sacred

formed. See M. Foucault, 'Nietzsche, Genealogy, History' in *Language, Counter-Memory, Practice* (1977, Ithaca). A more complex discussion can be found in P. Legendre, *L'Inestimable Objet de la transmission* (1985, Paris), pp. 197–205 and passim.

1   See M. Foucault, *The Order of Things* (1974, London), pp. xi–xiii.

time was the little-attended yet more scholarly systematisation of a 'logic' or method of common law, a mnemonics associated with Ramism and the movement to modernise and vernacularise all the classical arts. The second part of the chapter will trace the disciplinary development of jurisprudence in relation to its contemporary domains of scholarship. The argument developed concerns the relationship of a legal hermeneutic to the emergence of the other vernacular disciplines and most particularly poetics, rhetoric and dialectic. Scholasticism brought with it the theocratic dogmas of the Roman tradition.[1] The genealogical analysis of legal scholarship at the time that it produced its first properly jurisprudential literature indicates that the institutional expansion of the profession was accompanied by a comparable discursive imperialism. In developing a specifically legal hermeneutic, the new jurisprudence advanced juridical notions of linguistic contract and of linguistic notation, of bonding or of faithful tie between word and referent, that far exceed the specifically legal context of their initial elaboration.

The Polemical Context[2]

English jurisprudence arrived at its proper destination or found its appropriate dogmatic role somewhat late in history, arguably over three centuries after comparable developments within the continental legal tradition. While there are clear intimations of a desire to provide a defence of the legal faith in Fortescue's *De Laudibus Legum Angliae* of 1460, it is only with the advent of print that the threat of a legal reformation becomes sufficiently immediate to require the established institution to develop a systematic and systematically polemical legal apologetics. The development of a doctrinal defence of law adopts precisely the same strategies and the same structure of argument as had the defence of the established Church against the foreign popularising creed of Protestantism and the vernacular translation of the Bible. A dogmatic theology of law needed to base

1 See P. Legendre, *L'Amour du censeur* (1974, Paris), pp. 259–68; idem, *L'Empire de la vérité* (1983, Paris), Part II.

2 The classic example is *Ignoramus, or the English Lawyer*, (1621/1736 edn, London), a dramatic comedy centred around the sophistical duplicity and greed of its eponymous leading character who 'speaks English, Dutch, French and Latin; yet speaks nor English, nor Dutch, nor French, nor Latin; which writes laws that they may be misprisions, and which writes misprisions that they may be laws' . . . 'if all men spoke such gibberish, twere a happiness to be deaf', at pp. 24–5, 8 respectively. See also, John Day, *Law Tricks* (1608, ed. 1950, Oxford).

itself first upon a conception of sacral origination, of another time and place at the source of legal communication or from whence legal signs are writ and sent. It needed secondly to elaborate a rigorously esoteric hermeneutic that would guard the legal missive from profane interpretations. With respect to both requirements, contemporary theological polemics provided the requisite conceptual apparatuses.

Thomas More's Legal Theology

In the course of a lengthy polemic against the lawyer Saint German, Thomas More remarks, during a discussion of misinterpretations of his work, that 'if their books be once put abroad in print, it is a thing very hard to get them well in again'.[1] In a later addition to the same dispute, More echoes this fear of the ready diffusion of heretical ideas made available through print, in this case the criticism of laws and statutes, in remarking that 'be they of the church or the realm . . . to put out books in writing abroad among the people against them, that I would neither do myself, nor in the doing commend any man that does'.[2] More's fear was a commonly expressed one on the part of the established Church and it adequately captures one of the principal ingredients of the transformation in cultural communication introduced by the presses. While it has been convincingly shown in the work of Stock, Clanchy and others[3] that the scribal age had laid the foundations for a culture of books, the scale of dissemination of heretical ideas made possible by printing was an indispensable element in the Reformation. As is adequately noted by Eisenstein,[4] the shift in the mode of production of books took place at the expense of the monasteries and of the clergy, and one of its more immediate consequences was that of challenging the privileges of clerical and

---

1   Thomas More, *The Apology* in *Complete Works* (1979, New Haven), vol. 9.

2   Thomas More, *Debellacyon*, op. cit., at fol. q. viii. a – q.ix.a. It is worth recollecting that More would not simply condemn such critics but would advocate that they 'carry the faggots', in other words that they be burned.

3   M. T. Clanchy, *From Memory to Written Record* (1979, London), pp. 231–6, 258–65; B. Stock, *The Implications of Literacy* (1983, New Jersey); R. Pattison, *On Literacy* (1982, New York), ch. 4; Graff, *Legacies*, op. cit., n. 25, pp. 108–20.

4   Eisenstein, *Printing*, op. cit., pp. 389–90. The major studies are S. H. Steinberg, *Five Hundred Years of Printing* (1961, Bristol); L. Febvre and H. Martin, *The Coming of the Book* (1958/1976 edn, London); E. Eisenstein, *The Printing Press as an Agent of Change* (1980, Cambridge), 2 vols; N. Z. Davis, *Society and Culture in Early Modern Europe* (1975, London); H. J. Graff, *The Legacies of Literacy* (1987, Indiana), Pt. 3; D. R. Kelley, *The Beginning of Ideology* (1981, Cambridge).

legal élites.[1] The initial manner in which it did so was relatively indirect and took the form of the translation of the Bible. A coincident advocacy of national languages that would support a market for the vernacular scriptures became a principal object of doctrinal debate.

Scribal culture had been a preserve of the Church and had barely managed to supply the needs of the priesthood for liturgical and devotional works. Print technology shattered the restraints of the scribal culture and its limited distribution of texts. It was seen for that reason by some as an instrument of the Devil,[2] and bibliolatry (the inke-divinitie) entered the list of sins condemned by the Catholic Church. One of the main threats represented by print was that of secularisation and popularisation of religious and legal texts. In political terms, the Reformers threatened the established Church by preferring the authority of the scriptures to that of the hierarchy, of the patristic tradition: the word is before the faith, and faith makes the congregation. The primacy of the word returns to a belief in the 'living word', the word as a sacrament for 'the word was flesh, and dwelt among us . . . full of grace and truth'.[3] Scripture itself is the source of life; it is both tradition *and* text, signifier *and* signified. In doctrinal terms this threat of a democratic Church is manifested in acerbic debates on language, and most particularly on the primacy of the word as against the authority of the Church (*traditio*), debates which included elaborate analyses of the significance of signs, miracles and sacraments. For Tyndale, the Eucharist must be understood as guaranteeing the New Testament; it provides it both with depth and with feeling (intimacy), precisely because of the sacrifice which it recollects:

> God wrote his testament unto them [the sons of Adam] in all ways . . . for the sacrifices which God gave Adam's sons were no dumb puppetry or supersticious Mahometic, but signs of the testament of God. And in them they read the word of God as we do in books and we should do in the sacraments, if the wicked pope had not taken the significaciones away from us, as he had robbed us of the true sense of the scripture.[4]

The reformers were therefore textualists, believing in the literal and accessible truth of the scriptures and the sacraments. For Tyndale, the first translator of the Bible into English and eventually a martyr

1 Eisenstein, op. cit., pp. 71–2, 362–3.
2 Ibid., pp. 50–1, 472–3.
3 W. Tyndale, *An Answer unto Thomas Mores Dialogue*, fol. iva.
4 Ibid., fol. xivb.

for the vernacular, the Catholic Church 'teaches not to know the scripture: but hides it in the Latin from the common people'.[1] For that reason the impetus of reform was centred upon the demand that a translation of the Bible be made commonly available; the scriptures should thereby be removed from the 'mist of [papal] sophistry'[2] established by the Church. It should be placed in the hands of a 'feeling' faith, an immediate faith inscribed through the text on the heart, as opposed to an 'historical' (unwritten) faith based upon the authority of the Church.

For Tyndale, Barnes and their fellow reformers, the word preceded the Church; it was the truth, and the holy scripture was in consequence to be read as the truth, for 'the pith and substance in general of everything necessary unto our soul's health, both of what we ought to believe, and what we ought to do, was written'.[3] Similarly, the sacraments should be taken out of the hands of the Pope and their meaning made plain by the text as opposed to being hidden in the administrative power of the clerics and in puppetry and superstitious ceremonies, the 'howling, buzzing and crying out' of the Roman Church. In institutional terms, the demand that the scriptures be placed in the hands of the public had two radical implications. Firstly, it challenged the supremacy of doctrine and in Tyndale's metaphor took the Bible from under the feet of the Pope where it had lain hidden 'in the Latin from the common people'. Further, 'from them that understand Latin they hide the true sense with a thousand false glosses . . . And I say that the pope keeps the scriptures as did the pharisees, to make merchandise of it.'[4] The second consequence of the argument was to deprive the 'ordinaries', the Church lawyers, of their power of interpretation. The scripture had 'the authority of him that sent it, that is to wit God, which the miracles did testify, and not of the man that brought it'.[5] Of the ordinaries, Tyndale remarks appropriately 'that they be lawyers ordained by the pope and can no more skill of the scriptures than they that never saw it . . . they be right hangmen to murder whosoever desires for the doctrine that God have given to be the ordinary of our faith'.[6] Tyndale himself, of course, later met his Maker at the hands of the hangmen lawyers. For translating the Bible inappropriately, for

---

1	Ibid., fol. lxxxiiib.	4	Ibid., fol. lxxb.
2	Ibid., fol. iva.	5	Ibid., lxxxiiib.
3	Ibid., fol. xiiib.	6	Ibid, cvb.

translating *ecclesia* as congregation not Church, for alleging an heretical theory of immediate presence, Tyndale himself was absented.

For Thomas More, sometime reader at Lincoln's Inn and incumbent Lord Chancellor, Tyndale was proud, presumptuous and unwise. He was a victim of continental theories and of dangerous modernist pretensions. Above all, 'it is the known Catholic Church that discerns the words of God from the words of men' and in consequence 'the people may have every necessary truth of scripture, and every thing necessary for them to know . . . truly taught and preached unto them, though the corps and body of the scripture be not translated into the mother tongue'.[1] The historical faith, protected and transmitted by the unwritten tradition of a Church which admittedly had frequently changed its mind, preceded the scriptures and determined what in those writings was true and what was false and unholy. The greatest authority rested with the 'word of God unwritten' and with the holy tradition that kept and interpreted it in accord with its special and allegorical senses.[2] The doctrinal argument saw the written word as a sign of grace and as a figure of holy mysteries: 'for our matter is not of scripture, as it is taken for bare writing, such as every scrivener's boy writes in his master's shop, but as it signifies such holy writing as God causes to be written and binds folk to believe, upon the peril of their soul'.[3] In institutional terms, the argument reasserts the necessity that the text be kept and protected by the Church, which alone can search the visible, the laws and 'outward sensible signs and sacraments',[4] to reveal their inward signification of grace. Drawing on the negative conclusions of a Royal Commission appointed by Henry VIII,[5] More anticipates the very words of the defenders of law French in arguing that a scripture in the English tongue would cause the unlearned to draw conclusions that would do them deadly harm. As to the professional interpreters of the text, 'God whose plenteous spirit wrote [endyghted] the scripture,

---

1   More, *Apology*, op. cit., n. 1, at fol. 19b.

2   Ibid., fol. 26b–27b; cf. *The Confutacyon of Tyndale's Answere by Sir Thomas More Knyght Lorde Chauncellor of England*, in *Collected Works* (1973, New Haven), vol. 8 at pp. 150–52, 155–6, 226–7, 255.

3   *Confutacyon*, op. cit., at pp. 272. At p. 635: 'the allegory neither destroys nor hinders (letteth) the literal sense, but the literal sense stands whole beside . . . Luther and Tyndale would have all allegories and all other senses taken away, saving the literal sense alone.'

4   Ibid. at p. 78.

5   D. Wilkins, *Consilia Magnae Britanniae et Hiberniae ab anno MCCCL ad annum MDLXLV* (4 vols, 1737, London), vol. 3, 736.

foresaw full well himself that many godly allegories holy men should by his inspiration at divers times draw out thereof. And sometime he wrote it . . . that the letter had none other sense than mysteries and allegories.'[1]

The parallel between the defence of the established Church and its ordinaries and the legal institution whose 'inkhorn' texts were also made visible by print is foreseen by More at one point in the *Confutacyon*. Tyndale in his *Answer* repeatedly raises the question of why necessary points of the faith should have been omitted from the scriptures, to which More responds that the argument 'is much as Tyndale would affirm that all the laws of England be written, and whatsoever were unwritten were no law. And when he had long wrestled therewith and could not prove it, would then ask me, has the realm of England any laws that be not written? to what purpose I pray you should they be left unwritten?'[2] More's answer to that question in relation to the common law comes in his later polemic with Saint German in terms of the sovereign power of the judiciary: 'But surely (as I have often heard that great wise and right worshipped man Sir John Fineux say, late Chief Justice of the King's Bench) who so takes from a justice the order of his discretion, takes surely from him more than half his office.'[3] Elsewhere, in the course of a lengthy and repetitive polemic, the argument in support of the esoteric tradition and institutional interpreters of the law occurs again and again, primarily in relation to More's advocacy of the *ex officio* suit under the statute *De Haeretico Comburendo*,[4] whereby heretics could be summoned by the ordinaries upon suspicion of heresy and without the need for indictment or open accusation.[5]

Slaves of the Text and Slaves of Language

The movement for reform and the advocacy of translation into the mother tongue divided the European faith, and scholarship more generally, according to national linguistic boundaries.[6] The popularising impetus behind the translation of the Bible rapidly expanded

1   *Confutacyon*, op. cit., at p. 636.
2   Ibid. at p. 291.
3   *Debellacyon*, op. cit. at fol. Mvia–Mvib.
4   1401 2 Hen. 4, c. 15.
5   *Debellacyon*, op. cit. at fol. Fiib–Fiiia, Giia, Uiiib–Uiva. It is no worse, he argues, than arrest for suspicion of felony at common law.
6   Eisenstein, *Printing*, op. cit., at pp. 83–4, 117–19, 358–60; Steinberg, *Five Hundred Years*, op.cit., n. 25 at pp. 120–26; Lefebvre and Martin, *The Book*, op. cit., at pp. 319–32.

from its religious beginnings into a movement for the vernacular and for standardisation in all the disciplines. In his *Treatise Concerning the Division between the Spirituality and Temporality*, Saint German attacked the authority of the Church and the abuses of the canon lawyers in a vernacular polemic.[1] His theme and his method of arguing according to ordinary language (somesays) is reasserted in *Salem and Bizance*. In response to More's criticism of his having thereby grossly overpublicised abuses of faith and law, Saint German defends his tract and its vernacular presentation on the grounds that 'the said treatise was made for the people of this realm, and therefore the English tongue in this realm was the most convenient'.[2] The crucial aspect of the debate between Saint German and Sir Thomas More is that in this later polemic the object of controversy explicitly becomes the relation between spirituality and temporality. Arguments as to abuses of procedure, obscurities of language, misinterpretation of texts and of judicial powers on the part of the spirituality, the 'ordinaries', are now interlaced with discussion and criticism of the common law and its 'ordinaries', its judges. More 'would the temporality and the spirituality as the body and soul of one man, live well together and neither of them be glad to hear evil of the other . . . but drawn both by one line, according to both laws' cease all criticism of the hierarchy.

For Thomas More the arguments are the same whether it be one law or the other, the Church or the secular law of the realm, that is to be defended against misinterpretation and popular criticism. As regards the spiritual law, and equally the authority of its clerics and scribes, we saw in detail that the Church precedes the word. The argument is both historical and conceptual. In historical terms, the faith existed and was preached and taught by word of mouth, by custom transmitting tradition from age to age, long before the advent of the scriptures. Indeed 'the right faith which Adam had and such as in the same faith succeeded him long ere writing began, was taught by the word of God unwritten'.[3] In conceptual terms, the spoken word, the spirit (i.e. breath) that gives life, was often more effective and more appropriate to a context than the written: 'the apostles did more plainly speak, and more openly declared, many things by mouth among the christian folk because their audience was more mete . . . than they did by their writing, which might by chance come into the

1   *Division*, op. cit., especially fol. 6a–b, 16a–17b, 22a.

2   *Salem and Bizance*, op. cit., at fol. ixb. Earlier criticisms of the spirituality in Latin, he complains, had elicited no response (fol. xiva).

3   *Apology*, op cit., fol. 30b–31a.

hands of heathen men'.[1] The Church, in other words, was custodian and bearer of a hidden reserve of divine truths. The written word of God could thus not be trusted to imbue a reader with the correct faith unless such a reader also carried to the text the full panoply of esoteric interpretative wisdoms that the ages and institutions of the Church had handed out. Both laws must be protected and their substance, together with any criticism of it, should rest hidden or secret in the Latin tongue.

The contentious argument put forward by Eisenstein that printing most directly threatened and eventually had its greatest effects upon professional languages and literatures gains some support from the experience of the common law.[2] During the course of the fifteenth century the advocacy of English was powerfully asserted in the form of vernacular presentations of most of the disciplines. English works on theology, history,[3] rhetoric, poetics,[4] education and grammar[5] all stressed the popular benefits and the national virtues of English as against continued servitude to the 'darke' rhetoric of Rome. Although law printing was rapidly regulated and restricted by means of a system of royal licences,[6] print bestowed upon legal texts a visibility that both generated criticism of their language and also created a

---

1   *Confutacyon*, op. cit., p. 292.

2   Eisenstein, *Printing*, op. cit., pp. 117–120, 191. Cf. Graff, *Literacy*, op. cit., at pp. 116–18.

3   R. Verstegan, *A Restitution of Decayed Antiquities* (1605, London); J. Stow, *The Annales or General Chronicle of England* (1615, London).

4   See Richard Sherry, *A Treatise of Schemes and Tropes* (1550, London) at fol. Avib–Aviia. 'In speaking and writing nothing is more foolish than to affect or fondly labour to speak darkly . . . since the proper use of speech is to utter the meaning in our mind with as plain words as may be.' Even more striking is George Puttenham, *Arte of Poesie*, op.cit., n. 2, at pp. 3, 120–21: 'ye shall take the . . . usual speech of the court, and that of London and the shires lying about London within forty miles and not much above'.

5   Elyot, *The Governour*, op. cit., Richard Mulcaster, *The First Part of the Elementary* (1582/1970 edn, Menston), pp. 450, 73, 79, 101, 254: 'For is it not a marvellous bondage, to become servants to one tongue for learnings sake . . . whereas we may have the very same treasure in our own tongue . . . and our own tongue bearing the joyous title of our liberty and freedom, the Latin tongue reminding us of our tradition and bondage? I love Rome, but London better . . .'

6   H. Bennett, *English Books and Readers, 1475–1557* (1952, Cambridge), pp. 76–85. The first such royal patent was granted in 1552 and by the last quarter of the sixteenth century virtually all law texts are printed *cum privilegio regiae maiestatis*. See also E. Eisenstein, *Printing*, op. cit., at pp. 104–5, 120.

demand for a more stable use of precedent. One of the earliest of such critiques again comes in the context of a theological dialogue.[1] The dialogue between Cardinal Pole and Thomas Lupset is most often referred to as evidence of an argument in favour of a reception of Roman law in Renaissance England.[2] While the possibility of codifying English law is certainly raised, it occurs in the course of a critical discussion of the chaotic state of common law precedent and the haphazard nature of judicial decision making:

> There is no stable ground therin, nor sure stay; but everyone that can colour reason makes a stop to the best law that is before-time devised. The subtlety of one sergeant shall inert and destroy all the judgments of many wise men before-time received . . . The judgment of years be infinite and full of much controversy, and beside that, of small authority. The judges are not bounden, as I understand, to follow them as a rule.[3]

Far from advocating the abandonment of English law in favour of the Roman, Pole is concerned that the national law be standardised, its procedural abuses remedied and its method rationalised. While Roman law could provide an exemplar of method and conceptual clarity, his 'wish' was 'that all these laws should be brought into some small number, and to be written also in our mother tongue' rather than the barbarous tongue of old French 'which serves no purpose else'.[4] That his primary leaning was towards a national law is echoed in his repeated concern that the common law, this 'great blot on our polity', was a foreign import 'writ in a strange tongue, as though the law were written to strangers', and he is unrestrained in his reference to 'the great infamy and rot that remains in us, to be governed by laws given us of such a barbarous nation as the Normans be'.[5]

The other significant theme of the *Dialogue* is one which castigates the legal profession and judiciary for being pharisees and making merchandise of the law and of justice: 'lucre and affection ruleth all

---

1   T. Starkey, *A Dialogue*, op. cit., 172.

2   The classic text is F. W. Maitland, *English Law and the Renaissance* (1901, Cambridge) at p. 7. The same view is to be found in A. Watson, *Sources of Law, Legal Change and Ambiguity* (1984, Philadelphia). Cf. J. H. Baker, *Spelman*, op. cit., pp. 24–7.

3   *Dialogue*, op. cit., at p. 173.

4   Ibid., p. 174.

5   Ibid., pp. 189, 175 respectively.

therin'. The common lawyers inhabit a fantastical and delirious mental realm; blindness, reverie and babble supplant any order or rule of right reason as the profession 'apply themselves to fulfilling of their vain pleasures and foolish fantasy; wherefore they be taken, as it were, with a common frenzy'.[1] It was not, of course, Roman law but rather the Reformation and the printing presses that gained a varying reception in England and with them came an ever more vehement and popular denunciation of the 'dunsmen' lawyers and their 'dunsicalities'.[2] On the continent Luther condemned 'juristerey' as a 'doctrine not of grace but of wrath' and law itself as ugly dogma.[3] It may also be noted that a more general resistance to the growth of the legal profession in Europe saw civilian lawyers expelled from Hungary in the 1460s,[4] banned from the Spanish colony of Peru in 1529,[5] subjected to varying oaths most commonly forbidding immoral argument, lies and inflated fees,[6] and equally subjected to abuse and being labelled as *chicaneux*,[7] liars, blasphemers and fools.

In England the popular attack on the lawyers was only slightly slower and lacked none of the vigour of the continental reformists.[8] Its principal themes are those of the number of lawyers, delay, uncertainty, expense, autocracy, pomposity and incomprehensibility, to which more learned critics added rampant particularism with

---

1   Ibid., pp. 86–7.

2   'The sophistical trifles of dunsmen' appears first in Sir Thomas Challoner's translation of Erasmus, *The Praise of Folly* (1549/1965 edn, Oxford) at p. 82. See also Fraunce, *Lawiers Logike*, op. cit., at fol. 6a–b.

3   Luther, cited in G. Strauss, *Resistance*, op. cit., at p. 223.

4   F. Hotman, *Anti-Tribonian ou un discours d'un grand et renommé iurisconsulte de nostre temps sur l'estude des loix* (1567–1603 edn, Paris) at p. 144.

5   Strauss, *Resistance*, op. cit., at p. 23.

6   For Germany, see ibid. at p. 18; for France see D. R. Kelley, *Ideology*, op. cit., at p. 179; for England see Thomas Powell, *The Attourney's Academy* (1630, London), at fol. O.o.4.a.

7   The term comes from Hotman, *Anti-Tribonian*, op. cit., pp. 105–7. It was a work that greatly influenced Fraunce and others of the English Ramist movement.

8   Technically the literature attacking lawyers dates back much earlier, with the first English legislation appearing in the Statute of Pleadings, 1364. For that reference and further details see my 'Literacy and the Languages of the Early Common Law' (1987) 14 *Journal of Law and Society* 422. More generally, see C. W. Brooks, *Pettyfoggers and Vipers of the Commonwealth*, (1986, Cambridge), pp. 132–50.

especial reference to the law of misprision, procedural abuses,[1] excessive fines, poor scholarship and worse rhetoric. As regards the more popular criticisms, complaints as to excessive fees and malpractice[2] are sufficiently common for Anthony Munday in a formulary rhetoric published towards the end of the sixteenth century to include the argument that a lawyer is a profitable member of the commonweal as one of a list of paradoxes against common opinion which the aspirant advocate had to defend by way of learning by ordeal. The list also included exercises in praise of blindness, poverty, ignorance and deformity.[3] Another striking version of popular sentiments which stresses the excessive number of lawyers and the pervasiveness of their categories comes from the introduction to Fulbecke's *Parallele*:

> And I have had a very great desire to have some understanding of law, because I would not swim against the stream, nor be unlike unto my neighbours, who are so full of law-points, that when they sweat it is nothing but law; when they breath it is nothing but law, when they sneeze it is perfect law, when they dream it is profound law. The book of Littleton's Tenures is their breakfast, their dinner, their tea [boier], their supper and their rare banquet.[4]

The underlying current and theme, however, was that of legal language which precisely prevented acquisition of the knowledge for which Fulbecke's 'country man' pleads. The preponderant argument was initially simply that it made no sense to expect the subjects of the realm to know and obey a law so coloured, 'hotchpotch' and 'inkhorn' in its languages as to make little sense even to those learned in the mysteries of law.

---

1   Particularly the removal of causes by writ to Westminster and other delaying tactics; see Starkey, op. cit., pp. 171–2.

2   Thomas Powell, *Attourney's Academy*, op. cit., at fol. Gg3a, provides a striking example and makes 'the humble request to those who have the power of Reformation, in this crying reigning evil amongst lawyers, touching the disappointment, and defeat of clients causes, for which they are retained and feed, and yet fail to give attendance in the hour of tribulation, or to be near unto the client on the day of visitation'.

3   A. Munday, *A Defence of Contraries* (1593/1969 edn, Amsterdam), Liiia.

4   Fulbecke, *Parallele*, op. cit., at fol. B2a–B2b. See also Thomas Wilson, *The State of England*, op. cit., at pp. 24–5, on the oppression that comes in the form of swarms of lawyers. For a fairly comprehensive list of complaints, see W. Carey, 'Corruption and Deficiency', op. cit., at pp. 557–61.

The initial argument put forward by scholarly commentators such as Fulbecke and Fraunce, theologians such as Cardinal Pole and indeed Thomas More in his *Utopia*[1] and by Rastell in the introduction to his dictionary[2] gains considerably in intensity when it comes to be linked to the reformists' nationalistic advocacy of the vernacular. Law French was not simply the barbarous usage of an ominous guild of secular ordinaries, but its continued existence served to remind the inhabitants of the new commonwealth of the origin of law's mysteries in an earlier invasion and subjugation of the realm. The blight of lawyers imposed upon the realm was compounded by the fact that their pervasive laws were not even English laws. For John Hare this surviving 'tincture of Normanism' was a mountainous dishonour, a cause of shame and grief, as though some strange hero 'who being captivated, and marked for a slave, should have his senses so captivated also, as to be more ambitious to be chambered in his jail, and to glitter in gilt fetters, rather than to be restored to his lost freedom and reputation'.[3] A brief glance at the laws was enough to show that they 'still scorn to speak otherwise, than in the conqueror's language, and are for the most part, his introductions, shutting up the remaining liberties of our nation . . . as if we were no further to be accounted free, than infranchised'.[4] Others attacked the foreign 'ink-pot' terms of the *voces venales*;[5] the 'petty-fogging' Norman mentality, in John Warr's view, ensnared but did not remedy the people's ills. Law was the greatest of the commonwealth's wounds and of itself a sin for which only a 'reformation of the laws of England' could atone.[6]

1 *Utopia* in *Complete Works* (1963, New Haven), vol. 4, p. 195.

2 J. Rastell, *Expocisions*, op. cit., at fol. Aiib–Aiiia: 'If law is necessary to be had, and a virtuous and good thing, ergo to have knowledge thereof is a necessary and a virtuous and a good thing . . . it is necessary that the great multitude of the people have a knowledge of law, to which they be bound, ergo it follows the same law in every realm should be so published and declared and written, in such wise the people so bound to the same, may soon and shortly come to the knowledge thereof.' Without that knowledge the law is a secret thing, a 'trap and a net to vexation and trouble'.

3 'St Edward's Ghost', op. cit., at p. 91.

4 Ibid. at p. 99. See also pp. 103–4, 173–5.

5 'The Present State of England', op. cit., at p. 581.

6 'Corruption', op. cit., pp. 219–20, 221. At p. 215: 'The laws of England are full of tricks, doubts and contrary to themselves; for they were invented by the Normans, which were of all nations the most quarrelsome, and most fallacious in contriving of controversies and suits.'

Dogma and Heterodoxy: Language and the English Way

In a discussion of the temporal abuses of the clergy, Saint German remarks that 'as long as the spiritual rulers will pretend, that their authority is so high, and so immediately derived from God, that the people are bound to obey them, without argument or resistance, then so long the light of grace will not appear'.[1] The argument that the spirituality refuses to listen to criticism but rather denounces it in an oracular fashion is given a further twist when Saint German observes that 'if [prelates] preach heresy . . . it is certain, that they would look to be believed . . . for they would say, they were no heresies that they preached'.[2] Doctrine, in other words, though it may change, is always true as stated by the requisite authorities (sources) and must be obeyed. The key to understanding the authority of the spiritual judges is equally the key to understanding of temporal profession. The doctrinal defence of English law against the profusion of criticisms listed adopts a comparable strategy to the theologian's defence of the established faith and its clerical and ecclesiastical officiate.

The primary secular exponent of doctrinal apologetics is undoubtedly Coke, who manages in one body in one lifetime to defend the common law against foreigners, against scholars and against multiple forms of popular criticism. Criticism from any quarter is for Coke an undesirable attribute, and we might begin our account of this theology of English law by turning to that point in the *Reports* where he most strongly adopts the argument from the necessary authority of doctrine in relation to a newly founded Anglicanism, asserting that those who resort to Roman ways or who:

> bring over those books of late written . . . from Rome or the Romanists, or read them and justify them . . . run into desperate dangers and downfalls; for the first offence is a *praemunire*, which is to be adjudged outside the King's protection, to lose all their lands and goods, and to suffer perpetual imprisonment; and they that offend the second time therin incur the heavy danger of high treason.[3]

With such fervour directed against the continent and against Rome, against all that Rome represents in terms of Church, doctrine and

---

1   *Salem and Bizance*, op. cit., at fol. lxxxa.

2   Ibid. at fol. lxxxixa–b. Thomas More responded to this argument in the *Debellacyon*, op. cit., fol. svab.–svia, simply asserting that authority had never been used in this way.

3   Coke, *Reports*, op. cit., IV, Pt VII, fol. A5a.

law, it is unsurprising that interdisciplinary criticism, interest in continental philosophy or disparagement of the English judicial system should meet with outright dismissal. It is frequently as though any form of non-professional reading of law is a kind of 'petty treason', bad manners, poor form, un-English to be sure but also, and worse, unpatriotic and seditious.

The best known and most visible and enduring response to the critics of England's tainted laws and venal profession was to adapt the arguments as to their particularism and their history of foreign influence and to turn them into a eulogy of the spirit of the people enshrined in custom and legally presented in an idiosyncratic but wholly English garb. The common law was to be interpreted as the presence of God in England, an antique tradition dressed in a sacramental language of its own, existent outside history and beyond memory as the intimate knowledge of a chosen profession. If historians were likely to be unwilling to accept Coke's claims to a birthright extending back unalloyed to the first kings of the Britons (and even to the reign of Arthur), then 'to the grave and learned writers of histories, my advice is, that they meddle not with any point or secret of any art or science, especially with the laws of this realm, before they confer with some learned in the profession'. This is a view which is repeated when the records of the antiquity of the laws are said to be '*vetustatis et veritatis vestigia* . . . of that authority that they need not the aid of any historian . . . it doth appear most plain by successive authority in history what I have positively affirmed out of record, that the grounds of our common laws at this day were beyond the memory or register of any beginning'.[1] History and legal history, in other words, are far from being branches of the same discipline; they are to be carefully separated according to the dictates of doctrine to allow the lawyers, in an ironic and proleptic turn, to have a history of their own invention in praise of national law: a history of the unwritten word of the law, of the Church that comes before the word, of an historical faith which, following More's definition, is dependent upon the profession to discern the word of the law from the words of men, and further to reveal the inner signification of those words where they are written down. The tradition of an unwritten law passed by word of mouth or embedded in antique practice is in essence panegyric; it is a praise of indigenous law and a national faith, of a law

1 *Reports*, vol. ii, Pt iii, fol.B5a; vol. iv, Pt viii, fol. Liiia–b. For general commentary see J. G. A. Pocock, *The Ancient Constitution and the Feudal Law* (1987, Cambridge), pp. 30–55.

that has witnessed the origin of law. The model for such eulogies was Fortescue's *De Laudibus*, while its exemplars were Coke and Davies and to a lesser extent the Doctor and the student of the common law in Saint German's *Doctor and Student*.

The forging of the myth of a native legal tradition both in the face of a long history of hostility to law and lawyers and in contradiction of a number of apparent and known political and linguistic facts must, initially at least, have a distinctively polemical structure. It also, perhaps ironically, borrows much of its conceptual method and content from the civilians.[1] Elements of the general argument, however, are sophisticated and of importance to the parallel development of an English jurisprudential tradition. The most obviously polemical feature of all of the doctrinal apologia is their particularism: each work endeavours a detailed rebuttal of specific criticisms of English law and English lawyers. The points dealt with largely mirror the criticisms elaborated earlier in terms of delay, uncertainty, procedural abuse, professional integrity, antiquity, language and nationalism.[2] The latter three issues are of central jurisprudential significance as well as being constitutive of what might be termed the sacral myth of English law, a doctrinal myth that lives on to the present. At all events the three categories are linked. The myth of antiquity is best viewed as a theory of sources (*auctoritates*), of lost origins that serve to equate the law with the word both written and unwritten. For English lawyers the Church (*traditio*) comes before the word and assigns the text its allegorical and other senses. Legal language has therefore to be seen as something more than profane; it is no mere writing of 'any scrivener's boy in his master's shop'[3] but

1 The best study of civilian influence is Pawlisch, *Davies*, op. cit., at pp. 161ff. See also B. Levack, *The Civil Lawyers in England, 1603–41* (1973, Oxford), pp. 145–50; R. Schoeck, 'The Elizabethan Society of Antiquaries and Men of Law' (1954) 1 *Notes and Queries* 417; also 'The Libraries of Common Lawyers in Renaissance England' (1962) 6 *Manuscripta* 155; W. R. Prest, *The Barristers*, op. cit., at pp. 184–208.

2 In terms of particular issues, see, for example, Fortescue, *De Laudibus*, op. cit., pp. 34–5 (procedure), pp. 105–8 (language), pp. 116–21 (integrity), p. 125 (delay); Saint German, *Doctor and Student*, op. cit., pp. 69–71 (certainty), pp. 105–6 (procedures); Coke, *Reports*, op. cit., vol. 1, Pt 2, fol. A5b (certainty), vol. 2, Pt 3, fol. C4b–C5b (scholarship), C7b–C8a (language); Davies, *Le Primer Report*, op. cit., at fol. 3h–4a (language), 4b–5a (uncertainty), 5b–6b (uncertainty), and 6b–7b (immorality).

3 Coke, *Reports*, op. cit., vol. 1, Pt 2, A6a–b: 'the greatest questions arise not upon any of the rules of the common law, but sometimes upon conveyances and instruments made by men unlearned; at many times upon wills intricately,

rather the carrier of 'revealed', sacramental meanings that move in mysterious ways.[1] Finally, the idiosyncracy of law French, in comparative terms at least, requires a theory of national particularity whereby the oddity of legal language is explained by the privilege of national character and by its proximity to God. The arguments will be outlined in turn.

The attribution of authority to English law initially takes a conceptual form in the civilian manner. All of the authors under discussion are agreed that positive law has its origin in God's law. Saint German is the most explicit. Positive law is based upon law eternal, law of reason and law of God; it is 'a true sign constituted by human tradition and authority . . . with a view to some spiritual or temporal end consonant with reason [and] with the law of God'.[2] Fortescue likewise asserts the filial fear of God as the necessity underlying the study of law. Human laws are sacred and their science or profession is the art of what is good and equal, while those who administer the law, 'who sit and preside in the courts of justice, are therefore not improperly, called *sacerdotes* (being one who gives or teaches Holy things)'.[3] The genealogy of customary law renders arguments as to their antiquity in a different light. The assertion of the fact that English law is the very oldest and very best is only incidentally an historical argument. It is primarily a doctrinal notation of laws that are variously described by Fortescue as solemn, magnificent, exceeding valuable, excellent, sublime and 'superior to the civil law in that [they] accord more closely to the scriptures and the writings of the Church fathers'.[4] They are dispensed by literati who appear publicly for only three hours on *Dies juridicos* while spending the rest of their time studying the laws and reading the holy scriptures.[5]

absurdly, repugnantly set down, by parsons, scriveners, and other such imperites'.

1   For useful additional material on the symbolism of both word and book, see E. R. Curtius, *European Literature and the Latin Middle Ages* (1953/1979, London), pp. 302–46, 495–501; J. Gellrich, *The Idea of the Book in the Middle Ages* (1985, Ithaca), pp. 94–139.

2   Saint German, *Doctor and Student*, op. cit., at p. 27; see also pp. 107–13, 129–33.

3   *De Laudibus*, op.cit., at pp. 4–5.

4   Ibid. at pp. 89–91, 116.

5   Ibid. at p. 121. See Sir George Buc, *The Third Universitie of England* (1612, ed. 1615, London).

This patristic presentation of customary law gains its most explicit formulation in Davies' *Primer Report*. It is law most perfect, and most excellent, and without comparison the best:

> [A]s the law of nature, which the schoolmen do call *ius commune*, and which is also *ius non scriptum* being written only in the hearts of men, is better than all written laws . . . so the customary law of England, which we do likewise call *ius commune* as coming nearest to the law of nature, which is the root and touchstone of all good laws, and which is also *ius non scriptum*, [is] written only in the memory of man.[1]

Inscribed time out of mind in the collective memory of the legal profession, customary law is sanctioned, protected, transmitted through the ages and finally delivered by a tradition of the unwritten word, 'for the common law of England is a Tradition and learned by Tradition as well as by Books'. Even where there were records or writings, these were no more than affirmations of existent law, 'for indeed these reports are but comments or interpretations upon the text of the common law: which Text was never originally written, but has ever been preserved in the memory of men, though no man's memory can reach to the original thereof'.[2] It is precisely because tradition precedes scripture within the apparently Catholic profession of the law that when writing is referred to it must be understood as a sign, as bearing the authority of its author and source, and the meanings of the speech from whence it came. It is in consequence no ordinary writing but rather a mixture of senses literal, allegorical, mysterious and other. Once the primary position of tradition is settled and the institution and its bearers put in their proper place – they are those 'true and honest men' who guard the historical faith and consecrate its texts so as to reveal the substance of their words – then it should occasion no surprise to find that the language and even the script of the law will appear strange to the common or unlearned eye.

If the assertions of the antiquity and continuity of English law appear extreme, it is worth observing that the more philologically minded members of the profession were not reticent in dismissing such history as no more than pleasing myth.[3] The audience of the

---

1 Davies, *Le Primer Report*, op. cit., at fol. 2a.
2 Ibid., fol. 2b.
3 See particularly Sir Henry Spelman, *The Original of the Four Law Terms of the Year*, in *English Works* (1614/1723 edn, London), pp. 99–101, where Coke's views are summarily dismissed and English law is referred scrupulously to German, Saxon, French, canon and civil law. At p. 102 he makes the marvellous statement

discourse, however, was not primarily the profession but rather its critics. The language of the law had been an obvious and constant focus of popular indictment. It was also seen, not unreasonably, as lingering evidence of foreign and unreformed practices that could scarcely be justified in the new age of print and vernacular translations. The doctrinal answer to such criticisms parallels the annexation of history with an annexation of linguistics. Fortescue again sets the tone with the inventive argument that because law French is not a spoken tongue it has in effect managed to remain an original language, a pristine and pure scientific terminology, a tradition in its own right. If any comparison is to be made between legal language and the modern vernaculars, then the former must hold the day: 'modern French is not the same as that used by our lawyers in the Courts of Law, but is much altered and depraved by common use'.[1] Appearances to the contrary, even language turns to gold in the copious arms of the law.

Coke, Davies and others simply needed to expand the argument provided by Fortescue. Far from being illiterate remnants of a scribal culture, the legal profession was entrusted with the sacred duty of preserving the special coinage of law. For this purpose they had devised their own university, the Inns of Court, their own disciplinary technique of study and their own scientific lexicon. In the face of the popular experience of litigation as protracted and uncertain wrangling monopolised by the practitioners of *ars bablativa*, Coke and Davies simply assert the certainty of law and the clarity of its language. Where there are doubts as to law, Coke argues, that is because it has been interfered with by Parliament or tampered with by the unlearned: *in hominis vitium non professionis*.[2] Legal language thus explicitly served the exclusory function of keeping the law within the legal institution and subject to the singular techniques of its interpretative tradition. This, according to Coke, would spare the unlearned from immolating themselves and their possessions through

---

that the unwritten status of English law is to be explained by reference to the laws of Lycurgus of Sparta, introduced into England by the Saxons. See also W. Hakeworth in *A Collection of Curious Discourses* (1720, Oxford), pp. 2–3, for a refutation of Fortescue.

1   *De Laudibus*, op. cit. at pp. 108–9.

2   Coke, *Reports*, op. cit., vol. 1, pt 2, fol. A6a–b. See also Coke, *Institutes Part I* (1629, London), fol. C6a.

lack of a specialist and unwritten knowledge that came before the word: *in lectione non verba sed veritas est amanda*.[1]

The language of the law is a language of memory, of memorials and monuments, according to Davies and so appropriately shrouded in a documentary language never intended for human speech or the corruption of popular use. Similarly for Coke the hieroglyphic languages of the law, which included Greek, simply proved its age, its specialism and its integrity. It was *vocabula artis*, a compendious and technical language best fitted to serve the *longue durée* of legal use and record even though 'you shall meet with a whole army of words, which cannot defend themselves *in bello grammaticali*, in the grammatical war, and yet are more significant, compendious, and effectual to express the true sense of the matter, than if they were expressed in pure Latin'. His argument in fact goes further than is apparent. The law is its language; the language itself carries the law, for its peculiar words, removed as they are from use and speech, 'are so woven into the laws themselves, as it is in a manner impossible to change them, neither ought legal terms to be changed'.[2] The language of law is of itself the memory and the monument of law. Davies need simply add praise of that language to Coke's more sophisticated observations, his assertion being that 'we express the cases, arguments and judgments of the law in a form of speech so plain, so significant, and in a tongue so soon learned by any man . . . as I dare say there is no rational science in the world . . . that is so clearly delivered in any language'.[3]

When placed together these arguments as to antiquity and language are said to create the most English and excellent of all systems of laws. The English are more intelligent, of greater 'rank and distinction',[4] than the continentals and in Littleton's language of withernams, formedons, essoines, recaptions, vouchers, seneschalls and the like 'our native common lawyers'[5] had forged a hermetic science as close to perfection, to true reason and God, as any on earth. The study that Erasmus had observed to be 'as far as is possible from true learning'[6] was depicted by the doctrinal polemicists as being not

---

1 *Reports*, vol. 2, pt 3, at fol. C7b, which roughly translates as 'in reading, it is not the words but truth that is to be loved'. Compare Davies, *Le Primer Report*, op. cit. at fol. 3a–4a.

2 Coke, *Institutes*, Part I, fol. C6a.

3 Davies, *Le Primer Report*, op. cit., fol. 3a–b.

4 Fortescue, op. cit., p. 64.

5 Davies, op. cit., fol. 2b.

6 Erasmus, *Opus Epistolarum* (1922, Oxford), p. 17.

simply the purest of all legal sciences but also the queen of the disciplines, the highest branch of all knowledge. The profession was for Davies *lux in tenebris*, light in our darkness, and the oracle of justice, for 'doth she [our law] not register and keep in memory the best of our Nation? Does she not preserve our ancient customs and form of government . . . Are not the records of her acts and proceedings so precious, as they are kept in the king's treasury, like jewels of the crown, and reputed a principal part of the Royal treasure?' Further and perhaps more surprisingly, 'lastly, is not the professor of law a star in the firmament of the commonwealth? Is not his house as it were an oracle, not only to a town or city, but to a country?'[1] Unsurprisingly, criticism of the profession has transpired to be mistaken, vulgar and ignorant. Coke would not bother to 'sharpen the nib of my pen' against the critics of his histories or of Littleton, 'a work of as absolute perfection in its kind, and as free of error, as any book that I have known written of any human learning'.[2] In institutional terms, the profession also stands between justice, 'lady and queen of all moral virtues', and barbarism. Without the interpreters, in other words, justice would have no tongue.[3]

Law and Scholarship: Critical Commentaries and Lost Texts

The most remarkable feature of the doctrinal defence of law was its limited scholarship. Perhaps, like the most effective rhetoric, it was strikingly simple, not least because it stood sure of the centrality of the profession to the political development of the modern state. What is clear, however, is that as a genre of legal writing it did not greatly impress scholars either within or without the profession.[4] In addition to tracing the explicitly polemical elaboration of a native tradition, it

1   Davies, op. cit., fol. 9b.
2   Coke, *Reports*, vol. 5, pt 10, fol. Aaib.
3   Davies, op. cit., at fol. 7ba–b. 'lex est mutus magistratus' or 'lex est iustitia inanimata'.
4   To the examples already cited may be added Sir H. Spelman, *Law Terms*, op. cit., who, having marvelled at 'my Lord Coke's' refusal to address the historical and linguistic evidence of foreign influence, remarks that 'they beyond the seas are not only diligent but very curious in this kind; but we are all for profit and *lucrando pano*, taking what we find at market, without enquiring whence it came' (p. 99). See also Bacon, *Works* (1859, ed. Spedding, London), vol. 1, pt 7 at p. 359, and vol. 2, pt 7 at pp. 314–19, 321–2; and Baker (ed.), *Spelman*, op. cit., at p. 29 and references thereto.

is further necessary to account for the relationship of jurisprudence to the growth of the vernacular disciplines and to the sixteenth-century renaissance of learning in general. The differentiating feature of the more scholarly jurisprudential literature was, as was seen most clearly and exceptionally in the work of Fraunce, a desire to provide a theory of law as a discipline, a theory that would defend the legal order against the popular criticism of legal dunsmen and their hotchpot study as well as against the more academic criticism of a branch of learning that lacked a classical order and book. If law was to be properly presented as a reformed vernacular learning and as an order created through a revitalised national scholarship, then its obvious deficiency in comparison to the other disciplines was the absence of a disciplinary text, an Aristotle, Euclid or Galen,[1] or in legal terms a Gaius or Justinian, a Budé or Badouin. The Ramist concern with method and with the specific differentiating features of each of the disciplines within the greater order of the sciences was an ideal, though by no means exclusive, source for the emergence of a laicised conception of legal studies. For all the elements of vitriol and of exaggeration, of venom and of myth, that can be found in Coke and in Davies, there was an English tradition of learning which they were variously responsible for suppressing, distorting, ignoring or simply and perversely exaggerating.

The Poetic Contract

The defence of law against the popular indictment of lawyers and their language first received a learned representation in secularised terms in the work of the rhetoricians. For obvious reasons, rhetoricians were interested in and dissatisfied with the curriculum of legal study. From the available evidence of distribution,[2] as well as on the basis of textual references,[3] it would seem likely that most of those

---

1 For an elaboration of this point in another context, see H. Coing, 'Trois Formes Historiques d'Interpretation du Droit' (1970) 48 *Revue Histoire de Droit* 533.

2 On distribution, see Howell, *Logic and Rhetoric*, op. cit., at pp. 64–107; on curricula aspects of legal training, see Ong, *Ramus*, op. cit. at pp. 123 6, 131–9; R. Schoeck, 'Rhetoric and Law in Sixteenth-Century England' (1953) 50 *Studies in Philology* 120.

3 Elyot, *Governour*, op. cit., at pp. 62–9; John Ferne, *The Blazons of Gentrie* (1586, London), p.45; George Puttenham, *Poesie*, op. cit.: 'I have come to the Lord Keeper Sir Nicholas Bacon, and found him . . . alone with the works of

who studied at the Inns of Court would at some point have studied rhetoric in its Ciceronian and so forensic aspects. The first scholarly works to attempt to present an account of the form of law as argumentation were curricula rhetorical manuals. Works such as those of Cox (1530), Wilson (1553), Rainolde (1563), Sydney (1580) and Puttenham (1589) devoted extensive attention to law and to legal examples and, although they tended towards a formulary treatment of their subject, there are two senses in which their work may be adduced in relation to the emergent jurisprudence at a conceptual as opposed to a purely institutional level. The first is in terms of a poetic or rhetorical contract at the origin of the social and hence legal form, a theory of speech as *logos* which becomes incorporated into the dialectical conception of notation and at a more abstract level is repeated in the primary motive force of Ramist jurisprudence, the search for the imposition of a linguistic order upon the positive manifestations of a higher law. The second is in terms of topics or commonplaces of legal argument, organised according to criteria drawn from the rhetorical art of memory and subsequently and ironically developed in an explicit form in the jurisprudential account of method.

The initial demand was simply that lawyers and their schools of manners at the Inns of Court did not sever all links with scholarship. For Cox, 'judicial oratory belongs to controversies in the law and pleas, which kind of oration in time past belonged only to judges and men of law but now for the greater part it is neglected by them though there is nothing more necessary than to quicken them in crafty and wise handling of their matters'.[1] Such criticism is echoed and expanded in later works on the basis of both historical and conceptual lineages. In terms of its practice, law was the art of pleading and of arguing a cause. By virtue of that subject matter it was, and had always been, intrinsically linked to rhetoric: it was impossible either to plead or to argue skilfully without the aid of the art that set out and

Quintilian' (p. 117); Coke, *Reports*, vol. II, Pt III, fol. C4b: 'for the young student, who most commonly comes from one of the universities . . .'; Sir Thomas Smith, cited in Schoeck, op. cit., at pp. 117–18. See also John Earle, *Micro-Cosmographie* (1628, London), section 41; Sir George Buc, *The Third Universitie*, op. cit., p. 974.

1   Cox, *Arte*, op. cit., sig. Dva. Elyot, *Governour*, op. cit., refers to a 'shadow of the ancient rhetoric' and to 'the specious wit of logicians' (pp. 65, 66); see also Baker (ed.), *Spelman*, pp. 29–30.

explained the appropriate forms of all argumentation. That rhetoric was essential to law was indisputable. What occasioned concern was that the rhetoric employed was so frequently bad rhetoric. In such a fashion Puttenham argues that 'in all deliberations of importance where counsellors are allowed freely to opine and show their conceits, a good persuasion is no less requisite than speech itself'.[1] Good persuasion was impossible without a knowledge of the figures and order of speech. What was wrong with law was simply the appalling state of the rhetorical art in legal practice, a point which Wilson and Puttenham, both of whom were members of the Inns of Court, labour to the extreme. Pleadings were ambiguous,[2] narrations disordered,[3] figures inappropriate,[4] language 'inkhorn' and 'powdered',[5] style opaque and topics unseemly.[6] The consequence was that poor lawyering led to clients losing their possessions and their lives and the commonwealth was in consequence endangered.[7]

Rhetorical concern for the decay of legal argument was predicated not simply upon the immediate harm that was caused by legal ineptitude but more profoundly upon a notion of linguistic contract. To abuse language was a sin both against the order of disciplines and also against the linguistic fabric of social life. In an argument that in this instance stems alternately from the myth of Hegesias[8] and from Cicero's *De inventione*,[9] the original ground of language was poetry. Through the poetic apprehension of reality through language rhetoric, as successful communication, was to be understood as the

1   Puttenham, *Poesie*, pp. 117–18; Wilson, *Arte*, p. 22: 'An orator must be able to speak fully of all those questions, which by law and man's obedience are enacted'; Rainolde, *Foundacion*, fol. ia–b.

2   Wilson, *Arte*, pp. 203–4, under ambiguity 'the lawyers lack no cases to fill this part full of examples . . . in all this talk, I exempt always the good lawyer, and I may well spare them, for they are but a few'.

3   Ibid., pp. 199–200; Rainolde, *Foundacion*, fol. xiia–b; Cox, *Arte*, Dvia–Dvia.

4   Puttenham, *Poesie*, pp. 117–18, 128–9.

5   Wilson, *Arte*, pp. 325–30; Sherry, *Treatise*, at fol. Aviih–Aviiia.

6   Puttenham, *Poesie*, pp. 889 13, Wilson, *Arte*, pp. 339–41.

7   Wilson, *Arte*, p. 40; Rainolde, *Foundacion*, fol. 1a–b. See also Sir John Earle, *Micro-Cosmographie*, op. cit., sections 33, 41, 54.

8   Hegesias was a Greek philosopher and rhetor of the third century BC whose nihilistic philosophy of life was so persuasively articulated that large numbers of his audience would commit suicide. It is reported that Ptolemy II banished him from Egypt for that reason. See Puttenham, *Poesie*, p. 118.

9   *De Inventione*, 1.2, pp. 88–9; for discussion of this theme, see E. Grassi, *Rhetoric as Philosophy* (1980, Pennsylvania), pp. 68–101.

bond upon which all social order rested. In its strongest form, as presented by Puttenham, poetry creates and describes the social world through the use of images. Without the creative power of poetic language, society would never have been formed, knowledge would have been impossible and law irrelevant: 'The profession and use of poetry is most ancient from the beginning, and not as many erroneously suppose, after, but before any civil society was among men. For it is written that poetry was the original cause and occasion of their first assemblies.'[1] Observing that the speech of God was originally presented in metrical forms, Puttenham elaborates classical histories in which the first instances of all forms of knowledge, the first priests, oracles, seers (*videntes*), politicians and lawyers were all poets. Using the terminology of rhetoric and contract rather than that of poetics, the same theme is pervasive in Wilson's *Arte*: only by virtue of eloquence, the 'gift of utterance', was the state of nature transformed into that of civil society, such is 'the force of the tongue and such is the power of eloquence and reason, that most men are forced even to yield in that which most stands against their will'.[2] It is thus in a discussion of the second part of rhetoric, namely disposition, that Wilson specifies the linguistic basis of all law in terms of proper and proportionate – rational – speech: 'I know that all things stand by order and without order nothing can be. For by an order we are born, by an order we live, and by an order we make our end. By an order one ruleth as head and others obey as members. By an order realms stand and laws take their force.'[3]

The order to which Wilson attributes such primordial force is a rhetorical or argumentative one based upon the appropriate use and disposition of the figures and topics of the genres of speech. Without that intrinsically poetic order, laws would lose their force and governments would fall into disrepute.[4] In terms of the forensic art, this emphasis was spelled out in the demand that lawyers accept the originary linguistic mediation of all law and observe the appropriate forms of argument and proof. Although elements of emphasis vary as

1 Puttenham, *Poesie*, pp. 2–4. A comparable view can be found in Sir Philip Sydney, *A Defence of Poesy* (1595/1987, Manchester), pp. 103–7, well discussed in K. Eden, *Poetic and Legal Fiction in the Aristotelian Tradition* (1986, Princeton).

2 Wilson, *Arte* at pp. 17–18.

3 Ibid., pp. 316–17.

4 A point reiterated by Rainolde, *Foundacion*, ia–iia; Puttenham, *Poesie*, pp. 118–20.

between the formulary and the Ciceronian rhetorical schemes, a common theme to all vernacular accounts was that the mother tongue could be ordered and expanded to provide a national rhetoric equal to that of the classics.[1] The new national rhetorics were to pay considerable technical attention to law, with the judicial oration figuring prominently in the analysis of argumentative (sentential) and 'proving' figures.[2] With respect to future elaborations of dialectic, it is worth emphasising that the delineation of the legal genre pays especial attention to the political and so practical facility of rhetorical method which was taken to include both invention and disposition or judgment. Forensic rhetoric would therefore cover the topics and logic of proof, the figures of argument, the method of memory and the proportionate style. So too it would cover the order of narration, questions of law and of fact, fallacies (*elenchi*) of argumentation and vices (*cacozelia*) of style.[3] In short, a body of scholarship devoted to the cause of rescuing lawyers from the barbarity of their language and the sophistical casuistry of their argumentation already existed and lay open to exploitation at the time that Fraunce and other proponents of the new jurisprudence attempted to set out a distinctive method of legal studies and to expand the criticism of rhetoric into a more systematic analysis of the method of law as a scholarly discipline.

The Addiction to Law

The classical rhetorical concern with the primacy of language entailed a privileging of speech over writing and of communication over specialism. Its desire to apprehend and represent an original

1 In addition to references already provided – all of the rhetorics of the period included polemics in favour of the vernacular – see Wilson, *Arte*, pp. 25–6; Dudley Fenner, *Artes*, op. cit., n. 19, fol. A2a–b.

2 See, for example, Sherry, *Treatise*, fol. Dviib–Eviiib (figures of sentence and proof by means of signs); Puttenham, *Poesie*, pp. 127–31 (sententious and auricular figures intrinsic to judicial genre); Wilson, *Arte*, pp. 184–205, 236–50 (amplification); Peacham, *Garden*, op. cit., at fol. Cciiia–Cciva (sententia).

3 The clearest example is Thomas Wilson, *Arte*, pp. 64–5, 78–9, 236–40, where Wilson rehearses the places of logical argumentation as being appropriate to forensic rhetoric. In his *Rule of Reason* (1553, London), fol. 1a, 3a, 31b, 37a, logic is defined as the art of probable argument and the 'logician first and foremost professes to know words' (3a). In terms of the genealogy of the disciplines, logic thus comes after rhetoric and teaches through method the appropriate forms of a specific genre of argumentation.

linguistic order may have inserted the category of language as a mediating institution between God and humanity, but its theoretical basis is self-evidently theocratic. In terms of the disciplinary discourse of the various arts, the apparently democratic and nationalistic demand that the sovereign and its subordinate institutions communicate according to rules of rhetorical felicity, rules of visibility and clarity, is predicated upon a conception of pre-ordained truths that emanate, through the word, from the divine will. The order that language represented was an order that was already given and which words and signs should recollect but could not challenge or vary. The concern with argumentation and the accessibility of the various knowledges to their national audiences was similarly based upon a form of *anamnesis* or of knowledge as recollection of the already existent natural order. The utility of argument was not, therefore, that of analysing what it meant to think and to argue, but rather that of organising and dividing the categories of thought to reflect the pre-established order of their object.[1] In that important respect the rhetorical schemata must be understood as having a second-order status: the criticism of the legal institution was of its deviation or distance from an original bond between word and meaning, while the positive task of the rhetorical method was that of providing pedagogic rules whereby the relevant topics and appropriate words could be inculcated and remembered.

In broader genealogical terms, rhetoric thus took its place within an order of discourse concerned to remember and defend a primary knowledge. Superimposed upon that fundamentally theological enterprise, rhetoric came closest to being legitimately regarded as a jurisprudential discipline by virtue of both its object and its techniques. It had the advantage of being a classical art. One of its three parts was specifically concerned with the legal genre of argumentation. As the study of discourse, it comprehended the other disciplines that might be deemed relevant to law, most notably history, politics, logic and the nascent philology. It was not simply a learned art, but also and crucially a technique that was concerned directly with questions of practice and the spoken word. In that context it had a further virtue of inestimable value to the legal profession: it provided a practical tool that would enable lawyers to

1   Such a point, of course, holds true of all the pre-Cartesian disciplines. In terms of the role played by conceptions of method within contemporary jurisprudence, the pre-modern, systematising, impetus remains a dominant one.

challenge the popular protest against the profession and to elaborate a distinctive and persuasive map of a specifically legal curriculum. The Ramists may have changed the name of their preferred art from rhetoric to dialectic, but that change has to be understood in terms of contemporary academic debates and the attack on humanist scholasticism. In an era that had treated Aristotle as something of a sacred text, even the most minor deviation from the canon was a threateningly aggressive and somewhat blasphemous act.[1] It was, at all events, the Ramist Gabriel Harvey's lectures on rhetoric that Abraham Fraunce attended at Cambridge and it was to rhetoric and poetics that the bulk of his non-legal writings were devoted. If we now turn to examine legal Ramism as a collective phenomenon, as a movement towards establishing a particular form of educational curriculum at the Inns of Court, it is rapidly apparent that Fraunce's theory of legal reason as memory and the systematic quality of his critique of the contemporary legal curriculum were somewhat exceptional. His failure was, however, matched by the lesser failures of the movement as a whole. Where it did succeed despite its foreign provenance and its modernism, it was simply as a language of didactic certainty that could be added to the rather less rigorous style of the dogmatic eulogy of Englishness and common law.

Lost Innocence

The desire to introduce the rules of scholastic method to the scholarly study and teaching of law did not lack a precedent. The civilian tradition, of course, already provided a model for such an enterprise and a number of academic studies offered systematisations of English law based upon the theoretical schema of Justinian's *Institutes*. Cowell, in his *Institutiones Juris Anglicani*, thus argued that English law could acquire respectability by admitting the historical influence and utility of the Romanist studies, for:

> the civilians of other nations, have by their mutual industries raised this kind of work in their profession, to an unexpected excellency . . . And by this example would I gladly invite the learned in our common laws and antiquities of England, yet to lend their advice, to the gaining of some

1   See, for example, Fraunce, *Lawiers Logike*, at xiia–xiiib; 'A sophister of times past was a title of credit, and a word of commendation; now what more odious? Aristotle then the father of philosophy; now who less favoured?' More generally, see Ong, *Ramus*, pp. 214–23; Howell, *Logic and Rhetoric*, pp. 159–83; D. R. Kelley, 'Horizons of Intellectual History' (1987) 43 *Journal of the History of Ideas* 143.

comfortable lights and prospects toward the beautifying of this ancient palace, that has hitherto been . . . but dark and melancholy.[1]

The Ramist Fulbecke interestingly confirms both of Cowell's under-stated proposals, noting first, in terms of historical influence, that 'the common law cannot otherwise be divided from the civil and canon laws than the flower from the root and stalk' and second, in terms of method, exclaiming 'would that God would vouchsafe our Inns of Court with some second Budaeus, that is a third Varro, whose skill in the laws might be exquisite, whose pains extreme, whose reward excellent'.[2] In both instances, however, the invocation of Roman influence and methods was somewhat too explicit and direct for an embattled profession that was concerned to save its native history and to propound its national excellence. If there was to be a foreign influence, it had to be secondary and covert, subordinate to the polemically necessary exposition of a fully indigenous scholarship and its peculiar yet vernacular language. Even in Doderidge's thoroughly Ramistic logic, *The English Lawyer*, we find his formal recognition of civil law as a source of English law qualified by the crucial observation that 'those foreign [i.e. Roman] knowledges, are not inherent or inbred in the laws but rather a borrowed light not found there but rather brought thither and learned elsewhere by them that have adorned and polished the studies of the lawes'.

The civilian method had been the subject of unstinted nationalist attack in the work of Fortescue, Saint German, Coke and Davies. Although Coke and Davies had both made copious use of civilian concepts in their substantive legal elaborations, they had followed Fortescue in praising the superiority and appropriateness of the common law. English antiquity provided institutions of greater justice and customs of greater clarity, free of the inextricable web of glosses that had accrued to the written law – there was no need for commentaries on Littleton, Davies had pompously and inaccurately pronounced.[3] The theme was even taken up by Fraunce but to

1   Cowell, *Interpreter*, op. cit., at sig. 3a.Also, Cowell, *Institutes*, op. cit., at pp. 1–2. The argument is taken up and supported in Spelman, *Law Terms*, op. cit., at p. 99.

2   Fulbecke, *Parallele*, op. cit., at pt I, fol. 2a and pt II, A2b. See also his *Preparative*, op. cit., at pp. 13–14. Further evidence of a similar desire can be found in Sir Thomas Ridley, *A View of the Civille and Ecclesiasticall Law* (1607, edn 1676, Oxford), pp. 2–4, 117–45.

3   Fortescue, *De Laudibus*, pp. 32–3, 89–91; Coke, *Reports*, vol. II, pt IV, at Cvb; Davies, *Le Primer Report*, fol. 4b–5a, civilian law being 'gloss upon gloss, and book upon book, and every Doctor's opinion being a good authority fit to be cited'.

different effect. Extensively influenced by Hotman's superb indictment of glossatorial method and commentary, Fraunce could fully
agree that the sources of Justinian's law were too numerous and
unreliable and that 'as for Justinian's method, it does not so content
the civilians, but that they daily contend with new innovations and
continual printing of fresh methods, to bring it into better order'.[1]
None the less the stated weaknesses of the civilian tradition could
hardly be taken to exonerate the appalling lack of scholarship within
the Inns of Court. While Fraunce and the other Ramists all sought in
some manner to defend the substance of English law and to relate
custom to a nationalist notion of the principal legal institutions, their
criticisms of the state of learning at the Inns is detailed and damning.
While it might not be politically feasible to invoke directly the civil
law as a source of English law or even as a method of reasoning
applicable to English law, all the Ramists recognised the need to
develop a disciplinary method, a logic or scholarship of the common
law. In contrast to the somewhat incidental criticism of the profession
presented by Doderidge and Fulbecke[2] it was Fraunce who offered the
most detailed and substantive indictment of the legal curriculum with
the addition of an explicit presentation of a possible joining of law and
scholarship in the form of a properly legal hermeneutic governed by
the precepts of method. In historical terms, as we have already seen,
Fraunce failed in his attempt to propagate a logic of law. If we look
closely at the other Ramist treatises, they may lack the substantive
detail and rigour of Fraunce's argument but they none the less
advocated critical and comparative forms of legal study. Before
concluding with an account of the fate of the movement, its destiny
being that of absorption into a residually insular tradition, it is worth

---

1 Fraunce, *Lawiers Logike*, fol. xia–b. Doderidge, *English Lawyer*, op. cit., pp.
52–3, 61–2, attacks the civilian 'feudary tenurist writers' and praises Hotman,
Alciato, Budé and Cujas.

2 Ibid., fol. 119b–120a. For similar prescriptions see Finch, *Law*, op. cit., n.
11, fol. A3a–b. On the melancholic character of legal studies see Doderidge,
English Lawyer, p. 29: 'the study of law is *multorum annos opus*, the work of many
years, the attaining whereof will waste the verdure and vigour of youth'. See also
Coke, *Entries* (1627, London), preface: 'A learned man in the laws of this realm is a
long time a-making; the student thereof, having *sedentariam vitam*, is not
commonly long-lived; the study abstruse and difficult, the occasion sudden, the
practice dangerous.' Hotman, *Anti-Tribonian*, p. 111, talks of weariness of heart,
Fulbecke, *Preparative*, of addiction.

briefly outlining the more significant claims to method that the legal Ramists made.

From the Rule of Reason to the Letters of Law

The sources and the extent of Ramism in sixteenth-century England were hotly disputed at the time and remain somewhat unclear. There was already, most notably in Wilson's *Rule of Reason* and Lever's *Arte of Reason, Rightly Termed Witcraft*, a vernacular tradition of logic and the former work paid not inconsiderable attention to method (*methodus*).[1] Exempting the two vernacular translations of Ramus' *dialectique* by MacIlmaine and Dudley Fenner, it should also be noted that for all the scholastic vitriol aimed at the critics of the Aristotelian tradition the new school of logic was concerned with changes of emphasis rather than substance and that it was distinctly critical in its reception of Ramism.[2] Leaving points of detail aside, the most that can be said is that the Ramists introduced a virulently reformist style to the study of logic which, largely in response to the new technology of print, demanded a presentation of the vernacular discipline in a manner that could be seen to be ordered and discrete. It endeavoured not to change the substance of the discipline but rather to order its subject matter in a didactic and memorable way: 'the "Ramist man" must smash the images both within and without, must substitute for the old idolatrous art the new image-less way of remembering through abstract dialectical order'.[3]

In rhetorical terms, the Ramists were concerned to introduce English law and English lawyers to a new age of learning, a renaissance of the discipline based upon a critical reception of continental philosophy and upon a reworking of the order of disciplines. There was no reason why lawyers or law should fall behind in the reception of new learning, and indeed law might appropriately lead the renewal of classical learning. Both Doderidge and Fulbecke acknowledge that contemporary lawyers have been

---

1   *Rule of Reason*, fol. 17a–34b.

2   The *Lawiers Logike* pays attention to several other sources and at points dismisses Ramist classifications, as at fol. 51a. Fulbecke, *Preparative*, is similarly critical, see pp. 233–4. More generally, see Fenner, *Artes*, op. cit., n. 19 at A3b; Harvey, *Ciceronianus*, op. cit., pp. 69–72, 75–9, 81–4.

3   Frances Yates, *The Art of Memory* (1966, London) at p. 278; Eisenstein, *Printing*, pp. 71–4; Ong, *Ramus*, pp. 225–30.

justifiably criticised and even ridiculed for their lack of scholarship in general, and further for their sparsity of learning even within their own discipline. Fulbecke interestingly details such criticisms in terms of a 'science void of all proper definitions, artificial divisions and formal reasons', while for Doderidge lawyers are open principally to the criticism that they lack any conception of the place of law within learning in general. The generic and political function of method is therefore that of reintroducing law to its proper civic and discursive context. Knowledge is a question of dialogue between disciplines and, if one looks deep enough, historically and conceptually, then within the law can be traced the marks of all the disciplines. Henry Finch, in a frequently cited passage, thus discusses legal reason as coming 'out of the best and very bowels of divinity, grammar, logic; also from philosophy, natural, moral, political, economic, though in our year books they come not under the same terms, yet the things which there you find are the same; for the sparks of all sciences in the world are raked up in the ashes of the law'.[1] The whole of the first book of Finch's *Law* is thus taken up with outlining the appropriate disciplines from which the place logic of law should draw its topics, its arguments. These include those listed, with the significant addition of interpretation, 'law constructions natural', and fictions or 'law constructions feigned' as further sources of law or places of legal invention. Doderidge too offers the advice that the law, as the knowledge of all things divine and human, 'comprises all other knowledges' and that therefore the professor of law 'should be furnished with the knowledge of all good literature of most of the sciences liberal; for . . . a man may observe the use of those sciences to lie hidden in the law'. While Doderidge does not provide such an extensive or meticulously detailed list of relevant disciplines and learnings as Finch, his discussion of the sources of common law does spell out the argument that natural and moral philosophy are direct sources of law 'from whence, as from a fountain, all laws do flow',[2] and also includes the civil and canon laws as being parts of the law of nature and so also grounds of common law.

The generic context of legal knowledge, and most particularly of the logic of law, is that of discourse as such. Doderidge repeats at several points the claim that it is dialogue that founds learning and equally that both the arts and the sciences are but forms of discourse,

1   Finch, *Law*, fol. A3a.
2   Doderidge, op. cit., pp. 32–4.

the forms of discourse being the very instruments of knowledge: *sed scienda instrumenta sunt formae discenderi*.[1] When it comes to the logic of law we thus find this most basic underpinning of the method of legal science is itself, properly speaking, rhetorical. Logic is defined as the art of right definition and division; it is also the art of proper argumentation: *dialectica est recta definiendi, dividendi, et argumentandi ars*. When it came, however, to the order of 'artificial' reasoning of what Fraunce had termed 'the school at Westminster', it is a specific conception of logic, a discrete logic of law, that is stressed despite the more general advocacy of the plurality of knowledges relevant to law. In Doderidge the reader is treated to the exposition of the judgment in *Shellies Case* in the form of a syllogism and also to constant reiteration of the axiomatic character of legal precedents, legal maxims and the grounds of law in general. If we turn to Fulbecke it is also easy to see an element of defensiveness bordering the exposition of a logic of law. In the final analysis, the logic of law is based upon natural reason and unwritten tradition lodged in the *communis opinio* of the legal profession. In terms that extend but do not greatly differ from comparable definitions in Doderidge and in Finch, we thus find Fulbecke depicting the lawyer as an administrator of sacral customs and of unwritten truths, authorities to which he has access by virtue of the fact that 'both the lawyer and judge are the ministers and dispensers of justice, and of the gifts of God, and are servants to God himself'.

With regard to the 'unprecedented' introduction of logic to law, it is impossible not to conclude that the eventual effect of Ramism and of dialectical method more generally was that of placing logic in the service of authority and memory in the hands of the institution. The order of memory spelled out by Doderidge distinguished between memory and reminiscence, between *actus memorandi* and *actus reminiscendi*. The former, upon which method is based, represents the past as if it were present, 'representing the image of the thing forepassed in the same manner as if they were now actually and really present'.[2] Where *actus reminiscendi* was the discourse of memory and contained the possibility of discovery, criticism and the mixing of genres, the *actus memorandi* simply dictated the truths of a tradition, of that which was already established and in need of no further justification. Thus, for Fulbecke, 'the end and effect of law is to settle the property and right of things in them to whom they belong'. What

1   Ibid., pp. 64–5.
2   Ibid., p. 15.

was made present through the memory, the axiomatic places of legal logic, was an ancestral order, a hierarchy, a Church in the sense of an assembly in the Eucharistic presence of law. The point can be taken further in terms of the reception of Ramism in England. Where Fraunce had been wary of accepting the Ramist definition of a discipline, and particularly of its basis in received truths or in its own internal history, the less rigorous translation of Ramus' *Logic* tended towards the purely pedagogic. The three fundamental precepts of any art are enthusiastically spelled out by MacIlmaine in the introduction to the first English translation of the *Logic*. The first is that each discipline must be elaborated solely in terms of its own subject-matter and to the exclusion of all extraneous considerations; to write on law requires disavowing all considerations of grammar, divinity or physics, and if asked of contracts or obligations, it is a mockery of method to reply in terms of liberty or bondage.[1] Each discipline is, in other words, wholly discrete; a premiss that we may observe flatly contradicts the broader claims of law to divine wisdom or, indeed, to any great learning whatsoever. The second precept is that method proceeds through teaching necessary truths, through transmitting the ordained and accepted wisdom of the subject. According to the third precept, this transmission should follow an order of dispositive clarity from general truths of the discipline to particular and less absolute truths by means of a procedure of definition and subsequent specification in terms of available topics.

It takes little imagination to see that an uncritical version of Ramism could be of great service to Coke and others who wished to provide the mythologies of the legal institution with a veneer of scholarship. In Fraunce's text, the rule of reason could have provided reasoned tools for rational discourse in the realm of law. For Doderidge, Finch and Fulbecke, such learning was also present in their work, in the range of their references to other disciplines and to

1   Ramus, *Logike*, p. 9 (Epistle).
2   Classifications differ. That given is from Fulbecke, *Preparative*. Finch, *Law*, distinguishes law of nature, law of reason and positive law. The law of reason 'deduces principles by the discourse of sound reason . . . to which rules of positive law must either conform or yield' (fol. 5). The rules of reason are drawn from other learnings and include the precepts of divinity, grammar, logic, natural philosophy, politics, economics and morals, 'for the sparks of all the sciences in the world are raked up in the ashes of the law' (fol. 6).

other traditions. Had their work been taken seriously in its political dimensions, the standard of legal scholarship could only have been improved by recourse to precepts drawn from an array of disciplines other than law. For Fulbecke, the various types of law, namely the law of nature, of nations, the civil law, common law, customary law and equity all required argumentation in terms of very different disciplines and topics.[2] In that law should aspire through method to the status of reasoned discourse, it must make use of the learning relevant to the reasoning of any subject matter dealt with by legal argument, which includes, on even the most obvious counts, theology, natural and moral philosophy, politics, economics, history, rhetoric and grammar. In more classical terms, the accepted definition of law, repeated several times in Doderidge's *Engish Lawyer*, was *iuris prudentia est divinarum humanarumque rerum scientia*, knowledge of things both divine and human. The study of law was therefore, in Doderidge's terms at least, to be understood as both a speculative and a practical knowledge. In its speculative aspect, jurisprudence was to be the discourse that 'treats of the principles, ground-rules and originals of law and justice, being the chain of human society, without which it cannot consist'. In more pragmatic terms, speculative reason alone could 'purge English laws from the great confusions, tedious superfluous iterations, with which the reports are infested; [and] quit it of these manifold contrarieties, wherewith it is so greatly overcharged'.[1]

With the exception of Finch's *Law*, which provides a critical institutional account of the major divisions of English law specified in terms of possessions, wrongs and actions,[2] the exclusive focus of the jurisprudential literature was legal reasoning, understood as the discourse of law. Lodged historically at the point of intersection of a predominantly oral tradition and a new technology of print, jurisprudence grappled to provide an account of legal reason that would order an increasingly visible and contested literature, according to the intrinsic precepts of a vernacular or national hermeneutic. In doing

2 (see footnote 2 on page 103.)

1   Doderidge, *English Lawyer*, pp. 258–9; see also pp. 33–5, where the same argument is put forward in terms of the need for lawyers to study civil law and to be furnished with the knowledge 'of all good literature of most of the sciences liberal'. The view is repeated in relation to the division of topics at pp. 155–61.

2   The first book of the *Law* takes the form of a rhetorical place logic in which canons, maxims and rules (positive grounds) of the common law are explained and exemplified. The topics examined are drawn from all the disciplines of learning and the appropriate forms of logical argumentation are set out. Books 2–4 set out the divisions of substantive law according to Ramist principles.

so, the Ramists relied increasingly upon a veridical notion of language and upon a correlative conception of the truth of law as a sign of sacral depths. Fulbecke, for instance, presents the eminently practical view that 'the reason and conscience of the lawyer is not simply a question of the knowledge he has by the written law [for] when words are obscure . . . we imagine that more was spoken than written, and more intended than uttered . . . then the tongue yieldeth to the heart, and the words do give place to the meaning'.[1] In including this account of the rule of reason as it came to law, a number of themes can be drawn together by pointing to the fateful implications of Fulbecke's reinvocation of the tradition that precedes the word or of the Church that comes before the gospel.

For all the popular appeal and polemical value of the call to method and modernity, the superficial banner under which legal reason emerged as an independent domain of study should not blind historiography to the substance of its claims. In positive terms, the study of invention and judgment in law drew upon and expanded the scholastic rhetorical tradition of place logics or topics into a discursive theory of legal argumentation or dialectic. Principally concerned with the reasoning of legal argumentation, dialectic insisted on the probable character of the genre and in subordinating probable topics to reason allowed space for disciplines other than common law. The negative aspect of Ramism as a polemic in favour of method and doctrine was, however, always likely to be more amenable to the institutional and political needs of the profession. In its polemical guise, Ramism privileged dogmatics and gave pride of place to a purely custodial art of memory. Method organised the subject matter of any given discipline to the end of teaching and transmitting a series of dogmatic truths. If, as was subsequently to happen, the doctrinal aspect of Ramism was taken at face value, then jurisprudence could become what the ecclesiastics termed an historical as opposed to a feeling or 'lived' faith. As in theology, so also in law, tradition could be invoked as the guardian of an originary and unwritten word, and as the institutional custodian of a linguistic contract that now pre-existed memory and could be recollected only through the oracular pronouncements of professional dogmatics.

The argument from tradition to a notion of the special status of the legal word as a sign, as a secular sacrament, is not directly available in Fraunce's work. Its derivation can, however, be traced to an

1   Fulbecke, *Preparative*, pp. 86–8. Earlier he cites Celsus to the effect that *scire leges non est verba earum tenere, sed vim et proprietam.*

argument as to language which Fraunce uses in the analysis of definitions. Under the heading of secondary arguments is a lengthy analysis of notation or etymology, the interpretation of words according to their origins or, more accurately, their true and original meaning: *etymologia, id est, veriloquium.*[1] Fraunce's argument is the classical nominalist one that words are originally (by agreement) notes of things, and from all words either 'derivative or compound' arguments may be drawn and interpretations devised. Interpretation should agree with the name, a principle which Fraunce puts to interesting use in a lengthy analysis of legal terms ranging from contract, to mortmain, to wapentake, mancipation and manumission. He concludes by arguing that 'I have properly inserted a number of notations, for that I would make it plain, how the notion of the thing is oftentimes expressed by the notation of the word, contrary to the prejudiced opinion of some silly penmen, and illogical lawyers, who think it a fruitless point of superfluous curiosity, to understand words of a man's own profession.'[2]

In Doderidge[3] the same argument is put forward in relation to nominal definitions. However, it is no longer a secondary argument but a primary one: notation defines and explains the true signification and the effects of words, which are themselves but original signs of things.[4] The notations of a variety of legal words are then provided and the crucial significance of language to law is repeated by reference to the various different forms of language used in law proceedings, namely Latin, law Latin, neologisms from Saxon and French, and finally terms of art that were not known to the ancients. In endeavouring to explain the continued use of an archaic and arcane terminology, Doderidge puts forward two interesting propositions. The first is that all the arts were invented to further nature's operation through precepts. The precepts once put together form an art and such arts have devised 'many ways, by cypher, by counters and by

1 *Lawiers Logike*, fol. 51a, where etymology is also defined as *originatio, quod originem verborum explicet*. For an earlier discussion in terms of the originally agreed meaning of signs, see Wilson, *Rule of Reason*, fol. 48a.

2 Ibid., 56b–57a. Such a view was of course already extensively available in a general sense in the compilations of legal terms, particularly in Rastell, *Exposicions* and later in Cowell's *Interpreter*.

3 Doderidge, *English Lawyer*, op.cit., pp. 65–6: *definitio nominis est qua vocis significatio explicatur . . . sunt enim verba notae aut signa rerum*. At p. 73: *Etymologia est resolutio vocis in verum et proprium effectum, et verbi veritatem notificat.*

4 Doderidge, *English Lawyer*, pp. 31–2.

other forms to assist nature'. The peculiar terminology and form of legal record is justified as being such as 'serves to convey to posterity our memorials and records and not our debate or speech'.[1] The link between an immemorial nature and artistic language is exemplified, secondly, by references to language as the content of law: 'if a record once say the word, no man shall aver; speak against it; or impugn the same. No though such record contain manifest and known falsehood.'[2]

It is but a short step from the sanctity of records, of each letter and syllable 'significant and known to the law', to a conception of an original contract in which the unwritten word was bestowed to the custody of tradition. The connection between an originary language and customary law is made initially by Fulbecke, who refers to 'words of the law [which] may be compared to certain images called *sileni Alcibiades*, whose outward feature was deformed and ugly, but within they were full of jewels and precious stones'.[3] The theme is expanded in terms of the artificiality of legal writing whose words 'the inventors of art have devised for acquainting the mind with the mysteries and rules of their art, because words fitly and accomodately used, are the very images and representations of things which do lead . . . to the apprehension and perfect knowledge of the things themselves'.[4] It need only be added that the inward meaning of legal signs and of an 'image-serving' law was a question of authority and memory internal to the institution and unavailable to those without: *rationem ubique habet sed non ubique conspicuam*.[5] In Fulbecke's own words, 'speech is an external act, which is ordained for the declaration of inward meaning, and therefore words are said to be the limits of our meaning'.[6] Only those who hold the key to tradition and guard the

1   Ibid., p. 51.

2   Ibid., pp. 200–2: 'matter de record import in eux (per presumption del ley, pur leur hautesse) credit'. Thus 38. Ass. 21, where the testimony of Justices Greene and Skipworth of the King's Bench as to a misprision of the clerks was insufficient to reverse the same. The common law on misprision and errors – often of no more than a letter – was a constant source of conflict between the common law and Parliament. Lengthy discussions can be found in Finch, *Law*, pp. 226–32; and in *Vaux's Case* 4 Co. Rep. 39; *Arthur Blackamore's Case* 8 Co. Rep. 156; *Henry Pigot's Case* 9 Co. Rep. 26.

3   Fulbecke, *Preparative*, pp. 55–6.

4   Ibid., p. 77.

5   (Reason lives everywhere but is not everywhere conspicuous.) This fine understatement comes from Alberico Gentili and is cited by Fulbecke at p. 84.

6   Ibid. at p. 91.

unwritten meanings can properly determine whether or not the text is to be taken in its 'plain signification' or whether it is rather to be understood in an esoteric sense that accords more accurately with the hidden and immemorial reason of the oldest and most excellent of all laws. Finch provides the final and most explicit designation: positive laws are framed in the light of natural law and reason 'and from thence come the grounds and maxims of all common law, for that which we call common law, is not a word new and strange and barbarous . . . but the right term for all other laws'.[1]

Excursus

A genealogical study cannot claim to attribute causes, nor can it legitimately provide general conclusions that would somehow link the discontinuities studied to an explanation of their contemporary institution. Insofar, however, as genealogical analysis is the study of figures of descent, of the contingent affiliations and alien sources, the inessential qualities of emergence of specific textual communities, it raises properly hermeneutic issues. Those questions relate to the specific form of the legal textual community and the metaphysics of belonging to it or speaking for it. Hermeneutics is equally the study of tradition and, insofar as that textual community is 'our' tradition, that metaphysics will play a part in defining who 'we' are.[2] Even restricting analysis to the concepts of origin, essence, truth and transmission present in the earliest printed jurisprudential literature, we may none the less recognise a hermeneutic over which we still fight, a tradition of which we are still – however uneasily – the incumbents. I will end by simply listing certain of the more striking or inescapable features of that tradition, of that distance and those dark letters that are law for us.

1 *Origin and otherness.* The first principle of legal community is theocratic. It is the attribution of an originary status and authority to the speech of the law. Legal discourse and the texts through which it

1   Finch, *Law*, fol. 75.
2   See W. T. Murphy, 'Memorising Politics of Ancient History' (1987) 50 *Modern Law Review* 384, for a remarkable discussion of tradition and of what it means for us to belong to it. For the argument that we cannot claim to have escaped tradition, see J. Derrida, *Writing and Difference* (1978, London), pp. 284–92.

gains its positive formulations are simple representations of a primary speech that pre-exists and authorises the legal textual community. That origin is hidden, distant and dark. It is the *logos*, the source or oracle of law which our authors variously name as God, nature, time immemorial or that even more peculiarly English phenomenon, the unwritten constitution. Just as the constitution binds invisibly – it is simply 'how things are' – so the discourse of law remembers and repeats an ideal that is ever elsewhere, an origin or absolute other into whose face we may never look, whose back is ever turned towards us. In more contemporary terms, we may note jurisprudential preferences for sources rather than arguments or dialogues, for validity rather than value, for judgment rather than justification or accountability as the authenticating marks of juridical speech.

2 *Essence and absence.* Origin connotes essence as the survival of that quality which was first and which forms the basis of tradition. Tradition is the custody of that which is already there and its essence is expressed in the separation of spirit from substance. Legal hermeneutics thus distinguishes the material form or letter from the spirit of the text or the unwritten tradition by which doctrine alone may name the values and meanings of the text. The spiritual orientation of legal interpretation continuously subordinates the material qualities of tradition – the words, the texts, the notations as profane objects – to the search for their hidden meanings or essence: an essence that is always understood to be external, disembodied, an object of recuperation rather than of habit or of lived existence. Where it is a question of essence, then ceremony and ritual, theatrical framing and other emblems and insignia of the absolute (of that which is absent) are of greater importance than the simple materials of language. A language which consecrates is of interest only for that to which is refers.

3 *Truth and faith.* Tradition is predicated upon a notion of recollections of identificatory essences; through tradition we belong to communities. To belong is in some measure to be faithful to the creed. In legal terms, faith is faith in the origin, fidelity to the source of which the note or sign is the mere representation. To be lawful is to be true, by which enigma we may understand that truth is the faithful recollection of the message, the representation of the content of tradition in its own peculiar symbolic language. Literalism as a technique of legal hermeneutics has its place at this point in tradition: the legal sign may be taken literally, we may believe in the instrument

or deed or record, precisely because of its symbolic membership of the tradition. Its literality is simply the product of its power to exclude all other contexts, all other interpretations.

4 *Transmission and death*. The art of legal hermeneutics is essentially epistolary. It is a question of constantly replenishing a veridical language and simultaneously reaffirming the lawfulness of the message. Were one forced to offer a conclusion as to the significance of the legal tradition, it would be in terms of a system of transmission, of messages and so of texts, specialised writing systems or structures of notation. Were one to build a critique of that tradition of transmission, then it would have to start with the question of texts and of the linguistics of legal texts. In terms of grammatology, of the study of systems of writing, the critique might well begin by questioning the limited pretensions of the legal profession. It may well be that the full aspiration of legal hermeneutics is no greater than that of putting a certain textual system into social circulation, but those texts are sufficiently coercive, their notation of meaning sufficiently restrictive and life destroying to lend credence to the parable wherein only in death, *in articulo mortis*, can the subject perceive the secret of law.

4

Legal Writing Systems:
Rhetoric, Grammatology and
the Linguistic Injuries of Law

Introduction

The introduction to one of the earliest printed English law dictionaries, the *Interpreter*, contains the following statement of general principle: 'And indeed a lawyer professes true philosophy, and therefore should not be ignorant (if it were possible) of either beasts, fowls or creeping things, nor of the trees from the cedar in Lebanon to the hyssop that springs out of the wall.'[1] The dictionary is true to its declared principle. In addition to an extensive catalogue of technical legal items, of writs, offices and other terms translated from law Latin, law French and middle English, may be found also entries concerned with philosophic, economic and critical subject matter, together with entries defining spices, herbs, plants and a variety of other non-legal terms encountered in legal texts. Entries range from a definition of mystery to words such as surplusage, wage, barrator; caraway seed, turmeric, pepper and cassia lignea; perche (a long pole) and pelota. In each instance, the logic of inclusion was comparable. The discreteness of the legal lexicon required the translation of any term that fell prey to the genre or was touched by the law. On the other hand, there was a duty implicit in the classical definition of law as 'true philosophy' to account for the usages and discourse of the legal genre. It too should justify its place amongst the disciplines and so

---

1   Dr John Cowell, *The Interpreter or Book Containing the Signification of Words* (1607, Cambridge), fol. 4a. Compare J. Rastell, *The Exposicions of the Terms of the Laws of England* (1526/1527 edn, London), fol. Aiiia–b: 'ignorantis terminis ignoratur et ars* – he that is ignorant of the terms of any science, must needs be ignorant of the science'. For civilian models of this kind of work, see, for example, A. Alciatus, *De Verborum Significatione* (1530 edn, Lugudini).

manifest its subjection to reason or at least to the rhetorical order of probable argumentation.

The dictionary was one of many works that attempted in this and other manners to systematise the English common law and to bring some element of the sixteenth-century renaissance of learning to bear upon a burgeoning profession and its peculiar rhetorical, notarial and scriptural practices. In common with the other disciplines, the English legal tradition had to face the advent of printing and it was the élite scribal and notarial practices of the various tiers of the profession that became the object of the most extensive critical debate. Dr Cowell, the author of the *Interpreter* and professor of civil law at Cambridge, represented part of a vigorous but unsuccessful movement for the reform of English law through its subjection to some elements at least of comparative and critical historical method. In common with scholarly reformers on the continent such as Hotman,[1] Cowell's principal demand had been for the systematisation of common law and specifically of its various haphazard literary manifestations according to classically received civilian principles of philosophical, historical and rhetorical method.[2] In the event, the literary tradition that emerged in England lacked the breadth of scholarship, the range of reference, the order and rhetorical clarity, that Cowell and others had advocated.

The predominantly literary tradition that found its way into licensed legal print was a dogmatic one. It was produced within the profession, in the peculiar language of the profession, and was

---

1   F. Hotman, *Anti-Tribonian ou discours d'un grand et renommé iurisconsulte de nostre temps* (1567/1603 edn, Paris). As a leading figure of the 'post-glossatorial' or humanist movement, Hotman's principal theme was that of the need to return to history, to the original texts of Roman law and 'l'histoire du vray Empire Romain, lequel nous separons du bastard' (p. 20). The systematisation of law on the continent had to overcome in excess of three hundred years of glosses, 'such a vast literature grows up on the books that Baldus, at forty-seven, comments that he is still an apprentice; even the authorities admit to being dazzled by the authorities and to judging more by chance than by reference to assured and certain law' (p. 108). For Cowell's views on systematisation, see: J. Cowell, *The Institutes of the Lawes of England, Digested into the Method of the Civill or Imperiall Institutions* (1605/1651 edn, London).

2   For comparable arguments, see T. Ridley, *A View of the Civille and Ecclesiasticall Law* (1607/1676 edn, Oxford), especially pp. 367–70; W. Fulbecke, *A Paralle or Conference of the Civil Law, the Canon Law, and the Common Law of the Realm of*

circulated and stored almost exclusively amongst the various strata of the legal institution. Under very specific historical conditions and according to its own peculiar genealogy, the common law became a public system of written law. At the level of doctrine or ideology it emerged as a legal *écriture* or, to use the classical terminology, a system of written reason, a scripture. The elements of that English literary or linguistic genealogy are complex and obscure. The present chapter aims to provide no more than a depiction of certain aspects of the sixteenth-century emergence of the lawyer as a distinctive class of professional oracle and of lawyer's literature in particular as an exclusive and discrete genre. I will do so by examining three independent discourses concerned with the legal regulation of the inscription of social meaning, discourses that receive their first methodical or systematic treatment during the course of the sixteenth century. The discourses are those of armory, symbolaeography and etymology, dealing respectively with the laws of composition of heraldic insignia, the rules of legal writing and the lawful derivation or notation of words. In each instance, the most important questions to be raised concern the dialectic between law and philology. In the place of an oral tradition and its rhetorical art there emerges a linguistics of law and correlatively a legalisation of linguistics or, better, the juridical restraint of specific forms of inscription. I will begin with a brief consideration of the relation of an oral memory to literary forms, of speech to writing, of voice to print, and then move to consider the legal writing systems referred to above as examples of the textual linguistics of law.

In each instance, the question to be raised is material as well as linguistic. The development of a fully textual system of law first incorporates a question of the storage and circulation of legal texts. How are these texts produced, where are these texts kept, by whom are they used, how do they move or circulate, who receives them, who interprets them, who would understand them, whose office is it to understand and to send on that understanding, to transmit that custody? The specific material questions relating to the formulation of a legal archive, of a vast printed repository of law in the place of the ancient and hidden library, the *sacramentorum latibula* or sacred hiding places of earlier legal documents, the emergence of reports in the place

England (1602/1618 edn, London). More generally see F. Bacon, *Works* (1859 edn, Spedding, London), vol. 1, 7, pp. 359–61.

of rolls, tables and fines, is accompanied by a broader question of the science of legal writing or grammatology of law.[1] It is that of relating questions of language directly to issues of law: that is, to issues of the legal institution and its texts.

We are posing the question of a new genre of literature, of a printed archive of legal forms, of printed reports, treatises and compendia of statutory laws and of procedural forms,[2] and thereby we raise the question of the significance of this written form of law as it replaces the equally codified but materially distinct, predominantly oral culture of the early common law. For grammatology, the key question is precisely that of the form of law: a science of legal writing will look at law specifically as writing; it will define law by its opus, its work which is a body of writing, a special literary genre or species of writing that would have to be placed close – in the order of genres – to drama on the one hand and to the epic on the other. As such, a task is prescribed, one which Derrida defines in terms of an affair of form. It will be that of studying

> the [legal] text in its formal structure, its rhetorical organisation, the specificity and diversity of its textual types, its models of exposition and production – beyond what were once called genres – and, further, the space of its stagings (*mises en scènes*) and its syntax, which is not just the articulation of its signifieds and its references to being or to truth but also the disposition of its procedures and everything invested in them. In short, to consider [law] as "a particular literary genre", which draws upon the reserves of a linguistic system, organizing, forcing, or diverting a set of tropological possibilities that are older than [law] itself.[3]

1 On grammatology, see: J. Derrida, *Of Grammatology* (1976, Baltimore), pp. 15–20; idem, *Positions* (1981, Chicago), pp. 23–6, 36; also idem, 'Scribble (writing-power)' (1979) 58 *Yale French Studies* 116, at 118: 'struggles for *powers* set *various* writings up against one another. Let us not shrug our shoulders too hastily, pretending to believe that war could thus be confined within the field of literati, in the library or bookshop . . . the political question of literati, of intellectuals in the ideological apparatus, of the places and stockages of writing, of caste-phenomena, of "priests" and the hoarding of codes, of archival matters – all this should concern us.' On the history of legal records, see M. T. Clanchy, *From Memory to Written Record* (1979, London); P. Goodrich, 'Literacy and the Languages of the Early Common Law', (1987) 14 *Journal of Law and Society* 422.

2 See, for an example of the last mentioned, W. Rastall, Serjeant at Law, *A Collection in English of the Statutes now in Force* (1566/1615 edn, London). He was also author of *A Collection of Entrees. Of Declarations, Barres, Replications, Rejoinders, Issues, Verdicts, Judgements, Executions, Process, Continuances, Essoines and divers other Matters* (1566/1574 edn, London).

3 J. Derrida, *Margins of Philosophy* (1982, Brighton), pp. 293–4.

In place of Cowell's expansive art of true philosophy and natural law, grammatology must seek the more insidious legalism of artificial reason and positive written law. It will seek not only to trace the material written forms of the legal institution, its texts and their places of storage, but also to link those texts to the oral culture of their use, to the hermeneutics by and through which the written monument is repeated or made to live again.[1]

That repetition is a matter of memory to be sure, but it is also in law a question of fealty or faith to original (immemorial) yet forgotten meanings, a linguistics of textual recovery that does not simply reproduce the text but also makes it perform beyond its simple letters or literal form: to know the law is not to know the words of the law, but the force and property of the words.[2] The textual culture of law, indeed, brings with it an explicit linguistics, a linguistics of fidelity to sources, to originals, to supposed first usages and all that those usages implied. We will pose, therefore, the additional question of what law has done to language: it is not simply or only a matter of what languages, what stylistic and rhetorical forms structure (and betray) the legal text, but also, and in the long term more significantly, how

---

1   For contemporary discussions of hermeneutics as a conversation with the past, as the translation of dead written monuments into the lifeworld of speaking being, see H-G Gadamer, *Truth and Method* (1988, New York), pp. 331–41, at 331–2: 'Hence it is more than a metaphor, it is a memory of what originally was the case, to describe the work of hermeneutics as a conversation with the text', and it is through dialectic – the art of conversation – that 'that which is handed down in literary form is brought back out of the alienation in which it finds itself and into the living presence of conversation, whose fundamental procedure is always question and answer . . . This protects words from all dogmatic abuse.' For an equally influential though more sociological view of conversation, see J. Habermas, 'On Hermeneutics' Claim to Universality', in K. M. Mueller-Vollmer (ed.), *The Hermeneutics Reader* (1986, Oxford).

2   W. Fulbecke, *Direction or Preparative to the Study of Law, wherein is showed what things ought to be observed and used of them that are addicted to the study of law* (1599, London), p. 75: (citing Celsus): '*scire leges non est verba earum tenere, sed vim et proprietam.*' For commentary on this point in relation to Justinian's legislation on the point, see P. Legendre, *Le Désir politique de dieu* (1989, Paris), at p. 295: '[we here] enter the other world of interpretation, that is to say that world in which writing [*l'écrit*] is bound to power, where there is that which is written plus something else, something more, something *extra*. This *extra* was evoked by Justinian in *Novel* 146 in the form: *non solis litteris adhaerere*, word for word, not to adhere to the letters alone. Under the jurist's pen, to what would it be a matter of

has law entered language, how has law penetrated rhetorical and codified speech? These are questions which will be posed throughout. They imply that through a grammatological analysis, through the study of the history of systems of writing, we not only recollect the material movements, the residual geography, of positive law – the treasure chests, the archives, the libraries, the legal stationery offices – but we also consider how that material movement of law has marked language itself. We may note initially that, captured and made visible by print, the formation of a legal writing system or scripture and reportage of English law necessarily involves the sedimentation of a moving or nomadic law. The peripatetic tradition of a common law that came to specific places and applied its particular knowledges as a travelling law is replaced by a system of sedentary courts and available written texts. Does that change of form, that movement from nomadic to stationary, from oral to textual, from spirit to letter, aletheia to agon – does it not also imply new forms of faith in language and its fixity of meaning? Does it not imply a coming of age? A reduction of play? An application of a sedimented, textual law to mobile forms of transmission and correspondingly mobile forms of language use – does that not imply a new relationship to the earth and a corresponding change in the manner in which the languages of law refer to their objects, to their signified, to the tellurian reality of the lived world? We might finally ask how this change of form marks the language itself, not simply its words but equally the flesh that speaks it, the bodies upon which the law is always eventually inscribed, as a branding of names, an identification, a statement of the bodily *nomos* and the inner way, the prescription, in short, of legitimate speech. The unwritten law, let it be remembered, is 'ingrafted in us' by nature and before words, before speech, before writing; it commands 'the things that are to be done' and the things forbidden[1].

The Mixing of Oral and Literate Genres: Conversation and Law

If the institutional writers of our English law consistently agree upon any one thing, it is probably that the most fundamental law within the common law system is unwritten. It is custom and precedent rather

---

adhering, beyond the letter of the written law [*l'écrit*], if not to something that the law could not ignore.'

1   W. Fulbecke, *Direction*, op. cit. at p. 22, citing Cicero, *De Legibus*.

than statute or code that marks and defines our national law. Above all else, it is the antiquity of the native law that for Fortescue, Coke and Davies, but also for Finch and Fulbecke, for Thomas Smith and for Cowell, guarantees its provenance in natural reason, its proximity to God's will and consequently to natural law. The tradition, whatever its modes of custody in plea rolls, in formularies, in the various records and reports, is none the less an oral tradition; it is *traditio* in the ecclesiastical sense, an esoteric and authoritative knowledge handed on to the side of any manuscriptural or printed textual custody. In that sense, in the sense of the residually natural quality of common law, its antique inscription in the order of things themselves – in the human heart, in the legibility of natural forms –the common law will always exceed its particular texts, its particular references, its positive forms. To know the law, to belong to the company of the sages and the sacred judges of the law, is a matter of knowing an antique and unwritten tradition that exists outside of history, beyond all texts in the inaugural realm of things divine and to be divined (augured). In Coke's words, even where it is a matter of reading the law, it is a question of reading not simply the words of the text but also the tradition that accompanies them: the text is a mere representation of an external memory; it is a vestige in the classical sense of *vestigium*, an imprint, a footprint, a mark or trace of something, of some body, of some practice that passed on time out of mind or countless years ago. Where it is a question of reading, then it is not the words but the truth that is to be adhered to: *in lectione non verba sed veritas est amanda.*[1]

The customary basis of common law, the residually unwritten foundation of written law and so of all acts of interpretation, has the curious consequence of illustrating the subordination of both speech and writing, oral and written law, to a similar principle of fealty of meaning. Despite the differences in form, both genres of law respond to a comparable exigency and are subject to a similar demand. They are both systems of memory, traditions of precedent that use either their phonic or their graphic testimonies to reconstruct and represent an imagined past, a past of events and practices whose origins have been lost, whose credentials are presupposed, whose legitimacy is simply the product of collective faith (*communis opinio*) or latterly faith in the truth of texts (*de fide instrumentorum*). They are both in that sense

---

1   Sir E. Coke, *Reports* (1777 edn, London), pt III at C7b.

techniques or disciplines of faith as well as memory; as the judges constantly state, we no longer know why the law is as it is, but we are none the less certain that it is the law and that it is the best of all possible laws. It is in the first instance a rhetorical art and an oratorical practice. While it is futile to ignore the sense in which a spoken or non-literate language system is always already marked by writing – that is, by law and by the code that identifies its units, its syntax, its dictionary of meanings, its forms of repetition[1] – we may still also note the sense in which speech or a spoken form nevertheless determines the relation of the written to the life world. In the most general of senses, there is no application of a written text without some moment or modality of enunciation; what is written, in other words, will only ever appear in the present, in the event or in judgment through a reading or through some mechanism of oral delivery, of phonic application to a place and a person.[2] We must still ask of the text, who speaks this law?

The rhetorical question of the form of customary laws is well posed by Sir John Doderidge. In discussing the sources of common law, Doderidge makes explicit a point that is somewhat veiled in other authors of the same generation. The general definition of customary law is that it is a matter of use and of prescription based upon use. Cowell in the *Interpreter* offers the following definition: 'custom is a law or right not written, which being established by long use and the consent of our ancestors, has been and is daily practised'. The elements are age, usage and recognition or prescription based upon the former attributes. Interestingly, the slightly earlier dictionary by Rastell, *The Exposicions of the Terms of the Laws of England*, defines custom as a writ which is available 'when I or my ancestors after the limitation of assise . . . were not seised of the customs and services of

1 On which point see L. Marin, 'Manger, Parler, Ecrire' in *La Parole mangée* (1986, Paris), ch. 2; also M. Foucault, 'The Discourse on Language' in *The Archaeology of Knowledge* (1982, New York), p. 220: 'I suppose . . . there is barely a society without its major narratives, told, retold and varied; formulae, texts, ritualised texts to be spoken in well defined circumstances; things said once, and conserved because people suspect some hidden secret or wealth lies buried within . . . in short discourse which is *spoken* and remains spoken, indefinitely, beyond its formulation, and which remains to be spoken.' To references already given on the topic of orality may be added H-J Martin, *Historie et pouvoirs de l'ecrit* (1988, Paris); also W. Ong, *Orality and Literacy* (1982, London).

2 On which, see N. Z. Davis, *Society and Culture in Early Modern Europe* (1975, London), ch. 7.

my tenants'. It is, in other words, the authority of unwritten law, the original or the source that extends time out of mind or beyond memory, while the practice or use that constitutes custom is familiar and in this instance feudal. It is everyday life, the norm – desirable or undesirable – of quotidian service, of daily obedience, of submission, or in legal terms acceptance of unwritten law, everything from manners to modes of proper speech. It is, in Fulbecke's words, 'a determinate order established and ratified by common consent'. More than that, 'custom is law not written, by the manners and usage of certain people or the greater part of them upon good reason and judgment, begun and continued, and having the force of law. I said a law not written, because the bare memory of man is the register of customs' – it is communal assent (*communis assuetudo*).[1] Where Fulbecke, Coke and others refer to custom as being consensual, that consent is not meant to be understood, indeed cannot be understood, in a literal or political sense. It is consent in the sense of acquiescence in a given order, recognition of a deep structure, the inhabiting of an institution or the custody of tradition as a lived usage. It is consent in the same sense as consent to natural phenomena or divine decree, consent to thunder, to rain or to the sun. It is that inevitability which Doderidge ingeniously formulates in terms of a residual though fundamental source of law in 'custom, use and conversation of men'.[2]

Doderidge specifies his designation of conversation as a source of law in terms of linguistic use that is observed 'out of usual and ordinary speech . . . axioms and propositions of this [sort] are drawn from the phrase of speech, and deduced from the ordinary manner of conference by talk among men'. The only qualification which he offers in his discussion of this source of law is again a crucial one. Conversation as a source of law, as a source of 'general positions, maxims and rules proposed, and such like, cannot be properly reduced to any one peculiar title of law, extant in an abridgement, Table or directory; yet nevertheless they be brought under general

1 Fulbecke, *Direction*, op. cit., pp. 172–5. Also, H. Finch, *Law or a Discourse Thereof in Foure Bookes* (1627, London), fol. 77.

2 Sir John Doderidge, *The English Lawyer* (1600/1631 edn, London), pp. 161–3. One might note St German's frequent use of 'somesays' as an earlier equivalent of Doderidge's method. See St German, *A Treatise Concerning the Division between the Spirituality and the Temporality* (1534, London). Examples may be found on fol. 20a, fol. 22a. Sir Thomas More comments in a derogatory manner on the figure of 'somesay' in *Works* (1979, New Haven), vol. 9, p. 56.

titles or common places.'[1] Language thus carries the legal tradition, a tradition that is embedded in our very speech and of which our speech, our phrases, are the unwitting witnesses. Law in that sense is our grammar, the rule of our speech. It is the trace or imprint of the past in what we live and how we live, repossessed through iteration or diction. It is tradition as the law that is lived, as habitual body and daily routine, law as bond but also law as the trace of differentiation itself, or in more secular terms the mark of a pre-given script. In Derrida's terms, it would be the unwritten writing that precedes and structures speech, the 'arche-writing', the trace, that which acts as the imprint of an absolute past, a legal past, one beyond memory, one which could never be reactivated or awakened to presence: 'The trace refers to an absolute past . . . it obliges us to think a past that can no longer be understood in the form of a modified presence, as a present-past'.[2] Language is in grammatological terms always already marked by writing. For notation to be possible, language must already have been cut, recut and remarked by law. It must have been differenced, spaced, set out and its signs articulated prior to speech or any phonic linguistic substance. Doderidge surprisingly reminds us that, while the rhetoric of law may allow us to find a speech that resides in writing, a figuration and conversation within the text, we should not be oblivious to the underside of that source of law, namely the possibility of discovering a written law in oral representations. That is perhaps the ultimate price of tradition.

The metaphor of conversation as the art of an unwritten legal tradition directly poses a series of questions of a hermeneutic order: who are the participants in these conversations, who has access to their inscription – that is, who records them, in what form, in what library, to be recollected on what occasions, to be adjudged law in what subsequent conversation, in the order of which of all the possible interpretations, and according to what authority? It is, after all, hardly likely that every conversation becomes law. The contempo-

1   Sir John Doderidge, op. cit., p.164.
2   Derrida, *Of Grammatology*, op. cit., p. 66. See also, at p. 68 (discussing difference): '*Spacing* (notice that this word speaks the articulation of space and time, the becoming-space of time and the becoming-time of space) is always the unperceived, the nonpresent, and the nonconscious . . . Arche-writing as spacing cannot occur as such with the phenomenological experience of a *presence*. It marks the *dead time* within the presence of living present, within the general form of all presence.'

rary questions posed by the possibility of a rhetorical analysis of law are thus both grammatological and semiotic. To recapitulate briefly, they are material questions relating to the written form of law which may be approached initially grammatologically in terms of control over a system of encrypting and transmission. It is first a question of an archival kind: of storage of texts, of their production, access to them and legitimation through their repetition, a question of their destination. In semiotic terms a further question can be posed relating not simply to the legal writing system as an institution but further to the linguistic significance of legal dogmatics in the age of print: in place of the question of the language or rhetoric that legal doctrine uses we would rather pose the question of what law has done to language. To what extent were linguistics and rhetoric internally marked by the contractarian fidelities of legal writing and its dogmatic fixation of meaning and reference to what doctrine alone could present as the singular and original terms of the legal art?[1]

The lawyers taught specific and highly specialised forms of writing within a language of their own devising: part law Latin, part law French, part middle English. Foreign in its origins and arcane in its presentation, the language of law was a language of record, of documents and monuments, and not of speech: its language, according to Coke amongst others, was not one that could be 'pure or well pronounced' for the reason that it was written and read rather than spoken; it was formal and formulaic as opposed to being either dialect or dialogue.[2] Its uses, in other words, were scriptural and were first codified and published during the course of the sixteenth century when licensed legal printers published the first formbook evidence of the rules of legal writing (symbolaeography), the laws of composition and circulation of heraldic insignia (armory), the standard forms of writs (entrees) and the first vernacular curricula rhetorical hand-books. The early era of print also saw the first doctrinal defences or apologia for the legal profession, an early jurisprudential literature concerned to exorcise the remnants of rhetoric, of local oral traditions

1   As for example in Fulbecke, *Direction*, op. cit., p. 77, distinguishing artificial and inartificial words: 'artificial are these which the inventors of arts have devised for acquainting the mind with the mysteries and rules of their art, because words fitly and accomodately used are the very images and representations of things which do lead the understanding . . . to the apprehension and perfect knowledge of the things themselves. . . .'

2   Coke, *Commentary on Littleton* (1629 edn, London), C6a.

and jurisdictions, from the modern discipline of law. In providing a preliminary historical assessment of certain legal discourses concerned to regulate and restrict the inscription and circulation of particular forms of social meaning, I will concentrate upon the linguistic presuppositions of the exclusion of rhetoric. It will be argued that the exclusion in question – the banishment of rhetoric, of oral teachings and of conversation as explicit sources of law, in favour of a Ramist conception of logical method – did not drive rhetoric out of law but rather drove it within. The exclusion was in practice a repression, the full irony of which only becomes apparent when it is recognised that it was in the name, and for the cause, of the rhetorical art of memory that the repression in question was initially perpetrated.

Legal Writing Systems

The manner in which I intend to use a concept of the grammatological analysis of law draws directly upon a notion of a rhetoric of writing or of epistolary laws. It may be most easily formulated in terms of grammatological themes rather than by definition. Taking the sixteenth-century emergence of the first printed legal literature as a crucial point of reference and transmission, legal grammatology will be concerned with a series of broadly institutional questions: 'Who is writing? To whom? To send, to destine, to dispatch what? To what address?'[1]

First, there is the issue of the technology or mode of production of – and commentary upon – law. As with all the great transitions in English law, the emergence of a common law method or dogmatics owes its central tenets to continental jurisprudence and particularly to humanistic legal philology. A scribal culture of feudal chirography (handwriting), of the engrossing and tabling of fines and charges relating to land, was gradually systematised by doctrinal writers into a legal *écriture*.[2] In the hands of Coke and Davies the central doctrinal

1   J. Derrida, *The Post Card* (1987, Chicago), p. 5.
2   In classical legal terms we must note that the French *écrit* refers, like its English equivalent 'writ', both to writing and to law. The concept of *écriture* is one of the joining of writing to law within a system of texts. For Legendre, that is the lesson of the Roman concept of *ratio scripta*: 'the authority of genealogy has its provenance in the authority of texts founded on the principle of Reason. That is the great lesson to be drawn from the history of Roman law: the power and the

concept becomes one of a system of legal language and a corresponding method or technical discipline of national law. In the face of a new technology, the haphazard scribal practices associated with keepers of the rolls and with registers and custodians of instruments and writs had to be formally replaced with a national written law. In classical rhetorical terms, the first question is that of the institution to which legal discourse is tied, a question which Aristotle poses in Book One of the *Rhetoric* in terms of genre as the material site or locus of oratorical enunciation. In a more recent terminology, it is the question of who speaks, by what authority, in the name of what text, of what law?[1]

Law printing created a number of possibilities with regard to the visibility, accessibility and availability of law. It made possible what the Ramist Abraham Fraunce termed a 'logic of law', by which he meant a systematic presentation of general legal concepts under which particular rules of law might be subsumed. In the event, however, law printing was not a popularising or systematising innovation. Law texts were published by a restricted number of licensed printers. The texts were idiosyncratically selected for publication, and liable to be expensive and lengthy. They were written almost exclusively for the profession itself and consequently remained either in Latin or in law French. In terms of the production and transmission or sending of legal knowledge, the new form of inscription of legal texts did not challenge but rather reaffirmed the established order of the legal institution and its presentation of writing as governed by a dogmatics of the unwritten word. In Davies' words, the law remained explicitly a tradition as well as a collection of books,[2] in consequence of which legal writing had always to be approached as a representation, as an equivocal sign of hidden depths, and not as a profane, accessible or vernacular object of interpretation. Outside of the profession – and frequently within it as well – the newly printed texts could be received only as opaque or

authority of Reason are one and the same thing' (*L'Inestimable Objet de la Transmission*, 1985, Paris, p. 38). For a comparable, though much broader account, see J. Derrida, *Dissemination* (1981, Chicago), pp. 41–50, 134–55.

1 M. Foucault, *The Archaeology of Knowledge*, op. cit., pp. 50–1, 'Who is speaking? Who among the totality of individuals is accorded the right to use this sort of language? Who is qualified to do so? Who derives from it his own special quality, his prestige, and the presumption that what he says is true?' Discussed in P. Goodrich, *Legal Discourse* (1987, London), pp. 144–51.

2 Davies, *Le Primer Report* (1615, Dublin), fol. 20.

iconic representations of legality: awesomely particular collections of rules and procedures were most immediately recognisable as insignia of authority, of a system of arcane citations and repetitions, an epistolary art conducted in a strange tongue 'as thought the law were written to strangers'[1] or, perhaps, more simply, to the Other.

A third theme concerns an antagonism. In classical rhetorical terms there is no legitimate reason for supposing that law ought to be addressed outside of the legal institution. In terms of language, topics, audience and receipt, the circulation of legal texts can be understood as a matter internal to the various tiers of the legal profession. There are, of course, strong grounds of a doctrinal, sociological and political order for objecting to such a bureaucratic restriction of the written materials of civil disposition and penal government. There is, at least, a contradiction between the universal application of law or 'rule of law' and the rhetorical restrictions placed upon the availability and circulation of its texts. In grammatological terms, an additional question may thus be posed relating to the notational structure of legal writing systems and particularly with regard to the restricted rhetorical play of their eventual dissemination. The first codified systems of legal notation governed armory, instruments and records. In linguistic terms, they share a common theme: each notational system is legalistically regulated by a theory of origins and is semantically structured so as to restrict meaning to an imputed originary form. The legal note – whether emblem, ensign, enigma, instrument, syllable or word – was to be a note bonded to a singular and original referent. The legal use of signs was everywhere recognisable for its assertion of the canonic status of the first notation and for coincident theories of fidelity and custody of the original and lawful meaning.

Returning to the question of the rhetoric of writing, we may observe the inexorable subordination of rhetoric to law. The techniques of legal writing to be examined constitute a series of parallel systems of linguistic and graphic restraint based primarily upon classical etymologies and 'true' notations. The question of meaning was dealt with in terms of fealty or faith. Meaning was everywhere already decided, dogmatically determined in advance and so destined to immobility or semantic death. It is that principle of the death of meaning, or of the destruction of the sociality of meaning in favour of

1 T. Starkey (ed.), *A Dialogue between Reginald Pole and Thomas Lupset* (1535/1949 edn, London), p. 189.

an institutional dogma of the original and its protected images, that will be the object of the ensuing analysis. We begin with the inscription of images of birth, office, dignity and other forms of status: the law regulating the representation through 'exterior signs' of social place, fame and occasionally merit.

Emblemata

As an introduction to more complex and familiar systems of legal inscription, it is worth recollecting the rather exceptional issue of heraldry and the law governing the 'bearing of arms and the ranging of every man in his room of honour according as his place requires'.[1] At the level of social placement, arms and insignia function in the same way as names, they differentiate people: 'for as names were invented, to know men by them: so was the bearing of arms invented, for the knowledge of the deserts and names of the Noble'.[2] The bearing of arms or of 'coat-armor' in both military and civil contexts, together with the creation of symbols, emblems, enigmas, devices and other insignia of honour or 'generosity', were all subject to a series of legal regulations governing authorisation and the status of their bearers. The art was also subject to strict rules governing composition and content, inclusive of rules regulating the types of representation and of figuration that were permitted in relation to different statuses of honour and their symbolic representation. Thus, to take one example, the 'body', which is to say the image of a device, should follow natural forms in all its figurations with the exception of those that are mythological and subject to the invariable law that no device should show a human face.[3] The heraldic or armorial art was a

1   Ridley, op. cit., at p. 134. See also A. Fraunce, *Insignium Armorum, Emblematum, Hieroglyphicum et Symbolorum* (1588, London), fol. E2a, for Biblical reference on this point see Numbers 2.2: 'Every man of the children of Israel shall pitch by his own standard, with the ensign of their fathers house . . .' For general discussion see A.R. Wagner, *Heralds and Heraldry in the Middle Ages* (1956, Oxford); E. J. Jones, *Medieval Heraldry* (1943, Cardiff). For a recent and intelligent discussion of notes, notions and things from a slightly later era, see T. C. Singer, 'Hieroglyphs, Real Characters, and the Idea of Natural Language in English 17th Century Thought' (1989) *Journal of History of Ideas* 89.

2   John Ferne, *The Blazon of Gentrie* (1586, London), p. 225: *sicut et nomina inventa sunt, ad homines cognoscendum, ita et ista insignia, ad idem inventa sunt.* See also J. Guillim, *A Display of Heraldry* (1610/1679 edn, London), fol. 3a–b.

3   Fraunce, *Insignium Armorum*, op. cit., fol. Nib (no human face to appear on any symbol); A. Amboise, *Discours ou Traicte des Devises où est mise la raison et difference des emblemes, enigmes, sentences et autres* (1620, Paris), fol. Ava, Lviia.

complex and complete code of inscription or writing, and it received a number of systematic expositions and reformulations as a result of the Ramist impetus towards didactic or methodical presentations of all the arts. The most important of such presentations were either dedicated to or written by members of the Inns of Court.

The art of heraldry is most usually attributed a dual origin. In theological terms, it is derived from the story of genesis: Seth through signs or marks identifies himself and his family as true nobility, as 'having the place of his father' against his ignoble brother Cain.[1] In strictly theological terms, armory thus marks out the son that takes the place of the father and who is honoured in the eyes of God, although we should note that Cain too and all his descendants are equally marked; he is no less than 'destined to dishonour, a runnagate . . . condemned to a vagrant life, uncertain of his dwelling, without allotment or patrimony, or establishment of his family in any fixed place, or permanent inheritance . . . [marked] by signs and outward tokens, of servility, unnobleness and ignominy'.[2] On the positive side, Seth's honour is worn as a badge by the son and by his heirs for all time. In broader terms, 'it is known, that almighty God is the original author of honouring nobility who, even in heaven hath made a discrepance of his heavenly spirits, giving them several names as ensigns of honour'.[3]

In post-diluvian and more secular terms, armory concerned specific systems of military or royal communication (currours) and reward. The etymology of the word is generally agreed by systematisers of the art to indicate its original use, 'heralt' deriving from the Teutonic *here-healt*, meaning military champion or representative of the army who would carry messages of war and peace to the enemy in carefully staged forms.[4] More general definitions of the

---

1 C. Segoing, *Trésor heraldique ou mercure armorial* (1652/1657 edn, Paris), p. 4. The question is always one of descent, of race, of blood, a question whose theoretical dimensions are well discussed in Legendre, *Transmission*, op. cit., pp. 197–206.

2 Ferne, op. cit., p. 2.

3 Bosewell, *Workes of Armorie* (1572, London), fol. Biia.

4 R. Verstegan, *A Restitution of Decayed Intelligence in Antiquities* (1605, Amsterdam), pp. 320–1; see also N. Upton, *De Studio Militari Libri Quattor* (1655, London), pp. 20–1, on heralds as messengers or *nuncius regis*; and H. Spelman, *Aspilogia* (1654, London), pp. 2–4. The most interesting dimension of the classical definitions concerns the general function of the herald (and so of armory) as state messengers or state oracles. Armory covered all legal forms of communication – *arma sunt generaliter omnium rerum instrumenta* (cited in Bossewell, 1572, Aia) – and

art define arms as symbola or *symbola heroica*,[1] as 'signs, tokens or notes' distinguishing persons and units on the field of battle or alternatively identifying civil status and genealogy or blood by similar insignia and livery: 'arms, according to their original or first use . . . are tokens or resemblances, signifying some act or quality of the bearer . . . it is very probable that these signs, which we call arms [formerly they were emblems, pictures, hidden conceits, hieroglyphs, mysteries, enigmas] . . . were external notes of the inward disposition of the mind, manifesting in some sort the natural qualities of their bearers'.[2] In broader terms, we might say that, just as the standard or banner ('the signifier') identifies the military unit, so also armory would identify diverse other groups and statuses based upon either heredity or grant.[3] Specific insignia marked and distinguished geographical and political units of nation, city, town and villages; lineages or orders of nobility, from royal lineages to the orders of 'nobility princely' and 'nobility regall',[4] to the complex differentiating categories of gentility or generosity opposed to the various ignoble or plebeian statuses and accompanying 'marks' identifying the various ungentle forms of tenancy and trade: 'they are named ancient herehaughtes, who have made the distinction between gentle and ungentle, in which there is as much difference as between virtue and vice'.[5]

In its own terms, the art of armory is a language or semiotic system complete in itself and consisting of two parts: blazoning, which

thus, for example, to kill an enemy 'outwith the law' of arms was murder, while to usurp the arms of a dignity or office was forgery (*crimen falsi*). In grammatological terms it is interesting to note that by the sixteenth century, heralds are termed 'currours' in the vernacular and are defined as state messengers in a statute of 1547. Currours were centrally controlled by the master of the posts, an office of the king's court, and were charged particularly with maintenance of the public course of royal business and with the circulation of 'true reports' (Legh, op. cit., fol. 225a). For further details see Francis Thynne, *The Office and Duty of an Herald* (1605, London), fol. 35b.

1 Guillim, *Display*, op. cit., fol. 2a. Also C. Fauchet, *Origines des chevaliers, armoires et heraux* (1610, Paris), fol. 513a.

2 Guillim, op. cit., fol. 3a–b.

3 See for a definition in these terms, Bartolus de Saxoferrato, *Tractatus de Insigniis et Armis* (1475/1485 edn, Venice), at 2b. So to A. Alciatus, *De Notitia Dignitatem* (1651 edn, Paris).

4 Ferne, *Blazon*, op. cit., p. 88.

5 G. Legh, *The Accedens of Armorie* (1562, London), fol. iib.

governed the dictionary definition of armorial units, and marshalling which governed the syntax or association of elements.[1] It has first a lexicon of images or of signs, tokens and marks. The lexicon is supposedly universal and each element of colour, metal, precious stone, planet, beast, line and so on represented specific virtues and, in one theory at least, each was aligned to specific statuses such that the most precious metals, noble colours and propitious planets would rest only in royal arms.[2] There is secondly a syntax which governs the possible juxtaposition of elements in the lexicon with laws regulating the hierarchy of different signs within the coat of arms and the permissible relationship between independent elements. A particular syntax was either authentic or inauthentic depending first upon the originality and propriety of its derivation and differences, the accuracy of its presentation of ancestry and honour. The arms themselves were either *arma vera* or *arma falsa*, true or false arms, depending upon the relationship of colours to metals and the use of specific elements. It was false armory to misrepresent elements of the armorial code, such as to intermix in the same device natural and artificial signs.[3] It was also and for analogous reasons false armory to depict a higher status, legitimacy or other quality than that which the bearer occupied or to which the bearer was entitled. Most graphically, the individual's arms had always to be placed *in signum subjectionis* in relation to the sovereign's arms: 'any subject setting his arms in public in any undue manner, as, for example, above those of his prince or above the arms of any person to whom he owes obedience, they are lawfully to be removed and defaced. In the former case of the sovereign's arms it is treason.'[4]

The details of the various branches of armory – enigmas, devices, hieroglyphs, gryphs and symbols are all technically separate disciplines – will have to be ignored. The brief outline given refers simply to the general system of pictographic inscription or 'body' and accompanying words or 'soul', whereby a fully codified series of military, spiritual, civil and lineal degrees and statuses of honour were to be set down in arms and other devices. Viewed as a form of writing or notational system, heraldry clearly belongs within grammatology and in some senses is exemplary of certain of its historical

1 Guillim, *Display*, op. cit., fol. 8b.
2 Ferne, op. cit., pp. 169ff.
3 H. Estienne, *The Art of Making Devises* (1643/1650 edn, London), fol. G3a.
4 Ferne, op. cit., p. 270.

themes.[1] The heraldic use of signs functions legally to differentiate
and identify the individual according to a system of origins and proof
of origins. Its identificatory marks within civil contexts all refer the
identified individual to a corporate or civic place first by virtue of his
family and secondarily by reference to either a specific dignity (office)
or a form of tenancy and its accompanying fealties. Each place is
bonded to particular forms of representation or symbolisation and we
will return to the social significance of the code of honour and of
fidelity that governs that bonding and ultimately relates the human to
the divine and to death.[2] Prior to any examination of content,
however, the heraldic system raises questions of rhetorical form and
of epistolary use. Using the contemporary sixteenth- and early
seventeenth-century systematisations of heraldic method, I will
concentrate here upon questions of the legalisation of this imagistic
language, and the formal constraints imposed upon its system of
notation or writing; constraints that affect both the form of representation and its content, both its body and its soul.

The systematic armorial formbooks invariably precede their
doctrinal presentations of the substantive divisions and parts of the
discipline with a brief history and philosophy of the composition and
bearing of signs. In common with all the major humanistic reformulations of the disciplines, armory is granted a theological genealogy and
a first place amongst the orders of representation. The philosophical
origins of armory lie in pictograms and hieroglyphics, in a holy

1   J. Derrida (1976), p. 9: 'For some time now, as a matter of fact, here and
there, by a gesture and for motives that are profoundly necessary, whose
degradation is easier to denounce than it is to disclose their origin, one says
'language' for action, movement, thought, reflection, consciousness, unconscious-
ness, experience, affectivity, etc. Now we tend to say "writing" for all that and
more: to designate not only physical gestures of literal pictographic or ideographic
inscriptions, but also the totality of what makes it possible; and also, beyond the
signifying face, the signified face itself. And thus we say "writing" for all that gives
rise to an inscription in general . . .' See also idem, *Positions*, op. cit., p. 36: 'there is
no *scientific* semiotic work which does not serve grammatology'.

2   P. Legendre, *L'Empire de la vérité* (1983, Paris), p. 107 (discussing the parable
of the law in Kafka's *Trial*): 'What does it mean to say that the science of Law is
based upon a secret? . . . it is precisely a question of guarding the secret of the Law,
an inviolate secret, one that can only be represented aesthetically in a parable
whose last word is the last word of each human life *in articulo mortis*, at the point of
death; the secret of the Law is the death of every human being. That is eventually
what is both unliveable and necessary to life, that is the founding truth of the
institution.'

writing or art of sacred letters that makes use of a wide variety of enigmatic representations, of 'emblems, pictures, hidden conceits, hieroglyphs, symbols and enigmas',[1] to portray qualities or images of the soul. The images that exist in the soul are themselves impresses or marks, 'draughts and resemblances' of divine archetypes of all the species and objects. Within the human soul, God has imprinted the marks and symbols, the diverse characters or script, of that which, by virtue of its very divinity, cannot be directly presented. The science of those originary 'holy letters' is esoteric, 'abstruse and sacred', for the primordial reason that the name of God was consigned to the human heart in the veiled or shrouded form of symbols, enigmas and other figures that range from mutilation of the body to the symbolic inscriptions of religious ritual. At one level, the principle involved in the circulation of such holy letters or signs was one of opacity; these marks were either esoteric by virtue of the political status of the bearer or they were opaque as the signs of God. The formal principle of such inscription was clear only in the most general of terms, namely that the sign indicated formidable and occasionally sacred inner qualities: 'but armes shall be accompted, as the goods and riches of the soul. For they are the rewards, the significations, and outward marks of virtue, which have proceeded, from the soul or mind of the first bearer'.[2]

From hierography, the first ranked and most esoteric of the disciplines, there develops a general science of symbols. All the disciplines or mysteries encode their truth or originary reality in sacred signs; nor could the 'principles of other sciences be infused . . . into the minds of posterity, without these kinds of symbols and aenigmas which serve as rind or bark to conserve all the mysteries'.[3] A generalised principle of the esoteric transmission of sacred knowledge accepts that divinely given knowledge be restrictively disseminated through the mediation of signs. Knowledge of the code of the particular disciplines is thus to be construed as a privilege, as a dignity, nobility or honour. It is an honour, first, in a metaphysical sense because custody of the meaning of signs is a custody of an unseen and unwritten (divine) truth entrusted originally to holy heralds and only subsequently made available to the Church. In terms of subsequent traditions, it need simply be noted that the

1 Guillim, op. cit., at fol. 3a.

2 Ferne, op. cit. at p. 288. See further: Estienne, *Devises*, op. cit. at fol. B2a.

3 Estienne, op. cit., fol. Bia. Thynne, *Office and Duty*, op. cit. at 33a refers to *arcana imperii heraldorum*.

armorial insignia represent a system of social fealty based upon an invisible order of truth. In a profane or political sense, knowledge is encoded and is specifically kept from the general and ignoble public: they can neither know nor bear arms of honour or virtue. Of those that do bear arms, the appropriate term is *nobilitas* which derives from *nosco*, to know, to belong to an honourable lineage and so to be both the bearer of a tradition of knowledge and also known or noted, set apart. Conjoint with *nobilitas* is *dignitas*, the office which nobility must needs hold by dint of knowledge. In political terms, all offices are dignities and bear their own insignia or holy letters: *possessio dignitatis, probatur per insignia*, possession of a dignity is proved through its insignia.

The political force of the sacral nature of public office and dignity needs little emphasis; armory was simply the means of its notation. As a system of such notations, armory introduces and circulates two crucial notions, namely those of the authority and authenticity of emblematic signs.[1] The authority of the sign is a question of legitimacy, a matter of origin, of birth or descent, the lineage that will refer the sign either to an immemorial or to a divine source. That legitimacy – the absolute reference – precludes the need for justification outside of the benediction or *auctoritas* of faith itself: each politically established dignity or office has access to the sanctity of the sign and may therefore speak as something other than the human voice – as impersonal *officium* or function, as justice or law or right, as scripture or sign. Nobility is thus authority; it is a form of access to a particular right and function of enunciation while also allowing for the effacement of the sociality of that speech behind a classically dogmatic legitimation: *dignitas non moritur*, dignity (here truth) is immortal. The issue of authenticity, on the other hand, draws us towards a question of linguistics.

The authority of the sign derives from a metaphysical reference; it guarantees the truth of lineage or the authenticity of noble office by

---

1   P. Legendre, *Transmission*, op. cit., p. 205: these legal traits of authority and authenticity are the essential feature of emblems, they provide a basis for dogmatic discourse through the creation of a liturgical or inaugural setting for that discourse, they are in that sense the secular equivalent of the icon which functioned to create sacred space. For Legendre the liturgical is 'the theatrical staging (*mise-en-scène*) of the legality of the message, consisting of an address *to all those* who are supposed to have to deal with, in one manner or another, the discourse of legitimacy.'

reference to the dogmatic space of myth. Either God or sovereign gives these honours or alternatively they have always been there, it has always been like that, and there is no reason to change immemorial practice.[1] The notions of reference and authenticity indicate further issues of signification. The notational system established by the armorial code is strictly denotative: the emblem or sign in civil contexts belongs to a family, a dignity or a degree of gentility. The sign was a note that named and guaranteed the identity and quality of its bearer. It distinguishes and identifies the bearer and thereby had a nominal function, that of noting and publicly declaring membership of a social genre with all the attendant duties and privileges of that genre: *a nominibus, ad arma, sequuntur argumenta*, reasons or arguments taken from the name follow to their arms.[2] In this respect the sign is a complex form of proper noun. Its function is twofold. First, as a name, it refers uniquely to its bearer and distinguishes and names both his degree of nobility and his personal attributes or differences. The emblem as identificatory sign springs from the blood and in law can be neither sold nor otherwise granted or alienated. In familial terms, 'armes do attend both the body and the soul of the bearer'; they are a 'privilege perpetual' attending the person.[3] The sign is simply an outward mark or token that refers to an original nobility, a virtue or deed or quality of mind of the first bearer: underpinning the materiality of the sign is a corresponding state of the soul. Similarly, the emblem of dignity is attached as an incident or inseparable accident to the office it represents, 'even as a shadow waits on the body'.

Sufficient has been said to illustrate the rigours of emblemata and of their composition and use. The function of arms was that of a theocratic distribution of honour, of names and their social qualification or genre. Each sign tied its bearer to a specific identity and required that he remain so linked to the original meaning or immemorial quality of which the sign was the body, or outward mark.

---

1 Coke, *A Book of Entries containing perfect and approved president of Courts, declarations . . . and all other matters and proceedings . . . concerning the practick part of the laws of England* (1610/1671) edn, London), fol. A6A: (in a writ of mesne) 'et que cest forme avoiet touts foits este use ils ne voillent chaunger cest use, nient obstant que lour opinion [i.e. that of the prothonotaries] fuit al contrarie, quia non valet ratio contra experimentum.' (Ellice Case 39 H 6, fol. 30.)

2 Ferne, op. cit., p. 225.

3 Ibid at 287.

A special court, that of Constable and Marshal, was established by statute (13 Richard II cap. II) in the mid-fourteenth century with full incarceral and capital jurisdictions to oversee and regulate all disputes relating to arms.[1] Under the presidency of the Earl Marshal, the King Herald and diverse other heralds and pursuivants had judicial powers both to devise arms and to strip and punish those bearing false or falsely composed arms. Usurpation of the arms of another or the forging of the arms of a dignity were both serious crimes and punishable, either by death or by lengthy imprisonment, as *crimen falsi*.[2] To forgery can be added a string of further crimes relating to the possession, inscription and bearing of arms. The most serious relate to failure to respect the hierarchy of honours in the inscription of the device itself. As noted earlier, such an offence could be either treason or petty treason depending on the status of the party offended. More generically, an action *de scandalis magnatum* lay against those who injured the honour or name of a nobleman; an *actio iniuriam* against any ungentle person who detracted from the honour of a gentleman.[3] To the general title to actions for defaming the honour of nobility or gentility can be added various further specific crimes against the image. An action thus lay for *crimen iniuriae*, for any defacement, removal or taking down of arms from their authorised place. Further, to treat the arms of the sovereign in any disrespectful manner, 'to set them forth on a reversed escutcheon or to place them by any shameful and dishonourable matter, sign, emblem or writing', was also treason.[4] Amongst the more esoteric offences against honour we might end with an example drawn from war by noting that there was an action for *iniuria sermonis*, injury by words, which lay against anyone who asserted that insignia had been abandoned on the battlefield.

Symbolaeography

In rhetorical terms, the armorial system of notation or of authentic representation of the various forms of filiation creates a public sphere. The inscription of social meaning in arms established a liturgical or ideal realm of discourse, of legitimate representation, and simul-

1   Thynne, *Office and Duty*, op. cit., 38a–b.
2   Bartolus, *Tractatus*, op. cit., 2b.
3   John Logan, *Analogia Honorum* (1677, London), fol. 42a, 156b.
4   Ferne, op. cit., p. 270.

taneously marked out the space of public dignities and, in particular, those of politics and law. The armorial sign was addressed specifically to that public sphere and its institutions. It was addressed *erga omnes*, to all those with access to the public sphere. To the unaffiliated, those not possessed of such honour or nobility, it simply represented in diverse forms the mystic legitimacy of sovereign discourse and its various delegated public powers or offices. Those without public names or insignia were neither intended nor equipped to receive the discourse of the soul, a discourse emanating from the ideal and destined for the audience of either *nobilitas* or *dignitas*: 'according to their modern or present use, arms may be said to be hieroglyphic or enigmatic symbols or signs . . . external notes of the inward disposition of the mind, manifesting in some sort the natural qualities of their bearers, yet so as they were hidden from the vulgar sort, and known to the judicious only'; they were signs 'neither obscure to the learned nor over-familiar to the common sort'.[1]

As writing, the composition of insignia mirrors the ideal quality of their social function. In terms of their content, arms are either true or false. There are numerous technical compositional rules requiring particular styles of representation and reference,[2] particular hierarchies of signs and an enigmatic or 'strange' language of mottos, of the soul.[3] For present purposes, the generally significant rule was that the authenticity of the sign related to its origin or source; its lineage must be traceable either beyond memory or to some other foundational act. In that sense, the language of insignia is a ritual language of repetition and accretion, a language of liturgy or theatre within a strictly qualified social space. What qualified that public space was a mixture of divinity and antiquity, virtue and blood, whose discourse or insignia were governed by law against any false lineage, forged dignity or improperly composed (unnatural) arms. If we move now to the second writing system, symbolaeography or the rules for writing instruments and precedents, a close parallel may be drawn between the restrictive inscription of insignia and the law governing the linguistic content of contractual documents. Legal writing belongs to and develops from the symbolic tradition of holy letters or enigmatic transmission. In linguistic terms, the tradition is similarly nominalist and bonded: the meaning of legal script or scrivening is judged

1   Guillim, op. cit., fol. 3a.
2   Estienne, op. cit., fol. G2b–F1b.
3   Amboise, op. cit., fol. Biiia.

according to its lineage, *antiquitate et tempore*, by antiquity and time or in contemporary terms by reference to tradition and sources, a legitimacy of lineage, of descent.[1]

The term symbolaeography is coined by William West as the title of a formbook of legal precedents and rules of legal writing first published in 1592 and subtitled *The Art or Description or Image of Instruments, or the Paterne of Presidents or the Notarie or Scrivener*. In etymological terms, symbolaeography has an interesting duality. In one derivation from the Greek, *symbolum* refers to a contract and so symbolaeography would be the writing of contracts or contractual writing: either signs that bind or the bonding of signs. From the Latin *symbolus* there is a more general sense of the symbol as mark or token or seal. While general usage interprets the symbol as a material mark, figure or character that stands for, represents or denotes something else, it also bears a more restrictive religious and legal meaning. The symbol is a creed or confession of faith, a brief formal statement of the religious belief of the Christian faith or of a particular church or sect. The symbol as creed is a sign of identification of believers as against pagans or heathens. Symbolaeography would in that respect be the written statement of faith or, by transposition, the statement of legal faith in writing and in the truth of its characters and representations. In the hands of the legal scriveners and notaries, the symbol as sign of faith in law, as a form of belief and sanctification of the written, has a further powerful representation. In the words of Sir Edward Coke, legal writing is no ordinary or mere writing 'of any scrivener's boy in his master's shop'.[2] Legal writing is rather a learned art in a learned language. Nor does that documentary language signify as ordinary language, but rather as a code or system of legal scripts. As is quickly made clear in the symbolaeography, the predominant form of legal notation is epistolary; it is a system of charters, writs, registered formulae, inscribed tables, notes and fines that circulate within the various jurisdictions and archives of the legal institution.

The tradition that William West attempts to codify and methodise is properly described as notarial. It develops from the rhetorical *ars dictandi* and concerns the minute regulation of every orthographic, syllabic and other scribal detail of the production, storage or custody and circulation of documents for legal use. The significance of symbolaeography does not reside in novelty of content nor in any

1 Legendre, *Empire*, op. cit., p. 151.
2 Coke, *Reports*, II, A6a–b; see also, idem, *Institutes*, pt III, at fol. Liiia.

specific claim to coherence or completeness. It is a formbook and so the bulk of its content is repetitive; it provides a catalogue of the existing scribal standard forms for a variety of legal transactions. Such specimen documents are available elsewhere, either in earlier formbooks or in manuscript.[1] The significance of West's work is doctrinal. Accompanying the extraordinarily detailed presentation of written forms is an account of the theory of legal chirography, of the rules of composition of instruments, together with an account of the doctrine or 'causes' presupposed in the notarial art or profession.

As a writing system, symbolaeography may properly be described as symbolic. What is symbolised is primarily and simply a question of membership of a system of inscription, of belonging to the language of legal record.[2] In West's prosaic definition of the legal instrument, it is 'a formal writing made in paper or parchment, wherein are contained and described contracts, covenants, last wills, or other facts and things of persons for the testimony or memory thereof'.[3] This distinctive system of notation is first a formal system of representation. Its primary concern is with forms of bonding, of contract, in which 'any man confesses himself by his writing, orderly made, sealed and delivered'.[4] The confession or contract binds absolutely. It binds internally as confession and it binds externally as writing. In terms of confession or internal qualities, the instrument is *bona fide* and guaranteed true both by good faith – it is signed by and identified with the person – and by the Defender of the Faith, by the initial addressee of any instrument, God's representative, the sovereign. If we look at the form of address of the covenants, grants (feoffements) and wills listed in West, they are uniformly written in the name of God (*Dei gratia*) and addressed to the immediate custody of the kingdom of God or the defender of the faith (*fidei defensor*). While the precise formulation varies according to particular forms of instrument, no document is complete without a standard invocation of an eternal guarantee, be it the entire community of the faithful to whom the writing is presented (*omnibus christi fidelibus ad quos praesentes literae pervenerint*) or the one and universal king of justice (*reg. univers et singulis*

1 See C. W. Brooks, *Pettyfoggers and Vipers of the Commonwealth* (1986, Cambridge), p. 135.
2 See Clanchy, op. cit., pp. 151–74.
3 W. West, *Symbolaeography* (1603 edn, London), at fol. IB4a.
4 Ibid., IA8a.

iusticiariis), eternal lord (*salutem in domum sempiternam*) or some variant invocation of the same.[1]

The divine addressee of legal scripts might seem anachronistic or formulaic, an archaic epistolary ritual to which little significance should be attributed. The sacral quality of legal writing, which the Roman tradition has coined as *ratio scripta*, written reason, is best seen, however, as being directly performative: it symbolises and signals a peculiar and permanent discourse whose written marks are legally 'apt and significant' in each and every character or word.[2] It also announces a discourse which is in all ordinary senses hermetically sealed, the property of the institution to which it is tied and within which it circulates according to strict offices of ingrossing, tabling, noting, posting and custody of the various instruments and fines dealt with by West. That principle of restriction can be illustrated by further critical examination of the rhetorical form of written instruments. In addition to fairly obvious orthographic and calligraphic requirements of clarity of script and avoidance of interlinear glosses and abbreviations, the writing of instruments proceeds according to a classically prescribed order of place, person, occasion, manner of doing, cause, exception, (and) condition. Each topic in that order is governed by rules of citation, of repetition and precedent form.

To take but one example, the detailed regulation of legal inscription can be illustrated most succinctly by reference to the law of misprision or textual error. The bulk of rules relating to composition required precise repetition of standard formulae in the immemorial language of the law, together with procedures of naming, signing and delivering or ingrossing and proclaiming. As regards naming, or 'additions', a writ or instrument would fail if it lacked certainty of name, which certainty included additions of 'curtesie of place, dignity, estate, degree, misterie or occupation'.[3] A writ which designated a knight a gentleman (*generoso*) would thus fail, as would

---

1 The examples are all taken from West though the tradition of such forms of address to a divine auditor and judge is a venerable one in legal documents. For much earlier examples, see Robertson (ed.), *Anglo-Saxon Charters* (1956, London).

2 West, op. cit., IB7b. See also Doderidge, *English Lawyer*, op. cit., p. 46: 'without a knowledge of legal language, the student of the laws, the practitioner, and the judge must of necessity walk through a veil of darkness and palpable ignorance in the superlative.'

3 West, op. cit., II, ss. 25–26.

any writ in which any one of the listed additions formally addressing either the king or the recipient of the writ was omitted.[1] By an analogous logic, the symbolaeography also warns of the disastrous consequences of false Latin or law French and summarises a law of misprision (false spelling and inaccurate record) which was more litigated and legislated upon than virtually any other contemporary issue. Famous common law cases included the failure of a criminal count for using the word 'burgaliter' instead of the proper form 'burglariter', of a writ for recovery in waste for use of 'destrictionem' in place of 'destructionem', and 'haere' for 'haeredi' in a writ of *praecipe quod reddat*. The general rule with regard to written instruments may be summarised as requiring proper form, in the absence of which wording they will fail. On the other hand, once the instrument or other writing has been entered on record, that is to say formally knowledged, noted, proclaimed and then ingrossed, it is taken to be true and will generally be irreversible even where the record is manifestly false. In a case cited by Sir John Doderidge, the clerk to the court had mistakenly recorded an outlawry where the writ had in fact been rebutted. On appeal by the plaintiff in person, the justices, who had been present at the original hearing, recollected that the record was wrong but observed that the misprision was none the less on the record and testified outlawry.[2]

The *Symbolaeography* at several points specifies a requirement of plain style in legal documentation which should express 'all things certainly with apt significant words and therein eschewing all metaphorical, figurative, and borrowed speeches, and all words of divers or doubtful significations'.[3] The content of the documents exhaustively reproduced by West indicates that a plain style refers simply to accurate encrypting, together with a resistance to borrowing from non-legal discourses. The encoded character of legal documents is hardly questionable and in point of doctrine their encoding is their primary virtue, their language remaining pristine and unadulterated precisely be dint of never having been a spoken language or, indeed, a language used for any purpose other than law. What West presents is thus a language of originals, which are faithfully reproduced at extraordinary length and in the unrevised

---

1 Coke, *Reports*, VIII, 156b (*Arthur Blackamore's Case*). For a further compendium of examples, see Finch, *Law*, op. cit., pp. 226–32.

2 Doderidge, op. cit., p. 200.

3 West, op. cit., at 1B7b.

trilingual argot of the profession. These are the signs or written characters of the law; they have a hermetic logic of their own and are produced, proclaimed and stored by means of special rituals in the offices of the chirographer, the custodian of the rolls and the keeper of writs and of the post (*nisi prius* records forwarded – *postea* – to the common pleas). In point of use, these scripts and writs are talismanic if not holy letters which are posted or circulated within the various strata of the legal profession but have no immediate sense outside that institution. In short, principally in relation to the various statuses and types of property and property ownership, symbolaeography created a system of symbolic representation, of truths guaranteed by a principle of source and repetition, a system of notes or insignia that constituted a public sphere upon a logic of tradition, of immemorial documentations.

Laws of Notation

Legal writing was a ritual system of inscriptions. The text was necessarily true; it contained neither false Latin nor incongruous French, nor any words not already known to the law. It was a language not of speech but of memory, of memorials and of monuments addressed not so much to any immediate audience as to posterity and to God. For Coke, to take one example:

> a record is regularly a monument or act judicial before a judge, or judges, in a court of record entered in parchment in the right Roll. It is called a record, for that it records or bears witness of the truth . . . It hath this sovereign privilege, that it is proved by no other but by it self – *monumenta (quae nos Recorda vocamus) sunt vetustatis et veritatis vestigia* – a record is perpetual evidence.[1]

The record, the monument that bore immemorial witness of the arche-writing of the common law, of the traces of an absolute past, was presented by Davies and by Coke in a virtually identical language. The monumental text claimed to register and preserve from decay the antiquities of the nation, the ancient customs of the realm and forms of government:

> wherein the wisdom of our ancestors doth shine far above the policy of other kingdoms . . . are not the Records of her acts and proceedings so precious, as they are kept in the King's treasury, like jewels of the crown,

1 Coke, *Institutes*, III, at Liia.

and reputed a principal part of the Royal treasure? . . . Lastly, is not the learned Professor of law *lux in tenebris* – a star in the firmament of the Commonwealth? Is not his house an oracle not only to a Town or a City, but to a whole country?[1]

These are, in other words, no ordinary texts, nor simply scrivenings. They belong to a tradition in which the text is immediately a relic, a ruin, a truth or sacred item immediately surrounded by stone and anathemas or by the names of Coke and the other sages of the common law.

The claim to access to truth through legal signs has an interesting negative correlate, namely that other languages or modes of access to truth were stringently outlawed. Contemporary compilations of penal writs contain astonishingly detailed doctrinal condemnations of the various forms of metaphysical misuse of words and signs. To the obvious offences of blasphemy, heresy and treason by words can be added a whole series of illicit professions of signs, including magic, soothsaying, wizardry, divination, juggling, sleight of hand, enchanting and charming, witchery, haggery, sorcery and finally augury.[2] In relation to each such indictable offence the doctrinal issue is primarily that of the false oracle or of illicit characters, writings, pictures and images presenting hidden knowledge or illicit truth. Thus, to take one example, the magician is indicted for what appear to be false and unnatural representations, hallucinations that are the work of the outside, of the Devil. The magician is one 'which by uttering of certain superstitious words conceived, adventures to attempt things above the course of nature, by bringing forth dead men's ghosts as they are falsely pretended, in showing of things either secret or far off, and in showing them in any shape or likeness'.[3] The magician summons things that should not be seen, images that are not for mortal eyes, images that are outside the law of images, or *ius imaginarium*, images that are unnatural but real, idols or false augurs, and he is punished for leaving the everliving God and the prescribed images of his nature. In other indictments and writs of abjuration, enchanters and charmers are charged with (seemingly successfully) fulfilling wishes through 'words pronounced, characters and images'; they are termed inchantors or incantators because 'he is one *qui carminibus, aut cantiunculis Daemonem adjurat*. They were of ancient called carmina

---

1   Davies, *Reports*, op. cit. at 282. Coke, *Institutes*, III, refers to *thesauria regis*.
2   West, op. cit., II, ss. 13–14.
3   Ibid., s. 13.

because in those days their charms were in verse.'[1] In legislation referred to by Coke, 'if any person, or persons take upon him or them, by witchcraft, inchantment, charm or sorcery to tell or declare, in what places any treasure or gold or silver should or might be found, or had in the earth, or other secret places; . . . or to provoke any person to unlawful love', those things are punishable.[2] Jugglers, through words and writings called charms, can cure diseases. Soothsayers and wizards usurp the role of the oracle and foretell the future by evil means. A conjurer 'is he that by the holy and powerful names of almighty God invokes and conjures the Devil to consult with him, or to do some acts', while diviners could divine where lost or stolen things now rested.[3]

Where the law of arms paid particular attention to the crime of falsity, the usurpation of a dignity, the symbolaeography stresses crimes of verbal or scriptural falsity, the usurpation of the notarial art or office. What is particularly heinous in the listed 'offences by words' is not so much any direct contumely which they offer to God[4] but rather that they challenge or usurp the power to name which has increasingly come to define the principal territory of the legal profession. As oath swearers and notaries, it is the office of the lawyer to invoke and manipulate mystic words. It is the profession which knows and preserves the true meaning of alien signs, which can read the omens, the augurs, the fates, the insignia of other or future worlds. By diverse scribal and epistolary rules it is the legal oracle alone that can legitimately call up the immemorial past and through its originary signs, its self-presence in the legal text, can determine and limit the contours – the shapes and likenesses – of the future. In historical and philosophical terms, it can be argued that the legal writing system has become exemplary of writing as such. I will examine first the historical argument and will conclude with the philosophical.

1 Coke, *Institutes*, III, at Givb.

2 Ibid. at Hiib, reference being to 1 James cap 12.

3 Ibid. at Givb; and idem, *Entries*, fol. B1a. See also W. Rastall, *A Collection of Entrees* (1566, London).

4 Offence to God was, of course, a matter of canon law for the ecclesiastical courts and sanctioned by excommunication, which is to say literally by social denial of communicative competence. See Ridley, *A View*, op. cit., pp. 245–9. See also Coke, *Institutes*, III, G4b, who lists sorcery, divining, conjuring, charming and witchcraft as heresy.

What emerges most strongly in the printed curricula accounts of the legal discipline published from the early sixteenth century onwards, and associated with forensic rhetoricians such as Thomas Wilson and with Ramists such as Abraham Fraunce, Sir John Doderidge and William Fulbecke, is the fundamentally linguistic character of the developing 'science' of common law. In its early vernacular presentations, the discipline of law is defined – and arguably obscured – as a discipline of words. Using precisely the same terms and myth as the systematisers of armory,[1] the legal word is to be taken as a sign and in consequence 'may be compared to certain images called *Sileni Alcibiades*, whose outward features were deformed but within they were full of jewels and precious stones'.[2] Those jewels, according to the doctrinal writers discussed in Chapter Three, were the deposits of time immemorial, mined by the lawyer from the inexhaustibly rich seam of native custom extending beyond the 'memory of man'. Mystic notions of time immemorial, of forgotten sources or of a divinely inscribed natural law underwriting the frequently invisible history of positive law are conjoined in a theory of language itself as a contractually based system of notation.

At a superficial level the curricula authors simply reaffirm and generalise the arguments of symbolaeography. Increasingly, the predominant function of the lawyer is to document and to record. Grammar – meaning Latin and only by analogy correct usage – is in consequence the first art, the forms of discourse being the instruments of knowledge (*sed scienda instrumenta sunt formae discenderi*). The study of language, however, has further legal meanings and a constitutional significance. There is first an argument from myth, an argument common to the Ciceronian tradition and repeated by the forensic rhetoricians.[3] The origin of society is to be comprehended as a consequence of the grant or gift of language. The fallen state of nature was finally superseded and society established through the offices of poetry and rhetoric. Poets and orators were revealers and seers. They alone remembered the character of originals and through images and words presented objective memorials of true understanding, namely of the divinely ordained or natural order of law.[4] The lawyers could

1   Amboise, *Discours*, op. cit., G7a.
2   Fulbecke, *Direction* at 55.
3   T. Wilson, *The Arte of Rhetorique* (1553, London), pp. 17–20; Puttenham, *The Arte of English Poesie* (1589, London), pp. 4–8.
4   Puttenham, op. cit. at 15.

incorporate that notion of an original missive and coincident rhetorical order in the simple assertion that the legal tradition was precisely the custodian of the divinely ordained 'revealed' order and that its sources in immemorial time were those first words or notes agreed between God and Adam.

The substantive form that such an argument takes is classically nominalist: 'our ancient language consisted in the beginning of monosyllables and each word being of one syllable had his own proper signification put into the minds of such as first received it by almighty God'.[1] Words are notes – either sounds or marks – of agreed meanings. Each word (monosyllable) is attached to and stands for or names an agreed object or thing: 'For words be notes of things, and of all words either derivative or compound, you may yield some reason made [fet] from the first arguments, if the notation be well made. It is called, *Originatio, quod originem verborum explicet: et Etymologia, id est, veriloquium* [Origination, because it explains the origin of words: and Etymology, that is, true speech].'[2] The principle of notation is thus a principle of naming or defining the originary signification of the word and on the basis of that authoritative or given definition further compound arguments can be developed as deductions from or extrapolations of the founding axiom. Legal dogmatics is in this respect simply presented as the most authoritative – the oldest – social language of reference and its terms and axioms are therefore to be understood as closest to God and to natural law. It is law that silences the Babel of tongues and thereby first establishes or contracts the rhetorical bond of social order.

The theory of notation suggests a necessary correspondence between understanding and law. The basis of that correspondence lies in *anamnesis* or recollection of a primary reference attributed by lawyers to an original speaker and a constitutive social moment. There are, in short, true (authoritative) meanings to words, and dogmatic argument simply and faithfully develops those lawful bonds of reference. The linguistic faith of the lawyer is a faith in memory. It is memory that provides the definition of words and restricts all possible ambiguities and polysemy more generally under the strict notation or lexical meaning of each and every term. The theory of

---

1 Verstegan, *Restitution*, op. cit., pp. 242–3.

2 Fraunce, *The Lawiers Logike* (1588, London), fol. 51a. See also Doderidge, op. cit. at p. 73: 'etymologia est resolutio vocis in verum et proprium effectum, et verbi veritatem notificat.'

notes is a static faith of attachment or of belonging which establishes a complex series of specific fidelities as the signs under which we pay homage to law, to the restriction of social meaning to the dignities of legal office. In rhetorical terms, it may simply be observed that if the note is always in principle sent from the irrational space of the immemorial, and if it is God or some other originary legislator who invariably signs it and sends it to law, then there is little hermeneutic room left in which to argue as to its other meanings or as to its guarantees. In more technical terms, the semantic possibilities of the legal text are overdetermined by the issues of documentation and status that travel under the lexico-grammatical axioms and exegetical rules of notation.

Conclusion

The linguistic note is a sign or mark that is attendant upon and stands in for an object. The legal note similarly represents and guarantees a specific transaction. Both senses of note involve a proprietary relation in which the note is the mere mark or token of a real object, action or speech. In that respect it is the obvious duty of the custodians of the note, the notaries, to keep faith with the referent, to recollect the sender, of whose intention the note is never more than the symbol. Fidelity to meaning or to the conservation of authoritative prior meanings marks the legal writing systems examined in this chapter as systems of restriction: the note contracts; it reduces, it limits, it binds. It might also be said that in claiming to represent real properties it becomes a form of property, a unit in a system of exchange, a token of good faith, of propriety or of honour and traditional virtues.

The economic metaphor deserves a brief elaboration. The system of exchange that formed the content of the heraldic and symbolaeographic systems of notation was chivalric and feudal. It is precisely in terms of content, as the expression of an elaborate hierarchy of honorific forms of property holding or tenure, that legal notation finds its most characteristic place and use. In each instance of inscription studied the principal content of the system analysed was the marking of political faith. The feudal legal structure was primarily a hierarchically ordered system of property holding. The insignia of tenure were arms or the absence of arms, while legal writing developed to provide the proof of statuses and holdings and so inserted each form of tenure into its proper place with respect to the duties or fealties of tenancy. Those duties corresponded to the various degrees of honour and were carried with the holding of land, itself termed 'feodum' or 'feudum' from the Latin *fideum*, faith or trust. All land was held in fee (*fide*), which is to say, faithfully.[1] Tenancy was always ultimately of the sovereign and obtained by original grant and subsequently by the various forms of feudal donation or 'enfeoffment', the term again being etymologically derived from faith or fidelity, and connoting the passing of property by patronage and with fealty, *fide vel fidelitate*.[2] Each form of tenancy, from the lowest forms of villeinage and vassallage to the highest nobility, was taken upon oath of fealty to the superior lord and entailed some ceremony of homage (*hominium*), some sign or symbol of subjection to sovereignty, of fidelity and allegiance to the feudal lord.[3] In a literal sense the signs of law, the notes of property holding, were tokens of faith and emblems of the original grant which bound the tenant to fidelity to both lord and prince.[4] The note here has a further meaning from the Latin *nota* and can be interpreted as brand or stigma or mark of censorship and place within the hierarchy of political faith.

The content of legal writing systems obviously changed rapidly after their early systematisations. The second edition of West, for instance, is double the length of the first and the additional material reproduced is largely taken up with mercantile instruments. Even at the time of the first edition, much of the substantive content of the symbolaeography and allied works was already somewhat anachronistic, not simply in its language but also in its detail. The grants of manumission of bondswomen and villeins are the most obvious example.[5] The hidden motive for examining early forms of legal writing system, however, was simply to suggest that the development of a system of legal inscription owed most of its formal properties to theocratic conceptions of government and law. It was also intended to suggest that law, or the legality of the sign, was very much a part of the early systematisation of the vernacular disciplines and that in consequence it would be unfortunate to exclude the question of law when considering the development of linguistics and the other

1 Fraunce, *Logike*, op. cit., fol. 54b.
2 West, op. cit., I, s. 235.
3 Ridley, *View*, op.cit., p. 91.
4 Finch, *Law*, op. cit., fol. 143b.
5 West, op.cit., I, s. 381.

interpretative or human sciences. In particular, it raises the question of semantic faith, of the allegiance or contract that binds the note to its singular object and the word to its unitary referent.

The common theme to legal systems of inscription and the more general theories of notation developed, in particular, by English grammarians, philologists and logicians is the rhetorical art of memory as the condition of attachment to tradition and its linguistic community. The art of armory was explicitly a form of codification and symbolisation of ancestry, of lineage or blood and the dignities attendant upon them. The coat of arms was a systematically formulated note or reminder of ancient honours and fealties. It referred to qualities that were to be reinvoked and emulated for, in John Ferne's graphic depiction, the production of 'ancient statuaes, smoakie images, autentique coate-armors, torne and rotten guidons, of the valiant and virtuous ancestors' would not of itself subdue the enemy.[1] The systematic accounts of the discipline of arms simply set out the 'agreed' units or axioms of armorial representation, the lexicon and syntax of the proper composition of an esoteric tradition of filiation. The *Symbolaeography* similarly codified the scriptural rules for the composition of various forms of authentic record. The principal form that such records were to take was that of repetition. Documents were to be esoterically constructed according to lengthily established standard forms. The archaic language of those forms, a language that had never had any other use but that of legal inscription, itself testifies to the immemorial character of legal writing. The instruments of law were a writing apart from other linguistic usages and they circulated as much as symbols of belief in the legitimacy of the institution, as a recognition of its absolute source and as a ritual grammar, as they served any specific identificatory or testamentary functions.

Without attributing relations of cause or effect as between the disciplines, it is plausible to propose a general hypothesis. The formulation of the writing systems examined according to precepts of memory or, more technically, according to the classical divisions of the rhetorical art of memory, is profoundly dogmatic.[2] In the place of

1   Ferne, op. cit., p. 19.
2   Memory, of course, is the quintessential legal art, the foundation of precedent. Memory, however, as was argued at length in Chapters 2 and 3, belongs to tradition and not to history, a theme too rich to be pursued again here. As regards contemporary definitions of memory, see T. Wilson, *The Rule of Reason*

rhetoric as a discipline founded upon a concept of some species of public dialogue, and on occasion as a critical sphere of political discourse, is substituted an axiomatic system of insignia or scripts within a centrally controlled sphere of circulation. The points of transmission are institutionally designated sites of custody, archives from which the written guarantee of truth emanates as sign, 'writ' or promulgation. The order of writing is dogmatic in the sense of subordinating knowledge to memory: predicating its content upon received axioms the rules of writing simply order institutionally guaranteed definitions – the necessarily true precepts of a given discipline[1] – in that manner that best enables their retention and subsequent repetition. Together with the rhetoric of memory there is a linguistics of nominal definition. In the case of honorific and legal signs, that which they name or note ultimately belongs within the institutional tradition as esoteric memory and is open to no other forms of challenge or dispute. The meaning of the sign is a matter of faith, a question of law.

It remains to be observed that the law in question, and indeed the bulk of the subject matter of this chapter, has been presented as belonging resolutely to the past, to the premodern. The discourses in question, however, remain – precisely as memory, as tradition and precedent – as components of contemporary legal dogmatics. It would be surprising indeed if the legal discourse of tradition, the language of repetition *par excellence*, were somehow to have shed its own sources, its own validity as predicated upon the myth of an immemorial accretion of discourse. In that broader cultural context it seems fitting to end by mimicking the Cowell of the *Interpreter*. Where Cowell invoked nature and truth as the rhetorical ends of law, there might well be room in contemporary interdisciplinary dialogue to invoke the poetic possibility of a revival of the theory of notes. The premodern usage of the theory of notes concentrated upon the authority and antiquity of the sign: it was primarily a note in the sense of a token of legal record, indelible mark of the original or immemorial. In a postmodern context we could do worse than to recollect an alternative to that fealty of notation. The note is also a

---

(1557), fol. 37a–b, 49a; T. Wilson (1553), pp. 413–30; and A. Fraunce (1588), fol. 1a: 'An art is a methodical disposition of true and coherent precepts, for the more easy perceiving and remembering of the same.'

1 P. Ramus, *The Logike* (1574, London), pp. 8ff.

sign depicting a pitch and duration of musical sound. It is in that sense a tone, a strain of music, and no longer simply a name or dead letter of representation. In linguistic terms, the musical note may serve to remind us of the essentially rhythmic or syntactic quality of all marks: it is not the linguistic note but rather the combination and sending of such notes that constitutes the tenuous emergence of meaning.

5

Contractions: A Linguistic Philosophy of the Postal Rule

'Quid est epistola? Tacitus nuncius.'

'In history, this is my hypothesis, epistolary fictions multiply with the arrival of each new crisis of destination.'[1]

An early nineteenth-century common law doctrinal development, borrowed directly from Pothier, held that an epistolary acceptance of a contractual offer becomes binding once placed in the course of the post.[2] An epistolary acceptance thus need not be communicated or brought to the attention of the offering party. It is possible that the letter fails to arrive at its destination, or that it arrives late, and yet a binding contract none the less subsists. It is possible, in this as in numerous other instances of contemporary contract law, to be bound

1   Respectively, A. Alciatus, *De Notitia Dignitatem* (1651 edn, Paris), p. 190, literally: 'what is a letter? A secret messenger'; and J. Derrida, *The Post Card* (1987, Chicago), p. 232.

2   The doctrine was elaborated first in 1818, in *Adams* v. *Lindsell* [1818] 1 B & Ald. 681], and in the United States in 1819, in *Eliason* v. *Henshaw* [1819] Wheat 225, 4 Ed. 556. By 1880 the rule was sufficiently well accepted to be stated without authority: 'where an offer is made and accepted by letters sent through the post, the contract is completed the moment the letter accepting the offer is posted, even though it never reaches its destination' (*Byrne* v. *Van Tienhoven* [1880] 5 CPD 344). The rule is deemed to be 'an artificial concept' and applies to the postal service and to telegraph but not to telex or telephone (*Entores* v. *Miles Far Eastern Corporation* [1955] 2 AER). As regards communication by 'the normal course of the post' no authority, either express or implied, is needed for use of the service as the channel of acceptance, the legal implication of the act of posting being sufficient evidence of communication: 'the acceptor in posting the letter, has . . . put it out of his control and done an extraneous act which clenches the matter, and shows beyond all doubt that each side is bound. How then can a casuality in the post, whether resulting in delay, or in non-delivery unbind the parties or unmake the contracts? . . . if he [the offeror] trusts to the post he trusts to a means of communication which, as a rule, does not fail' (*Household Fire Insurance* v. *Grant* [1879] 4 Ed. 216). In more recent decisions, the fax machine and its facsimile mail have been held to be outside the postal rule.

by texts that one has not read, to be engaged in a relation with the institution on terms that have been established in advance, or to be addressed – interpolated – by the very means or avenue of communication selected for contracting. The postal rule, a product of the classical law of contract, paradoxically reminds us that the system of circulation of messages, the means of communication or objectified text, is often of greater significance than its apparent subjective content. When it is a question of contract and so of law, the postal rule may serve to indicate that the letter, the contractual act, may have an existence independent both of its sender and of its destination.

The paradoxical character of the postal rule is emblematic of a more general series of questions that need to be raised as part of a postmodern account of contract and of the contractarian tradition. Even at the height of the ascendancy of *laissez-faire* economics and of its corresponding doctrine of freedom of contract, the postal rule uneasily testifies to the intrinsically social character of the contract. It is a relationship made by reference to and via the avenue of the law. It is a communication that passes from one subject to the other via the objectification – the textual relay – of the post and of all the qualifications and supplements that are the inevitable consequences of a centrally organised system of social communication. It entails thereby a series of epistolary and more broadly linguistic questions that are the essential subject matter of any critical history of the contractarian tradition and its concept of law. We will approach those questions of contract and transmission, of law and meaning, through a reading of the work of Jean-Jacques Rousseau on the origin of language and on contract as the origin of law. Our analysis will be rhetorical and will imply no necessary adherence either to the terms of the contract spelt out by Jean-Jacques or to the laws of transmission by which the contract remains our tradition. First, however, we must make a series of preliminary advertisements concerning language, contract and communication.

Our concern with the postal rule is with a metaphor for the institutional character of contract, within which institution it is frequently impossible rigorously to distinguish legal contract from social contract. They are both legal forms of association, of *societas*, and both equally imply participation in a tradition, within a system of communication or, better, of transmission governed by law. As regards the institution of the post, we will simply note certain institutional details concerning its centralised role. Military and civil messages of state were classically the province of heralds (*fetiales*) and governed by the law of arms or armory. The English post (currours) receives its first definition in a statute of Edward VI in 1547.[1] The post is the 'public course', the avenue of circulation of royal business, of the king's messages, and particularly of law, of edict and of writ.[2] The office of master of the posts is attached to the king's court and takes the form of responsibility for keeping the public course, the network of communications, open for royal use.[3] More specialist offices are subsequently attached to legal forms of postage, the term *postea* referring to writs returned from provincial courts to the royal courts to be decided and then engrossed (enrolled) and stored in the office of records (*custos brevium*). It may also be noted that every detail of such writs, from their orthography to the exact Latin phrasing of their

1   The reference to 'currours', who are simply defined as 'sure messengers for the expedition of state business' appointed by the Prince, is from the barrister G. Legh, *The Accedens of Armory* (1562, London), fol. 69b, where virtue and godliness are described as the two chief requisites of carrying royal messages. The herald is *nuncius regis* and is responsible for the law of arms which governs all aspects of military and civil communication (*arma generaliter omnium rerum instrumenta sunt*) including what were termed the *arcana imperii heraldorum*, extensive areas of 'secret intelligence' and of foreign languages by means of which sacral knowledge and other honours could be kept from common eyes (Bossewell, *Workes of Armorie* (1572, London), fol. Aia). For comparable continental accounts see also the historian C. Fauchet, *Origines des chevaliers, armoires et heraux* (1610, Paris), fol. 515a.; and C. Segoing, *Trésor heraldique ou mercure armorial* (1652, Paris), pp. 4–7. More general discussion can be found in Legendre (1985), pp. 197–206.

2   Legh, *Accedens*, op. cit., provides the most interesting depiction of the role of the currour, including surprisingly detailed description of what the heralds should wear – to reflect the importance of their mission – and how they should travel ('they ride on their sovereign's messages'), their faith, their perception and their memory also being discussed (fol. 225). Legh's emphasis on the necessary expedition of state business gains considerable attention in Braudel, *The Mediterranean and the Mediterranean World* (2nd edn 1972, New York), pp. 360, 372, which emphasises that 'a state had to wage not one but many struggles against distance' and that 'delays in the mail were a *structural* feature of the [seventeenth] century'. In philosophical terms, see Derrida, *The Post Card*, op. cit., p. 65: 'If, on the contrary (but this is not simply the contrary), I think the postal and the post card on the basis of the destinal of Being . . . of language, and the inverse . . . then the post is no longer a simple metaphor, and is even, as the site of all transferences and all correspondences, the "proper" possibility of every possible rhetoric.' See also J-F Lyotard, *L'Inhumain* (1988, Paris), pp. 64–7, commenting on the notion of 'passage' as a working through, as labour.

3   Cowell, *Interpreter* (1607, Cambridge), 'Master of the Posts': 'is an officer of the King's court, that has the appointing, placing, and displacing of all such through England, as provide post horse for the speedy passing of the King's messages and other business, in the thorough-fayre townes where they dwell . . .'
T. Ridley, *A View of Civille and Ecclesiasticall Law* (1607, Oxford), 'Post-masters, those to whom the care of the public course doth appertain.'

content, was scrupulously supervised: each letter and syllable was to be 'significant and known to the law'. At this point we may simply note that postal communication entailed – by virtue of statutory and case law provisions[1] – that each word used was fixed in advance, that it belonged to a standard or recognised form, that it referred to its proper, legally designated referent.

The institutional implications of the post do not stop with the objectified form or language of the writ or letter. To use the post is in the first instance to enter into a specific, centrally regulated jurisdiction, a specific domain of discourse subject to rules of both lexical and semantic scope requiring, at the minimum, a specific textual form and more normally a legally prescribed and recognised content as well. Post or *postea* also, of course, means after or afterwards. A second aspect to our invocation of postal communication concerns the temporal charter whereby our communication comes, in a dual sense, afterward. In a somewhat technical sense, well elaborated in the work of Jacques Derrida, we would note that speech has generally been formulated in terms of representation: the phoneme is a note of inner qualities that are variously formulated by the scholastic tradition as *formae imaginariae*, or as *intellectus*, inchoate senses or reason, that the notes of speech will order and represent.[2] In social terms, speech is also already a part of tradition, a participant in a conventionally regulated network. As regards tradition and its transmission, we are involved in the receipt and sending on of received forms; we are both recipients and custodians of the lawful knowledge of tradition and of its representation, its language. The letter or *signum* becomes a token of participation in a juridically defined sociality. It betokens at the very least that we come after and are faithful to – are users of – the postal network, or more generally of the tradition, of the system of commerce and communication:

> The charter is the contract for the following, which quite stupidly one has to believe: Socrates comes *before* Plato, there is between them – and in general – an order of generations, an irreversible sequence of inheritance. Socrates is before, not in front of, but before Plato, therefore

1   See H. Finch, *Law or a Discourse Thereof* (1627, London), fol. 295–98.

2   On the relation of law to representation, and representation to law, see the excellent M. T. Clanchy, *From Memory to Written Record* (1979, London), pp. 199–200, 320–26; also B. Stock, *The Implications of Literacy* (1983, New Jersey), pp. 370–83. The appropriate maxim probably comes from Celsus, '*scire leges non est verba earum tenere, sed vim et proprietam*'. Sir Edward Coke, *Reports* (1777 edn, London), vol. 2, pt 3, improved upon the formulation '*in lectione non verba sed veritas est amanda.*'

behind him, and the charter binds us to this order: this is how to orient one's thought, this is the left and this is the right, march.[1]

Finally, however, post may refer to an ending, to the last post, to death: it is possible that postmodernity precisely implies a break with the temporal charter of tradition, a breach of the contract, a free or irreligious association of words.

To recapitulate, the form of tradition and the form of our participation in it are both linguistic and symbolic. They are governed by certain rules of reference but also by a theory of origin and image that is concerned as much with temporality, with a charter designating lineage or lineal relations between before and after, as with reference. In a purely descriptive sense we may chart the contract in terms of its progression from theocratic pact or covenant of biblical derivation requiring obedience to an unwritten law (nature), to the more positive and legalistic contract or social treaty establishing political sovereignty and a coincidental power of secular nomination. The desire to elicit and question the more fundamental forms of the social contract, to enquire as to the linguistic contract or the veridical language that underpins juridical rule, leads us from the post to the letter: that is to say, from the institution to the word, from the network to its elements of conduction.

The theme that governs the various notions of pact, covenant, compact, convention, treaty and contract in their traditional forms may be spelled out and developed etymologically.[2] The contract binds words to meanings, it institutes and polices reference, it decides in advance the terms and conditions of interpretation, of meaning. This fundamentally scriptural function of contract institutes certain conditions of faith, of keeping faith, well captured in the concept of *pacta sunt servanda*. The contract may here be interpreted in the sense of *con-traho*; it draws together, it binds, but we may note that in doing so

1 J. Derrida, *The Post Card*, op. cit., p. 20.
2 The principle involved is grammatological and is one which treats first of the material of language itself. It receives an interesting depiction in Derrida (1987), p. 8: 'In that I still love him, I can foresee the impatience of the *bad* reader: this is the way I name or accuse the fearful reader, the reader in a hurry to be determined, decided upon deciding (in order to annul, in other words to bring back to oneself, one has to wish to know in advance what to expect, one wishes to expect what has happened, one wishes to expect oneself). Now, it is bad, and I know of no other definition of bad, it is bad to predestine one's reading, it is always bad to foretell. It is bad, reader, no longer to like retracing one's steps.'

it also implies contraction, it abridges, shortens, encodes and represses. As the chapter progresses we will pursue the contract from present to past tense, from *contraho* to *contractus*. The etymology of contract includes a tropological connotation of dejection or depression associated with a secondary meaning of *traho*, to withdraw or pull out. In its past tense the contract fittingly connotes diminution or elimination of the trace or track, of the mark or spoor. Tract or trace imply writing; the tract – tractate or treatise – protracts: it treats or examines but it also prolongs, defers, puts off, delays. The social contract, like its cognates the legal contract and the various other testamentary writings or deeds, endeavours to send a message to the future, to control posterity, to ordain both issues of record (of property) and of meaning. In the final instance, by leaving its track, its impression or imprint, the contract presents a memorial, a vestige, a mark that will endure, that will stand for its sender long after his demise. In both a social and a symbolic sense, the contract calls us to belong and thereby to survive death or at least to exclude the signs of death, those of historical temporality, of a finiteness that tradition alone can transcend. By fixing meaning in advance, by deciding the forms of interpretation before reading the material text of tradition, we are asked by the contract to keep faith with a temporal charter – a particular sense of time as deferral of death – and to belong to a specific track, a stretch of text or territory, a space or expanse of land, a region or nation, that will serve as the sign of our identity and as the mark of that through which 'we' will live on.

Literary Contracts

An orator uses ink to trace out his writings; does that mean that ink is a highly eloquent liquid?[1]

The contract: a particular writing, an instrument, a text, tract or trace. Early legal definitions of contract (*contractus*) treat the contract as a form of writing, an instrument which is differentiated from its oral equivalent of stipulation precisely by virtue of its scriptural quality. It is a work of writing, that of the notary or expert in notation whose highest office is that of chirographer, the royal amanuensis who tables

---

1   J-J. Rousseau, *Essai sur l'origine des langues* (1970 edn, Paris), p. 149. (Hereafter cited as *Essay*.)

fines, enrolls writs and posts or notes other charges and fines on land. To take but one example, the contract is defined by William West as a bond or deed 'whereby any man confesseth himself by his writing orderly made, sealed and delivered'.[1] The confession, we may suspect, has the status of serious speech, of iterability, and may be approached initially as a matter for grammatological analysis. The contract is a text or record, an instrument (*symbolum*) of a special status, an authentic sign inscribing in formal terms a legally designated object.

In the material terms with which grammatology is initially concerned, the contract as mark, note or grapheme has a dual significance. On one hand, the instrument is a physical object, a symbol in the sense of a sign or token that circulates within the institution and according to an economy of writing or politics of scriptural accumulation and exchange. In crude material terms, the contract is produced by and is by and large accessible to the legal profession alone; it belongs to a specific textual community and its institutional significance should be traced in terms of that community. On the other hand, the contract is an epistle or note and as such is an act of communication; it is not simply a form but also a content. As regards the content of contract, the relevant grammatological themes concern writing and repetition, reference and faith; in short, the question of linguistic content concerns the rhetorical and more broadly semantic conditions under which a particular writing system becomes monumental and its texts become party to a tradition, thereby escaping history to join the repetitive permanence of institutional language. We will deal first with the latter issue, that of language as the content and so also the condition of possibility of contract. It is an issue that is dealt with most directly in the *Essay on the Origin of Languages*.

The first order of justification of the contract is linguistic. The contract acts as simple writing, as a mark or note that is capable of representing and preserving the ephemeral phonic substance of speech. In this view, speech is prior to script and is the substance of the contractual mark which notes and remembers the anterior event. Such is the fable (*histoire*) presented in Rousseau's theory of the origin of language, a work which states at its very beginning that 'speech, being the first social institution, owes its form to natural causes alone'.[2] The invocation of nature as the source of speech immediately

1 W. West, *Symbolaeography* (1590, London), fol. A8a. 2 *Essay*, p. 27.

establishes the elements of a hierarchy of oppositions which moves in Rousseau's text from the natural to the artificial, from passion to reason (law) and from rhetoric to writing. Aligned to those oppositions we may note, respectively, the familiar figures of institutionalisation: laicisation, progress and truth. During the course of the *Essay* a divinely ordained natural order will give issue to a laicised modern polity, passion will be displaced – though not without a certain nostalgic regret – by the inevitable progression of reason, while in reducing rhetoric to writing figurative signs and melodic verse will come to be excluded from the prosaic public discourse of truth.

The rhetorical structure of the *Essay* is markedly progressive. In each instance cited the terms of the oppositions are causally related and broadly indicative of the necessary terms of a teleological institution of the social. Such is not least the case in the opening declaration that speech is the first institution, a move in which Jean-Jacques links language to the origin of society in an inexorable and portentous manner. The argument is a complex one in that it mixes a number of different myths of origin so as to allow for an overlay of romantic pessimism upon the traditional myth of the fall and consequent ejection from the Garden of Eden. The rhetorical structure of the 'origin' of language can be simply outlined. The original language was edenic, it was born and lost with residence in the Garden of Eden. We have no idea of what the language was other than that 'Adam was taught by God himself'[1] and that it was irredeemably lost. The first language was that in which God and man named the beasts and nature more generally. It would seem likely that it was a noun-based language and further that it represented the true or deepest nature of language towards which all later endeavours must aim to return.[2]

---

1   Ibid. at 103.

2   *Essay*, p. 53 (discussing the roots of language): 'If you understand these ideas in all their ramifications, you will find that Plato's *Cratylus* is not as ridiculous as it appears to be.' A much more direct exposition of the point can be found in Hobbes, *Leviathan* (1651), pp. 100–1: 'the first author of speech was God himself, that instructed Adam how to name such creatures as he presented to his sight', adding subsequently that 'all this language gotten, and augmented by Adam and his posterity, was again lost at the tower of Babel, when by the hand of God, every man was stricken for his rebellion, with an oblivion of his former language.'

What is crucial to the conception of an originary, theocratically given language is neither its lexical nor its syntactic features, nor its grammatical composition, but rather the simple fact of its loss. The origin of language transpires to belong to the sphere of the divine; it is therefore prior to or outside of history and equally significantly hidden and secret, a matter of myth and of ritual, of the hieroglyphs or holy letters of initiate (sacral) knowledge and therewith immune to historical or political examination. The origin becomes in this way a simple insignia of the absolute, an emblematic representation of an absence from which and, it might equally be suspected, towards which language is directed. Any further discussion of the origin of language or of the development of individual languages is subject or secondary to this prior model hidden from humanity in the mind of God. That it is hidden allows for the creation and justification of an unwritten doctrinal tradition to underpin and govern manifest language or the apparent meaning of simulacra, while the fact that it is lost attaches a variety of sentiments of guilt and remorse to the apprehension of national or historic languages – they are not the Father's tongue – and equally suggests the possible visitation of the penalties of sin upon those who endeavour to suggest any free-play or purely secular genesis of the meaning of words. Such freedom is always likely to be seen as an atheistic breach of the originary (lost) pact or of the primordial meaning of words known to tradition alone.[1]

The absent origin of language serves several essential rhetorical or argumentative functions. It suggests a 'contrat d'ordre langagier' (a

1   The disputes between Romans and Reformers over the translation and proper interpretation of the Bible provide good examples of this theme. Sir Thomas More, *The Confutacyon of Tyndale's Answere*, in *Collected Works* (1973, New Haven): 'for our matter is not of scripture, as it is taken for bare writing, such as every scrivener's boy writes in his master's shop, but as it signifies such holy writing as God causes to be written and binds folk to believe, upon peril of their soul.' Much later in the same *Confutacyon* More goes so far as to observe that 'sometime he [God] wrote it . . . that the letter had none other sense than mysteries and allegories' (ibid., p. 636). In a contemporary context, see U. Eco, *Semiotics and the Philosophy of Language* (1984, New York), who, discussing deconstruction, refers dismissively to an atheistic and mystical multiplication of readings, to an 'ultimate epiphany of the symbolic mode, the text as symbol is no longer read in order to find in it a truth that lies outside: the only truth is the very play of deconstruction' (pp. 155–6). For an extended discussion of such a theme, see P. Goodrich, 'Simulation and the Semiotics of Law' (1988) 2 *Textual Practice* 180 at 183–90.

contract of a linguistic order)[1] that is not simply the first institution but also, by virtue of being first, the model or prototype of all other institutions. In the influential terms of Hobbes' *Leviathan*, the priority of speech is explicit and crucially indicative of the order of sociality: 'but the most noble and profitable invention of all other, was that of SPEECH, consisting of *Names* or *Appellations* and their Connexion; whereby men register their thoughts; recall them when they are past; and also declare them one to another for mutuall utility and conversation; without which, there had been amongst men neither Common-wealth, nor society nor Contract, nor Peace'.[2] In the absence of the divinely ordained order of proper names, the theory of the origin of language must endeavour to imitate a lost model and to establish in human speech an order of notes or marks, tokens, emblems or signs that will remember, guarantee and recall to phonic or graphic representation an external order of reference, be it of things, fantasies or thoughts. In structural terms, we may thus observe a first – though absent – moment of speech, an archetypal instant in which language was called upon by God to name or nominate, to refer to an order that God had created and guaranteed prior to the attachment of names.

The natural causes of speech referred to at the outset of the *Essay* are thus more complex than might be suspected. They involve a fallen or historical nature,[3] a golden age of savagery[4] in which a humanity expelled from the Garden lives in individual isolation and forgets its original tongue: 'the first common tongue [*langue commune*] died with the first society'.[5] In place of language various ostensive and gestural semiotic systems develop to indicate in a visual manner the contents of the mind: 'what the ancients said in the liveliest way, they did not express in words but by means of signs. They did not say it, they showed it . . . the most vigorous (*énergetique*) language is one in which the Sign has said everything before one speaks.'[6] Heraldic symbols and other emblematic or figurative depictions had developed prior to speech for the simple reason that the task of any system of notation is taken to be ostensive; it is that of imitating its object or referent which is later transposed into that of marking and calling to memory objects of a more abstract kind. The principle of composition and function is in each case of notation identical. From heraldry to 'la langue

1   J. Derrida, 'Préjugés', in *La Faculté de juger* (1985, Paris).
2   Hobbes, *Leviathan*, p. 100.   3   *Essay*, p. 103.   4   Ibid. at 95.
5   Ibid. at 103.   6   Ibid. at 31.

épistolaire des Salams' (the epistolary language of salaams),[1] from melody – 'it imitates the tones [*accens*] of languages, and the twists produced in every idiom by certain movements of the spirit (*mouvemens de l'ame*). It does not simply imitate, it speaks'[2] – to the representation of nature in painting or indeed the more complex musical notations of verse,[3] the note or mark identifies a referent, an object designated by agreement, by 'le concours d'autrui' (by agreement with the other)[4] in advance of any individual use. The lost Adamic pact is replicated, one could venture to say, in a generalised semiotic or notarial contract which Rousseau locates distantly either in terms of 'l'enseigne de leur père' (the tutelage of their father)[5] or in the more explicit habitus of the other as that rhetorical space from which and to which the sign or letter is posted.

The laicisation of language is represented by Rousseau in terms of the replacement of a divinely ordained linguistic pact by an originary semiotic contract. In both cases the principles of signification, of incremental addition to primary lexical or semic units of denotation, are identical: 'most of the root words would be imitative sounds or accents of passion, or effects of sense objects'.[6] The biblical pact is mimicked in the contract or rather in that series of contracts in which are agreed the proper notes (the names) of visual, emblematic, phonic and scriptural orders. The relationship between those several contracts is one not only of functional identity but also of a strictly ordered progression from signs to notes, from orality to literacy, from rhetoric to writing, from natural to positive law or from the invisible scripture of the heart to the prosaic notation of a written constitution. The progression is towards reason and is formulated in terms of the displacement of figure, trope and passion by the order of grammatical law in a permanent textual form. In relation to each of the oppositions cited, an examination of the terms in which Jean-Jacques formulates the progression towards the reason of 'peuples policés' (political societies)[7] indicates a weighted interdependency of the terms involved.

---

1 Salaams are tokens of courtly love, mundane objects such as ribbons, charcoal, fruits, which are sent as cryptic messages to loved ones. The meaning of the salaam was known to the lover and would find its exemplary use in being sent via the eunuch to a lover in a harem. Rousseau's concern is with the fact that one speaks most passionately by means of signs: 'one speaks more effectively to the eye than to the ear' (*Essay*, p. 22).

2 *Essay* at p. 159.   3 Ibid., pp. 175, 139.   4 Ibid., p. 139.
5 Ibid., p. 127.   6 Ibid., p. 51.   7 Ibid., p. 57.

The initial proposition which locates the source of the social in systems of notation or linguistic bonding is not novel. Cicero in *De Inventione* and in *Pro Archia* provided an account of a state of nature, of savagery, ignorance, error – of blind aimless passion – from which humanity escapes only through the office of poetry. Poets, variously termed *vates* and *videntes*, speakers or soothsayers and seers or revealers, are understood by the Ciceronian tradition to have been the first ground of society, the first source of eloquence and the first means of social communication or assembly.[1] Thus Rousseau takes up a recognised though now somewhat recondite tradition in arguing that 'the first histories, the first speeches [*harangues*], the first laws were in verse. Poetry was created before prose. That must have been the case, since feelings speak before reason.'[2] An epoch of primitive ignorance, of inarticulacy and brute gesture, a state of nature depicted as a universal state of war,[3] comes to sociality only through poetry or eloquence, rhythmic speech which subordinates grammar to music, to euphony and harmony or beauty of sounds. In the context of the first language we learn that 'in place of arguments it would have aphorisms, it would persuade without convincing, and would represent without reasoning'.[4]

Certain obvious points deserve brief mention. The office of the poet is a priestly office while the eloquence that draws humanity together, that arouses, impassions and persuades, is an oracular or magical use of the tongue. The first institution, that of poetic speech, is uniformly mythic in its qualities and practices. It aligns the first law to religious

---

1   For illustration of such a point, see, for example, Sir Philip Sydney, *An Apology for Poetry* (1581–3/1987, Manchester), pp. 103–7, where it is explicitly argued that poetry precedes law ('the lawyer saith what men have determined') and is alone amongst the arts in improving upon nature. George Puttenham, *The Arte of English Poesie* (1689), pp. 2–4: 'The profession and use of poetry is most ancient from the beginning, and not, as some erroneously suppose, after, but before any civil society was among men. For it is written that poetry was the original cause and occasion of their first assemblies.' The issue is always that of the linguistic basis of order, for only through speech, through poetry and rhetoric which are its first practical social forms, can any form of communication, namely *communis* or commonality, emerge. It is to language, to a rhetorical order, that Thomas Wilson, *The Arte of Rhetorique* (1533/1982, London), pp. 316–17, famously refers: 'I know that all things stand by order and without order nothing can be. For by an order we are born, by an order we live and by an order we make our end. By an order one ruleth as head and others obey as members . . .'

2   *Essay* at 141.   3   Ibid. at 97.   4   Ibid. at 53.

modes of representation and persuasion, while the first contract – that which constitutes civil society – transpires to be more a concession by divine right, a hieroglyphically encrypted use of sacral tradition, of *traditio* in its theological sense of custody of the unwritten word, than a movement of enlightenment or reason as such.[1] At various points of the *Essay* it may be observed that the origin is opaque or enigmatic; it is hidden and much of its originality is thereby lost.[2] The postulation of an origin that is hidden and variously described as symbolic, poetic, emblematic, oracular and irrational has further connotations. It serves to distinguish the savage or primitive, the first (*prémiers*), from the civilised and modern.[3] More importantly, it serves to associate and to bind the characters of the primitive – of linguistic figurativeness or seductive symbolics – to the past. The symbolic dimensions of words, the delirious rhythms and figures, the eloquence, passion and politics of language are all ineluctably bound (contracted) to the past. Thereby they are banished from the present: its powers of speech are rational and enlightened; they are social yet separate from the origins of sociality. In the place of history, the search for origins substitutes the sepulchral and repetitive figures of tradition; in the place of linguistics it inserts the dead letters of truth; in the place of rhetoric it signs the notarial contract of law. It does so, it must be admitted, with every appearance of regret. Music has

1   On the hidden or arcane nature of letters and particularly of 'holy letters' or hieroglyphics see A. D'Amboise, *Discours ou traicte des devises* (1620, Paris), p. 109, where the early function of signs is depicted in terms of secret figures, hidden meanings and with regard to visual signs, we are referred to 'intentions soubz le voile des chose, qui comme des Silenes d'Alcibiade parroissent en dehors tout autrement que ce qui est au dedans' (intentions covered by the veil of things, which like Sileni Alcibiades have an outward appearance quite different to what lies within). The English lawyer William Fulbecke, *Directive or Preparative to the Study of Law* (1599, London), interestingly pursues the same analogy in relation to legal signs, refering directly to the 'words of the law [which] may be compared to certain images called *sileni Alcibiades*, whose outward feature was deformed and ugly, but within they were full of jewels and precious stones' (pp. 55–6). In linguistic terms, Fulbecke presents the same point by differentiating speech, which is an external act, from inward meaning. Words are the limits of our meaning (p. 91), which, in relation to writing – to written law – indicates that 'the reason and conscience of the lawyer is not simply a question of the knowledge he has of the written law, for when words are obscure . . . we imagine that more was spoken than written, and more intended than uttered . . . then the tongue yieldeth to the heart, and the words do give place to the meaning' (pp. 86–8).

2   *Essay* at p. 51.   3   Ibid., p. 91.

degenerated, passion has been lost, the government of prose and of grammar has inaugurated an absolutism of its own. Let it simply be observed that it is far easier to present tradition under the guise of nostalgia than it is to locate history in its proper place – the present.

Legal Letters and Social Contracts
(*De Fide Instrumentorum*[1])

The *Essay* concludes with a brief discussion of the relation of language to government in which Jean-Jacques momentarily raises the question of how speech relates to popular politics, and philology to law. Following certain other readings of Rousseau, we have elaborated the thesis that the theory of the origins of language places a linguistic contract at the basis of the occidental juridico-political tradition. Language is the first contract of sociality, the original bond or institution, and it lies therefore at the basis of tradition as its hidden source. The implications of the relationship of language to law, of speech to norm and of text to institution can be analysed initially in terms of the governing relation of rhetoric to writing specified in the closing chapters of the *Essay*.

It is the paradoxical function of the theory of origins to invoke a symbolical representation of a vanishing point: the origin can be presented only in terms of the retrospectively glimpsed last trace, the moment where the self becomes the other and the identical broaches the different. The logic of such a move is simple and binary: before life, death; before history, God; before society, nature; before language, silence. The antithetical latter terms annihilate their opposites; they are points of closure at which representation ceases in enigma or more profoundly *in articulo mortis*, in the founding moment of myth. As regards the origin of language, that movement to annihilation follows an exemplary pattern. At the origin of language

---

1 *Digest*, 22.4. 'Of the faith which attaches to instruments'. Writing is to be believed because it simply reflects, without translation or addition, the speech of its source. The scribe, and in consequence that which is written, is no more than the innocently represented speech of another, the author of the law: 'he who writes makes himself part of that which is written, by his name and by graphism, but he writes as an innocent instituted by the message. He is the hand. He is the person who writes in the name of the Guarantor . . . the innocent instrument of account . . .' (Legendre, *Paroles poétiques echapées du texte* (1982, Paris), p. 133.

is a fall from grace, a lost grace that cannot be recovered in any more direct manner than through faith in God through the intermediaries – the 'ordinaries' or *sacerdotes* – of the established Church.[1] In the beginning was the word, but that word was secret, a matter of initiate knowledge at best available only to the seers, the revealers, the priests and those with the wisdom of law:

> [T]he effect would have to become the cause; the social spirit, which should be created by the institution, would have to preside over its very foundation; and men would have to be before the law what they should become by means of it . . . This is what has, in all ages, compelled the fathers of nations to have recourse to divine [*du ciel*] intervention and to credit the gods with their own wisdom.[2]

Whatever the asserted intention behind depicting the source of the institution or of law as being the divine mouth or mystic oracle, its function is necessarily also that of making law a question of memory, of that invisible scripture written upon the evanescent parchment of the soul.[3]

The originary word is an unwritten word. It is placed in the mouth of God. It comes with its meaning attached to it, its meaning being prior to its use. It is already contracted, bonded, canonic. The rhetorical contract precedes any written law in precisely the same manner that each trope of progression used in the *Essay* evokes increased civility: signs become words, feelings become reasons (abstract ideas), persuasion becomes conviction, song becomes prose, the audible becomes legible as the spoken comes to be written down, the note noted. What is crucial is that, for all the appearance of a linear progression towards truth, the principle involved in the ascription of a development from origin to truth is one of repetition, of

---

1 In doctrinal terms it is a question of 'grace', an issue that is extensively disputed by Sir Thomas More, *The Apologye* (1533, London), as for example at fol. 31a–b, 'the church of Christ has been, is, and ever shall be taught and instructed by God and his holy spirit with his holy word of either kind, that is to wit both with his word written and his word unwritten, and that they which will not believe God's word but if he put it in writing, be as plain infidels . . . since God's word takes his authority of God that speaks it, and not of man that writes it.' It is thus argued that only through the tradition of the Church can the 'light of grace' or the 'blessed spirit of God inwardly taught' appear.

2 J.-J. Rousseau, *Du Contrat social* (1977, Paris), p. 210.

3 For commentary on the civilian maxim *omnia scrinia habet in pectore suo*, see

memory, of keeping faith (*fidelitas*) with the invisible (natural) spoken word. The principle is that of tradition, of a circular or repetitive instantiation of the institution in the nostalgic belief that the divinely ordained meaning of words can be kept from history in the custody of unwritten law. The shift from speech to writing might equally be formulated as a shift from politics to law in which writing plays the role of note or reminder, a new symbol of a prior bond. What is at stake in such a move is both a repetition of the contract in a more permanent form and also a vital restriction of the rhetorical domain. The two are closely and surprisingly connected.

Jean-Jacques emphasises the restriction inherent in the movement towards philology and philosophical grammar. The 'restraint' of rhetoric is portrayed first as a loss of eloquence and of melody 'which began by being no more than an aspect of discourse, imperceptibly takes on a separate existence, and music becomes more independent of speech'.[1] It is also portrayed, following Tacitus in the *Dialogus*, as a loss of style, a fettering (*aux fers*) of linguistic feeling in philosophical reason or a sermonising grammar fit only for 'le bourdonement des Divans' (murmuring on couches).[2] Eloquence could be heard and understood from a great distance (*de fort loin*); it could arouse the emotions and move to action in a way that is, in Rousseau's view, simply not possible in the dead prose of a written grammar. In place of eloquence and style which were traditionally the third part or division of rhetoric, it is memory (*memoria*) that now explicitly comes to dominate the rhetorical scheme of written communication. Memory is here a dialectical and didactic instrument, teaching, after the manner of Ramus,[3] the 'truths' of a discipline, and is no longer the

---

Legendre, *L'Empire de la vérité* (1983, Paris), pp. 144–5, and more generally Kantorowicz, *The King's Two Bodies* (1957, New Jersey), pp. 224–32.

1 *Essay*, p. 189.

2 Ibid., p. 199. The reference to 'le bourdonement des divans' deserves a study of its own which might well trace a lineage from the 'langue épistolaire des Salams' and the various other common items or objects 'the meaning of their sending was known to all lovers'. The analytic couch and the murmur of the unconscious suggest that the hidden language of the divan might form an alternative network, an underground relay, which cannot be as easily separated from public discourse as Rousseau implies. For the present, see P. Legendre, *Paroles poétiques échappées du texte* (1982, Paris), pp. 91–123 ('Protocole de la lettre de l'amour').

3 The literature on memory, and particularly on the didactic function of memory in dialectical schemata, is extensive. On the humanist use of memory see

probable organising logic of the places or topics of rhetorical argument associated with Simonides and oral disposition.

That memory comes to dominate the new dialectical order of written discourse has further connotations, specifically concerned with dictating the form of tradition as repetition and recollection, as custom (*voluntas populi*) and law (*lex posita*). If we move to look at the rhetorical structure of the *Contrat Social* we would emphasise the charter that makes it a secondary contract, which, wittingly or unwittingly, Rousseau depicts in the self-same terms that were used to characterise writing as coming after speech, namely that both writing and law are abstract, generalised, ideational, conventional, cold, univocal and uniform. The contract, in other words, has come to take a new form as written prose or as an instrument, a symbol or *symbolum* in a dual sense, one which associates the contract as writing both with the act of writing, with the mark, token or graph of 'symbolaeography' – of contractual writing – and with the symbol in its theological sense of creed: the symbol here being interpreted as a formal authoritative statement or summary of the religious belief of the Christian (or some other) Church, a creed or confession of faith. In etymological terms, the symbol, and by extension the contract, is the sign or mark that differentiates the Christian from the heathen and the believer or the faithful from the heretic.

In linguistic terms, the creed referred to by the etymology of *symbolum* is the order of original linguistic meanings; it is belief in the contract of origin in which the order of words was announced to the faithful and subsequently maintained by tradition and declared by the law. Only by virtue of a prior agreement as to the reference of signs is the social compact, and consequent creation of foundational or fundamental laws (*lois fondamentales*), remotely feasible. In terms of writing, we may thus postulate that there is implicit in the development of language from speech to script a comparable development from faith in a spoken creed or mark of belief and belonging to a more

---

T. Wilson (1553), pp. 343 and 413–22, where tropes, and particularly those based on similitude, are described in terms of aiding memory and as 'digesting images' through the application of a proper order. The Ramist Abraham Fraunce in *The Lawiers Logike* (1588, London), pp. 116–18, treats memory as the art of 'logical disposition'. For general discussion of the implications of *memoria*, classic discussions are contained in F. Nietzsche, 'Homer and Classical Philology' and 'We Philologists', respectively in *Complete Works*, vol. 6 and vol. 4, and in Frances

prosaic written contract in which belief is transferred from the creed to the instrument, and from sound to silent letters. In terms of the social contract, we may suspect that law (*lex*)[1] itself is now to be defined as a derivative of *legere*, to read, and that the contract is in consequence best understood as an indissociable combination of law and writing, of lawful writing which for Jean-Jacques means cold, clear and writ for all time.

The specific features of the *Contrat Social* may be dealt with quite swiftly, their rhetorical order mimicking that of the *Essay*. The social contract is announced by means of a massive simulation: '*I suppose* men to have reached the point at which the obstacles standing in the way of their preservation in the state of nature show their power of resistance to be greater than the resources at the disposal of each individual for his maintenance in that state.'[2] There follows from this hypothetical depiction of an imaginary historical necessity a further passage in which the logical necessity of the compact (*pacte social*) is spelled out in the equally simulated terms of problem and solution: if there is such a problem its solution is necessarily as follows by implication of the terms in which it is posed: 'the clauses of this contract are so determined by the nature of the act . . . *so that, even though they have perhaps never been formally announced* they are everywhere the same'.[3] The principal function of such a simulated origin is that of hiding and so making sacred the source of tradition and law: 'it is not

Yates, *The Art of Memory* (1966, London). For further references and discussion, see notes to Chapter 2.

1 See Legendre (1988, pp. 289–91). Law derives from *legere* to read. That something is written is, in dogmatic culture, sufficient proof of its lawfulness; it is then binding, both instrument and scripture. See also E. Benveniste, *Le vocabulaire des institutions Indo-Européenes II* (1969, Paris), pp. 267–75. The etymology given is based on Isidore of Seville. It is possible to make a contrary argument on the basis of the Greek verb *legein*, to say, from which the Roman *legere* can also be derived. Such a derivation links law to speech, or more precisely to declaration. See P. Stein, *Regulae Iuris* (1966, Edinburgh), pp. 3–25. There is an interesting polemical discussion in G. Rose, *Dialectic of Nihilism: Post-Structuralism and Law* (1984, Oxford), pp. 24–6. The contrary argument, however, fails to take account of the textual context of legal declaration: *traditio* or oral tradition and authority, as we have earlier argued, has always accompanied and interpreted the written law. Further, the law has always been 'announced' but that does not alter the character of the tradition itself, on which see P. Goodrich, *Reading the Law* (1986, Oxford), ch. 4; also idem, 'Review' (of *Dialectic of Nihilism*) (1985) 12 *Journal of Law and Society* 241.

2 *Contract* at p. 182.   3   Ibid., p. 183.

anybody who can make the gods speak, nor get themselves believed when they proclaim themselves their interpreter'.[1] Only the 'as if' of the absolute reference can adequately simulate the originary moment, the instant of genesis, of otherness, in which meaning is forged and the first words, the first notes or letters, are sent, the first contract signed and the first of a series of simulations inaugurated. The two crucial moments of such simulation are that of the deferred origin of meaning – of the point of the first, the unitary reference – and of writing, which simulates the law of origin or, in Rousseau's words: 'Thus in the task of legislation one finds two seemingly incompatible things: an enterprise beyond human power and, for its execution, a non-existent authority [*qui n'est rien*].'[2]

In positive terms, the simulation of a point of origin, the postulation of a contract as the source of tradition, suggests a move from the rule of God to the rule of law, from covenant to contract. The shift is one of laicisation rather than of secularisation, a change of terminology rather than of function: law as the direct expression of God's will, as concession or donation, is replaced by an apparently positive notion, that of reference to a contract, an agreement, a mutual bond upon the strength of which a new series of institutional guarantees – of points of transmission – can replace an antique Christian order with the rational universalities of law. It is the people, by means of the general will, that now guarantee sovereignty, order and law. It is the people, in the split form of the contract, that now send and receive the message of law: the contract establishes the two parties to an exchange and then indicates the bond or tie that binds them together in the form of obligation. We will pursue briefly the terms of this contract by reference to its rhetorical context and form.

In both historical and linguistic terms, the immediate context of the contract is a divinely imbued nature. The state of nature, as it affects the contract, is a fallen state in which only the ambivalent memory of genesis and of Eden can potentially restrict unbounded aggression. It is in consequence a split state in which instinct opposes justice[3] and self-interest precludes moral sentiment. There is in such a condition no guarantee, no recognised bond of mutuality in God, that will preclude either personal compulsion or general tyranny. In instituting the social, as in instituting language, it is rhetorically evident that the ultimate source of the first social action is to establish the human

1   Ibid., p. 211.   2   Ibid., p. 209.   3   Ibid., p. 187.

in the image of the divine. The task is that of instituting society as a simulated natural order, a point on which Rousseau is explicit: 'the social order is a sacred right [*droit sacré*] which acts as the basis of all others. Nevertheless, this right [or law] does not come from nature, it is therefore to be founded upon conventions.'[1] In historical terms it may thus be observed that that which precedes the social is the spiritual, directly referred to at one point as 'the homeland [*la patrie*] of the Christian [which] is not of this world'.[2] The other world must be brought down to or directed towards human ends and for such a purpose a simulacrum of the divine order is to be instituted in the fictional form of the state. There can be no doubt that the language used to depict the instituting act, the creation of 'the moral person which constitutes the State as a rational being',[3] is redolent of earlier theological conceptions of social order and indeed explicitly states that 'all justice comes from God, who alone is its source'.[4] Yet neither justice nor written law nor the moral *persona ficta* of the state can claim to be copies or models of the divine. They cannot, without idolatry ('image-serving'), be images of God and therefore they must be taken as simulations, impossible images or icons that represent an absent and unknowable God:

> [T]he simulacrum is an image without resemblance. The catechism, so much inspired by platonism, has familiarised us with this notion: God made man in his image but, through sin, man lost the resemblance while keeping the image. We have lost moral existence so as to enter into an aesthetic one ... the simulacrum is built upon a disparity, on a difference, it interiorises a dissimilarity.[5]

The individual subject of law, the citizen, takes on the same simulated characteristics as the exemplary moral personality and does so for the same reasons. The legal subject is likewise split between a precedent (and lost) spiritual essence and a positive legal form. In the moment of its institution as subject, the individual is bound to an implied instituting term: 'in order then that the social compact may not be an empty formula, it tacitly includes the undertaking, which alone can give force to the rest, that whoever refuses to obey the general will shall be compelled to do so by the

---

1   Ibid., p. 172.   2   Ibid., p. 309.   3   Ibid., p. 186.
4   Ibid., p. 204.
5   G. Deleuze, *Logique du sens* (1969, Paris) at p. 297; idem, *Différence et*

whole body'.[1] At other points in the text a more simple and explicit designation of the simulated source of the contract, and specifically of the subject who contracts, observes that 'the body politic or sovereign [draws] its being wholly from the *sanctity* of the contract',[2] or with equal lack of equivocation 'the sovereign power [is] absolute, sacred and inviolable'.[3] The crucial point is that, while the source of such sanctity is external to the social, as nature, unconscious or 'effroi primitif' (primordial fear)[4] – it is expressed appropriately enough by Jean-Jacques in the spiritual language of the divine – its attributes subsist in and underpin the polity requiring of the subject a faith or 'fidelity'[5] to the sovereign and to the established order,[6] an obedience,[7] a duty owed towards the 'sacred name of the public good' by virtue of a 'lien social' (social bond) inscribed indelibly 'in all hearts'.[8] The individual, in other words, never had a chance; the individual was always already the product of law.

The theological figures used to depict a simulated deity, the *corpus mysticum* of the people, should not detract from the sense in which the contract renews and so lends a new life to the dogmatic tradition. Prior to an analysis of the contemporary significance of the contract, it is worth observing – again in conformity with the earlier depiction of the poetic bond – that the social contract also represents a movement from rhetoric to writing, from a law written invisibly in the heart (*ius*) to a positive social bond legislated in written form (*lex*). In the place of the rhetorically conceived natural laws (*imago Dei*), the social contract introduces the law of the state in terms of generality, abstraction and, by implication of indestructibility, permanence. The conditions of writing are the conditions of law: 'the object of laws is always general, I mean that the law considers subjects as bodies and actions as abstractions, and never a particular man as an individual nor a particular action'.[9] In theological terms, one might view Rousseau as replacing custom, the unwritten tradition of Church and law, with a textual tradition, with a law that writes and a corresponding demand that the subjects of law keep faith with writing and with the notarial

répétition) (1969, Paris), pp. 354–65. See also, J. Baudrillard, *L'Echange symbolique et la mort* (1976, Paris), pp. 77–118.

1   *Contract*, p. 187.   2   Ibid., p. 186.   3   Ibid., pp. 200, 263.

4   Pierre Dauchy, 'Identité individuelle, conception du monde et réseaux d'appartenances' in *La Société civile* (1986, Paris) at p. 119.

5   *Contract*, p. 186.   6   Ibid., p. 190.   7   Ibid., p. 276.

8   Ibid., p. 275.   9   Ibid., p. 205.

law of writing that the civilian lawyers had early formulated in the maxim *de fide instrumentorum* (of the faith that attaches to instruments). To keep faith with the instruments of law is also to keep faith with the contract and with the word or mark by means of which the contract is remembered and so binds. In writing (*lex posita*), therefore, we have a further simulation in which the note or legal mark achieves the effect of resemblance:

> [T]he specificity of writing would thus be intimately bound to the absence of the father. Such an absence can of course exist along very diverse modalities, distinctly or confusedly, successively or simultaneously: to have lost one's father, through natural or violent death, through random violence or patricide; and then to solicit the aid and attendance, possible or impossible, of the paternal presence, to solicit it directly or to claim to be getting along without it, etc. The reader will have noted Socrates' insistence on the misery, whether pitiful or arrogant, of a *logos* committed to writing.[1]

Metaphysics of Contract

The sovereign, by virtue of what it is, is always all that it ought to be.[2]

The connection between the *Essai* and the *Contrat social*, between language and law, is presented by Rousseau in terms of a rhetorical structure that moves from the natural to the social and from the unwritten to the written. That movement is cast in terms of secularisation; in terms, that is, of a movement towards a constituted, written, human law which abandons the 'metaphysical ideas' that had formerly attached to the concept of a law of nature.[3] We are presented rather with a definition of the manner in which the self-sufficient principle of sovereignty communicates with itself, the manner in which the body or social corpus identifies (names) and manipulates its various parts by means of 'the law [which] unites universality of will with universality of object'.[4] That process of communication involves a relationship of internality: 'when the whole people legislates for the whole people, it is considering only itself; and if a relation is formed, it is that between the entire object

---

1 J. Derrida, *Dissemination* (1981, Chicago) at p. 77. Consider also P. Legendre, *Le Crime du Caporal Lortie: Traité sur le père* (1989, Paris).

2 *Contract*, p. 186. 3 Ibid., p. 61. 4 Ibid., p. 205.

seen from one point of view and the entire object seen from another point of view, without there being any division of the whole'.[1] In short, the sender and receiver of the message are one and the same; the contract separates the parties to the exchange simply so as to unite them indissolubly, textually, legally. That is to say, in metaphysical terms, the contract internalises both origin and end. For Rousseau it is, however, always a question of the origin or of the first, of a contract which is also metaphysically first, namely which is One or of the One, a unity, a canonic referent, outside of which there remain only the possibilities of irrationality or death, of that which remains after reason or life are gone.

The principle of self-sufficiency represents the process of communication as a circular one: semiotic and juridical subjects alike are destined eventually to refer only to themselves, their message simply and ceremonially reflecting its origins, its sender. It is possible in consequence to observe that within the contours of the contract as depicted the possibilities of language, of truth and of law are both exorbitant and extremely limited. The realm of contractual communication which structures the possibility of both knowledge and law is possessed of the truth – of a name, a referent, a cause – but is endlessly destined to repeat theatrically the signs of that dogmatic truth in ever more various veridical and juridical forms. If the tradition speaks, it is because it already knows. If the law rules, it is because it has immemorially designated both the office and the referent of such rule: it rules its own creation, it proclaims *erga omnes*. Finally, if the subject of communication seduces, it can only be in the sense of a radical narcissism – it is 'our' tradition and it is 'we' who love, nationally, patriotically and unto death. Alternatively, it is we who love, but within the prescribed limits and according to law. We love but that desire is allowed no better object than that of *pro patria mori*.

Such is the nature of our contract; it is that which binds us to discourse and ties us to the institution and to law. Equally, the contract is that which excludes; it is that which immunises us against other discourses and precludes that we even think of any other law. To pursue the meaning of the contract to its end, to its desuetude or death, would be a suicidal venture: by definition nobody escapes the institution. The problem is rather an anthropological one: the

1   Ibid., p. 205.

contractarian tradition expresses a specific enlightenment project, a particular conception of modernity – of *modus*, of rhythm, path or way. To pursue the meaning of the contract is to question how the tradition has scripted and circulated the law; it is to question the codification of meaning – its reduction to the contract – and its exclusion of the other as alien figure or foreign law, which is, in the last instance, either 'dark words' or plain force, the other either as death of meaning or as loss of life, either semantic or physical annihilation. That exclusion can be formulated in legal terms as a question of privity of contract, of belonging, of entering into 'consideration', as against the non-recognition of third-party rights or of a *ius quaesitum tertio*. The third party, it may at this point be hinted, is the meaning that the contracting parties cannot appropriate, that for which they cannot speak, the limit of the contract, the end of its life, its last mark, death. It can be simply noted in conclusion that a postmodern account of the contractarian tradition, and specifically of the contract as a contract, does not escape the tradition or evade its law. It can do no more than hope to add further meanings to the contract and to historicise in a supplementary fashion the terms in which the legal tradition presents itself as dogma: that is to say, as truth.

The issue of postmodernity can itself be formulated as that of systematically raising the question of how we have been contracted, which is to say how we have been made to speak and upon what terms we participate in the institutional text. We will end by reviewing in general terms the principal tenets of the contract as writing, always noting that here the contract has further connotations as something put out. To put out a contract is to send a missive, to advertise an intention and equally to threaten with death, to put out a contract on someone meaning prospectively to sign his death warrant and by extension to symbolise his end. The crucial relations are here temporal and spatial. The contract endeavours to govern the future and as writing it seeks to communicate beyond the lifetime of its author: the legislator 'should found his judgment not upon what he sees, but upon what he foresees, nor should he stop so much at the actual state of the population but rather at that which it ought naturally to attain'.[1] To write is to preserve, to delay, to create a monument to posterity whereby the simulated figure of the father can continue to lay down the law on no stronger ground than that of

---

1 Ibid., p. 217.

tradition: that is the role (*officium*) of paternity, that is why the contract must be obeyed.[1]

To the temporal text can be added a spatial territory. The *topos* or place of the text is both that of the *longue durée* of tradition and the space within which it is disseminated.[2] The image of the early metaphysics of the book,[3] of the symbolical manner in which texts were treated, can help elucidate certain of the grammatological and semiotic issues involved. The book was, in the high Middle Ages, no more than a collection of disparate texts which could well include charters, donations of land and other royal concessions. Before being stored in the sanctuary of the abbey, in the chapel or the treasure chest, the text would be placed upon the altar, offered to God and blessed. It would then be removed to the safest – and most remote – possible archival space, to a sacred hiding place or *sacramentorum latibula*, where, blessed and abandoned, the text would remain for posterity under the guardianship of heaven. It was, it may be noted, an immediate relic surrounded by stone and anathemas and thereby it joined immediately the other time of tradition, eternity or myth, and the other place of the sacred, the utopia of the *sanctum sanctorum*. The text, as bearer of the juridical tradition – as *corpus* of law (*iuris*) and of society (*civilis*) – was hidden instantly from time as history and removed from political or profane space. It remains to argue that in the place of the contract of linearity, of eternal progression, post-modernity implies a notion of temporal intensity; in the place of the utopia of tradition, of no place, it indicates a notion of heterotopias. In

1   It is interesting to note that God was the explicit addressee of all contractual instruments as listed in West (1590), passim. Instruments would all begin with invocations of *dei gratia* and would proceed to forms of address such as *Salutem in domum sempiternam* or *omnibus christi fidelibus ad quos praesentes literae pervenerint* or some variant thereon. For further details see the examples and discussion in Chapter 4.

2   Compare R. Debray, *La Puissance et les rêves* (1984, Paris), p. 95: 'socialist doctrines rest upon either latent or explicit philosophies of history, reactionary doctrines – those of "national security" or of "living space" – on the metaphysics of nature.'

3   General references are Curtius, *European Literature and the Latin Middle Ages* (1953, London), pp. 957, 310–26; Clanchy, *From Memory to Written Record* (1979, London), pp. 202–30; and Stock, *The Implication of Literacy* (1983, Princeton). For an interesting discussion of the fetishising of the law books, see F. Hotman, *Anti-Tribonian ou discours d'un grand et renommé iurisconsulte de nostre temps sur l'estude des loix* (1567/1603, Paris), pp. 105–6, and 120–21, the original books of Justinian 'being guarded   like   a   precious   and   sacred   relic,   only   being   very   rarely

the shattering of demarcations and boundaries suggested by such temporal and spatial displacements, it implies finally that the internal contract of the split self, of the first, of one or *origo*, be displaced by a play of one and other, in which sender and receiver be interrupted by the excluded other of the contract, the third party, language itself as the endlessly varied failure of presence: 'in the ineffable [*insaisissable*] instant where it plays the law, a literature goes beyond literature. It finds itself on both sides of the line which separates the law from that which is outside the law; it divides the being before the law, it is at the same time, like the peasant, "before the law" [*devant la loi*] and "prior to the law" [*avant la loi*]'.[1] To allow literature to play the law, to refuse the immunising properties of writing – of positive law – returns the contract to its emblematic or symbolic space: the simulation that makes the Rousseauite series of unitary contractual orders possible is no more than a metaphor, a symbol in the Greek sense of a splitting of the self – of the one or some other representamen of God – within the internal space of repression: in legal terms, *fictio, figura veritatis*.

To contract is both to include and to repress (to bury) that which cannot be included as part of the system. The contract, in establishing the genre of law, acts as an antidote to other discourses. The written law comes to represent the idea or ideal whereby original and image, real and imagined, inside and outside, conscious and unconscious, society and nature, take their places within the tradition. We receive the tradition 'in the normal course of the post'. The contract, as was observed at the outset, is binding once posted, once placed in the hands of the state messengers, or passed over to what Legendre terms 'les messages-messagers'.[2] When literature plays the law we are entitled to expand the invocation of the postal rule determining the formation – the communication – of a contract. The emblem of the postmodern contract would be that of the undelivered letter, of the letter that does not arrive or, in terms of Thomas Pynchon's *The Crying of Lot 49*,[3] that joins the other, the alternative postal network.

shown accompanied by candles and torches, thus did the ancient mystagogues show their law to the faithful [*sacrez*]'.

1 Derrida in *Préjugés*, op. cit., p. 134.

2 Legendre, *Empire*, op. cit., p. 119: 'power without celebration is inconceivable: we would be incapable of moving for the political, of making the distinction between ordinary speech and the speech of power, of entwining ourselves with what I have called the message-messengers, which is to say of entering into the poetical and sacred game of social communication . . .'

3 T. Pynchon, *The Crying of Lot 49* (1967, Harmondsworth).

Pynchon's fiction is concerned with what is left once the contract has gone, when we are left only with the underground relay, the other postal network, that of the repressed, of what has been left to one side or thrown within. *The Crying* depicts a modernist society (America) as a social form that is closed to the outside world and at the same time inwardly petrified. Governed by the contract, by law, it is immune to life and rejects all forms of dialogue. It is sclerotic and so maintains itself through the explusion of life: it places life on the outside with the waste, the refuse, the dispossessed, the inarticulate, the other, the trace. Life is condemned to expend, to squander itself on the other side, formlessly, subterraneanly and buried from sight as refuse or waste. The refuse may also, however, refuse. It may form its own network of communication, and it is largely in the name of the other, of that which remains, that the heroine Oedipa pursues the signs and clues, the marks or traces, the dross outside the contractual network, as indices of an underground postal network. The emission and relay of the repressed, of WASTE, the silent transmission of the messages of the disaffected, form the object of a fictional detection.[1] The book ends by leaving the question of the underground postal system un-answered, the last and undelivered letters of the tradition unopened – *poste restante*. It may be hallucination or it may be there; at all events only the future will decide the existence, the coming to being, of the other, of the underground relay buried within law's body.

1 Pynchon, at p.71: 'Oedipa wondered whether at the end of this (if it were supposed to end), she too might not be left with only compiled memories of clues, announcements, intimations, but never with the central truth itself, which must somehow each time be too bright for her memory to hold; which must always blaze out, destroying its own message irreversibly, leaving an overexposed blank when the ordinary world came back.' Compare Derrida (1980, p. 58): 'Once intercepted – a second suffices – the message no longer has any chance of reaching any determinable person, in any [*déterminable*] place whatever. This has to be accepted, and I accept [*j'accepte*]. But I recognise that such a certainty is unbearable, for anyone. One can only deny this self-evidence, and, by their function, those who deny it most energetically are the people charged with the carrying of the mail, the guardians of the letter, the archivists, the professors as well as the journalists, today the psychoanalysts.'

Part Two

LANGUAGE, IMAGE, SIGN AND COMMON LAW

6

Modalities of Legal Annunciation: A Linguistics of Courtroom Speech

'[T]here is no cultural document that is not also a record of barbarism.'[1]

Let Us Compare Mythologies: Questions of the Legal Other

The Queen Charlotte Islands form a small archipelago off the coast of mainland British Columbia. Lyell Island is the largest of the group and has been inhabited since before the Dutch and subsequent British discovery and colonisation of western Canada by the Haida Indians. The island is covered by primordial forest and its traditional economy is based upon woodcraft and fishing. In early 1985, without consulting the inhabitants of the islands, the government of British Columbia granted a logging licence to an American company, Western Forest Products Ltd, to exploit the islands for lumber. By a variety of means which included inserting metal spikes into the trunks of trees and a non-violent blockade, the Haida Indians prevented Western Forest Products Ltd from commencing logging. On 6 November 1985 Western Forest Products Ltd issued a writ naming the president of the Council of Haida nations, Chief Richardson, as defendant in an action for an injunction seeking to prevent any further interference with logging on the island. The case of *Western Forest Products Ltd* v. *Richardson and Others*[2] came before the Supreme Court of

1   W. Benjamin, *One Way Street* (1979, London), p. 221.
2   The case was unreported in the Supreme Court of British Columbia law reports and the only available record is the trial transcript which is available for personal inspection but cannot be copied or removed from the Supreme Court building. A general account of the issues involved in the protest can be found in M. Johnstone and D. Jones, 'Queen Charlotte Islands, Homeland of the Haida' (1987) *National Geographic* 102.

British Columbia and was heard by Justice McKay in the following week.

At the preliminary hearing of the case the Haida Indians appeared before the court unrepresented by lawyers and endeavoured to argue their preliminary case without legal assistance. The first linguistic issue raised in the case was thus posed as that of whose language was to represent the litigants, the question of whose speech was to be heard within the institution. Such is always the first question of law, that of authority and qualification for legitimate speech, but here it was also the first question raised, the primary question in the case. It was the key question of representation in its fullest sense: how and by what means, by what insignia and in which words, or by reference to which texts, will I appear before the law. The issue, which could also be labelled that of voice,[1] was dealt with elliptically by the court. During argument Justice McKay on several occasions attempted to persuade Chief Richardson to employ counsel and eventually adjourned the case for three days during which time he urged the defendant to obtain representation. For the period of the recess, Chief Richardson persisted in refusing legal representation, partly on the ground of cost but primarily on the ground of not wishing to create an illusion of justice: 'the issue of our lands is too important to leave in the hands of lawyers who are unfamiliar with our people'. That resistance to indirect representation, to the translation of law, was made explicit in remarks of the defendant to the press, which included the statement that in the defendants' view and 'for whatever reason, [Justice McKay] does not want us to speak for ourselves'. It should be noted also in this context that Haida custom and institutions included mechanisms and customary languages for dealing with this type of dispute. Firstly, it may be observed that in Haida custom any dispute over land or the use of land was traditionally settled by consent, negotiation and participation rather than by adjudication; secondly,

1 As posed by Bakhtin, *The Dialogic Imagination* (1981, Texas), ch. 4, the question of voice is that of who speaks, a question that includes issues of the internal stratification of language and the 'inner dialogue' of the word. The question of voice is also the question of which or whose language it is that is being spoken, a question of who speaks, of who is qualified to speak and also of whom they speak for. For a case study see J. Brigham, 'Right, Rage and Remedy: Forms of Law in Political Discourse' in *Studies in American Political Development* (1987, New Haven), at p.306: 'Legal forms are evident in the language, purposes, and strategies of movement activity as practices. When activists speak to one another their *language* contains practices of, about or in opposition to the legal system.'

logging of the islands threatened not simply the community and lifestyle of the Haida but their existence as a nation insofar as its economic consequences would force large numbers of the community to leave the islands. If we now move to read the text, the 'unrepresented' arguments put to the court by the defendants, we may read the transcript most thoroughly by examining all those places in which the discourse of the Haida comes into conflict with and even subverts the language of an essentially colonial law.

On the first day of the trial Chief Richardson appeared before the court in full ceremonial dress accompanied by eighteen elders of the Haida nations but without lawyers. The first argument, the first representation, the first address, was that of dress: to the judges' robes can be contrasted the button blankets of the defendant.[1] The significance of the ceremonial dress, a button blanket, is that the embroidery on the blanket symbolically both depicts the status of the wearer within the Haida nation and also denotes the wearer's relationship to and rights over traditional lands. No comment was made as to the ceremonial dress, nor was evidence allowed as to its significance. It was passed over in silence, it was not seen, it was not a language which the court was prepared to countenance: before the law there are only individuals, subjects that can be reconstructed as legal actors, abstract subjects, individuals without clothes, certainly without all that clothes imply, namely the social and ceremonial dimensions of collective and ethnic life, the material and social habitus of the individual. Despite subsequently expressed doubts, Justice McKay allowed Chief Richardson to speak to the court and to call witnesses. At the risk of vastly oversimplifying a court transcription that runs to over a thousand pages, the following sequence of arguments were heard – though arguably heard only in a notional sense – by the court. Draped in red and black button blankets, all the witnesses called addressed the issue of the Haida's arrival in and occupation of the Queen Charlotte archipelago. Noting that the writ

1   The classic study is T. Carlyle, *Sartor Resartus* (1893, London), p. 45: 'The beginning of all Wisdom is to look fixedly on Clothes, or even with armed eyesight, till they become *transparent*.' ('As Montesquieu wrote a *Spirit of Laws*, observes our Professor [i.e. Teufelsdrockh], so could I write a *Spirit of Clothes*; thus, with an *Esprit des lois*, properly an *Esprit de coutumes*, we should have an *Esprit de Costumes* . . . In all his Modes, and habilatory endeavours an Architectural Idea will be found lurking; his Body and the Cloth are the site and materials whereon and whereby his beautified edifice, of a Person, is to be built.' (p. 23).

served on the Haida made reference, as was until recently the standard form for common law writs, to the 'grace of God' (*Dei gratia*), Chief Lightbrown and others retold at length the mythological history of the Haida arrival in the islands. God, whom they referred to as the 'Great Spirit and Creator' had granted the islands to the Haida at the beginning of time for their use and occupation. They had a right 'to stand on the islands' and to act as caretakers from that moment at the dawn of time when the first Indians had emerged, according to Haida legend, from a clamshell carried by a raven and dropped on the sands of the islands.

A series of further anecdotal narratives, tellurian mythologies and traditional poems were presented to the court as evidence of the ancestral claim of the Haida to the islands. Several Haida artists explained at length the character and symbolism of their art forms, of their totem poles, masks and carvings, all of which spoke to the integral relationship of the Haida to the land, of their love of it and respect for it. They had been there since time began; this was their land by custom, by the prescription of use, by precedent even, yet ironically they were threatened by a common law writ and a property right that ran only to a hundred or so years. And it was a writ, let us say, that had neither history nor art nor poetry, nor even the logic of common law memory, to protect it. After the island had been reduced to stumps by the modernist anti-aesthetic of the loggers, the intruders would leave but the Haida would remain to inhabit what was left of their destiny and their island. They would have nowhere else to go. Of the other anecdotes and histories presented, the most striking occurs towards the end of the evidence when one of the women elders sang traditional songs to the court for a full afternoon. The songs repeated ancestral legends and evidenced again that, in Haida custom and art, inhabitant and nature were one; that as occupiers of the islands the Haida do not differentiate themselves from their environment but rather see their culture and community as being inextricably and intrinsically bound up in the land. She ended her songs weeping. Chief Richardson concluded his defence by appeal to natural justice, to a law of nature, an ethics, which he argued invested the Haida cause with a spirit of truth that pre-existed and would long survive any ruling as to mere law.

The testimony presented to the court was extremely novel in legal terms. It took the form of symbolic dress, mythologies, masks and totem poles as well as the legends, stories, poems, songs and other forms of interpretation that such art and mythology implied. The argument was both lyrical and visual, narrative and aesthetic, and it extended far beyond the contours of contemporary Western languages of law, although the defence – perhaps simply as a matter of respect and most frequently in response to judicial questioning – did also include more prosaic forms of argument as to Haida customary law of dispute settlement and land claim. Unreserved[1] judgment was given by the court the day after argument ended. Justice McKay observed that the court would not normally have allowed argument of the political kind heard but that, in view of the fact that the Haida had no other arena available to them, he had been prepared to listen and generously recommended that a record of the evidence presented should be kept for posterity. The judgment itself was extremely brief. The evidence presented as to the Haida title to and relationship with the islands was not legally relevant to the case being heard, which simply concerned interference with a valid logging licence. In law it was simply a matter of the wrong forum, perhaps of *forum non conveniens* too, and he had no alternative but to grant the injunction. He proceeded to do so while absolving himself of any moral responsibility by remarking in time-honoured form that 'while people sometimes think that judges have the power to do what they want, they must in fact act according to law; they administrate the law but cannot make policy'. Of course, this moral self-absolution of the court, this washing of hands, had as its underside the annihilation of the opposing language, the non-legal language in which the defence had been conducted. That language was annulled in the simple, direct and brutal sense that it was not even referred to save as a curiosity, a relic, a primitive remnant of a more savage past. The court would not compare mythologies, *it refused even to countenance the question of the 'other'*, because to do so would raise questions of its 'self', of the social and mythic construction of its own body, its social role and actions, its own clothes.[2] In short, although it was the only arena available to the

---

1   In legal terms the case simply concerned the formal validity of the logging licence and there was, in consequence, no need to take time to consider judgment.

2   That refusal of the 'other' is intrinsic to law: 'The law supposes a Grand Subject which must encompass or act upon something in the exercise of its grand project, and this something cannot any longer be taken to be simply itself, a reflection of itself, as it were. The "Other" is that upon which the "Law" acts, that which it completely absorbs, but which remains when the "Law" has spent itself. The "Other" may be called "Society"' (from A. Carty, 'Enlightenment,

Haida, the court was not prepared to countenance their argument which related not to law but rather to those more intangible courts of politics, history and moral reason. In those arenas the Haida might well be vindicated and justice be seen to lie down on their side; but in the meantime the trees and their livelihood would have been prised from their lands and their nation dispersed.[1]

The apparently emotive example of legal deafness presented in *Western Forest Products Ltd* v. *Richardson and Others* is at its most profound level an example of a deep structure of common law. It exemplifies an habitual logic of law, one which throughout its history has systematically obliterated difference in all its manifestations, in all its discourses. Like the inquisition, and the 'ordinaries' of the Counter-Reformation, like the Church which has historically either annexed or destroyed the other, the logic of the common law has been one of a comparable lack of alternatives, of a refusal to recognise that vast host of the other: the outsider, the stranger, the vagrant, the marginal; the Irish, the coloured, the foreign. What is their place in the law, what is their voice, whose language do they use? In its immediate linguistic technology, the case is in fact a vivid illustration of the procedural peculiarities and stringent evidential rules of relevance and admissibility that pertain to all forms of legal dialogue. Routine hearings for rent arrears, repossession of goods bought on credit, unfair dismissal, maintenance, breach of the peace, social security appeals or incompletely performed contracts exhibit identical disparities between expectations of audience and the reality of routine processing of claims before tribunals and the lower courts. As is reasonably accurately articulated in popular presentations of the legal community, the law, both as an institution and as a profession, represents itself as an arcane and élite pursuit; its image of a language is that of a peculiarly legal reason, that of the logic of rules, and its forms of utterance reflect the idiosyncracies, the obscure presuppositions and the generic inaccessibility of a language that is 'learned' in

Revolution and the Death of Man: A Postmodern Approach to Law' in A. Carty (ed.), *Postmodern Law*, 1990, Edinburgh, p. 6). For an implicit elaboration of a similar argument, see P. Fitzpatrick, 'Racism and the Innocence of Law' (1987) 14 *Journal of Law and Society* 119.

1   The Haida continued to protest and to blockade the island, and in a subsequent action for contempt of court several protesters received custodial sentences. On 11 July 1987 South Moresby finally became a national park but not

both senses of the term. In the most obvious of senses, legal dialogue is exclusory in the same manner that medieval usage of Latin was exclusory, namely that the language of legal communication is not a vernacular usage but rather a closely guarded and professionally governed specialist register whose lexicon and syntax reflect the historical influence of two alien and one obsolete, specifically legal dialects.[1] Against the background of that history it should be borne in mind that before any lawyer is equipped to 'estreat recognisances', 'escheat' property, pass 'fee simples', attend to 'res judicata', counsel in 'voir dire' or plead 'ex turpi causa non oritur actio' they have applied in excess of six years to the acquisition of the language and techniques of the legal register. As the case of the Haida Indian land claim well illustrates, however powerful the arguments or cause, however justified the case in terms of natural justice or moral competence, it is unlikely to be to the advantage of the laity to speak for themselves in legal settings; they are unlikely to be heard. More specifically, they cannot be heard in the sense that any recognition of the vernacular, and of all that the vernacular implies in terms of values and references, would place the court in a position of relativity; the language of law would itself become just one more dialect, one more register or code, a further vernacular to be weighed in the scales of legitimacy. In purely pragmatic terms, the vernacular must therefore efface itself and the non-legal speaker learn through that erasure of voice to benefit from complicity in the community of legal language, a complicity that takes place through representation and lodges both civility and fate in the hands of the profession.

It is to that profession and language, to the complex particularity of a legal audience, that the present Chapter will turn in endeavouring to outline certain of the more salient features of listening in legal settings. Throughout our theme will be that, irrespective of the aura of rationality and of specialism that surrounds legal hearings, they are best depicted not in terms of the law's own image, that of impartiality

---

before considerable parts of Lyell island had been extensively and irreparably logged.

1   For general accounts, see: D. Mellinkoff, *The Language of the Law* (1963, Boston); P. Goodrich, 'Literacy and the Languages of the Early Common Law' (1987) 14 *Journal of Law and Society* 422; G. E. Woodbine, 'The Language of English Law' (1943) 18 *Speculum* 396; B. Danet, 'Language in the Legal Process' (1980) 14 *Law and Society Review* 445; J-L. Sourioux and P. Lerat, *Le Langage du droit* (1976, Paris).

and the inexorable necessity of the application of pre-existent rules of statute and precedent, but rather in terms of the uneven exchange that characterises the flawed dialogue or 'distorted communication' of the most contemporary bureaucratic discourses. What underpins and prolongs the unilateral monologue of most legal auditoria is not the exquisite precision of scientific expression but simple political expedience and the linguistic manifestation of the vested interest of economically and sexually dominant social groups.[1]

Legal Auditoria

The books of the law run to many volumes. If one includes the full panoply of historical and contemporary law in force, together with the synopses, commentaries, doctrinal and procedural writings, updates and treatises on method, it runs to many libraries.[2] It is a literal impossibility to know the law, and even if one expended an entire existence in legal repositories one could only ever know part of the law. While much law is available in literary form to those trained in the art of finding and reading it, it should also be observed that many decisions are not reported and that many that are transcribed are not published but are available only in court libraries to which the judiciary alone has access. Even were one to accept for the sake of argument that the physical availability of law rendered the majority of legal rules accessible, in a broader sense the unequal distribution of legal knowledge gives the profession or community of lawyers an inevitable advantage or superiority in the forms and utility of legal discourse. In both linguistic and rhetorical senses, dialogue before the

1   On which point, see, for example, R. Fowler, *Language and Control* (1979, London); D. Cameron, *Feminism and Linguistic Theory* (1985, London). In specifically legal terms, see R. Benson, 'The End of Legalese' (1984–5) 13 *Review of Law and Social Change* 519; P. Goodrich, 'The Role of Linguistics in Legal Analysis' (1984) 46 *Modern Law Review* 523.

2   On the metaphor of the Alexandrian age of the printing press, see W. T. Murphy and S. Roberts, 'Introduction' (1987) 50 *Modern Law Review* 677; the other classic discussion is in M. Foucault, *Language, Counter-Memory, Practice* (1977), pp. 92–3: according to Flaubert's *The Temptation* the dubious honour of being 'the first literary work to comprehend the greenish institutions where books are accumulated and the slow and incontrovertible vegetation of learning quietly proliferates . . . [he] erects [his] art within the archive . . . all literary works are [now] confined to the indefinite murmur of writing.'

law is likely to be heavily weighted in favour of legal actors, a point which we will pursue in terms of legal audience by examining first the pragmatic contexts of legal address and second the specific linguistic forms of legal argumentation.

The image of law as a pre-eminently rational enterprise, as the inexorable application of axiomatic rules, is predicated in the main upon doctrinal systematisations of statutory law and the reported decisions of a very small number of higher courts. It is primarily upon the strength of textbook studies of a relatively small number of appeal court decisions – most notably those of the High Court, the Court of Appeal and the House of Lords – that notions of the certainty and completeness of legal regulation are derived. Invested with a high degree of public visibility and symbolic prominence, those courts inspire the mythology of legal certainty and of the mystery of legal presence which textbooks reformulate for didactic educational purposes without ever evidencing either the necessity of the decisions reported or their relevance to the preponderant domain of law's public presence. The presence of law as social discipline and authoritative regulation intersects with public life at a wholly different and largely unrelated level, that of enforcement agencies, tribunals and courts of first instance, within which arena those sitting in judgment are seldom legally trained and in which those who 'come before' the system of justice are rarely if ever successful in their pleas. The conviction rates in 1978, for example, were 84 per cent of English Crown Court cases; and 93 per cent of indictable offences and 95 per cent of non-indictable cases in the Magistrates' Courts. It is the bureaucracy, in the form of the police, administrative agencies and large corporate enterprises that are overwhelmingly the victors in the adversarial process of trial. In criminal cases, for example, the majority of defendants are unrepresented and statistically the vast bulk of them plead guilty as charged, sample studies indicating that 76–93 per cent of defendants in Magistrates' Courts and 57–75 per cent in higher courts enter guilty pleas.[1] The defendant's day in court is seldom a voluble one; the hearing is brief and the processing swift.

Assuming that the process of justice, of receiving a hearing, is best understood in terms of that point at which law is created and applied

1   Figures given in D. McBarnet, *Conviction* (1983, London). See also J. Baldwin and M. McConville, *Negotiated Justice* (1977, London); J. Baldwin, *Pre-Trial Justice* (1985, Oxford); A. Desbruslais, 'Pre-Trial Disclosure in Magistrates' Courts: Why Wait?' (1982) 146 *Justice of the Peace* 384.

to members of the public – that is, at the point at which it becomes law for them – then the image of legal rationality as a phenomenon of texts and rules has only the most indirect of relevances. The day in court is likely rather to be experienced in terms of confusion, ambiguity, incomprehension, panic and frustration, and if justice is seen to be done it is so seen by outsiders to the process.[1] Nor is justice likely to be heard to be done by participants in the trial. The visual metaphor of justice as something that must be visible and seen enacted has a striking poignance in that it well captures the paramount symbolic presence of law as a façade, a drama played out before the eyes of those subject to it. Any attempt to depict the nature of a legal hearing does well to begin by examining that visibility, the physical structure and architecture of a peculiar auditory space.

Legal dialogue, and particularly the verbal creation of law, occurs in very specific formal institutional settings.[2] Although the architecture, the spatial arrangement, symmetries and positionings, of the contemporary courtroom are variable, certain general structural features can be singled out. By way of introduction we may observe briefly that the relationship between culture, communication and the built environment has not been the object of very extensive study.[3] To the relatively obvious issue of acoustics, contemporary architectural studies have, however, added an impressive list of signifying dimen-

1   For a small survey of consumer views, see M. Cain, 'The General Practice Lawyer and the Client' in R. Dingwall and P. Lewis (eds.), *The Sociology of the Professions* (1985, London); S. Harris, 'Defendant Resistance to Power and Control in the Courtroom', in H. Coleman (ed.), *Working with Languages* (1987, The Hague); W. O'Barr, *Linguistic Evidence* (1982, New York). See also M. Atkinson and P. Drew, *Order in Court* (1979, London); P. Carlen, *Magistrates' Justice* (1976, London); W. L. Bennett and M. S. Feldman, *Reconstructing Reality in the Courtroom* (1981, New Brunswick). Classically, see H. Garfinkel, 'Conditions of Successful Degradation Ceremonies' (1956) 64 *American Journal of Sociology* 420.

2   Atkinson and Drew, op. cit., ch. 2. More generally R. Kevelson (ed.), *Law and Semiotics I* (1988, New York), ch. 4; A. Garapon, *L'Ane portant des reliques* (1984, Paris); idem, 'Forme Symbolique et Forme Linguistique du Droit' (1988) 2 *International Journal for the Semiotics of Law* 161.

3   D. Preziosi, *The Semiotics of the Built Environment* (1979, Indiana); M. Foucault, *Discipline and Punish* (1979, London); P. Hirst, 'Constructed Space and the Subject' in R. Fardon (ed.), *Power and Knowledge* (1985, Edinburgh); J. Bender, *Imagining the Penitentiary* (1988, Chicago). More generally, see B. Hillier and J. Hanson, *The Social Logic of Space* (1984, Cambridge); A. Vidler, *The Writing of the Walls* (1987, New Jersey); G. Hersey, *The Lost Meaning of Classical Architecture* (1988, Boston).

sions to public spaces: buildings variously store information, hierarchically arrange communicational relations, separate and align visual axes, strategically facilitate the administration of their occupants and above all, in Foucault's terminology, construct and constitute 'enunciative modalities'.[1] The latter concept refers to the fashion in which social discourse or discursive formations are tied to particular sites and roles, bound to specific institutional settings within which specifically delimited subjects are socially authorised to present a qualified specialist speech. The enunciative modality determines both what can and what should be said within a particular form, that of, for example, a lecture, a political speech, a sermon or a judgement, as well as delimiting the context and conditions of its reception and appropriation in, respectively, the lecture theatre, the hustings, the church or the courtroom. Intrinsic to such enunciative modalities is not simply an analytic space but equally a physical architecture which both delimits and contributes to the symbolic effect of carefully regulated genres of speech. The building hosts and echoes the semantic import of discourse while also strategically facilitating and administrating its subjects.[2]

On the portals of the court building will be inscribed the royal motto, 'Dieu et mon Droit', while in other regimes it would be 'Fiat Iustitia' or some variant thereof. The windows to the buildings are likely either to be barred or to be somewhat higher and narrower than is usually the case: the building does not see out, it is blind to the outside like an archive or a bunker, its reality is exclusively within. Access to the rear of the building will be likewise barred and the entrance to the courts will be in some varying measure imposing not simply by virtue of its size but also by dint of its elevation from the street. Whatever the form it takes, and the degree of emphasis or imposition is likely to vary according to the date of design and the status of the courts within the legal hierarchy, the threshold to the court building will be marked and physical access to the seats of justice will involve both a visual and conceptual ascension from the quotidian street to ritualised space. That the situation and external structure of the courts signify a degree of distance from the everyday and the mundane concerns of public space gains further emphasis upon entry into the ritualised internal spacing of the courts, of the judicial world secreted in the heart of the city and wrapped in an

1   M. Foucault, *The Archaeology of Knowledge* (1981, London), pp. 50–56.
2   P. Hirst, op. cit., pp. 182–3.

archaic and sacral atmosphere of special functions and the silent unravelling of other times.

Semioticians of architectural form have tended to distinguish between the 'formal' and 'material' syntax of buildings.[1] The formal syntax of buildings, as the linguistic metaphor suggests, is concerned with the study of the formal properties of the built environment: that is, with the geometry of organisation which may be reduced to (i) sets of items or formal properties of space; (ii) sets of relationships amongst these; and (iii) a set of rules or laws obeyed by the latter. In a necessarily simplified account, the fundamental issue involved in formal syntax is the study of the 'empirical overall style' through which the built environment communicates by organising visual relationships, symbolising subject positions (placements) and controlling avenues of circulation and visibility according to generally functional criteria, be they those of devotion, (panoptic) surveillance, isolation, communion or some other alternately disciplinary or hedonistic design.[2] As an adjunct to formal syntax, material syntax concerns the study of a set of rather more necessary features to the surface of buildings, the materials used, textures, colours, scales, modulations and insignia that range from gargoyles to heraldic crests.

Summoned by writ, subpoena or condition of bail, even before arriving at court the subject of legal proceedings will have already had to traverse the linguistic complexities of what were until recently archaic and verbose standard legal forms of interpellation that variously invoked God and monarch and threatened sanctions of fine or imprisonment. The subject is called and arrives in the ill-demarcated open hallway of the courts to an atmosphere of hushed routine efficiency of business combined with a confusion engendered by a general absence of clear indicators either of the order of proceedings or of where the relevant court is sitting. While lists are displayed, the order and place of proceedings will generally have to be explained save in the case of defendants in custody who either arrive under police escort or are brought from the sparse environs of the court cells up to the lavishly contrasting well of the court. At this point

1   D. Preziosi, 'Environmental and Linguistic Structure', in R. Fawcett et al. (eds.), *Semiotics of Language and Culture* (1984, London).

2   As discussed in A. Vidler, op. cit., ch. 5 (on the architecture of libertinage). Also Foucault (1979), op. cit., pp. 195ff (on the panopticon); more generally, L. Martines, *Power and Imagination* (1979, London).

generalisation becomes difficult in view of the diversity of courts and their arrangement. Viewing and listening positions will also vary markedly according to the role that is to be played within the proceedings. While there are significant procedural and architectural facets to the roles of juror and of witness – the latter, for instance, with the exception of expert witnesses, are not allowed into the court until they are called to give testimony – I will limit my remarks to defendants.

The strategic organising principle of the courtroom is a didactic one. It is that of the visibility of justice rather than of its audibility. The ritual character of proceedings in court have, first, an obvious material character in the higher courts in the form of the ceremonial dress of legal participants, in judicial robes and wigs, barristerial gowns and wigs, the use of royal red and emblazoned royal arms on and frequently also above the judicial seat or throne. To the aged pomp of the furniture and scale of the courtroom can be added the not altogether incidental features of procedure and address. The 'court' is silent and rises to its feet upon the entry of the judge. The judge is addressed never by name but either in metonymic form as 'the court' or 'bench', or sacrally as 'your honour', 'your lordship' or 'your worship'. It is not a human being, in other words, that sits when the court returns to their seats but rather justice (*jus*) and law (*lex*) that take their place at the pinnacle of a strictly ordered hierarchical space, surrounded by a veritable debauch of symbols of majesty and order. The sitting is accompanied by a strictly controlled order and tone of speech: speakers are called upon to speak and cannot do so volitionally, nor is it in general possible to interrupt that order and decorum. The court must remain silent and indeed obedient to procedure, with stringent sanctions attaching to the common law offence of 'contempt in the face of the court' which punishes any who 'scandalise' the court *in praesentia*, while the powers enacted in the Contempt of Court Act 1981 not only create wide-ranging offences of strict liability but have also on occasion been used to imprison observers or participants who have done no more than laugh in court.

In an interesting discussion of genres of discourse, Mikhail Bakhtin observes that where discourse performs as authoritative discourse it no longer performs as information, direction, rules, models and so forth but rather strives to determine the very bases of our ideological interrelations with the world, the very basis of our behaviour. In this respect we encounter the authoritative word:

with its authority already fused to it. The authoritative word is located in a distanced zone, organically connected with a past that is felt to be hierarchically higher. It is, so to speak, the word of the fathers. Its authority was already *acknowledged* in the past. It is a prior discourse. It is therefore not a question of choosing it from among other possible discourses that are its equal. It is given [it sounds] in lofty spheres, not those of familiar contact.[1]

The social distance and unfamiliarity of the courtroom within which justice 'sounds', as opposed to conversing in any more vernacular manner, gains further emphasis in the formal syntax of the court.

While the judiciary are in a nominal sense the servants of the public, of a public which seems when invoked to be peculiarly of their own making, their position within the spatial organisation of the courtroom is one of absolute separation, of elevation and of privilege. Judges or magistrates will appear in court by means of a special entrance to the rear of the bench and, formalities completed, will take their seat on the 'bench', from which elevated location they look down upon the court protected by a series of barriers (bars) in the older courts and by court officials and stenographers in more modern architectural structures. No one approaches the bench except on request, and any exhibits or documents are passed up to the bench by the court clerk. The adversarial process of the trial unrolls below the bench and its agonistic or gladiatorial character lends an atmosphere of the classical games in the amphitheatre, in which the Emperor decided life or death from a situation above the arena and in the form of concession or donation. In less allusive terms, juridical space is a separate and obligatory space for its occupants; a space hierarchically organised in the image of the Law: 'It suspends, for an instant, all the habitual differences of rank between men, so as to substitute others. *It incarnates order, it creates order, it is order.* Within the imperfection of the world and the corruption of life, it realises a temporary and limited perfection.'[2]

In the court below, in those designed for jury trials, a certain symmetry prevails in which the dock, itself an elevated and enclosed space, faces the bench, and to either side rise tiers of seats to accommodate the jury and on the other side reporters and other official court observers. Prosecution and defence counsel take their place on either side of the open well of the court and conduct the

1   Bakhtin, op. cit., pp. 342–3.   2   Garapon, op. cit., p. 45.

combative game of trial directly in front of the bench. Witnesses, when called, will appear to the side of the court and, while the dock is visually a focal point from the public gallery at the front of the court, it is frequently at such a distance from proceedings, the exchange of arguments, that irrespective of whether or not the legal wrangling between counsel and bench could be understood, it is near impossible to hear: 'spatial arrangements, however, which might signify to the onlooker a guarantee of an orderly display of justice, are too often experienced by participants as being generative of a theatrical autism with all the actors talking past each other'.[1] Defendants, *accused* of acts of law breaking, are set apart from other actors and frequently distanced from proceedings in which their contribution will seldom be more than that of responding to formal questions and projecting answers concerning intimate details of their lives across the auditory gulf that separates the dock from the elevated pinnacle of the court, the bench.[2]

The Language of Annexation and Reformulation

The thematic unity of courtroom architecture is to be found in elements and relationships of visual display in which the defendant is an isolated and usually unfamiliar witness of archaic and formulaic proceedings. Much of the argument in court, where it concerns points of procedure, evidence or law, will neither involve defendants nor be comprehensible to them. The language used will appear learned and technical and references will be to sources of law generally inaccessible to the public. Where defendants are called to speak, it is not so as to present their own narrative of events or of motives and causes, but rather to respond on cue to formal questioning which, while it may be less archaic in lexical terms, is concerned with legal categories of relevance and intention, is subject to interruption from the bench and bears an apparently indirect relation to any perceived narrative of real events.

The principal linguistic task of legal speech is to translate and reformulate vernacular dialects into the apparently separate and unitary genre of legal discourse.[3] To analyse the linguistics of that

---

1   Carlen, op. cit., p. 20. See also T. Mathieson, *Law, Society and Political Action* (1980, London), pp. 89–105.

2   S. Harris, 'Language, Power and Control in Court' (1982) 3 *Crosscurrents* 33.

3   I. Stewart, 'Law and Closure' (1987) 50 *Modern Law Review* 908.

process of reformulation and annexation would involve an account of the historical development and disciplinary techniques of legal textual culture, its use of foreign languages and its exemplary forms of rhetorical organisation, that far exceed the boundaries of an account of legal auditions.[1] It remains true, however, that courtroom speech is underpinned by many of the more general and manifest inequalities of relationship that exist as between legal discourse and non-legal discourses within the development of legal language as a whole. In terms of legal dialogue, the 'imagined community' of the legal genre as an administrative discourse evidences its discursive power through an explicit superiority of attitude towards and exclusion of other discourses and usages. Authoritative (professional) languages demand, as was observed above, an allegiance on the part of their listeners which accepts the authority of the language as an inert and indissoluble whole irrespective of its content. That authority is linked initially, or at least most obviously, to a specific political power, that of sanction, to an institution, the court, and to a person, the judge. In a less direct but easily apparent sense, linguistic authority is manifest in the imposed forms of dialogue and silence and in the irrefragable truth of legal definitions that variously annex, reformulate, appropriate or exclude competing usages: 'what is important [in relation to professional languages] is the intentional dimensions, that is, the denotative and expressive dimension of the "shared" language's stratification. It is not in fact the neutral linguistic components of language being stratified and differentiated, but rather a situation in which the intentional possibilities of languages are being expropriated.'[2] The intentional possiblities of utterance are annexed and reformulated in a particular direction and with a particular content that conforms to the specific objects, belief systems, forms of expression and value judgments of the relevant profession. For the speakers of the language, the reformulation involved is directly intentional whereas, for less powerful outsiders to the given purview, the intentions permeating these languages become '*things*, limited in their meaning and expression; they attract to, or excise from, such a language a particular word – making it difficult for the word to be utilized in a directly intentional way, without any qualification'.[3]

While it would be useful to present a comprehensive typology of the

1   See P. Goodrich, *Legal Discourse* (1987, London); also, idem, 'Traditions of Interpretation and the Status of the Legal Text' (1986) 6 *Legal Studies* 53.

2   Bakhtin, op. cit., p. 289.   3   Ibid., p. 290.

forms of definition, annexation and reformulation endemic to dialogue between legal and extra-legal genres, this discussion will be limited to a more manageable analysis of examples drawn from dialogue in the lower courts. The examples will be loosely arranged according to the order of proceedings. In each instance the concern will be with the explicit manifestion of an image of legal community and sovereignty at the expense of other usages: that is, with the subordination of the listener to an imposed form and to purportedly pre-established definitions. By way of introduction to the preponderant number of examples, drawn from defendant's responses in Magistrates' Courts, it should be noted that prior even to the initial courtroom scene of entering of a plea defendants have likely been subject to considerable pressure in relation to their plea, in terms either of informal plea bargaining or of straightforward persuasion to plead guilty.[1]

The initial stage of criminal trial takes the form of pleading, while in civil cases it generally takes the form of a statement of claim and counter-claim. In both cases, though markedly less so in civil proceedings, the initial speech in the proceedings will be legally formulated and will concern neither the events nor the perceived wrong at issue, but a legal category and definition of offence or civil claim. The question posed will concern not issues of what was done, why it was done or the contexts and motives of its doing, but simply the legal statement of charge to which the defendant must reply either guilty or not guilty. The discursively interesting aspect of this initial ritual of legal recognition is that the statement of charge or wrong may well appear so irrelevant to the actions concerned that the option of pleading guilty or not guilty is perceived either as peripheral or as coercive. Its function, however, is largely one of recognition and submission to the arena of trial, as the following examples from the Magistrates' Courts well illustrate. The first case[2] involves a charge of trespassing with intent to steal:

> *Clerk*: Do you plead guilty or not guilty?
> *Defendant*: Well, yes and no.
> *Clerk*: Do you plead guilty or not guilty?
> *Defendant*: Yes – I was guilty of trespassing – and no – I wasn't intending to steal.

1 See Carlen, op. cit., for a theoretical argument to that effect. See also J. Baldwin, op. cit., ch. 7.

2 Carlen, op. cit., pp. 115–16.

Clerk: So you plead not guilty?
Defendant: That's not what I said.
Clerk: Not guilty.

A not guilty plea was entered on the record, no attempt being made by the court, the clerk or magistrate to establish the grammar of the phrase and so to separate the two themes. In another relatively obvious example of reformulation[1] the defendant is concerned to ignore the specific wording required by the court as formal pleading, in view of a legally ulterior purpose to the discussion:

Clerk: Do you plead guilty or not guilty?
Defendant: Yes, I did it. I said I did it.
Clerk: No. Do you plead guilty or not guilty?
Defendant: Yes, I did it. I just want to get out of here . . .
Magistrate: Do you plead guilty or not guilty?
Defendant: Yes, I did it.
Magistrate: No. I'm asking whether you plead guilty or not guilty. You must use either the words 'not guilty' or 'guilty'.
Defendant: [Looking towards probation officer] She said, 'Say guilty'.
Magistrate: No. You must say what you *want* to say.
Defendant: Yes, I'll say what you like. I did it.
Magistrate: No. You must use the language of the court.

In broader terms, the central issue of the case may well be that of what the legally formulated charge means in commonsensical, political or moral terms. The question of who defines whether peace activists demonstrating are guilty as charged of behaviour likely to cause a breach of the peace, or whether, in *R*. v. *Ponting*,[2] passing information to an unauthorised person constituted an offence under s.2(1) of the Official Secrets Act 1911 which makes it an offence to 'communicate . . . information to any person, other than to a person to whom he is authorised to communicate it', is hardly encompassed in the option of pleading guilty or not guilty. The point is well made in terms of the semantic ambiguity of the plea in a case from Lancaster Magistrates' Court,[3] where the defendant, who was unrepresented, was charged with resisting arrest and hitting a policeman. He admitted that he had hit the policeman but later claimed that the

1   Ibid.
2   (1985) *Criminal Law Review* 318; discussed at length in C. Ponting, *The Right to Know* (1985, London). For discussion of the Official Secrets Act 1989, see J. Griffith, 'The Official Secrets Act' (1989) 16 *Journal of Law and Society* 273.
3   J. Thomas, 'The Language of Power' (1985) 9 *Pragmatics* 765.

policeman had hit him first, in which case self-defence may legally be pleaded as a defence to the action:

> *Clerk*: How do you plead – guilty or not guilty?
> *Defendant*: [Silence]
> *Clerk*: Did you do it or not?
> *Defendant*: Well, I did hit him, yes.
> *Clerk*: So that's 'guilty' then.
> *Defendant*: Yes, sir.

The control of dialogue by court officials, counsel and judge is a significant feature of subsequent discursive sequences. While I will refer to that strategy of formulaic and definitional control in subsequent discussion, the principal discursive operator in court-room dialogue is undoubtedly that of paraphrase reformulation. Paraphrase, of course, may involve either a relation of equivalence or symmetrical substitution between elements (words, expressions, propositions) such that the elements *a* and *b* 'mean the same thing' in the relevant discourse, or a relation of implication or orientated substitutability such that the relation of substitution *a* to *b* is not the same as the relation *b* to *a*.[1] It is the latter form of paraphrase that is of greatest discursive and ideological significance in two respects. Firstly, the choice of implication will organise the meaning attributed to the given statement; secondly, the content of that implication is not explicit but depends upon a pre-established discourse and meanings that are not necessarily equally available to both parties to the dialogue – nor are both parties always equally equipped to contest the pertinent implications.

The most explicitly and significantly orientated types of para-phrase tend to take the form of implicating the respondent's statement, by lexical or referential means, in legally and often also morally opprobrious results:

> *Prosecutor*: And you say this before us is not the proceeds of shoplifting?
> *Defendant*: No, not that stuff, no.
> *Prosecutor*: And the police have invented this case against you, it must follow, mustn't it?
> *Defendant*: Well I suppose so.
> *Prosecutor*: Well it's the only thing possible isn't it?
> *Defendant*: Yes . . .

1 M. Pêcheux, *Language, Semantics and Ideology* (1982, London), pp. 112–27; C. Fuchs, *La Paraphrase* (1982, Paris).

> *Prosecutor*: You think that they created the whole case against you?
> *Defendant*: *I am not calling them* liars but that's what happened.
> *Prosecutor*: It's not good enough to say you are not calling them liars, because that is the only possibility if you are telling the truth.

The reformulation in the above example[1] is legally an effective and frequent one. The implication adduced is by no means a necessary one; the positive assertion could equally imply mistake as to the identity of the goods, as to the identity of the accused or as to certification of payment, and it certainly makes no necessary attribution of motive with regard to the police evidence. The further implications of the reformulation also draw upon the moral credibility of the police as routine witnesses in courtroom dialogue and the further legal implication that, if the character of witnesses is attacked by the defence, the character of the defendant can then be placed in issue. The process of reformulation thus acts to control the topic of discourse and to particularise a generic account of behaviour in a damaging yet, for the unrepresented defendant, unforeseeable manner. In the following example,[2] the defendant has explained at length to the Arrears and Maintenance Court how, after two years' unemployment, he has recently found employment again:

> *Magistrate*: In other words what you're really saying to us is that you started to wake up to the fact.
> *Defendant*: Yeh.
> *Magistrate*: That uh you've got certain obligations to meet and it's vitally important that you should start to think about them – that's what you're saying I take it.
> *Defendant*: Yeh.
> *Clerk*: You did – you do accept that you should be paying ten pounds a week?
> *Defendant*: Oh yeh, yeh I do accept it.
> *Clerk*: Uh – are you really asking that uh some of these arrears be remitted – is that what you're really asking?
> *Defendant*: Yeh.

The defendant's simple description of two years' unemployment followed by a short period of self-employment is reformulated by the magistrate into a set of moral obligations and motives of legal relevance which the clerk proceeds to translate into a further acceptance of a specified amount and period of remission of arrears.

---

1 McBarnet, op. cit., p. 79.   2   Harris (1982), op. cit., p. 541.

Aligned to control of topic in the form of paraphrase and definition can be added a series of rules of relevance, prohibition of hearsay and admissibility. The ability to negate or to challenge adverse paraphrase and damaging implications depends throughout upon knowledge of their relevance, their preconstructed force within the legal form of discourse, and the status and credibility of the witness or respondent. An interesting contrast in status and the power to reformulate can be explicitly seen in the following examples. The first[1] is a rape trial:

Defence: When you first saw him he was in company with another man and you approached both of these men?

Complainer: No.

Defence: *And* talked to them?

Complainer: No.

Defence: *And* that was at your suggestion that in fact, you went up this close in the first place?

Complainer: That is ridiculous, utterly ridiculous . . . no.

Defence: Was it not the case that the man in the dock did talk to you at some point in the street and offer to walk to wherever it was you said you were going?

Complainer: How could he possibly do that if he was in . . . Road?

Judge: Don't argue with counsel; at the moment all *we* want *you* to do is to answer the question.

Complainer: No.

Note the connective 'and' in the defence's questions, implying as they do a connection or continuous logic to the discourse of the defence despite the assertion of the precise opposite in the complainer's replies. The 'and' connects the monologue of the defence, it connects a discourse that ignores the dialogic implicatures of the exchange and retains a cohesion through simply denying the dialogic character of questioning. When the judge intervenes it is also noteworthy that a 'we' is invoked that can only refer to a complicity between judge and defence established against the complainer – after all, the defence could easily have been instructed to ask relevant questions in the light of the answers given. The second example[2] of an even stronger exclusionary power predicated upon an accusatorially conceived concept of relevance may be briefly elicited from proceedings in the Magistrates' Court. Two youths are accused of suspicious activities

1 Chambers and Miller, *Prosecuting Sexual Offence* (1986, Edinburgh), p. 123. (emphasis added).

2 McBarnet, op. cit.

around cars. They claim, in defence, that they were in fact being arrested for nothing in order to be questioned about a stolen television, but were interrupted as follows:

Magistrate: I'm sorry – I'm not prepared to listen to information about a television.

Accused: But he said he didn't ask us about a TV and he did.

Magistrate: It's irrelevant to the charge.

In dramatic contrast to the preceeding instances of annexation, the final example involves a much greater degree of parity of paraphrase, as might be expected to be associated with the titled head of the civil service, Sir Robert Armstrong, giving evidence of government actions in *Her Majesty's Attorney General in and for the UK* v. *Heinemann and Wright*.[1] Counsel is cross-examining Sir Robert Armstrong as to a letter he had written to W. Armstrong of Sidgwick and Jackson requesting a copy of their book *Their Trade is Treachery* so that the Prime Minister should be in a position to make a statement to the House of Commons and saying 'clearly she cannot do so until she has seen . . . the book itself':

Q: . . . That conveys the very distinct suggestion, the explicit suggestion that she has not had access to the book before this letter, does it not?

A: I don't know whether she had access to the book itself at that stage, but that is beside the point. I did not wish to disclose that we had obtained a copy of the book.

Q: You misled Mr William Armstrong in order not to disclose the fact –

A: I did not disclose to Mr Armstrong the fact that a copy of the book had been obtained.

Q: You misled Mr William Armstrong, did you not?

A: If you put that interpretation on it. I was bound to do so, but I wished to protect the source.

Q: That letter was *calculated to mislead*. Was it not?

A: It was *calculated to ask for a copy* of the book on which we could take direct action.

Q: It was *calculated to mislead* Mr Armstrong as to whether the Government had a copy of the book or not?

A: It was *calculated not to disclose* to Mr Armstrong that the Government had obtained a copy of the book.

Q: It was *calculated to mislead* Mr Armstrong to believe that the Government did not have a copy of the book. Correct?

1   Transcript day 2.

A: It was *calculated not to disclose* to Mr Armstrong that the Government
      had a copy of the book in order to protect the confidentiality of the
      source from which it came.
Q: And the Government did have a copy of the book?
A: The Government did have a copy of the book.
. . .
Q: I put it to you that the letter contains an untruth. That is the
      question.
A: It does not say that we have already got a copy of the book, that is
      quite true.
Q: So it contains an untruth.
A: It does not contain that truth.
. . .
Q: So it contains a lie?
A: It is a misleading impression, it does not contain a lie, I don't think.
Q: What is the difference between a misleading impression and a lie?
A: You are as good at English as I am.
Q: I am just trying to understand.
A: A lie is a straight untruth . . .
Q: What is a misleading impression – a sort of bent untruth?
A: As one person said, it is perhaps being economical with the truth.

Suffice it to observe that Sir Robert Armstrong's refusal to accept the
proffered reformulation of the implications of the letter in question
was dependent upon a confidence and knowledge as well as a
tolerance from the bench that are rarely found in lower court criminal
proceedings, a conclusion which is well borne out by studies of
witness credibility in relation to status carried out by O'Barr and
others at Duke University.[1]

Forms of Closure: The Modalities of Annunciation

If it is correctly argued, as I believe it to be, that implicative
or orientated paraphrase at both semantic and lexico-
referential levels is the most common form of argumentative

---

1   See particularly W. O'Barr, *Linguistic Evidence*, op. cit. For further discus
sion, see B. S. Jackson, *Law, Fact and Narrative Coherence* (1989, Merseyside), pp.
63–71; W. L. Bennett and M. S. Feldman, *Reconstructing Reality in the Courtroom*, op.
cit., pp. 166ff; also R. Charrow, 'Linguistic Theory and the Study of Legal and
Bureaucratic Language', in *Exceptional Language and Linguistics* (1982, New York).

manipulation, then the ability to challenge the legal control of topic and terms is primarily a matter of contesting the discursive preconstruction of questions. In general that ability will depend upon access to the 'shared knowledge' which acts as the precondition of the propositional content of the statement. In legal settings it also depends upon a knowledge of procedure and conversational forms as well as a more general capacity or confidence that will allow the respondent both to question or oppose legal dialect (the community of legal language) and to risk the possibility of sanction.

The question of the accessibility of legal preconstructions to those without the linguistic community of lawyers is amenable to a relatively swift answer. At its most general level, the discourse of law is that of an authoritative prior discourse which for the bulk of its history has been encoded either in an alien language or in an archaic register of the vernacular. While the function of that restricted coding is primarily that of authorising particular speakers or enunciative modalities – irrespective of the specific content of their speech, as is most obviously the case with a lay magistrature who are forced to rely upon legally qualified court clerks for esoteric points of law – a few comments may also be passed on the general semantic features of law as prior discourse. Restricting the discussion somewhat, the over-whelming empirical evidence is to the effect that the language of statute, precedent, jury instructions and argument on points of law is inaccessible even to those non-lawyers with several years' experience of higher education.[1] The available tests of comprehension are by no means precise but the CLOZE test, to take one example, is considered an adequate measure of comprehension for commercial, educational and publishing purposes. The test simply involves the deletion of every fifth word of a text which then has to be completed by the respondent. In tests conducted at Loyola University, Los Angeles, by Professor Robert Benson,[2] codified jury instructions and a Federal labour relations statute were amongst the documents used on a group of highly educated non-lawyers, 90 per cent of whom had attended higher education and 28 per cent of whom had done

1 See, for example, R. P. Charrow and V. R. Charrow, 'Making Legal Language Understandable: A Psycholinguistic Study of Jury Instructions' (1979) 79 *Columbia Law Review* 1306; A. Lind and W. O'Barr, 'The Social Significance of Courtroom Speech' in H. Giles and R. St Clair (eds.), *Language and Social Psychology* (1979, Oxford).

2 R. Benson, 'The End of Legalese', op. cit., at 536–47.

some post-graduate work. The CLOZE criterion of minimum adequate comprehension is a 55 per cent score. The jury instructions scored 48.6 per cent and the Federal statute 39.2 per cent. Translated on to the rather more vivid Flesch scale, an educational test based upon word and syllable counts, legal documents fared even worse. The Flesch criterion of minimum adequate comprehension is a score of plus 40. Amongst the documents tested, the trust clause from a 1983 federal case scored minus 55, a 1982 Vocational Education Act scored minus 83, a 1982 Social Security Act scored minus 132, while the winning score of minus 219 went, not entirely inappropriately, to a 1976 Ethics in Government Act.

Whatever the variations in reliability of the tests used, the general conclusion is that legal documentation, as a reservoir or lexicon of pre-established meanings within the discourse of law, is satisfactorily proven to annul ordinary discourse – in the case of a score of minus 219, it does so to the point of absurdity. In considering the significance of such data for the analysis of legal dialogue and specifically of audience, two further observations pointing in a contrary direction are pertinent. The first is that tests of comprehension are generally based upon lexical and syntactic features of discourse and do not directly test comprehension in terms of 'gist' or effect. In that respect it is interesting that, when Charrow and Charrow tested jury comprehension of formally drafted instructions in Maryland by means of a paraphrase test, the fact that they scored between 45 per cent and 54 per cent did not preclude the conclusion that in the overwhelming majority of cases, even where the instructions were clearly not understood, the jurors, inventing their own meaning for the instructions, acted (unwittingly) within the spirit of the formally drafted instructions. The point is an interesting one in terms of the assumptions to be made with regard to listening or viewing positions more generally. The second qualification of the results summarised above concerns the degree of acquiescence that is to be imputed to audiences. Recent important studies of audience reception[1] clearly indicate that, even where programmes are very

1 D. Morley, *The Nationwide Audience* (1980, London); Morley, 'The Nationwide Audience, A Critical Postscript' (1981) *Screen Education* 39; K. Richardson and J. Corner, 'Reading Reception' (1986) 8 *Media, Culture, Society* 458; J. Corner and K. Richardson, 'The Documentary Viewer and the Discourse of Interpretation', in J. Corner (ed.), *Documentary and the Mass Media* (1986, London).

clearly framed to present a particular ideological bias, audiences are frequently competent to view such presentations in a 'mediated' or 'oppositional' manner which takes full account of the framing or structured preferences of presentation.

   In the context of legal dialogue it should not, therefore, be assumed that the annexation of non-legal dialects is universally successful or unopposed. In an example again drawn from Arrears and Maintenance,[1] the defendant recognises yet ironically challenges the assumptions of the court:

> M: Well if you flatly refuse to accept the order of the court there's only one alternative – then you'll go to prison.
> D: Yeh.
> M: Is that what you're saying?
> D: Yes.
> M: [To the usher] Will you fetch a policeman?
> D: You can't do it now . . . I'm still uh under psychiatric treatment.
> M: You can receive that in prison Mr A.
> D: Oh thank you.
> M: You can't tell – you can't refuse to do something and tell us what we can do at the same time you know.
> D: That's the system isn't it?

The magistrate makes explicit that the defendant has broken the rules of courtroom discourse in challenging the power of the court to use force. An underlying assumption of the court is called into question and elicits a coercive response. In general the contestation of legal preconstructions does not and for obvious reasons cannot take the form of a response to the details of what is implied in the legal evaluation of behaviour. It tends rather to hinge upon generically expressed dissatisfaction with the fairness or justice of decisions in which, as in matters of legal meaning, the magistrature are arbiters of moral rectitude as it impinges upon legal obligations:

> M: Do you think it is a reasonable thing that a wife and child shall be without your support whilst you still enjoy the additional pleasure of colour television in your home . . . does that seem a reasonable thing to do?

---

1   Harris (1987), op. cit., p. 211; see also, Harris, 'The Form and Function of Threats in Court' (1984) 4 *Language and Communication* 247.

D: Depends on which way you look at it don't it?

M: Well looking at it from any reasonable point of view – is it reasonable for anybody to have the pleasure and the luxury of a colour television when a wife and child could be going without food ... whichever way you look at it is that reasonable?

D: Well I don't know because if I didn't have a colour telly I'd just spend my time – in the pubs then wouldn't I?

M: Well you're not forced to do it – I don't have a colour television and I don't spend my time in the pubs – there's no compulsion to make you go to the pub because you don't have a colour television ...

...

D: No I don't agree with you.

In formal terms, counter-questioning by means of tags endeavours, ineffectively, to challenge the preconstructed meaning of the possession of a television and to draw the magistrate into agreeing with the proposition expressed in the declarative part of the utterance.[1] In the circumstances of the case, as reported by Sandra Harris, the defendant wished (justifiably or not) to introduce evidence of the wife's current, relatively affluent, circumstances as relevant to the question of reasonableness. In its magnificent generality, however, the question of reasonableness is pre-eminently a matter for the closely guarded confines of specifically legal discourse, which means in effect that, whatever the mundane moral content of the discourse of the law, it is pronounced *ex cathedra* and as a consequence of its judicial source cannot be challenged even though the definition of 'fairness', 'reasonableness' or 'common sense' would not seem to be an exclusively legal skill.

The case of *Masterson and another* v. *Holden*[2] constitutes an interesting and fairly typical example of moral valuation dressed up as legal knowledge. Under s. 54 (13) of the Metropolitan Police Act 1839: 'Every person shall be liable to a penalty ... who shall use any threatening, abusive, or insulting Words or Behaviour with Intent to

---

1 For a study of these terms, see D. Rokosz, 'Cross-Talk: Pragmatics and Courtroom Questioning' (1988, Edinburgh).

2 [1986] 3 All ER 39.

provoke a Breach of the Peace, or whereby a Breach of the Peace may be occasioned.' What is to be constructed as behaviour intended to occasion a breach of the peace is pre-eminently a matter of value-judgment concerned with norms of interaction, the justification of behaviour, the reasonableness of responses and the semantic import of an 'insult'. In the case in question, two men 'cuddling each other and kissing each other' in Oxford Street at 1.55 a.m. were found guilty of the offence of insulting behaviour intended to provoke a breach of the peace and were bound over to keep the peace. On appeal to the Divisional Court of the Queen's Bench Division before Justice Glidewell, the decision at first instance was upheld on the strength of the legally sanctioned reasonableness of the reaction of two other couples:

> Two couples were walking along the south footway of Oxford Street. First there were two young men about twenty-one years of age [AB] and second two young women of about twenty . . . The case finds that the two young men appeared not to notice them [the defendants] but the two young women stopped opposite the defendants and one of them raised a hand to her mouth and both of them ran up to the two young men [AB]. After a short conversation one of the girls pointed at the defendants who were still cuddling . . . Both of the young men [AB] then walked towards the defendants and one of them shouted: 'You filthy sods. How dare you in front of our girls?'[1]

While the issues involved in *Masterson* were pre-eminently political and moral (and as such will form the basis of the analysis in the next chapter), doctrine has always sought to separate such issues from the putatively normative sphere of legal argument. Although the predominant categories of legal argument and judgment concern broadly drawn and necessarily changing notions of reason, fairness and justice as the criteria of interpretation of legal rules, and despite the didactic epithets of approval and disapproval that ground the majority of judgments, challenges to that legal pedagogy on forms of behaviour and lifestyle must take the form of extra-legal, political protest and lobbying. To be heard in court, arguments must be reformulated in the abstract legal terms of the case, presented on cue and subject to the potentially censorious intervention of the court. By way of conclusion, it may be noted that resistance to the legal imposition of order and forms of argument in court is generally

1   Ibid., 40.

disadvantageous. There is, however, an occasional yet interesting history of lay participants in trials disregarding legal forms.

That history centres around the changing role and presence of the jury in the common law tradition. In its earliest form the jury was chosen from amongst the peer group of the accused and was arbiter of both fact and law (generally custom). More recently, its role has been restricted to that of fact finding, but on occasions where the law to be applied has appeared too out of keeping with contemporary mores or when the sentences likely to be passed are felt to be too draconian, the jury still retains a right to find the accused not guilty irrespective of the legal direction that they have received from the judge. One such instance would be the earlier-mentioned case of *R*. v. *Ponting*, where the judge had at one point in the trial threatened to stop proceedings on the ground that no legally relevant defence had been presented to the charge laid under the Official Secrets Act. In the event, the jury acquitted Ponting in the face of a judicial summing-up that had made it quite clear that in law the defence presented had to be disregarded. In the more recent American case of *State of Massachusetts* v. *Allain, Carter, Clay and others*,[1] a defence of necessity was pleaded to a charge of disorderly conduct and trespass. Students were charged in relation to demonstrations at the University of Massachusetts which had attempted to draw attention to and protest against Central Intelligence Agency recruitment techniques on American campuses. The defence of necessity involved arguing that the misdemeanours committed were justified on moral grounds as being necessary to prevent the commission of graver crimes by the CIA. Evidence was brought by the defence of subversion, political murder, terrorism and other illegal acts committed by the CIA in the course of 'intelligence gathering' worldwide. Although it was made plain in summing up that the CIA were not a party to the case and that much of the defence argument was in consequence irrelevant, the jury acquitted. The case is interesting in that it represents the first reported occasion on which the defence of necessity, which has been regularly ruled out in nuclear weapons protest cases, has been allowed. It is unlikely that its admission in a first-instance case in Massachusetts will greatly alter its status in common law, nor is it likely that rare occasions of what are generally legally regarded as 'perverse verdicts' will do anything to

1 Transcript, 1987, April 14–15.

radicalise the structural constraints within which the overwhelming majority of cases receive their momentary legal audition.

7

The Enchanted Past:
A Semiotics of Common Law

'Other countries, my prince, are not in such an happy situation, are not
so well stored with inhabitants. Though there be in other parts of the
world, persons of rank and distinction, men of estates and possessions,
yet they are not so frequent, and so near situated one to another, as in
England.'[1]

A semiotics of law studies all the different means by which law is
communicated.[2] One of its principal objects is obviously the language
of law. In relation to common law it must thus provide some account
of the paradoxical fact that English law comes clothed not in the
English language but in Latin, French and Middle English, an
archaic form of English itself. The language of law, however, is only
one medium of transmission of law. The fact that the language of
English law is in many aspects a foreign dialect indeed indicates that
it is unlikely to be widely read outside the profession. The texts of law
are thus likely to have symbolic rather than an immediately semantic
– i.e. linguistic – content. For a semiotics of law this point is crucial. It
is through symbols, through the forms of appearance and

1   Sir John Fortescue, *De Laudibus Legum Angliae* (1737, London), p. 64.

2   There is no standard introduction to semiotics, but M. Blomsky (ed.) *On
Signs* (1985, Oxford) is a good guide. There is also interesting material in J. Deeley
(ed.), *Frontiers in Semiotics* (1986, Indiana). Specifically on legal semiotics, see : D.
Carzo and B. Jackson (eds.), *Semiotics, Law and Social Science* (1985, Rome/
Liverpool), and R. Kevelson (ed.), *Law and Semiotics*, Volumes 1–3 (1987–89, New
York), for essays on all aspects of legal semiotics. See also, R. Kevelson, *Law
as a System of Signs* (1988, New York), and B. Jackson, *Semiotics and Legal Theory*
(1985, London), for more sophisticated works from very different perspectives.
For specialist work in law and semiotics, refer to the *International Journal for the
Semiotics of Law* which is now in its sixth volume.

representation of law in the public sphere, that the public generally recognises law as the speech and action of either a legitimate or simply a *de facto* sovereign social power.

In this chapter we will concentrate upon the Englishness of English law and particularly upon the images, symbols and other icons through which common law as a tradition is transmitted. In cultural and so also semiotic terms a tradition, legal or otherwise, is not an historical discipline, it is not a rational, proven or evidenced sense of the past but much more a mythology, an unconscious reservoir of images and symbols, of fictive narratives and oracular (or immemorial) truths. A semiotics of common law must thus pursue the tradition through its images, through the forms in which it is seen, precisely because it is as an image, as a sign that law is recognised, accepted and lived. It is not as a system of rules that the individual is born into and adheres to the law as an aspect of everyday life. The law as a structure of material life, as an institution, is a system of images, and it is through its symbolisation of authority and through its signs of power that the law dwells within the subject. The law is in that sense nothing other than its image, no more and no less than a sign; it is the spectacle of the scaffold, the aura of judgment, the sense of the normal.

Introduction: The Very Idea

Instead of presenting a theory – another theory – of semiotics, language and law, this chapter will approach the question of law as a sign, as a symbol and as a word in its copious particularlity. The path followed will be that of an analysis of a specific legal system, that of dear, vile England, of the common law, and of a specific text, a single case in public law. The theme to be pursued in this particular manner is that of the politics of the legal text: what is this language that we call law; what is this speech that lasts longer than non-liturgical or non-legal annunciation; what is this place, this text, this mouth, from which law speaks; who speaks when law speaks? To answer such questions will take us into the realm of what is technically termed legal grammatology: that is, the realm of law as a system of material signs, of things that circulate. We will find the law in particular words inscribed on particular things, codes for example, or statute books or the notice boards that replaced the town crier, or in the lists that name the law terms, the courts and the litigants in cases to be heard. It will be found in created objects, nomadically, according to the places and times at which the law sits. If we are here to present an analysis of the various forms in which law is encoded, of the signs or the languages through which we have access to it, then we might list four levels of legal appearance, of material objects or of sites of legal presence: the iconic, the symbolic, the textual and the spoken will be the avenues of approach adopted here.

Imagine for an instant a particular ideal object, law for example, the law spoken of by Coke in the *Institutes* and the *Reports*. As it is found there, it is more than anything else English law: that is, it is related immediately to the English, to a language and the history of that language as it has coalesced in hereditaments, in forms of property and in forms of collectivity or government. That the law is English law is a site to which this chapter will return many times; England, and more especially English as the peculiar elocution of a national geography, is the particular soil and the specific representational form that the common law adopts. Initially, however, we should think of the law as a language and as the context, the materiality, of a language. In Coke we thus learn to consider the law as a peculiar 'grammar', as a 'special language' unknown to the grammarians but significant to the lawyers: it is 'no ordinary scrivening' of any scrivener's boy in his master's shop.[1] Interesting what ties the law (in Coke) to a language, to English, even though that English is not English at all, but part law Latin, part law French and part middle English – an archaic vernacular.

That the language of English law transpires not to be English at all, that the common law is indeed a foreign law, a nomadic incursion that came with the Celts, the Romans, the Angles, the Saxons, the Vikings

1   Sir Edward Coke, *Reports* (1777 edn), Pt II, fol. A6a–b refers to questions of law as being more often than not errors of transcription, the produce of instruments made by unlearned men or 'wills intricately, absurdly, and repugnantly set down by parsons, scriveners and other such imperites . . .' In its proper sphere and memorised through perfect inscription, the literature of the common law is *testi temporum, veritatis vitae, nuncio vetustatis* – the witness of time, the life of truth, the herald of the age old, of the *longue durée* (pt I, A4a). To take it one step further, Coke even presents a theory of the eternal return of the same common law, arguing in pt II, C3a, that even where ignorance or impetuosity have deplorably led to 'some points of ancient common law [being] altered or diverted from his due course, yet in revolution of time, the same . . . have been with great applause, for avoiding any inconveniences, restored again . . .'

and then the Normans, allows for some interesting observations as to movement, boundaries and ethnicity.[1] Just as the language of the common law was and is a much-travelled heteroglossia, just as it is at the very heart of its insularity foreign, so also we should recognise that, as a language, law does not refer to any anterior realm of legal things; it refers simply to the system of legal notation, to other signs of law, to other legal texts.[2] In this sense, if we wish to think of language and law, or of signs and law, we can do so only through recognition of the difference that constitutes that language or system: the language of law is a language that is subject to law, that is a servant to legal forms of reference, to the rattle of juridical definitions in the form of arbitrary yet obligatory reference to precedent texts.[3] The law is a form of writing, but it is also a form of speech. In both instances it is necessary to understand that at the heart of the legal text (graphic or phonic) lies a foreign body, an alien or nomadic meaning, the

1   There is an extensive debate on Englishness and law, which ranges from popular assertions of the need for a break with Rome and with tincture of Normanism to eulogies of the antiquity and excellence of a peculiary English, an eternally English, law as found by Sir John Fortescue, for example, in *De Laudibus Legum Angliae*; (1737 edn): 'I am convinced that our laws of England eminently excel, beyond the laws of all other countries . . .' (p.64), or again in *De Politica administratione et Legibus Civilibus florentissimi Regni Angliae*, '. . . wherefore the contrary is not to be said nor thought, but that the English customs are very good, yea of all other the very best'. Coke, pt VI, Z2a, makes the argument that 'if the ancient laws of this noble island, had not excelled all others it could not be but some of the several conquerors and governors thereof, that is to say the Romans, Saxons, Danes, or Normans, and especially the Romans . . . would have altered or changed the same'. Sir Henry Spelman, *The Original of the Four Law Terms of the Year* (1614/1695, London), p. 99, marvels that Coke did not realise that such was precisely what the Romans, the Saxons, the Danes and the Normans had done: 'I do marvel many times, that my Lord Coke, adorning our law with so many flowers of antiquity and foreign learning, has not yet turned aside into this field [that of foreign law] from whence so many roots of our law, have of old been taken and transplanted.'

2   The point is elaborated well in Pierre Legendre, *L'Empire de la vérité* (1983, Paris), p. 103: 'aesthetics further teaches us this: truth is a place, by hypothesis an empty place, somewhere where there is nothing, if not for texts. We constantly re-encounter this point, because if dogmatics has a constant theme, it is in relation to a truth which is resident precisely in texts. Reference is reference to texts.' More generally, see B. Rotman, *Signifying Nothing, The Semiotics of Zero* (1987, London).

3   On the general form of such reference see my *Reading the Law* (1986, Oxford), chapters 4 and 5. For a recent and interesting collection of materials see S. Levinson and S. Mailloux (eds), *Interpreting Law and Literature* (1988, Evanston).

possibility in short of its being read against itself, illicitly or in a supplementary manner. The formal procedure of this chapter will be one that moves from a specific system of law to a specific report and attempts no more than a depiction of those two ideal entities in terms of their visible presence, their attachment to objects and places, to a text and to a language. The order of movement will be from structure to speech, from place to position, from plastic elocution or iconic form to the order of its representatives, its subjects.

The Iconography of English Law

Take as a starting point the notion propounded by one contemporary philosopher that we 'recognise' law in much the same manner that we recognise a language even if we have no conscious grasp of its grammatical rules. The question is, what is it that we recognise, with which we are familiar or at ease? At the level of greatest generality, it can be suggested that what is recognised initially – both in historical and psychological senses – is Englishness, a particular systemic context, a specific system of law tied to a unified sense of geographical and national–political identity. It can be suggested thus as a point of departure that we look precisely for an identity, for that which differentiates common law from other laws, the law of a nation (*ius commune*) from the law of nations (*ius gentium*). The answer is likely to be found in the language and particularly the imagery in which the common law establishes itself as a tradition, as having a separate yet identifiable history, an insular and unique sense of the past. Only once we have identified the elements of that sense of the past, of that time out of mind which is also time immemorial, the basic source of common law, can we endeavour to understand the nature of the English constitution or the character and colour of English law.

In virtually all its pre-classical definitions, the word 'law' – as, for example, halachah, shari'a, Dike or dharma – refers either directly or incidentally to the path, the way or the road: the law is the order of our going; it is the map, the compass, the route taken across a landscape, the direction by which we find the next encampment.[1] The common

---

1   Specifically on dharma, see B. Jackson's interesting comments in 'From Dharma to Law' (1978) *American Journal of Comparative Law*. On law as the road or way, see G. Rose, 'Architecture to Philosophy – The Postmodern Complicity'

law does not differ in its desire to map both a territory and a history, at the same time to provide a path, a series of fixed points across a realm (*lex terrae*), and also to indicate a conceptual lineage, to trace a genealogy or indicate an origin and a line. In this very generic sense, the qualities of Englishness and so of an English law are well established: the common law is the law of the land, a rustic law for rural types. Despite innumerable conquests, the English law is sacred and stretches back to the halcyon times of King Arthur, to Cornwall, to Camelot. It can be traced also beyond the time of memory, beyond the imaginings of 'the best historians',[1] to an originary time and a lost place, the place where dwell the vast hosts of the dead, the ancestors. The time of the law is constantly specified as that of ancient custom, a time of inheritance, antiquity and establishment about which we learn through the arcane and wise books of the law. Despite the Greek, the Latin and the French, which even Coke recognised as elements of legal language, these books and their disparate knowledges are said to have survived all the invasions of England and have perpetuated the ancient realm, the sceptred isle, the immemorial knowledge.

The legal knowledge with which we are here concerned is that of an English law which enshrines the particular national code, an inheritance that is closer to nature and to divine law than any other existent system of laws.[2] It is the law of the land, of old England, a land peopled by the freeborn, by the gentle and honest, by justice and juries, by liberties and the continuity of immemorial custom, its

---

(1988) 5 *Theory, Culture, Society* 357 at 359–60. On dike, see E. Benveniste, *Le Vocabulaire de institutions Indo-Européenes* (1969, Paris), vol. II, pp. 107–10.

1   For Coke indeed the antiquity of the common law is so apparent and well attested that the books and records, the annals, 'need not the aid of any historian' [pt VIII, L3a–b]. Elsewhere we find both King Arthur and King Brutus as the first English Kings, as the originary authors of our law. Thus, referring to the *Mirror of Justices*, he remarks that 'in this ancient mirror you may also clearly discern as far as the reign of the often named King Arthur, the great antiquity of the officers and ministers of the common law, and of their inferior courts' (pt IX, C2a). The reference to Brutus 'the first king of this land' is in *Reports*, II, B1a. For more popular expressions of similar sentiments see, for example, *The Englishman's Right* (1680, London).

2   Fortescue's *De Laudibus* is the earliest explicit proponent of this view. Further expressions of interest can be found in Sir Thomas Smith, *De Republica Anglorum* (1583/1906, Cambridge); and especially Coke, as for example in *The*

speech, its books and other records. It is a countryside and the English, 'a rustic, active and generous people',[1] are there bathed in the king's peace in which very Englishman's home is his castle and in which Magna Carta secures for all time and unto heaven the innate right of the Englishman to his property and his person. The imagery is distinctive. There is first and foremost an inviolable soil: 'No man can set his foot upon my ground without my licence, but he is liable to an action, though the damage be nothing; which is proved by every declaration in trespass, where the defendant is called upon to answer for bruising the grass and even treading upon the soil.'[2] To the inviolability of a native soil should be added the sanctity of a place, the peace, the quiet, the tranquillity of a home that is castle, fortress and refuge, a space both of repose and of defence. The home is the safest of escapes,[3] so safe indeed that even after the sheriff has made a lawful entry his right to break down 'such inner doors as may happen to be shut' was still worth litigating,[4] so safe that as regards unlawful entry Chief Justice Wilmot ventured that 'the plaintiff being a butcher, or inferior person, makes no difference in the case'.[5]

The immemorial law is an unwritten tradition, an eternally present collective legal memory, something that passes by word of mouth and that is in consequence a tacit knowledge, an attribute of honour and a criterion of manners. The tacit quality of a knowledge, together with decisions that are always already made, already made behind the scenes, are both extremely English phenomena. It is manners or 'good form', chivalry or a sense of fair play, that have traditionally been supposed to act as the bulwark protecting the subject of law from the tyranny of judgment: it is the aristocracy in the upper house of Parliament who have traditionally been supposed to mediate between the sovereign and the governed,[6] a point to which we shall return. For

Second Part of the Institutes of the Laws of England (1681 edn, London), at A2a: 'the best inheritance a subject has is the law of the realm.'

1   Sir T. Smith, *De Republica Anglorum*, op. cit., pp. 60–71. See also the useful discussion in A. Fox and J. Gray, *Reassessing the Henrician Age* (1986, Oxford).

2   *Entick* v. *Carrington* [1765] 19 St. Tr. 1030, at 1066.

3   *Semayne's Case* [1605] 5 Co. Rep. 91a–91b, *domus sua cuique est tutissimum refugium*.

4   *Ratcliffe* v. *Burton* [1802] 27 Eng. Rep. 123, 126.

5   *Bruce* v. *Rawlins* [1770] 95 Eng. Rep. 934.

6   Coke, *Political Catechism* (1680, London), A3b, 'the Lords being trusted with a judicatory power, are an excellent screen and bank between the Prince and the

the moment, consider that the emblems of freeborn Englishness, of ancestral honour and liberty, are the *Magnae Chartae libertatum Angliae*,[1] the Charta de Foresta and particularly the Magna Carta itself, a concession extracted from the Crown, a royal grant primarily concerned with the relationship between Church and monarch and only incidentally with the 'amendment of the realm'. Ironically, as far as liberties are concerned and so as far as the great charter can genuinely be labelled *communis libertas (quia liberos faciunt)* or *chartre de franchises*, Magna Carta simply extorts from the monarch the promise not further to diminish or arbitrarily to extinguish customs and liberties that had formerly been recognised by the Crown. Thus the city of London is guaranteed 'the old liberties and customs', knight's fee will not be further raised, free men will not be forced to build bridges to their homes nor walls around their property and merchants are guaranteed safe passage through the kingdom.

The rights and liberties symbolically affirmed in Magna Carta are all subject to the law of the earth, of the realm, *lex terrae*, which is nothing other than the judgment of the king as *justiciarum regni*, as maker or voice of the law. In that respect even rights as fundamental —that is to say, as ancient[2] – as the writ of habeas corpus (who has the body?) or the inviolability of land or of home are all provisional and defeasible. In *Darnel's Case* the writ of habeas corpus was of no use in the face of committal to prison *per speciale mandatum domini regis* (by special command of His Majesty).[3] Where the realm requires it, the

---

People, to assist each in any encroachments of the other, and by just judgments to preserve that law which ought to be the rule of all three.'

1   Coke, *Institutes II*, Proeme, also termed '*Chartae libertatum Regni . . . quia liberos faciunt*' and '*communis libertas*'. At all events, according to Coke, *Reports*, VIII, L6b, the two charters together contain the bulk of the ancient customs, the inheritance, the antique laws, the birthright of our land: '*quae ex parte maxima leges antiquas et regni consuetudines continebant*'.

2   On the notion of the ancient, see particularly J. G. A. Pocock, *The Ancient Constitution and the Feudal Law* (2nd edn 1987, Cambridge), pp. 30–56. To take one other example, Henry Finch, *Law, or a Discourse Thereof in Four Books* (1627, London) establishes the antiquity of the source as being on the one hand 'time out of mind', brute age, but also and significantly links that disappearance into the immemorial to the aura of the divinity: 'positive laws are framed in the light of natural law and reason and from thence come all the grounds and maxims of the common law, for that which we call common law, is not a word new or strange or barbarous . . . but the right term for all other laws' (Bk I, fol. 74–5).

3   [1627] 3 St Tr 1.

king has also always had a prerogative right of access to soil and to property, to papers, to diaries, even to the post.[1] The very title given to Magna Carta, *Charta libertatum Regni*, indicates that these are liberties by and of the ruler, of the sovereign and not of the governed. We are left with an image of freeborn and gentle, and indeed natural, Englishness which is notable less for its antiquity than for its insecurity: the ancient order is an order of vassalage, of dominium and service, a feudal order in which every subject is a tenant of the Crown and liable, when the realm requires, to serve and to die for a soil that is not his or her own.[2]

If we return to the question of the iconic unity of law as that which we recognise when we first recognise law as being our law, the image is of old England, an England that is eternal: it is our environment, our landscape, our nature, both mystical and thoughtless. It is at one level a purely internal history, the history of the survival of the English line, the history of the exclusion or repression of all forms of foreigness, even (or especially) when such foreigness is in our midst as language, as conqueror or, indeed, as royal family. In a secondary sense, the internal character of the history of the English is a product of the fact that it is not a considered or explicit history; it is nature in the sense that it is given and indisputable. What is English, be it law or any other institution, is first and unquestionable. The history is therefore something that can be assumed; it is internal in the sense of being inside all true English, all free English, mystical and inexplicit. In the end it is a family history, a history of a domestic constitution, a constitution that is unwritten because gentlemen do not need to put their word in writing – it is enough simply to give one's word.[3] It is an

---

1 As, for example, in *The Case of the Prerogative of the King in Saltpetre* 12 Co. Rep. 12 at 12–13, allowing access to property for purposes of the defence of the realm, 'although the king cannot take the trees of the subject . . . and he cannot take gravel . . . he cannot charge the subject to make a wall around his own house, or for to make a bridge to come to his house. The ministers of the king cannot undermine, weaken or impair any of my wall or foundations of any house, be they mansion, houses, or outhouses or barns, stables, dove houses, mills or any other buildings . . . for that my house is the subject place for my refuge, my safety and comfort of all my family . . .'

2 On *pro patria mori*, see E. Kantorowicz, *Selected Studies* (1965, New York), pp. 308–24, and idem, *The King's Two Bodies* (1957, New Jersey), pp. 232–73.

3 See for example, *Kingston v. Preston* (1773) 2 Doug 689, 99 ER 437, where Lord Mansfield famously argues to the effect that provided that there is

unwritten constitution also because domestic agreements are outside the law; they are irreducible to law for the simple reason that no one would wish to jeopardise the harmony or honour of family agreements by taking them to court, just as it is still the case even today that no one can threaten a marriage by taking a husband to court for rape of his wife.[1] The question remains as regards the constitution, whose body, whose family, which line?

The authors of the ancient tradition are quite explicit: the constitution is one of 'regulated monarchy' and, as Coke also puts it, the Crown is the hieroglyph of all our laws. If we turn to the icon itself, the licit representation of our nation and of our national legal system – the two are inseparable[2] – it is the monarchy that paradoxically coheres both the identity of our character and the unity of the national legal system. The point is one which has been made variously in historical terms through the analysis of the *corpus mysticum* or undying royal body and its various forms of portraiture,[3] while in the specific terms of the common law as it exists today, there is the exhaustive and excellent study by Tom Nairn[4] of the quintessentially monarchical character of the historical and contemporary English constitution. What he also makes abundantly clear is the dependency of the national psyche, the media, the communications industry, the entire fabric of social placement and personal differentiation, upon one icon, one family, one Crown. If we move now to examine what it is that we belong to, what constitutes our culture and our law, before we read any individual text, it is the monarchy that will emblematise the space of law, the depth of structure, the waking and the sleeping dream. It is precisely to a monarchical culture that we belong before we read; it is from that culture that we make our decisions as to interpretation and

contractual intention, a parole contract is binding, even though consideration is lacking – the word is enough.

  1   See for example *Balfour* v. *Balfour* [1919] 2 KB 271; on rape in marriage, see *R.* v. *Miller* [1954] 2 All ER 529.

  2   Coke, *Institutes II*, p. 74: '*major hereditas venit unicuique nostrum a iure et legibus quam a parentibus.*'

  3   For excellent studies of the portraiture of monarchy, and analysis of the appropriately iconic forms of such presentation, see particularly L. Marin, 'Le Corps Glorieux du Roi et son Portrait' in *La Parole mangée* (1986, Paris) and L. Marin, *Portrait of the King* (1988, London).

  4   Tom Nairn, *The Enchanted Glass* (1988, London). Interestingly reviewed by A. Carty, 'Of Crabs and Constitutions' (1989) 5 *International Journal for the Semiotics of Law* 215.

state with each judgment our allegiance to a literal Englishness, to an identity that excludes all consideration of any other culture or any other way.

The elements of an unwritten constitution can be listed with relative brevity. The key to the English constitution – to how we 'stand together' (*con-statuere*) – is precisely that it is unwritten, that it is tacit and traditional; it is law as dharma, as way or path or road, as a manner of doing things, as good form, and not as an idea or a dialogue or even as anything to be thought about. In that sense it is pure tradition and can in consequence be understood only by those with a head for the symbolical. To begin the list of elements we should thus note that precisely at its head, as the pinnacle of the constitution, is the monarchy. Not a day passes without news of the monarchy in all the media: it may be deemed trivial but in quantitative terms there is an irrefragable significance to the circulation of one symbol, of one icon, of one family, of what we are as represented in the comings and goings, the doings and sayings, the court news and the state functions of the royalty, the royal family. The search for an identity could thus well begin with a statement of the obvious: the constitution as it exists today was primarily the product of the arrogation of the powers of the Church to the Crown in 1532. The monarch became both spiritual and secular sovereign, Leviathan twice over, the inerasable and singular image of a national legal system that had broken with Rome and with the Roman Church. Law, as the frequently misread philosopher John Austin had no hesitation in specifying,[1] was best defined affectively as being no more nor less than the command of the sovereign: a command that could be positive and direct or could take the more subtle form of adoption of existing law or tacit command in the form of the judgments of the sovereign's judicial representatives.

As regards the realms of adoption and tacit command, we move into the realm (the *regalis*) of the unsaid or unstated of a legal system that has accumulated or found law far more often than it would claim to have directly devised it. Law as tradition depends upon the notion that what is established requires no further or no rational justification; it simply belongs, it is there, part of the system of symbols that constitute a legal identity and system of law. Insofar as it is surprising and could be amusing, we can borrow some statistics from Nairn's

---

1   For discussion of such misreadings of Austin, see R. Moles, *Definition and Rule in Legal Theory* (1987, Oxford).

Enchanted Glass to suggest the extent to which the monarchy as symbol pervades the national consciousness, and its unconscious as well. Taken from surveys in the late 1960s and the 1970s, we learn that 77 per cent of Labour (socialist) voters would retain the monarchy (the royal family does no harm), 50 per cent of the unemployed would retain the monarchy, over 50 per cent of the population believe that God took a special interest in England, 'that God guides this country in times of trouble', and finally over a third of the population has dreamt about the royal family. The statistics can be added to the other indices of a quiet but obsessive national concern with the Crown, with its omnipresence in public life, and the question to be posed is that of how serious that pervasive regality is in terms of the constitution of our laws.

In a perfectly literal sense, the Crown heads the constitution and is the author of our laws: it is the Queen in Parliament that is the constitutional legislator, the sovereign body. Parliament is opened by the Queen, the Queen's speech announces the legislative programme and the government itself is the Queen's government, a government appointed by the Crown and terminable by it as well. If we move to the text of legislation itself, the preamble of every statute takes the form of the words: 'Be it enacted by the Queen's most excellent majesty, by and with the advice and consent of the Lords Spiritual and Temporal, and Commons, in this present Parliament assembled, and by the authority of the same . . .'. It is interesting that the 'upper house' is the House of Lords, where by virtue of a principle of heredity, a principle of pure genealogy, peers of the realm – which is to say of the Crown's jurisdiction, of the *regalis* – both spiritual and temporal sit as of right, and as of birthright, to legitimate the enactments of the Crown's government initiated from 'the other place'. The key to an understanding of the significance, the absolutism, of a monarchical and wholly pre-revolutionary constitution does not lie in the literal manifestations of monarchism, in its ordinariness or its triviality, but in the impossible and unspoken realm of everyday power that circulates alone lines of force that emanate from the throne. Let us continue the list, but now in terms of symbols that refer the citizen, the litigant, the subject, to the liturgical or inaugural space of the monarchy, of that mystic body that never dies: 'King is a name of Continuance, which will always endure as the Head and Governor of the People (as the Law presumes) as long as the People continue . . . ; and in this Name the King never dies.'[1] We may go further than Justice Brown and observe that not only does the King, as mystic body, or body politic, never die, but the political and legal attributes of that body, its mystic members, its offices and honours, statuses and creeds do not, cannot, die either. To adopt a classical civilian motif, *dignitas non moritur* – dignity, meaning office and honour, do not die, though we may certainly die for them: we may die for an office, for a country, for honour, for a mask.

What descends most immediately from the Crown is the system of honours and of political privilege. In addition to a complex system of inheritance of title and honour, of status and wealth, there is also and crucially the continued creation of new honours lists: the reward for a life in politics is the conferment of any one of an infinitely varied and nuanced hierarchy of honours, of dignities and estates that stretch from simple membership of the royal court, to the various orders of merit and Empire, to knighthood, baronetcy, peerage and hereditary peerage, to the greater estates of Viscount, Earl, Marquis and Duke. These are estates and offices that do not die; they are the members, the limbs, of an eternal or mystic body, part of old England, of England as tradition and as class; they are part of our gentility, our status, our honour. The hierarchy of honour, of an honour that speaks, that pervades all aspects of cultural and institutional life, from products manufactured 'By Appointment to her Majesty the Queen'[2] to the Queen's awards for industry, to the innumerable titular directors and titled members of company boardrooms, to the ennoblement of members of the judiciary and the right of Law Lords to sit in the upper house as a court, as a club and lastly as a political body. Finally, consider how it is precisely those people who belong most immediately to the political system and who have thereby the power to change the institutions and the constitution, to introduce some element of reality, of democracy, who are precisely those who stand the greatest chance of preferment or privilege through the honours list.[3] They have, in a word, a vested interest in that

---

1   *Willion* v. *Berkley*, Plowden Reports, 3 Eliz 177a, discussed in Kantorowicz, *The King's Two Bodies*, op. cit., at pp. 11–15. For an extended discussion of the metaphor of the body and the continuance of dignities, see P. Legendre, *Le Désir politique de dieu* (1988, Paris), pp 39 42.

2   Meaning that a jar of black treacle once got lost in the Royal pantry or that the crown prince once smoked a pipe.

3   See Nairn, op. cit., for extended discussion, pp. 311–15. 'Honour is the

continuance which the law bestows upon the name of authority, the name of the Crown and its essentially feudal demesnes and domains.

Much if not all of what is done, in terms of appointments and institutional and political decision making, bears some relation to that system of monarchical culture, even if it requires either inside knowledge or extensive archaeology mixed with intuition to discover quite what that relation is. We will return to other aspects of that symbolism. If we remain in search of the *regalis*, of the Crown in public or abroad, we must look to the courts. In one of its earliest guises the court was the Royal Court, it was the Royal Household or 'the body of persons who form the [sovereign's] suite or council' and accompany the king's person on its constant journey through the kingdom and other possessions.[1] As *curia regis (coram rege)* it was also the first court of the common law, though the notion of the court as that which follows the Crown, as a suite or continuance, provides a useful insight into both senses of court, as sites of etiquette and decorum in their proper senses – that of ceremonies of court – as well as being sites of judgment or mercy, preferment or punishment. The court follows the Crown; it is peripatetic as part of the royal entourage and later itinerant through delegation: the provincial courts and assizes are simply the Royal Court 'sitting elsewhere', the king's person in its capacity of body politic rather than natural being.

That the court is the Royal Court sitting in the absence of the monarch does not in any sense preclude the presencing of majesty. The labyrinthine structure of the Royal Courts of Justice amply indicate an architecture of place, a pageantry and regality that constitute in the most direct of senses a plastic elocution of an iconic authority: the name of the law is to be found endlessly repeated in the alternative space and the other time of the court.[2] Consider the iconic

spiritual money of Monarchy: a coinage which, though now distributed by governments, owes its real value to the Royal source . . . Through ennoblement or recognition the symbol world constantly repenetrates reality, re-transforming it into the spiritual commodity of place' (pp. 311, 314).

1   See, for example, S. F. Milsom, *Historical Foundations of the Common Law* (1981, London), pp. 31–3.

2   On the iconicity of authority see P. Legendre, *La Passion d'être un autre* (1978, Paris), pp. 257–71; also idem, *L'Inestimable Objet de la transmission* (1985, Paris), at p. 38: 'the authority of genealogy comes from the authority of texts, founded upon the principle of reason. That is the great lesson to be drawn from the history of Roman law: that the power and the authority of reason are the same thing.' If we ask how that power of reason is instituted, the answer is through the iconic image,

order of licit representation as it is to be found in the architectural organisation of a court, in the symbolics of its physical places, in the aura of its furniture and gargoyles, in its inscriptions and devices (crests and arms), in its modes of dress and of address, and finally in its terms, its moments of appearance and disappearance, of sitting and of dissolution. The list could be indefinitely extended but our concern is with that panoply of symbols that exist to create a legal place, a space of law, of legal annunciation[1] in which a discourse becomes solemnised, a language approaches a liturgy, and the signs are all there to indicate the distances necessary to a place, the distances that will allow the judge to speak in the mask of the Other, to speak innocently as a mouth of the law.[2] The places are mapped according to criteria of ascension and both physically and verbally all points look up to and are directed towards the bench, upon which, after the ushers have demanded silence and respect, it is the Law that sits down in the place of merely human demands. Consider too the forms of dress, the apparel of justice,[3] the order of its coming and

through the placement of the subject in relation to that image. In Legendre's more aphoristic style, 'the institution of the image is the medium by which genealogy [i.e. Law] gets under our skin' (p. 55). It takes possession, we will argue, of the emotional body.

1   Annunciation of course is enunciation but with a phonetically indiscernible difference. The biblical annunciation brought news of her pregnancy to Mary via the Archangel Gabriel. It was both the announcement and simultaneously the presence of the Holy Spirit in her womb. In secular terms the annunciation of an institution refers, I would suggest, to the aura of authority, the mode of presence that has to be brought to law for it to be law.

2   There is a very little work on the details of courtroom architecture from a semiotic perspective. There is A. Garapon, *L'Ane portant des reliques* (1985, Paris) and P. Hirst, 'Constructed Space and the Subject' in R. Fardon (ed.), *Power and Knowledge* (1985, Edinburgh). For an interesting development of Foucault's concept of the panopticon and panoptic visibility, see J-A. Miller, 'Jeremy Bentham's Panoptic Device' (1986) *October* 3.

3   The classic study of dress is, of course, T. Carlyle, *Sartor Resartus* (1893 edn, London), and contains some magnificent passages of criticism of the mentality of the outside, of the cloth: 'the beginning of all wisdom is to look fixedly on Clothes'. The philosophical underpinning of such criticism is less sound if no less commendable, and it is summarised in the following observation from early in the study: 'Happy he who can look through the clothes of a man (the woollen, and fleshly, and official Bank-paper and state paper clothes) into the man himself; and discern, it may be, in this or other dread potentate, a more or less incompetent digestive-apparatus . . .' (p. 45). The argument against such a clinical dismembering or at least divestment of the subject from his apparel, is put by L. Marin, *La*

going and the restriction upon the forms in which it can be addressed, the various metonymies as well as the sacral appellations: the court, the bench, your honour, your worship, your lordship.

Insofar as it is a specific web of monarchical symbols that we are pursuing in the name of a nation and its laws, the specific dignities or offices or roles that are played in the court can be left as details to be added by others. For our list, the other point of importance concerns the geography of the court: the Royal Court is based in London, originally at Westminster and now on the Strand,[1] and when it has sat elsewhere, it has sat away from London, as London in the provinces. What the Court takes with it is the awful logic of the centre, the English tradition, the custom of the realm, which is of course the custom of the Crown. Consider again that English is first a language and second a law, the common law. Immediately prior to the era when Sir Edward Coke, Sir John Davies and others were forging the records of the English legal tradition and creating the secular myth of the common law, Richard Mulcaster, Henry Peacham, Thomas Wilson, Sir Thomas Elyot and others less well remembered were nurturing English as the national and the best of all language.[2] Consider then the work of a barrister, George Puttenham, on the geography of correct linguistic usage. You:

> shall follow generally the better brought up sort, such as the Greeks call [*charientes*] men civil and graciously behaved and bred. Our matter therefore at these days shall not follow Piers Plowman nor Gower nor

Parole mangée, (op. cit., pp. 217–25, arguing that the image is only comprehensible as an impossible unity, as embedded in a history, as a deep structure or habitual body.

1 'Strand': (i) the margin or beach of the sea or of a lake; v.i., to drift or be driven ashore; v.t., to run aground. (ii) one of the strings or parts that make up a rope . . . (OED).

2 A useful introduction can be found in C. Grayson, 'The Growth of Linguistic National Consciousness in England' in *The Fairest Flower* (1985, Firenze). See also W. S. Howell, *Logic and Rhetoric in England 1500–1700*. Of the contemporary works, see R. Mulcaster, *The First Part of the Elementary* (1582, London), pp. 254–5: 'For is it not a marvellous bondage, to become servants of one tongue for learning's sake [i.e. Latin], the most of our time, with loss of most time, whereas we may have the very same treasure in our own tongue, with the gain of most time? Our own bearing the joyful title of our liberty and freedom, the Latin tongue reminding us, of our thraldom and bondage? I love Rome, but London better, I favour Italy, but England more, I honour the Latin but I worship the English.'

Lydgate nor yet Chaucer neither shall [you] take the terms of Northern men . . . nor in effect any speech beyond the river Trent, though no man can deny but that theirs is the purer English Saxon at this day, yet it is not so courtly or so current as our Southern English, no more is the far Western men's speech . . . ye shall therefore take the usual speech of the court, and that of London and the shires lying about London within 40 miles, and not much above.[1]

Just as the courts follow the Court, English law follows the English language in respect at least of the geography of correct usage, the centrality of records, of places, and the pre-eminence of manners, of forms of correct behaviour and speech as determinative of propriety or, more strongly, of normality. The phonetic basis of class identity is comprehensible only to those who have lived in England: a certain tone, an accent, use of received pronunciation and standard English vocabulary are together the most powerful of indicators of class and determinative of institutional place. It is frequently the case that no more is needed than a few choice, well-spoken words.

The unwritten constitution, the English constitution, is a court-based custom, a series of conventions transmitted through an unwritten knowledge of forms and tacit rules of behaviour associated with the better classes, the better educated, with the honourable and the gentle. Just as the court has its place, namely London, so the people have their places with 'every man in his room of honour according as his place requires'.[2] The distinction of blood, of breeding, of genealogy, has been as important as, possibly more important than, any particular behaviour: 'the distinction between gentle and ungentle, [is one] in which there is as much difference, as between virtue and vice'.[3] It was the lawyers in the main who systematised and spelled out the system of honours, of manners, of proper speech and of social law.[4] We can learn from them. The system of honour depicts or better represents the various forms of ancestral or acquired nobility. As Sir John Ferne defines it, that nobility is derived as a word from the Latin *nobilitas*, which in turn has a root in *nosco*, to know. By extension we might thus argue that the system of nobility

1   G. Puttenham, *The Arte of English Poesie* (1589, London), pp. 120–21.
2   Ridley, op. cit., p. 134.   3   Legh, op. cit., fol. 11b.
4   The major works by members of the Inns of Court include: J. Ferne, *The Blazon of Gentrie*, op. cit.; H. Spelman, *Aspilogia* (1654, London); G. Legh, *The Accedens of Armory* (1562, London); A. Fraunce, *Insignia Armorum*, op. cit.; J. Logan, *Analogia Honorum* (1677, London); J. Bosewell, *Workes of Armorie* (1610, London).

not only signifies 'generosity', namely nobility, of blood and degree which is known by its insignia, which is represented in the 'devise' or mark or crest, but it is also a form of codification, an encoding of knowledge, a hidden language or initiate wisdom even if that wisdom is of manners and mores and of little else. Through their arms the gentle, the honoured, those of social standing, are known and noted. They bear their status on their breast as *symbolica heroica*, as signs of dignity and of birth. What is known and noted, however, is strictly and opaquely encoded. All the treatises of armory emphasise: it is a secret science, known of God;[1] it is the art 'of hieroglyphical or enigmatic symbols and signs, testifying the nobility or gentry' of the bearer;[2] they are 'true symbols',[3] and being 'abstruse and sacred', enigmatic and holy in origin, the meanings of arms of honour are best protected by dark and foreign words.[4]

Retain the notion that, while status is known by a variety of outward forms or signs, the content of breeding, blood or honour is enigmatic; it is itself esoteric knowledge protected by the very symbol that proclaims it. While nepotism may no longer be so obviously related to family or to upbringing, while its forms may be marginally more diffuse, the system has hardly changed. The unwritten constitution simply symbolises the tacit character of our governmental arrangements and of our law-making élite. Government, like everything else genuinely English, is something arranged behind the scenes and according to the orders of esoteric knowledge. The domesticity of the constitution operates thus according to a simple law of inclusion and exclusion: the brute distinction between 'them and us' is precisely what differentiates the establishment from the hordes of the governed, the knowledgeable from those whom jurisprudence has generally termed the 'ignorant majority', the well spoken from those who are not well spoken.[5] The unwritten constitution spans equally the political and legal domains. It establishes a power that is both unknown and nomadic, a moving target in that the generic secrecy of the institution means inevitably that for every success in eliciting information countless documents disappear, oral culture reasserts

---

1   Legh, op. cit., fol. vb.   2   Guillim, op. cit., fol. 3a.
3   Fraunce, op. cit., fol. H3b.   4   Estienne, op. cit., fol. Biia.
5   H. L. A. Hart, *The Concept of Law* (1962, Oxford), pp. 60, 111, on the ignorant. On the phonetic characteristics of class identity and the uses of standard English see Nairn, op. cit., pp. 267ff.

itself, archives sink without trace, new laws of secrecy are passed or old laws are exorbitantly enforced.[1]

The two principles of English constitutionalism, those of monarchism and secrecy, of an aura or display of power that simultaneously hides the logic of its practice, can be traced without difficulty or too great a degree of digression into the common law itself. The aura of majesty that is put in place by the architecture of the court, by the placement of the judiciary within the courtroom, by the direct ennoblement of the judges, by the appropriate modes of addressing the bench, by the order of speech, by the rules of evidence, by costume, pageantry and language, all these display the makings of a liturgical, legal setting. These are the servants of the Crown, they issue their writs by the grace of God and in defence of the faith and in the name of the Crown; their space is the regal space of the Law. Like the constitution, the Law that they carry is unwritten, it is custom, it is tradition, it is *ius non scriptum*, unwritten reason that can be terroristically applied as and when the judicial memory of the immemorial or of 'time out of mind' happens circumstantially to be activated. The notion of 'time out of mind' describes legal method most exactly: it is time unbound to any object, free of any specific temporality, a time of repetition and so a thoughtless time; it is the delirium of the institution which unravels itself within the discrete confines of the legal form, as a prisoner not of life but of normative governance. In that respect the delirium of the institution hallucinates standard forms of procedure and norms of usual behaviour on the strength of half-remembered arguments,[2] through the dazed recollection of unreported cases or largely forgotten conversations. These were the tools of the common law; these were their memories, a *communis opinio*, a collective memory, as law. The hallucinating mind is in strict terms a mind that wanders, that 'lucinates', that goes astray. That is the source of common law, of unwritten law; it is the meandering of the legal mind, a temporal and geographical

1   Nairn, op. cit., at p. 268: 'From the 1680s up until the 1980s the right of those in power to disclose nothing about the exercise of power but what suited them has been a constitutive principle of British tranquillity and decency.'

2   See J. H. Baker (ed.), *The Reports of John Spelman* (1970, London), vol. 2 at p. 159: 'In those cases where judges were declaring law it was a transient, oral, informal process and only those present at the arguments could hope to achieve a wholly accurate impression of what had been decided, and then only when the judges spoke loudly enough.'

nomadism that snakes its path across the justificatory texts, the judgments, of the Year Books and the law reports. It is the circular logic of repetition, an uncodified (unsupported)[1] reason that was traditionally more lyrical than rational but that now travels under the disguise of a linear and pragmatic logic of decision making, that now travels as the lie of reason.

To complete an inevitably incomplete list – we have touched only upon the phonetics of class, or upon the concept of *generoso*, of the gentleman and his acolyte the Lady as forerunners or figures of social order, of law – consider the protection of the emblematic image of law. If we read the law it is obvious that the place of the reader is of one positioned as the subject – as the subjection – of a text. Neither a statutory text nor a case report nor a textbook nor a practitioner's manual invite any dialogue or opinion.[2] They are stylistically gauged to state the law through an awesomely boring and repetitive panoply of citation, quotation, footnoted references, names of cases, names of statutes, names of judges, names of reports, names of other 'jurisconsulta' and experts, sages of the 'unwritten' written law – all presented, it must be added, in a tongue that has never suffered the blandishments of usage anywhere but in court and in its diverse tiers of reportage.[3] As regards the more visible and popular display of justice being done at the appointed hour in the appointed place, in terms of our right to our day in court, the order of law is announced by the court usher who appears from behind the bench of the court and commands 'silence in court and all rise' before the appearance of the judiciary. All further speech throughout the trial or civil hearing must be on cue and as requested by the bench.[4] The interesting point as to the visibility and audibility of the hearing, as to the necessity of justice

1   A code from the Latin *caudex* meaning structure or support, as well as table or tablet.

2   A point well made in P. Legendre, *L'Amour du censeur* (1972, Paris), arguing that in structural terms it is only possible to understand the discourse of law as a liturgical speech: one reads the texts of the law so as to make them speak, they are in that sense oracular, Delphic, and not dialogic.

3   See Sir John Fortescue, *De Laudibus*, op. cit., pp. 198–9, on the persistence of law French for pleadings, argument, reports and many statutes. He observes that 'modern French is not the same as that used by our lawyers in the Courts of law, but is much altered and depraved by common use, which does not happen to the law French used in England, because it is oftener writ than spoken.'

4   The classic analysis of the annexation of linguistic subjectivity in Court is P. Carlen, *Magistrates' Justice* (1978, Oxford).

being seen to be done in open court, is that these requirements are met only in the most immediate of terms: those who are present, who are allowed to be present, for whom there is either room or reason for presence – many, it should be noted, are excluded – they can indeed see justice being done, but what they see will inevitably be gesturally and rhetorically opaque and linguistically enigmatic. What occurs in court is emblematic; its image is protected both in the occasion of its appearance and even more so in the public relay of that appearance through the press and the other media.[1]

The law which governs 'contempt of court' is unique in that it allows summary indictment of offenders without the option of jury trial: to take some recent examples, people laughing in the courtroom, witnesses too frightened to give evidence against people they know, persons too confused to respond to judicial questions, have all been imprisoned on the spot for common law contempt of court *in praesentia*. The protection of the sacral aura of courtroom process is one of the oldest powers known to the common law. It is indeed 'coeval with their first foundation and constitution; it is a necessary incident to every Court of Justice'.[2] Its basis is interestingly enough forgotten, it belongs to time out of mind, it is part of the *lex terrae*, part of the very soil, the earth from which the law comes unseen and unremembered till now. This immemorial usage has no origin, the Chief Justice admitting readily that 'I have examined very carefully to see if I could find out any vestiges or traces of its introduction, but can find none. It is as ancient as any other part of the common law, *there is no priority or posteriority to be discovered about it*'.[3] It is simply there, established and unchallengeable, part of precedent, part of the law even if we have no reason, no justification, no memory of why that might be – or, better, might have been – the case.[4] Two points need to be made, one spatial and one temporal. From early on in its history, the court was not geographically limited to the courtroom. It was a 'place' and it was to be protected as such: that is to say, in its other offices, in its chambers, in the Inns of Court, in the chancelleries, the libraries and all the other sacred hiding places (*sacramentorum latibula*) and treasure chests in which the records and the writs of the law were either forged or kept.

---

1   On the history of which see J. H. Baker, *The Legal Profession and the Common Law* (1986, London).

2   *R.* v. *Almer* [1765] Wilm 243, 97 Eng Rep 94.   3   Ibid. at 99–100.

4   There is no doctrine of desuetude in English law save for the very restrictively interpreted maxim of *cessante ratione cessat ipsa lex*.

In *Thorpe* v. *Makerel*, to take a geographically extreme example, a clerk of the King's Court was urinated on in Fleet Street on his way to Westminster, in the company of other men of the court. In the writ issued, a *venire facias*, the trespass charged was stated as having been *in presencia curiae*.[1]

The point of that little history, however, is larger than is perhaps apparent: all aspects of the honour of the court and of its aura are protected: what cannot be geographically charged as contempt in the face of the court can be indicted as scandalising the court *in absentia*. The emblematic image, the reputation, the representation, of the court and of what occurs within it is rigorously, not to say draconianly, controlled. Nothing can be published that would be, in the eyes of the court, prejudicial to any civil or criminal trial. Their vision is often surprising and it has been held, for example, to be contempt for a lawyer to show documents that had been read out in open court to an investigative journalist, even though the journalist could have obtained a transcript of the trial.[2] It has been held more recently that publication of information that was already in the public domain could be a contempt of court.[3] Further, 'any act done or writing published calculated to bring a Court or a judge of the Court into contempt or to lower his authority, is a contempt of court'.[4] Thus any adverse criticism of any aspect of a trial, of a judge, of a court, of a verdict, is potentially in danger of meeting the strictures of the law. It is to be reported, in other words, according to and in its majesty. It is to be reported reverently, darkly, emblematically, for such are the characteristics of the institution. They are also embedded in its language.

Behaviour at Bus Stops; Queues and the Manner of a Case

The motive question that underlies any extended discussion of the iconography and symbolism of a legal order is that of the context of a specific linguistic and textual practice of law. The question can be broken down into two parts. Firstly, there is a metaphysical question,

1   1318 Selden Soc, vol. 74, at 79.

2   *Home Office* v. *Harman* [1982] 1 All ER 532.

3   *Attorney General* v. *Newspaper Publishing PLC and others* [1989] Guardian Reports, May 8.

4   *R.* v. *Gray* [1900] 2 QB 36 at 40.

a question about how law hangs together: if the road to law is pathed with images of faith, of specific loyalties, of allegiance, of an ancient, honourable and continuing order, then is it reasonable to expect the language of law – the language of oath swearers and of notaries public – or the practice of judgment to be free of such iconic and symbolic dimensions?[1] Put differently, we might argue that law is a form of representation, that it *is* as it is represented. At the core of its representation is language, at least in the structural or architectural sense in which law can be defined adequately as legitimate social speech: can we then expect that the language used in such legitimate speech will represent differently or escape the lyrical irrationality, the murderous *arbitrium*, of the monarchy and its common law tradition? A second mode of asking the same question is more obviously practical: reading is never innocent and so what institutions, what honours, what images of reverence or of sacrifice, what other texts, do we bring as legal readers to the object being read? Can we remember?

The aura of majesty that surrounds the legal system, the symbols and tokens of regality that lead the individual to the appropriate place and the appropriate perspective or attitude, to a hegemonic place or even style, should not be too easily dismissed when it comes to questions of reading the law as a professional, as a lawyer. Indeed, if we pay even glancing attention to the history of legal language, there is little room within which to deny the symbolic character of both language and text as they have existed to represent the law. We could even usefully pose very simple material questions as to what and, more importantly, where are the books of the law, the libraries, the archives that store the traditions of the common law? What demotic access does the populace have to such places or storehouses?[2] Even if the materials of the positive law, the texts and the speech, were readily available, of what use would it be if the words used are separate from ordinary language and can only be understood, only properly exist, within the discrete thesaurus of the legal tradition? The tradition is

1 There is nothing particularly terrifying about the term metaphysics, it is simply the umbrella term for that which 'holds' a frame of reference or form of life in place. It thus obviously has a variety of sacral connotations in so far as that which holds things together is necessarily external to the individual and in excess of the ego, it is even deserving of either praise or imprecation. More prosaically, metaphysics determines both what there is and what it means.

2 See P. Goodrich, 'Literacy and the Languages of the Early Common Law' (1987) 14 *Journal of Law and Society* 422.

doubly protected: it is protected by virtue of being tacit and unwritten, by virtue, that is, of being an initiate knowledge that can be understood only in esoteric terms; it is also protected by symbols, by the enigmatic or emblematic form in which it appears. In the latter respect it is protected not least by the language of the tradition, the 'bark' or 'rind' within which legal meaning is encoded and kept: the foreign tongue, the Latin and French, the *vocabula artis* by which we recognise the outward appearance of law.[1] In such a context the lawyer is a prospector, a miner, an archivist, a diviner of laws like others are diviners of water, save that the danger that threatens is not so much drought as boredom.

A series of knowledges, of pre-existent texts or of what Gadamer terms prejudices, namely pre-judgments, are the terms of entry into the discourses of law, as indeed of any theology or tradition.[2] In that it is not possible to follow all the various parameters of the legal encyclopedia, nor to measure all of the constraints that law imposes upon its own discourse and particularly upon its circulation, one text will have to suffice as an illustration. The report is in the All England Reports for 1986, volume 3, pages 39–44. It is an appeal on a point of law from a decision of Marlborough Street Magistrates' Court to the Queen's Bench Division, and is heard by Lord Justice Glidewell and Mr Justice Schiemann. It takes the form of a law report and because of the legal familiarity of such a form it is worth noting certain features. The volume will be found virtually exclusively in law libraries or in law offices. As regards libraries, the reports are subject to their own system of classification – they are not in other words part of the Dewey system or indeed of the 'main' library – and they are distinctive as books. The law reports come in sizeable uniform volumes. They are bound in single and normally dull colours: navy

1 See W. Fulbecke, *Directive or Preparative to the Study of Law* (1589/1829, London), pp. 55–6.

2 H. Gadamer, *Truth and Method* (1979, London), p. 240: 'Actually "prejudice" means a judgment that is given before all the elements that determine a situation have been finally examined. In German legal terminology a "prejudice" is a provisional legal verdict before the final verdict is reached. For someone involved in a legal dispute, this kind of judgment against him affects his chances adversely. Accordingly, the French préjudice, as well as the Latin praejudicium, means simply 'adverse effect', 'disadvantage', 'harm'. But this negative sense is only a consecutive one. The negative consequence depends precisely on the positive validity, the value of the provisional decision as a prejudgment, which is that of any precedent.'

blue, jet black, military green or, for the older reports, Moroccan leather, beige, deep red. Each set of reports stretches with bland numerical indifference over seemingly infinite shelving. Each volume is extensive – not to say palimpsestic – in terms of its number of pages and the type of paper used: it is likely to be printed on thin India paper in smaller than average typeface. The reports are just that, a chronological accumulation of cases reported in the form of a reference book under the names of the litigants and providing a formulaic account of what happened in court, nothing more nor less, nothing to the side nor before nor after.

There is no logic to the list of cases. This one travels under the name of *Masterson and another* v. *Holden*.[1] As is normal, the pages of the report are accompanied by marginal letters every seven lines which allow for the easier identification of citations. The report begins cryptically with a list of legal keywords, something of a telegram: 'Public order – Offensive conduct conducive to breaches of peace – Threatening, abusive or insulting words or behaviour – Insulting – Nature of insulting behaviour . . . Defendants engaged in overt homosexual behaviour at bus stop – Defendants' behaviour observed by passing couples – Defendants unaware of other persons in vicinity – . . . Metropolitan Police Act 1839, s. 54(13).' The cryptic keywords, page 39b to c, are followed by a précis of the case and its 'holding', the rule of law that applied to determine the decision. Here the reader is presented with a short history, a retrospective narrative of a decided case, a judgment upon what lawyers are wont to term the facts, a *ratio decidendi* according to the textbooks. At this point it is possible to pause and summarise our progress. Where it is a question of the institution, it is not matter of who you are but *where* you are. Here the reader is within the contours of the legal text. There are already references to other sources of law: there is the Metropolitan Police Act, the relevant section of which is provided in footnote 'a' of the opening page. Aside from certain words and phrases that are indicatively legal, there are further references to cases and to sources, as for example: 'for insulting behaviour in London, see 40 Halsbury's Laws (4th edn) para 452', or 'for cases on [the offence of using insulting words or behaviour likely to cause a breach of the peace], see 15 Digest (Reissue) 908–910, 7797–7807', or, more laconically, '*Parkin* v. *Norman* [1982] 2 All ER 583 explained'.

1   [1986] 3 AER 39.

Where we are institutionally can also, however, be understood in terms of public space and the circulation of bodies, of persons in this case, in the public thoroughfare. It would be extremely inaccurate to suppose that by virtue of being outside – outside the library, outside the courtroom, free from the cell – that one had escaped either the institution or the law. It may even be worth observing that the bulk of the law of persons and of property is solely concerned with the demarcation and regulation of inhabited space as a geography, as the route of royal messages, as the 'public course' of all forms of circulation, which avenues have also always been the courses of manners or behaviours. The law of persons exists largely to protect the spheres of personal circulation or mobility, the nomadism of individuality, of organs: the body is protected from the various forms of illegal invasion or of civil or criminal trespass upon the attributes of a body, its members or limbs, or alternatively upon the house, the garden or the land that surrounds a body. To take one vivid example, the tort of false imprisonment is solely concerned with the individual's right of 'egress': that is, of entry and exit of any given space. The plaintiff could be drunk, asleep, catatonic, meditating, stupefied or voluntarily chained to a table, and yet if the defendant deprives the plaintiff of the possibility of leaving the room or the house or the street, that will constitute false imprisonment.[1] The immediately relevant writ, if it is a criminal matter, would be that of habeas corpus, the question being who has the body, where is the body, in which house, in whose room? What is preventing the circulation of a body in public space, what is limiting its freedom of movement? It is not a question of who occupies the body and so of an individual's spiritual or metaphysical rights, but rather a matter of what surrounds the body and so of its possibilities of movement in public space. To what market, to what trade route, to what public course, does this body attach itself? If it is arrested in some form, then by what right, for an inhabited body is 'quick', it exists as movement, it circulates, it has

1   See *Bird* v. *Jones* [1845] 7 QB 742, per Coleridge J: 'If, in the course of a night, both ends of a street were walled up, and there was no egress from the house but into the street, I should have no difficulty in saying that the inhabitants were thereby imprisoned.' The only restriction imposed by the majority decision in the case was that the constraint be total, in other words that there be no alternative available route. Lord Denman, dissenting, observes interestingly and radically: '. . . I had no idea that any person in these times supposed any particular boundary to be necessary to constitute imprisonment . . .'

places, a geography? So if we are concerned more generally with institutional questions, with where we are, then particular attention needs to be paid to specific geographies. Indeed, a parallel needs to be drawn between a cartography of the public sphere and the articulations, the signs, that lay out the body and refract its gaze off into the street.[1]

Here it is a question of a town, a metropolis, London, and certain places within it. Magna Carta, as will be recollected, guarantees to London its liberties and customs, and in the present case they are protected or enforced by local legislation, an 1839 Act governing offences 'in any Thoroughfare or public Place' within the limits of the Metropolitan Police District.[2] We will return to that point. The issue of place is too important to be abandoned. The headnote begins as follows: 'In the early hours of the morning in a public street in London the defendants were seen by two passing couples . . .'. If we move to page 40b, a paragraph headed 'Case stated' and then to the judgment of Glidewell LJ, we learn that it was on 11 June 1984 that the particular public street was occupied by the defendants in the manner subject to the present legal challenge. It was 1.55 a.m. on the 'south footway' of Oxford Street: 'it was in the open street, one of the busiest streets in the United Kingdom, although it was 1.55 a.m.'. Although it is mentioned only twice, the two men, Simon Thomas Masterson and Robert Matthew Cooper, were at a bus stop. That this site is passed over so quickly is important: in England the bus stop is not simply what Sartre describes as a serial place, a group space where the only connective bond or form of group membership between individuals is the purely abstract one of the bus route, the cohering power of the third being the teleology of public transport.[3] It is also

1   See A. Lingis, *Excesses, Eros and Culture* (1978, New York), pp. 24–30; also, *Fragments for a History of the Human Body* (1988, Boston).

2   Metropolitan Police Act, s.54(13): 'Every Person who shall use any threatening, abusive, or insulting Words or Behaviour with Intent to provoke a Breach of the Peace, or whereby a Breach of the Peace may be occasioned.'

3   The key philosophical analysis of queues at bus stops is to be found in J-P. Sartre, *Critique of Dialectical Reason I, Theory of Practical Ensembles* (1976, London), pp. 256–70. The *Critique* is highly suggestive of alternative possible interpretations of the offence – or objectionable character of the behaviour – in *Masterson*. First, there is the isolation of the bus stop 'which everyone lives as the provisional negation of their reciprocal relations with Others' (p. 256). The ideal-typical queueing individual turns his back on the other, or is unaware of him: his practical field is anticipatory, it is defined by waiting, by his 'real membership' of other

the traditional place of courtship, it is where young lovers meet, it is where the enamoured embrace overtly in public – as opposed to the darkened back row of the cinema or the back seat of a car or the relative seclusion of the park bench. It is, moreover, where Simon M. and Robert C., 'wholly unaware of other persons in the vicinity', happened to cuddle and kiss each other on the lips: 'then, the justices find, Cooper rubbed the back of Masterson with his right hand and later Cooper moved his hand from Masterson's back and placed it on Masterson's bottom and squeezed his buttocks. Cooper then placed his hand, on Masterson's genital area and rubbed his hand round this area'. (40g–h).

Here we must compare geographies, those of the city and of the body, different zones and so too, it transpires, different fares.[1] There are also two different forms of transport involved, public and pubic, that of the omnibus and of the erogenous. If we are seriously to investigate what was happening in this text, namely what it is that is reported, then the issue is precisely that of this double geography. There are innumerable questions. Think of a few in relation to each issue. The scene of the crime was a bus stop. There is a night service provided by London Transport – part of Oxford Street's business – so

groups, the office, the factory, or the home. At the level of practical interest, the members of the queue are interchangeable, they are mere instrumentalities of the city: for 'isolation becomes, for and through everyone, for him and for others, the real, social, product of cities' (p. 257). The individual at the bus queue is a participant in an instrumental rationality, an absence, an interchangeable point of conductivity, exterior to himself and to the other members of the queue. In the final analysis it is the bus that defines the queue, the object that temporalises and locates the place, the space, of the queue: 'the object takes on a structure which overflows its pure inert existence; as such it is provided with a passive future and past, and these make it appear to the passengers as a fragment of their destiny' (259). In using the bus stop as an emotional space, in breaking down the isolation of the queue, in turning not the back but the face to the other, in ignoring the anticipatory temporality of the queue, by refusing simply to wait, by refusing to be defined by the object, the lovers in *Masterson* threatened the instrumentality of the city and its segregation of the group. Consider finally Sartre's friend Paul Nizan, *Aden Arabie*, 'you think you are innocent if you say "I love this [man] and I want to act in accordance with this love" but you are being revolutionary. Besides your love will not succeed.'

1 The magistrates had bound each defendant over to keep the peace in the sum of £100 over twelve months. A season ticket on London Transport between Clapham and Oxford Street was at that time £120 for three months. What are the respective pleasures?

was there a bus coming? Did the defendants know of any bus? Were they waiting? Is the time of the offence, the breach of the peace, related to the likelihood or the regularity of buses coming down Oxford Street? The Justices had, after all, remarked that 'quite different criteria apply to behaviour at a bus stop in the street than apply to behaviour in a gentleman's public lavatory' (41c–d). And Glidewell LJ remarks generically that 'every decision must be read in the light of the [geographical] facts on which it is based' (43c–d). So we might note that a decision in relation to an Oxford Street bus stop cannot be assumed good even of other types of stop or station: would the decision have included behaviour at a railway station, an airport, the docks, an underground station?

We might note also that the map of the city that the case presents also includes the route, the relationship between the Magistrates' court and the scene of the incident. The one contribution of Shiemann J. to the text is to remark that 'this type of case in my judgment is one peculiarly suitable for decision by the justices. They are the ones sitting at Marlborough Street who are most likely to know what is insulting behaviour at 1.55 a.m. on a June morning.' As Marlborough Street is considerably closer to Oxford Street than are the Royal Courts of Justice on the Strand, it can only be assumed that it is the geographic proximity and so 'street credibility' of the magistrates at Marlborough Street that is their attraction. As to the geography of the body, it is a question not so much of when the transport comes, as of how far can one go? Glidewell LJ concludes by stating: 'So it comes back to this. Was it conduct which within the ordinary meaning of the word could be said to be insulting? . . . Overt homosexual conduct in a public street . . . may well be considered by many persons to be objectionable, to be conduct which ought to be confined to a private place' (44c–d). The erotic geography of the body is implausibly asserted to be a private one and, while it may exist only by virtue of the relation of a private eros to public space, to others, it is also an inevitable part of the imagery of the street. In that respect even a judge could surely recognise that the private, the erotic, the body as sensation and as desire, is thoroughly manufactured by public goods, by symbols, by prohibitions, by law both violated and remembered, by the touch of the other, the gaze of the other, the knowledge transmitted by others. How many buses, one could even ask, carry advertisements displaying variously attired erogenous zones? How many newspapers blowing as rubbish along the Oxford Street 'footpath' carry photographs of lips, of breasts, of nipples, of buttocks? How many advertising hoardings endeavour to sell their products by direct reference to or through images of the erotic? How many bus shelters now carry advertisements?

The issue of reading posed by the above analysis can be reformulated in terms of a supplement to one of the best known of legal metaphors. Behaviour at a bus stop is the issue. The questions it raises concern manners and reasonableness in public places, although the judgment will not present these questions in a direct way. We are, in other words, already involved in a supplementary reading which can be depicted again in terms of buses. For the common law, reasonableness is an attribute that is frequently defined in terms of 'the man on the Clapham omnibus'. The Clapham omnibus indeed has for long provided the criterion of legal rationality where it is a matter of fact: would a reasonable man find this behaviour negligent, offensive, reckless, immoral? becomes, in law, would the man on the Clapham omnibus react in such a manner? The reasonable man is on the bus, not at the Clapham omnibus stop. He is certainly not at an Oxford Street bus stop, although there are several routes between Clapham and Oxford Street. The point is that the reasonable man is already travelling; reason itself is teleological, it is on its way, it has a purpose, somewhere to go – whereas those at the bus stop have yet to embark upon the rationality of social circulation; they are outside the omnibus, dark figures who are in this instance to be judged from the bus; they are not reasonable, they are common, vulgar, to be bound over, to be punished. To institute a reasonable public life requires certainly that the lawyer can differentiate precisely between the reasonable and the merely vulgar, between the innocuous reverie of the passenger and the dangerousness of any appearance of eros in the public course: 'overt homosexual conduct in a public street, indeed overt heterosexual conduct in a public street, may well be considered by many persons to be objectionable' (44c–d). The comparison of homosexual and heterosexual conduct does not hold in the text; we will return to it. For the moment the issue is one of security and threat: the demand for ordinariness or predictable and routine behaviour in public, the legal demand for good manners, returns us to the starting point of this chapter and of the case, that of Englishness and of the need of the English to secure not only their home but also – through ritual, through honour, through ceremonials such as those of the common law, of the law of the land – to secure the sense of distance, of coldness and courtesy, that make the public realm secure in the Queen's peace and allow us to believe that life is proceeding as normal.

I will move now to separate out the elements of the judgment itself according to its textual laws, which is to say according to a semiotic schema of the forms of transmission that are used in a case. The question to be answered is a classical one. The legal institution institutes social life. The logic of the law that institutes such life is supposedly a discrete one; it is circular or syllogistic according to the exponents of English jurisprudence. The analysis of a case as pure text, pure law, as a sign, will allow us to raise the issue both of the circularity of the judgment – its literal discreteness, for no one talks or writes like this – and also, and more usefully, the indications of supplementarity, the flaws and silences, the marks or traces of other discourses, the breaks and faults in the seams of the circle. Those faults are precisely the basis of a supplementary reading: how does one read a case against itself? Figure 7.1 provides a list of elements to be checked in any attempt to depict the significatory logic of a text, particularly a legal text. These are elements, it must be stressed, of description and no more; they describe a singular text and they may well need to be revised for the analysis of others. At the same time,

Figure 7.1 The legal institution of public life

	A	B Lexico-	C	D
	Text (author)	grammatical (reference)	Semantic (contract)	Iconic (Law)
1 Instance	Statute (1839 Act s. 13)	Index	Fact	Annunciation
2 Inscription	'May be occasioned'	Agency	Definition	Judgment
3 Intertext	Precedent (Insult)	'Objectionable'	Rule	Sovereignty
4 [Institution]	(organs as virtual objects)	(speech as symptom)	(repression as repetition)	[Instituted] (new norm/ bus stop)

however, it is part of the argument of this chapter that there is unlikely to be a need for any extensive revision of this chart or grid. In that the common law operates according to a logic of repetition, the deconstruction and mapping of its elements, its structure, is unlikely to differ greatly in formal terms from case to case. The institution, as row 4 depicts it, institutes itself, it discovers and passes on the established norm.

Our reading of the case has already been elaborately introduced in terms of the geography and manners of public places; the legal sites of certainty and of security in the public course of circulation have been canvassed. The details of an alternative reading of the case, of a supplementary reading against the text, have thus already been set out. We now need to fill in the more formal means by which such a reading or interpretation can be represented persuasively by reference to a variety of linguistic and symbolic dimensions of the chosen text and the narrative of security or insecurity, of zones, that it supports.

The overall movement to which our reading will subject the text is an apparently linear and historical progression depicted horizontally in row 4 of Figure 7.1 as the teleological movement of the textual narrative from the institution to the instituted, from the generality of the law to the particularity of its implementation, from the normal (the reasonable) to the correction of the abnormal. If we take up the last formulation, it is easy also to invoke an argument as to the circularity of the text: the institution institutes a generalised normality, it applies rules, it exacts a standard from a particular behaviour, it abstracts from the night, from Oxford Street, from a bus stop on the route of the 88 from Clapham to Tooting Mitre, the permissible zones of touch, the proper role of the body on a 'footpath' in a metropolis. The movement from 1A to 4D is a circular one; it is a question of a variety of forms of legal abstraction, both of a taking-out, a removal like that of a tooth, and of a variation in levels of generality: what is read in the text as section 54, subsection 13 of a specific statute becomes in iconic terms a question of sovereignty, of sources of law, of the statute as an emblem of a culture, something that we wear, that we inhabit, a portrait.

The terms of the analysis schematised in Figure 7.1 are relatively simple. The horizontal rows represent a list of functions: that of instancing or particularising, that of inscription or rewriting the text, that of intertextuality or of establishing, possibly coercing the relation of law to other discourses, and finally that of outcome, of restating the institution in its various forms, and on a particular occasion. Starting with 1A, we will follow the terms of the reading already begun and pose the question not of who is involved, but of where are we, in which text, in which law, properly speaking, in the space between the lines of which book, of what report? We start with a section of a statutory text. Section 54, so far as material, provides:

> Every Person shall be liable to a Penalty not more than [level 2 on the standard scale], who within the Limits of the Metropolitan Police District, shall, in any Thoroughfare or public Place, commit any of the following Offences . . . 13. Every Person who shall use any threatening, abusive, or insulting Words or Behaviours with Intent to provoke a Breach of the Peace, or whereby a Breach of the Peace may be occasioned . . .

That statute is a choice on the part of the prosecution and also on the part of the court; there are numerous other public order offences, including the Public Order Act 1936, as well as a variety of residual common law offences of indecency and immorality that lie in the power of the court as censor of moral values and as keeper of public conscience.

Position 2A concerns the inscription of the statute in relation to a particular sequence of facts, the question being not what is read, but how is it to be read? The precise inscription will determine, or at least is likely to be indicative of – to signal ahead – the outcome of the case. In this instance, the textual inscription does precisely that: the 1839 Act is distinguished from non-metropolitan legislation on breaches of the peace through use of the verb 'may'. Glidewell LJ observes:

> I note in passing that the wording of the offence under the 1839 Act uses the word 'may' have been occasioned in relation to the question of breach of the peace. Grammatically it should be 'might' though nothing turns on that, but in that way the section is to be distinguished from the similar offence under the Public Order Act 1936, where the wording is 'likely to be occasioned'.

Nothing turns on the word 'may' save the fate of a particular behaviour, save the outcome of a case, save the destiny of an appeal on a point of law. Nothing hangs, nothing turns, on the tense of a verb except the question of what it is that has to be proved in a successful prosecution. Nothing turns on 'may' rather than 'might' because the case is already decided once the words are selected. Now we know the outcome: anything, any behaviour, particularly homosexual behaviour, 'may' – as a present tense, as a present or continuing possibility – provoke a breach of the peace, whereas whether or not it did, whether in the past tense it might (have), is a separable question, a stronger thing to have to prove. 'May' connotes a possibility and no more, an ability to do something, a purpose or concession which may or may not be realised. On the other hand, 'might' is redolent of probability; it connotes a power to do something, a force that will penetrate, something real and not simply imagined. If Simon M. and Robert C. are to be disallowed their appeal, if they are to be held correctly convicted in law upon facts that were found by those best situated, at Marlborough Street Magistrates' Court, then it will be best to read section 54(13) as requiring that there be proof of a possible breach of the peace, proof of nothing more than that a breach of the peace 'may be occasioned'.

If we stopped at this place, at the inscription of the text in relation to the adjudicated facts of the case, we would still need some account of the nature of a 'breach of the peace'. In classical common law terms, a breach of the peace is a breach of the king's peace, a disruption *vi et armis* or by force and arms of the law of the land, of the custom of the realm. Even an elementary analysis, however, would require that we look further at the nature of a breach: it is a breaking of the law, a breach of contract, a breach of promise, certainly, but it is also perhaps additionally a breach as in the breaching of a wall so as to invade a city, so as to end a siege, a manner of moving in, of invasion or intrusion, a breaking through. The breach itself is a wounded spot, a broken space, a disputed place, a gap or fissure in fortifications made by a battery. According to that broader lexical definition, the gap exists to be closed, something must be erected to fill the breach, to make the wall whole, to make the city secure, to reintroduce order, the order of the conquerors – a new law perhaps.

The second moment of inscription thus occurs in relation to other discourses. Position 3A is therefore concerned with intertextuality, which is to say with all the possible forms of behaviour that the decision will imply for the order of the city; more prosaically, with how it is to be explained or represented to those subject to the law. The question now is that of the nature of an insult, of 'insulting Words or Behaviour . . . whereby a Breach of the Peace may be occasioned', and the fashion by which it may provoke an infringement of the pre-existent order of the street. Here the judge must refer to the contexts in which insults have been held previously to have made their mark, to have infringed the serenity of the 'Thoroughfare or Public Place'. The question here is directly that of what is the law? What do the books, the reports, have to say? The question is metaphorical insofar as the precedents examined concern other, differently worded legislation and involve places other than bus stops. The cases referred to as establishing the law had dealt with a demonstration at the All England Lawn Tennis Tournament at Wimbledon (*Brutus* v. *Cozens* [1972] 2 All ER 1297) and with allegedly homosexual behaviour – masturbation, the sin of Onan – in a public lavatory (*Parkin* v. *Norman* [1982] 2 Al ER 583). The metaphor that operates in the judgment given by Glidewell LJ must transport the discussion of insulting behaviour, openly indulged masturbation in a public space which was willingly observed by a police officer, to fondling and cuddling in a thoroughfare or on a footpath by appellants 'wholly unaware of other persons in the vicinity'. It must abstract from the time and place of a public lavatory and an explicitly intended but essentially solitary act to a quite different circumstance and place. It does so by finding a 'surprising likeness' or resemblance[1] of behaviours in the definition of an unwitting insult as being constituted by behaviour which 'albeit it was not deliberately aimed at a particular person or persons . . . [could] be insulting to any member of the public who might be passing by' (44b–c) and later as conduct in a public street if such conduct 'may well be regarded by another person, particularly by a young woman, as conduct which insults her by suggesting that she is somebody who would find such conduct in public acceptable herself' (44d–e). The authority of this view, let it be well noted, is the argument given in the House of Lords decision in *Brutus* v. *Cozens* that the behaviour there in question could have been insulting if it 'was tantamount to a statement, "I believe you are another homosexual", which the average heterosexual would surely regard as insulting' (43a–b). So how does this metaphor hold together other than by a quality of sheer surprise? The answer is that it does so only by virtue of the institution, by virtue of being a part of a system of rules that identify and delete behaviours according to a tacit structure of reasonableness, in this case of travel: the institution, the law, creates a manner of doing things, creates a fiction in the form of a list of the

1   Aristotle, *Rhetoric*, Bk III, 2, 'metaphor must be drawn from things that are related to the original thing, and yet not obviously so related – just as in philosophy also an acute mind will perceive resemblance in things far apart.'

permitted and the excluded. It operates by a moralism of forms, a moralism of justificatory argument, and insinuates a content that we must now recreate or recall from the boundaries, the slips of the text.

There is no recognisable logic to the analogy created. Nothing binds one case to the next, there is no identity between the public toilet and the bus stop, there is no homology between the singular, though visible, act of masturbation and the dyadic forms of a caress or a kiss, there is no knowable logic that would allow us to assume that a young heterosexual woman might see herself as being designated homosexual by the sight – unwittingly presented to her – of two men kissing on a footpath almost two hours after midnight. The legal relevance of this past, these precedents, these differences, is iconic: the images represented in the pages of the judgment have another function, that of identifying potentially illicit instances of eros in public places so as to symbolise the awesome power of law, the sovereignty of an order that comes from elsewhere, from the logic of the immemorial, from time out of mind, from an authority that requires no justification beyond the manner of its own statement, its annunciation, its power to presence an absent spirit, that of the common law. Everything in the judgment says that this behaviour with which we are concerned, this conduct – outside of the bus, away from the bus conductor – this behaviour which 'made one [young woman] raise her hand to her mouth', is not good.

Between the vertical columns A and D in Figure 7.1 are listed the mechanical or linguistic elements of a report that will introduce the legality or legalisation of an issue. The syntax and grammar of law is one of the deletion of all extraneous or immaterial subjectivity and its translation by means of metaphor, by means of the metamorphosis of institutional placement, by means of abstraction and the consequent deletion of identities of time and place, into the generality of a text, a law report, this case. These can be run through here quite quickly. Column B lists the lexico-grammatical features of the text in a formal manner suggestive of a syntax. Position B1 concerns legal forms of designation, the reference to a field of connotations and a specifically legal vocabulary. It is a question of treating the language of the report in a very particular way to indicate where we are: anaphorical and other indexical items to the text indicate both an existent and artistic (i.e. technical) juridical vocabulary and a tradition of statement and interpretation. What most specifically inscribes the words (the lexicon) as those of the law is not simply the archaism of the terms, of a 'footpath' on Oxford Street, of a 'thoroughfare' in London, of 'binding over' or 'breach of the peace', of 'proper construction', 'appellants' or 'absolute discharge', but also and more emphatically the form of referencing to a statute, to cases and to determinations in other texts. For Lord Reid (*Brutus* v. *Cozens*), 'the proper construction of a statute is a question of law. If the context shows that a word is used in an unusual sense the court will determine in other words what that unusual sense is', while for McCullough J. (*Parkin* v. *Norman*), in more substantive terms 'one cannot insult nothing. The word presupposes a subject and an object and, in this day and age, a human object.' For Viscount Dilhorne (*Brutus* v. *Cozens*), 'There was no need to consider whether an intention to insult was required. Having regard to the tenor of the 1936 Act as a whole, we believe that no such intent need be proved.'

Having established a realm of reference, of true texts and proper meanings, appropriate determinations, it is necessary at the level of specific inscription (B2) to delete agency from the justification of a decision: the language of the law must acquire an objectivity, a universality that cannot be limited in its presentation to the contingency of a particular behaviour. We move to a decision that tells us about insults and the manner of insulting, to persons in general and no particular person: the question for Glidewell LJ is thus framed as follows:

> How does one reconcile the clear statement that an intention to insult somebody else is not necessarily a part of the offence with the later passage that an insult is something which is directed by one person at another? Reading the two together, what the second passage must be understood to mean is that words or behaviour cannot be insulting if there is not a human target which they strike, whether they are intended to strike that target or not. [44a]

For there to be a breach, in other words, a specific projectile would have to have hit a specific wall.

Moving to B3, the answer to the question of why the judge interprets this behaviour as being such a projectile, as breaching this early morning peace, as being an offence, is recuperable through the word 'objectionable'. The passage reads opaquely and indeed tautologically and needs to be cited in full:

> Overt homosexual conduct in a public street, indeed overt heterosexual conduct in a public street, may well be considered by many persons to be

> objectionable, to be conduct which ought to be confined to a private place. [That] the fact is objectionable does not constitute an offence. But the display of such objectionable conduct in a public street may well be regarded by another person, particularly by a young woman, as conduct which insults her by suggesting that she is somebody who would find such conduct in public acceptable herself. [44c–d]

We will pass over the obvious circularity of the statement, the proposition that what is objectionable is objectionable to a person because it is unacceptable, and enquire instead into the objectionable in an intertextual sense.

All maps are based upon a projection, any cartography, in other words, is founded upon a particular gaze, literally a throwing of vision towards a space, *projicere* as opposed here to *objicere* or objection, which throws in the way of, or constitutes an obstacle, a hindrance. The body that constitutes the offence is not something already there, something natural; it is a product or projection of the legal gaze, and its map of the body, its human geography, is a geography constructed upon the basis of 'the movements that men make and the relations that those movements imply'.[1] What is objectionable, then, is not a body, nor is it the parts of the body, the lips, the buttocks, the genitals – the genitals cannot even be seen. What we are invited to see is the movement of a hand: 'Cooper then placed his hand on Masterson's genital area and rubbed his hand around this area' (40h–j). The circumscribing hand defines, identifies and creates the erogenous object, the offending zone, the objectionable publicised place, an imagined swelling, a putative tumescence: it is the judicial stare that locates, that maps, an imaginary or projected erotic site, lips used and hands wandering after illicit or licentious ends. The objectionable transpires to be as much the erotic effect of the legal gaze, of a particular description of a caress, of what the rubbing motion is made to imply, as of any object or behaviour. The gaze informs, it delineates a movement in a particular way, it maps a hidden swelling, an objectivisation of a specific touch. We are left to consider what Bataille terms the 'place of all eroticism – the blending and fusion of separate objects'. A young man's hand travels across, marks, the unmarked sartorial surface of another's groin, and a young woman

1   F. Braudel, *The Mediterranean and the Mediterranean World in the Age of Philip the Second* (1972, New York), observing that no space has any 'unity but that created by the movements of men, the relationships they imply, and the routes they follow' (p. 276).

puts her hand to her mouth. It is the judicial eye that places these actions, that makes an obstacle of a movement, that objectifies the dual parabola of hands searching separate surfaces. It is the hand that seeks a mouth, a motion which the legal gaze fixes as a gesture of outrage rather than as one of excitation, that will in the end determine the character of objectionable conduct. If we go further, the two women leave the scene along with the two men they were walking with; they leave the law to take its course: 'although asked to wait by the police, [they] in fact did not, perhaps not wholly surprisingly, and when the police turned their attention to them they had gone' (41a). It is left to the law to announce a verdict; it is the judge who determines what the movement of two bodies together means; it is the law that will objectify the conduct, that will literally object in the sense of throwing something in the way of a specific act.

The form that legal objectification takes is tabulated in column C in terms of the semantic operations that constitute a legal judgment in its classical justificatory form. The form is that of generalisation, the deletion of specific subjectivities in favour of a universal law that will here govern a particular set of facts by redefining them as legally relevant facts, as evidence, as the object to which a rule is applied. The rhetoric of written reason is a familiar one; it here establishes a *ratio decidendi* whereby what happens in the case is finally presented as a holding, as the definition of a statutory clause and the framing of a general rule concerning the nature of insulting behaviour in London as it is relevant to the generalised conduct of the appellants. There is little need to dwell on the categories of that reasoning process, the question posed here is that of how to read them against themselves, how to indicate the mythic quality of that rational frame by relating the semantic operations to the iconic functions tabulated in the final column. We will define the iconic supplement both as the licit representation of an image of law, of authority, reason and source, and also as the emblematic quality of all legal judgments: the text necessarily exceeds both the occasion of its annunciation and the literal or repeated content of its judgment. The text is a manner of doing something; it is classically an instrument and should in that sense be understood as something inhabited and subject to the law of numbers; it is demographically sensitive, it is populus and as an instrument it exists to organise, to arrange that population. Understood as an instrument, the text produces effects: it intervenes in the lives of its subjects and it remakes the actions of the actors in its narrative sequence. If the text is a manner of doing things, it is the question of how it is done that the semiotician follows, observing amongst other things Nietzsche's injunction that the aesthetic perception is essentially one that views form as content, the only content, the materiality of a body, the surface of a skin, its extension, its egress into the world.

In iconic terms, the opening question is that which asks of what the legal text is actually a sign, what does it represent, what manner of order, what specific life? The icon separates licit and illicit modes of representation; it establishes a regime of similarity, of repetitions, of the permitted forms of figuration of an absent God, and so also of a law in abeyance, an immemorial tradition. The iconic function is thus that which inaugurates the social as representation and meaning as a sign of something else, as reference to a presence beyond – external to – the sign. The icon introduces the principle of spirituality into Western interpretation or hermeneutics; it separates the text from its referent, and in law that separation takes the exemplary form of an order of legitimate reference – every text is a sign of further texts, of memory as a hierarchy of texts and of sociality as the inscription of that textual order. We can begin the examination of the function of annunciation (D1) by looking to the dual character of that text as instituting an order of reference and as inscribing a principle of interpretation. The term annunciation can be taken first in the sense of its root meaning of the Latin *annunciatus*, that which declares beforehand, that brings a message, a message which is classically from Rome, from the Papacy via the papal messenger or nuncio. In this initial sense, our concern is with all the mechanisms already depicted which differentiate legal discourse from those other social discourses which are not law, which will fade in the very moment of their statement. The discourse with which we are concerned does not simply remain, it is emblematic; it establishes the site of the true sign that is thrown within, the sign that will capture a subject, that is emblematic in the sense of the Greek *emballo*, of throwing inside, of expending from within.

In Christian doctrine, of which the law is a part, the annunciation is also taken to be the process which presences the Holy Spirit: the archangel Gabriel is sent to tell our Lady that she was chosen to be the mother of God. The annunciation is in that sense the Immaculate Conception; the Holy Spirit presences the divinity in the womb of the virgin mother of Christ. It is *logos*, the word as incarnation of divine presence, the spirit made flesh. For the law, the spirit made flesh takes the form of a text, vellum or skin in which is inscribed the form of the institution, of society and its subjects as the unified members and membrane of a body, the *corpus iuris civilis* or civilised body, the *corpus mysticum* or body politic, Leviathan or law. Let us see. In common law doctrine what the court announces in its references to precedent, to the books, to unwritten memory and unremembered cases,[1] is no more nor less than the spirit of the law as present in the breast of the judges, *traditio* in the language of Christian dogmatics, an unwritten, inherited, oral authority, the Holy Spirit or living voice of the law. That indeed is the definition of common law given by Coke and by Davies: *lex est mutus magistratus* (the law is a mute magistrate) or again *lex est iustitia inanimata*[2] (the law is inanimate/breathless justice). In other words, it is the living who give breath to a silent, textual law, through their memory, through the inventions of speech. Glidewell LJ's judgment does not rely primarily upon the citations and quotations of authority or the sources of law that are given in the judgment as rational forms of content or as logical justifications; they are metaphors related to or borrowed from other circumstances and other occasions of the law. They have little if any direct relevance, they are not the law in this case, and the judgment is therefore better understood as slipping across a surface of texts, of references to invoke the sagacity of law, to discover how to invoke the law to justify a specific decision as to the objectionable and why behaviour is to be screened, to be veiled with this pejorative or perverse term in the eyes of the royal peace.

At the level of inscription the legal annunciation takes the form of a

1 See, for example, Fortescue J (1458, YB 36 Hen. VI 25b): 'Sir, the law is as I say it is, and so it has been laid down ever since the law began; and we have several set forms which are held as law, and so held for good reason, though we cannot at present remember that reason.'

2 Davies, *Le Primer Report des Cases and Matters en Ley Resolves and Adjudges in les Courts del Roy en Ireland* (1615, Dublin), fol. 7b, 8b: 'the matter of our profession is justice, the lady and queen of all virtues and our professors of law are her counsellors, her secretaries, her interpreters, her servants . . . how needful is the service of learned men in the law without which justice itself cannot stand? for *iustitia poriret si deesset qui iustitiam allegaret*. For if no man did study the reason of law, if no man kept in memory the rules of the law, if no man knew the forms of pleading, or the course of proceeding in the law, what would become of public justice? for: *lex est iustitia inanimata* or *lex est mutus magistratus*.' See also Coke, *Reports*, II, A3a–b, A6a.

judgment (D2). In terms of legal method, the judgment here simply states that authority justifies the designation of this objectionable behaviour as insulting within the meaning of the statute. In iconic terms, the court has heard the case and resumes to state the law as conclusive; an itinerant law stops to mark a place, fixes a gaze on a bus stop and establishes a commensurability of a public course and private parts. In intertextual terms (D3) what is manifest in the ruling, the 'holding' – a Teutonic word meaning to watch over – is a spirit, the spirit of the law, taking flesh in a sovereign act. The judgment recreates a frame of reference, a frame of reason as *universitas*, as the only reason, the only law. The frame determines both perception and interpretation; it is the frame that will hold a vision, a gaze, in place. The gaze that discerns and diagnoses the dimensions of an essentially elastic space locks in the possibilities of pub(l)ic life like a speculum; it creates the very object it claims only to observe in the mirror of the law.[1] The objectionable act and the objectionable object are born simultaneously under this mirror, this speculum of the law: it is the judicial imaging of what is happening to the flesh under the surface of clothing that institutes the mask of subjectivity, the person possessed by the law. The gaze fixes a particular geography of the body, it organises erogenous space, it articulates imaginary being, it converts a swelling into an object, a surface into a persona: it turns the hand inside out. The circling of a hand around a groin is seen not as an act of eroticism, a passion, but rather as a vulgarity of behaviour, an insult and an offence. The decision decides – it cuts off, *decidere* – and the frame thus institutes an order of movement; it imposes an itinerary on the movement of a subjectivity in order to intercept a hand; it defines its object and its objection by means of denial. The denial is a denial of the frame itself: the judge, Lord Justice Glidewell, arrives at his decision by outlawing the very eroticism of vision that enabled him to reconstruct the event, to see behind the cloth, to reconnoitre the erotic body and to map the movement of a hand as transgression. If the text is read against itself, in iconic terms, it is apparent that what the law announces in its judgment is its own death, the death of its own reason, the institution of its own life.

1   Coke, *Reports*, IX, A3a–b, discussing the *Mirror of Justices*: 'so in this mirror you may perfectly and truly discern the whole body of the common law of England', and elsewhere, 'the law whereof this summary is made, is of ancient usages warranted by holy scripture, and because it is generally given to all, it is called common'.

Conclusion

Finally, there is the question of the difference that a semiotic reading makes. This text has pursued two geographies, the geography of eros and the geography of public space. It is not obvious to us that the intensional/intensive regions of the body and the extensional space of the bus stop are isomorphic: it is not obvious to us that they share the same space or that they can be mapped according to the same projective principle, that that organ framed by the legal speculum is the same space, the same place, the same material life which swells in an order of intimacy, an order of touch.

If we return to Figure 7.1 and to the movement of row 4, the question is that of what does the institution of law institute? How does the law map out the body as a public space, how does it involve itself supremely in one's private parts? In a critical sense, a semiotics of law can provide an analysis of the various means by which a specific system of law, the common law of England, institutes a specific life, a specific body, a specific concept of security, a specific relation between public and private space. More than that, a semiotics of law can further depict the implicit rationalism of legal method and can instance the relationship between the legal gaze, the visual measure of conduct seen and circumscribed from the outside, and a Cartesian or modernist reason, a heliotropic rationality that since Descartes has silenced the imaginary and frozen its images in the name of logical schemata. Enlightenment reason constantly constructs the world from the outside, as an external thing. In doing so, it loses the very tradition and temporality that it claims as its frame or as its source, replacing temporal movement with spatial categories and with a forensic gaze that is essentially a panoptic surveillance of a space inhabited by others.[1] The forensic speculum,[2] the mirror or tech-

---

1   'The [panoptic] configuration sets up a brutal dissymmetry of visibility. The [observed] space lacks depth; it is spread out and open to a single, solitary, central eye. It is bathed in light. Nothing and no-one can be hidden . . . except the gaze itself, the invisible omnivoyeur' the law. 'Surveillance confiscates the gaze for its own profit, appropriates it, and submits' the street to it. (J-A. Miller, 'Jeremy Bentham's Panoptic Device', op. cit., p. 4.)

2   The speculum, from *specere*, to look, via *specula* meaning that which looks, the thing or place from which one looks, a watchtower or height, but also (from *spes* – hope) meaning faint hope. In its medical meaning the speculum 'sees parts that are otherwise hidden', most notably the cervix and the womb.

nology of that surveillance, is diagnostic and distanced: the law opens up the body to the public eye but forgets itself. If we look at a body through a speculum we are given the illusion that the body remains unoccupied, that the inroad of the law occupies no space. The legal judgment mimics in the realm of the text the technology of the speculum; its judgment refuses to take account of its own frame, perspective and history. It thus makes no use of the tradition, it provides no historical account of it own instrumentation, and it refuses to do anything with the memories of law that constitute or, better, are the constitution of the thoroughfare, of the unwritten text which subtends both the institution and the street.

At the level of a literal reading, Lord Justice Glidewell's judgment is simply banal. The report tells us that, after the two young women had recovered from the initial shock of seeing the interaction between Masterson and Cooper, the young men accompanying the young women approached the defendants 'and one of them shouted, "You filthy sods. How dare you in front of our girls?"' (40j). The expression does not lack clarity: it can be paraphrased without difficulty in terms of two propositions, two offences. On the one hand you are filthy, dirty, unnatural, abnormal since a sod is both 'a slice of earth', dirt, and also a practitioner of sodomy, of 'unnatural sexual intercourse, especially that of one male with another'. When used of places, it can also be noted, the sodomitical refers to things polluted or infected by sodomy. Were we to doubt that meaning, the second sentence repeats the accusation of sexual abnormality. It is specific: you are doing this in front of our girls. Might it not be all right if it had been done in front of our boys, the boys who play rugger and who, like Lord Justice Glidewell, went to all-male private boarding schools, who shared baths and slept in dormitories and suffered initiation rites at an early age? Small wonder that Glidwell does not wish to dwell upon the revulsion of the sodomitical; it might well summon not the im-memorial law as to the peace but highly specific memories of a very English institution and a very profane body wherein 'time out of mind' would refer to systems of corporal punishment and the very particular hothouse regime in which our judges and politicians are usually trained and in which buttocks, bottoms and fundaments feature constantly: they are birched or caned, they are smacked, they are seated, they are squeezed, very occasionally they are caressed, and there is nothing more frightening (or exciting) to the rustic Englishman than the intimacy of that particular caress. The buttocks here are iconic; the icon separates the text from its referent: it is the genitals that are being rubbed, but it is the buttocks that are offending. In law that separation is a means of disassociating organs through a gaze that will screen the judge from the lived act; it is also the interpretative deceit that makes possible an order of legitimate reference, a reading from memory. The question of interpretation is that of *whose* memory, whose order of reference does the law institute?

So Glidewell evades the issue and simply signals in the properly elliptical way what the law has always known: there are those who are like us and those who are not, there is the establishment and there are those who are uncouth, there are chaps who are discreet in their homosexual preferences – and the establishment is not lacking in examples – and there are those who flaunt an unacceptable difference, who go over to the other side – quite often they are also communists, traitors, betrayers of the Crown. Indeed, Lord Justice Glidewell, who seems to attract homophobic litigation, later took the opportunity in the case of *Regina* v. *Director of the Government Communications Headquarters ex parte Hodges* (1988, Guardian Law Report, 20 July) to rule that simply being a homosexual could legitimately be treated as being a threat to national security. Hodges had openly declared himself to be homosexual. At a routine security review his positive vetting clearance was withdrawn on the grounds that 'he might be vulnerable to pressure or blackmail from a hostile intelligence service due to his current homosexual lifestyle'. Glidewell LJ was expansive and wholly unmoved by any apparent contradiction between the openness of Hodges' erotic self-declaration and the requirement of secrecy for blackmail successfully to threaten disclosure: it was enough that Hodges was homosexual and 'it could not be said that the decision to withdraw security clearance was absurd, perverse or irrational'. If, as seems plausible in the light of the decision in *Masterson* v. *Holden*, it was Glidewell's view that homosexuality should always be hidden, that erotic perversity should never be openly declared, let alone displayed, then Hodges' sin was a lack of discretion: he would have done much better before Glidewell if he had remained in the 'closet' – or, indeed, the public toilet – where homosexuality has its traditionally scatological place.

In formal terms, the logic of the judgment in *Masterson* is circular; it is dead in the sense that it institutes a life that masks the life that is lived, that denies the lives that are actually led. The institution quite literally has nothing to say. So who is it who speaks, who is speaking?

In interpretative terms, the text sees nothing, it hears nothing, it says nothing. It runs scared, scared of its own desire, scared of the possibility of speech, scared of life and possibly scarred by the memory of sin, of Sodom, of corruption, of those things which happened long ago or 'time out of mind'. An institution which has lost the desire to speak, that has abandoned the surface of the text, that tyrannises with the emptiness of reason, is a dead institution, an entombed law, no more than detritus, relic, remains. My suggestion is that a semiotics of law can show us some of the forms of dying; it can read the signs and interpret the law so as to laugh at it, so as to seduce, to play by invocation of other worlds and more rigorous and living languages: surely a doctor staring up a speculum sometimes wonders how that uterus feels?

It is a question finally of value, of the value of life, and correlatively of the value of an interpretation, of what it can do. If we pose that question seriously, then we need to take up the position of accountants and be explicit about the material expenditure of specific lives and more particular about the values – the passions, the movements, the risks – through which being is accumulated and through which being is spent.[1] The very word 'interpretation' bears an important actuarial connotation since the Latin *interpres* from which interpretation is derived has at its root the word *pretium* or price.[2] Interpretation haggles before it fixes prices, it negotiates with the law, it seeks to make a bargain, it endlessly poses the question of how much does this cost, what should we pay, by what underlying measure should the price be fixed, what does the measuring imply? We are left then to balance the books, to audit the existing stock of meanings, to adjudicate profit and loss, to decide which interpretation to buy and for what quantity of promissory notes, for how many coins, for what futures?

The question is, what does an interpretation do? In that sense it is necessary to make comparisons, to calculate, not according to an order of truth – the law has always represented the truth – but

1   For elements of an actuarial analysis along these lines, see J. Simon, 'The Ideological Effects of Actuarial Practices' (1988) *Law and Society Review* 111.

2   See Benveniste, *Le Vocabulaire*, op. cit., I, at 140: 'In Latin . . . the term *pretium* 'price' has a difficult etymology; the only certain link within Latin is with *inter pret*, the notion was that of merchandise whose price was fixed by common agreement.' P. Legendre, *Le Désir politique de dieu*, op. cit., p. 300, comments interestingly.

according to an economy of texts and interpretations. Why look at it that way, why use that frame, why take a speculum to a body in love, why vulgarise an object or make a relationship, a motion, into a disinvested thing? Those are the values, the questions of life or of living, that are at stake in each judgment, that ideally give interpretation its value or, alternatively and more critically, that constitute its costs, its penalties, the losses attendant upon a method of interpretation that has lost its way, that has abdicated the role of merchant or haggler over meaning and the material and rhetorical forms which meaning takes.

Returning in conclusion to the character of a semiotic reading of common law, to the difference that it makes, to the question of what it does, it is helpful to recollect the particular character of any semiotics. If it is meaningful to talk of a general semiotics, it would refer simply to the signifying structure of all social life.[1] At the level of structure, the economic motif can be extended and it can be observed that societies form around systems of exchange, for it is only as material signs, as currency, that the elements of a culture can circulate, that a path can be formed in the moveable space of the imagination. All elements of culture circulate by means of such a symbolism, by means of an economic representation of value, by representing in material form a token of exchange, something, a woman, a text, a body, a word, for which we are prepared to accept a substitute. In each case the generality of a system of signs, of an economy of values, is specific in the sense that it is only on the basis of an order of legible and so negotiable, interpretable signs that exchange is possible: there has to be something to negotiate, there has to be a partially closed system of equivalences, of substitutions, of forms of paraphrase, for an economy to function, for goods to move. Precisely because it exists to be exchanged, because it exists as a value, the sign is irreducible: to be a sign is nothing other than to be mobile, to exist as the possibility of movement, as a means of accumulation and circulation.

Take up the last notion, that it is the materiality of signs that allows

1   'As in the case of women, the original impulse which compelled men to "exchange" words must be sought for in that split representation that pertains to the symbolic function. When a sonorous object is simultaneously perceived as having a value both for the speaker and the listener, the only way to resolve this contradiction is in the exchange of complementary values, to which all social existence is reduced.' (C. Levi-Strauss, *Structural Anthropology*, 1963, London, p. 62.)

elements to circulate, values to be exchanged, goods to move. Projection, as we have seen, is necessary to any movement; a map, a route, a road, a way are only possible according to an articulated landscape, a geography of movement, songlines or laws, depending upon where one is in the world. Our argument has been that where one is, is in the West a question of law, of the *lex terrae*, a question both of a territory and of a time, a memory. To take the territory first, we saw that it was England with all that such implies, not least a landscape of legally secured private spheres, bodies locked in castles, in homes, in gardens. We suggested that it might help to understand the law to comprehend it as a path, a way across that landscape, securing that rusticity, joining or articulating the borders of incommensurable spaces, a land of imperialist settlers, a slumbering earth. When the path becomes a highway, when the market becomes a mall, what has happened is simply that the law has designated an artificial space, a reality unbound from any particular earth, any particular soil, an immaculate conception. Being is replaced by projection, a flush by a mask, persona by legal subjectivity or, better, by possession and all that possession implies in terms of property, propriety and place. Of course, those who are possessed are also absent, mad, in theological terms diabolical and in need of exorcism. The law promises to invert this diabolism: the legal subject is possessed, yes, but possessed by reason, by 'rights', by property, by law, by debt. The institutional locus is carved from no more than the debris of living. Thus what is needed is a pathology of the body in law, of the body possessed by law from inside, of the law as an inroad to the body as a text, a hierarchy of texts, an institution of texts.

The existence of a path or a road is also initially a matter of memory, for how else could movement become sufficiently imprinted to indent a route, how else could vestigial being be tracked to its lair, how else would a lawyer discover the law? Consider the irony that underlies a rationalist conception of legal method: to discover the law is nothing less than to examine the past in the forms in which it has been inscribed, in precedent, in texts, in established institutions. The lawyer is explicit in his task; he seeks monuments stored in a monumental language and yet what the monument memorialises is precisely death, the absence of the living, the relics or remains, the debris of all that has disappeared. The language of the legal past shares with other histories the characteristic of being entombed, of existing only in the form of traces that have to be read, decoded, unveiled as traces of lives formerly lived according to specific routines. Insofar as the past is dead it does not speak, it is no longer currency, it is no longer 'quick', it is no longer a sign of anything beyond being a paradoxical reminder of that which is not or at least is no more. I will be quite blunt. If the law is to recognise itself as a way, if the legal past is to become a human history, then it can do so only on the basis of life, of presence, on the basis, that is, of a geography and a memory that will retrack the traces, that will repeat the routines, that will recollect the way. Those are the irreducible tasks of interpretation and of law as interpretation. They are tasks that Lord Justice Glidewell has signally failed to undertake. Even the concept of annunciation – the religious notion that through a spectral presence, through the angelic summoning of the law, the human can be equated with the divine – can be read blandly, lifelessly, legally, so that it loses whatever sense of presence or of striving for presence that *logos* or the incarnate word formerly connoted: read profanely and without fear the biblical text was layered, it was poetic, it had innumerable meanings for which men lived and for which they died. It had blood and it had skin, it instigated reform and counter-reform, revolution and revision upon the bodies of men. Like the secular law, it was interpreted many times, again and again, in solitude and in congregation: at least it was loved, at least it was hated. In its own terms it was not simply the truth it was also the light and the way. Where Glidewell LJ presences the law he ceases all attempt at freeing the space of interpretation. The annunciation he offers is institutional and cold, it explains nothing, it does not relate to the subjectivity of any behaviour and it lacks even a rhetorical presence; it is a pure annunciation and simply places the law, unmediated, without bargaining, upon the page. It is a style that is best typified by the mixture of decorum and boredom that resonates for those who wish to listen in his bloodless dismissal of 'counsel for the appellants, who, if I may say so, has put his argument in a most attractive and moderate way, [but] advances the same arguments as he did in the magistrates' court. He says that the conduct described in the facts found by the magistrates cannot have come within the meaning of the words "insulting behaviour" . . .' (41f–g). That is the tone of the judgment. It is scarcely interpretative; it does not aspire to meaning but only to a ritual and to symbols that were vacated some considerable time ago in favour of a law reduced to reason, reduced to writing as opposed to being, as it was, irreducibly written.

Because it is with the movement of two bodies that the case is concerned, any legal rule that emerges, any norm or abstract standard of behaviour that is to be gleaned from the decision, cannot escape the brute particularity, the libidinal surface, upon which an idea (of tenderness, of transgression, of violence, of insulting, of the proper) is inscribed, across which or through which an idea makes itself felt, makes itself life. The case deals with the movement of a hand, but it is not obvious that the violation is not that of the eye. It is not obvious that the decision makes felt a concurrent opposition between a geography which maps out and reconnoitres the body and the city on the basis of the eye and its specular judgments, and a geography mapped out by the hand, that hinges on a space traversed by the flesh, accessible only through touch – a terrain of which the hand has proprietary knowledge, a soil only the hand can legitimately enter, a dimension that can be traced only by sensation, a map that only the skin can remember.

Were we to pursue, to deepen, our analysis of the case it would be necessary to proceed to a semiotics of gesture and the equivocal history of the hand. The hand is the index of the flesh of the world: it has freed the flesh of slaves in the Roman law of manumission, it has cured sick flesh through faith, it has made the earth flesh through the common law ritual of *seisin*, it has measured the bodies of animals with reference to its own private parts – a horse, for example, is fourteen hands or more. The hand will always be a throwback to an older signature, an older form of possession, an older understanding of proximity, an older measure of distance, of space, of movement, of labour, of value. The hand still carries the world with its own palmy scale. The hand can measure the age of a thing through its fold, its moistness, its tendernesses. The hand shares in the intimate life of things.

The difference between law as a result of bargaining or a mediated, non-universal reality and law as an absolute, written text that maps out the body and the city once and for ever and for always is ultimately the difference between two forms of reason, two approaches to a text, two histories. The judgment analysed exists only within the space of a linear reason; its approach is progressive, it abolishes the possibility of interpretation by its refusal to recognise the irreducibility of writing, the history of the institution of writing as a political history of the struggle over differing forms of life. Explicitly, the issue is one of an opposition between reason and rhetoric, the visual and the sensuous, the inside and the outside. The opposition can also be posed in terms of the difference between a semiotics of law and the diagrammatic logic of contemporary forms of legal reason. Semiotics is concerned with the irreducibility of forms; its mode of interpretation is one which is based upon bargaining precisely because neither writing nor gesture nor geography can be reduced to literal contents. What we see in a sign is the possiblity of movement, the mobility of value, the circulation of goods. In that sense movement is fluid; it continuously remakes the institution and it bargains as to where and when the human can appear. That bargaining concerns the inside, the *hamartia* of material life as it is faced in the sensuous apprehension of thought: semiotics does not survey the surface of things so as to read an inner will or a unitary intention behind the thing; it reads the surface as a surface, as a sensuous and material field of force which extends outwards, which imposes its form upon the world. The concept of the inside, of *hamartia* or the tragedy, the historical plenitude of lived history in its numerous memorised forms, is all that there is to interpretation. It asks, where are we, according to what law, at what cost, in what history, and in whose speech?

In the specific terms of our analysis, can the law move in between the hand and the eye? Can it understand its maps as *pro*visional? Can it see the bus stop as a collapsible space: a city space for the women, an order of intimacy for the two men? Would it be possible then to map out an interpretative strategy, or a set of strategies, whereby the law could move in between a geography mapped out by the eye, a panoptical space held up by the projections of those who inhabit it, and a geography navigated by the hand, accessible only through touch, a dimension that can be traced only by sensation, a map that only the skin can remember?

The law would then recognise itself as always and already a deep structure of the erotic body: it would not follow the movement of life from behind, or hover over it from above, but would see itself surface through the body itself, the gestures themselves, the actions, the manipulations, the betrayals, the desires and the demotic of everyday life. If such a semiotics of law, such an interpretative strategy, were possible, it would be able to read the inner body, the body that lives and feels the world through the law, the emotional underside of a flesh that has many seams, many corridors, many waiting rooms, many archways, many altars.

8

Law's Emotional Body: Image and Aesthetic in the Work of Pierre Legendre

'The king is only truly king, that is, monarch, in images. They are his *real presence*. A belief in the effectiveness and operativeness of *his* iconic signs is obligatory, or else the monarch is emptied of all his substance through lack of transubstantiation, and only simulacrum is left; but inversely, because *his* signs are the royal *reality*, the being and substance of the prince, this belief is necessarily demanded by the signs themselves . . .'

'Quid est pictura? Veritas falsa.'[1]

'Take off the paint of Rome and you undo her.' Cast down the icons, remove the images or portraiture of the Roman Catholic faith and the Reformers believed that dissembling doctrine would also be undone. The war of images had begun, for the Church, at the Council of Nicea in 787.[2] It was a struggle over forms of representation, over the ceremonies, sacraments and texts – the rituals – through which the Western Church would present the moral law and inaugurate the bonding of human souls to Law. The external image or theatre of

---

1   Respectively, L. Marin, *Portrait of the King* (1988), p. 9; and A. Alciatus, *De Notitia Dignitatem* (1651 edn), p. 190.

2   See S. Runciman, *Byzantine Style and Civilization* (1987) ch. 3; also A. Grabar, *Christian Iconography* (1968), ch. 3. For an interesting introduction to the law of images in an English context, see M. Aston, *England's Iconoclasts* (1988), ch. 1. Legendre provides an account of the classical law of images in *Le Désir politique de dieu: Etude sur les montages de l'état et du droit* (1989, Paris, hereafter cited as *Désir*), pp. 233–6, an account that follows closely the essay on painting in J. Lacan, *The Four Fundamental Concepts of Psychoanalysis*, particularly (at p. 113): 'What makes the value of the icon is that the god it represents is also looking at it. It is intended to please God. At this level the artist is operating on the sacrificial plane – he is playing with those things, in this case images, that may arouse the desire of God . . . a certain pact may be signed beyond every image. Where we are, the image remains a go-between with the divinity – if Jahveh forbids the Jews to make idols, it

doctrine would bind the inner mind and the first act of reformation was consequently that of iconoclasm or 'defacing' of idolatrous representations – the simulated presence of God.[1]

What the Church recognised in the war of images was that forms of representation and of ritual were played for real stakes. Faith was predicated upon the symbolic presence of an absent God and the forms of that presence would determine both the character of the faith and the forms of adhesion or of love through which alone the individual could believe and so obey. In secular terms, the 'other Rome', that of the written law of Justinian, reports an early recognition in Roman law of an identical issue. Justinian's *Institutes* (2.1.34) had decided the case of an artist who paints upon a canvas owned by another in favour of the creator of the image and against the owner of the canvas. The twelfth-century glossators subsequently reversed that decision and assimilated the picture to the canvas by means of an analogy between painting and writing. From the twelfth century onwards, text and painting were to be treated as analogues: *pro lectione pictura est*, the picture is to be read.[2] The transposition was to prove crucial to the history of Western law. The work of art – whether it was a painting, a poem, a heraldic device or a book of law – was to be viewed or read as an act of creation or of authorship.[3] Behind its paint or its letters was another presence, the presence of one absent, that of God or Law, of nature or reason from whence the image came, from whom – or in whose name – it was sent. Precisely because the image was more than its simple appearance, because it

is because they give pleasure to other gods.' An interesting historical text is E. Troubetzkoi, *Trois Etudes sur l'icone* (1986).

1 See *Désir* at pp. 234–5: 'The distinction between image and idol fixes classification. In classical dogmatic theory, the idol is not an image . . . It is a reflection tied to a lie. A popular expression gives an exact account of the etymology (*eidolon*): something is thrown into full view. That is the idol, a false product of pure appearances. Anything else is in the register of the image, of the icon. There it is a question of the true . . . of the interrogation of identity, in the space of discourse were the *legal* representation of Reference takes form.'

2 Literally, 'the picture takes the place of knowing how to read'. See, T. G. Watkin, '*Tabula picta*: Images and Icons' (1984) 50 *Studia et documenta historiae et iuris*, 383–93.

3 In its classical formulation, the honour that should be manifested toward the image refers to the prototypes (*honosqui eis exhibitur, refertur ad prototypa*); the author is in other words not the artist but those further images (of God, the Virgin mother, the saints) of which the human is simply a resemblance. See *Désir*, p. 228.

belonged to the emotive body of a natural or unwritten tradition of law, to a secret knowledge of the heart, it could threaten or hold the invisible body, the emotional body, the affective subject or soul of those subject to the law.

The vast symbolic residue of the text is, according to Pierre Legendre, the indispensable condition of a knowledge of Western legal structure. It is a lost knowledge of the icons, images and Names, of the rites and myths, through which Western law becomes effective upon its subjects. It is to an aesthetic knowledge of the signs of law that the extensive writings of Legendre[1] have been dedicated. They have endeavoured to recover a lost poetic or mythic dimension of legal institutions and it is therefore as an aesthetic theory of the legal form that his work will be presented. This is admittedly to follow only one of several possible trajectories through his work. Other possible approaches would include the presentation of his writings as a history of the Roman and Canon law traditions,[2] a history of their presence in contemporary law, and as an application of psychoanalysis to legal theory. In the latter respect, Legendre, who has trained and practised as a psychoanalyst, has certainly contributed extensively to a Lacanian theory of the possession of the legal subject by Law, a theory of subjective adhesion or love of law as faith in the Other, in Knowledge and in Text.[3] Such approaches, however, provide accounts of no more than elements of a much larger philosophical project, that of a genealogy of legal institutions.[4]

In philosophical terms the originality and the coherence of

---

1 Legendre, *Paroles poétiques échappées du texte: Leçons sur la communication industrielle* (1982, hereafter *Paroles*) at p. 202: 'I have endlessly laboured my name.' It can be noted parenthetically that the name, Le-gendre, means the son-in-law, one who has chosen to enter the family by contract of marriage.

2 For which see *La Pénétration du droit Romain dans le droit canonique classique* (1964), and the essays collected in *Écrits juridiques du Moyen Age occidental* (1988). For different approaches, see J. Lenoble and F. Ost, *Droit, mythe et raison*, pp. 219–94, and N. Duxbury, 'Exploring Legal Tradition: Psychoanalytic Theory and Roman Law in Modern Continental Jurisprudence' (1989) 9 *Legal Studies* 94.

3 *La Passion d'être un autre: étude sur la danse* (1978, hereafter *Passion*), as well as the earlier works, *L'Amour du censeur: essai sur l'ordre dogmatique* (1972, hereafter *Amour*) and *Jouir du pouvoir: traité de la bureaucratie patriote* (1976, hereafter *Jouir*).

4 A project most explicitly formulated in *L'Inestimable Objet de la transmission: étude sur le principe généalogique en occident* (1985, hereafter *Transmission*) and most recently in *Désir*, op. cit. *Le Crime du Caporal Lortie* (1989) was published too late to be taken into account in this study.

Legendre's project is that of the immoralist before the law.[1] The account that he renders, the debt he pays, is that of coming to terms with Nietzsche as philosopher and genealogist of law. Situating his own work as that of one who writes in the twilight of the enlightenment, Legendre pushes forward the project of a subjectivist philosophy of the forms of attachment to law.[2] The question is initially that of the theatre of attachment, an issue of the mask or role or identity that will bind the individual to law, that will tie together in legal form the unity of a lived existence and so secure the political agency of the human subject through representation:

> Note that one of the central constructions of civil law, that which, following Justinian's terminology, we call *the law of persons*, literally derives from *persona* – referring initially to an actor's mask – and authorises me to translate the formula *de iure personarum* by 'of the law of masks'. In all institutional systems the political subject is reproduced

1 Legendre frequently remarks that his writings are not intended for an academic audience and resist the policing of discourse that is the contemporary role of the university. In *Paroles* at p. 12 we are informed that his theoretical effort to locate the dogmatic function in ultra-modern society has often been judged absurd: 'it has to pass outside the ridicule of certain retrograde academics (the self-same who tried to obstruct my teaching at the Sorbonne, judging it immoralist), but also the artificial division of the insufficiently criticised traditional knowledges. The indolent pedagogues, partisans of a systematic brainwashing, doubtless hope that the discoveries made by Freud and Lacan will disappear from circulation.' At ibid., p. 227: 'I have learned to arrange my life by the side of poets and of all those whose discourse wavers, and not in the company of intellectuals.' See also *Jouir*, p. 11: 'This book is devoid of any utility in the university.'

2 It is a pleasing enigma of early printed legal texts that no one has yet been able to divine the reasons for the use of capital letters. I will follow that convention, though as a guide to the reader I would specify that I use the upper-case Law to mimic Lacan's definition of symbolic Law, and the lower case to refer to positive law; see Lacan, *Ecrits* (1977): 'It is in the name of the father that we must recognise the support of the symbolic function which, from the dawn of history, has identified his person with the figure of the law' (p. 67). Similarly with Text, the upper case denotes Legendre's usage, Text referring to the textual system as a unified whole, the Text without a subject, the lower-case text referring to the no less unified textual instance. See *L'Empire de la vérité: Introduction aux espaces dogmatiques industriels* (1983, hereafter *Empire*), pp. 36–7: 'The Text without a subject signifies that institutional history is dependent upon a logic of symbolic transmission, that is to say upon a legal logic . . . in the perspective of the history of Roman law, the Text without a subject is a notification of the principle of paternity.'

through masks. This translation contributes to the rehabilitation of the problematic of the image at the heart of the legal order.[1]

Three indices from Nietzsche may serve to map the direction that will be traced in Legendre's studies in terms of genealogy, forms of reason and tragedy.[2]

Firstly, reference should be made to the development of Nietzsche's genealogical project. Its basic proposition was that to understand the past was not to understand something that happened, a truth, but rather to comprehend forms of life or modes of living – all those forms of inheritance, of emotion, habit, experience and seduction, that reproduce the human as a specific life. The value of history was precisely that of its modes of appearance: it was through its myths, its symbols and its rites that the past lived. In the early and little recognised essays[3] on philology, Nietzsche inveighed against the historical disciplines for studying a dead past, a past annihilated by the 'Gorgon head of the classicist',[4] the priestly imitator and supine servant of an idealised Latinity.[5] What is dead is simply dead and in that sense there is no history, no consecrated order of death. What lives in the past is that which ignored death, which through art transfigured life and became image and myth *in articulo mortis*: not history but tradition. The positive project of a genealogy is developed later as a study of the elements of life:

> Hitherto all that has given a colour to existence has lacked a history; where would one find a history of love, of avarice, of envy, of conscience, of piety, of cruelty? Even a comparative history of law . . . All that up till now has been considered as the 'conditions of existence', of human beings, and all reason, passion and superstition in this consideration – have they been investigated to the end?'[6]

1   *Désir*, pp. 225–6.
2   M. Foucault, 'Nietzsche, Genealogy, History' in *Language, Counter-Memory, Practice* (1977), is here a useful and unusual guide. For a specific application, see Foucault, 'On Governmentality' (1979) 6 *I & C* 5.
3   In particular, Nietzsche, 'We Philologists' in *The Case of Wagner* (1911) and idem, 'Homer and Classical Philology' in *The Future of our Educational Institutions* (1909). The guiding text, however, is *The Birth of Tragedy* (1909). For discussion of a similar view, see G. Rose, *The Dialectic of Nihilism* (1984), pp. 131–70.
4   'Homer and Classical Philology', at p. 147.
5   'We Philologists', at pp. 117, 126, 133, 139–40.
6   *The Joyful Wisdom* (1910), pp. 42–3.

Genealogy, in short, would study the descent of the conditions of existence to expose 'a body totally imprinted by history'.[1]

Secondly, as the invocation of genealogy suggests, reason is no longer to be viewed as the only order of the disciplines. It belongs rather to the many histories of sentiment and passion, albeit that it is our passion, our inescapable tradition, our institution. To uncover the body of that institution in genealogical terms is to study its ancestry, its descent. It is to study also what is lost in this transmission; to understand that a history of inscription includes the history of the surface, of that which was scratched out in order to make a certain mark, that which was covered in order to paint a certain sign, that which was mixed in order to make a certain image stick, that which was burned in order to make a certain brand. Behind the order of disciplines, screened by systems of knowledge, Nietzsche had from early on discerned, behind the figure of the scholar, the shadow of the lawyer. The classical tradition was a legal tradition, its writings were notarial, its knowledges were clerical catalogues, filing systems of distinctions, for these 'are philosophers who are at bottom nothing but systematising brains – the formal part of the paternal occupation has become its essence to them. The talent for classifications, for tables of categories, betrays something; it is not for nothing that a person is the child of his parents. The son of an advocate will also have to be an advocate as investigator'.[2] In more formal terms, the discourse of truth has always appeared in the guise of law.

There is finally the question of that which lives and lives on, or in Nietzsche's phrase: 'he who has no sense for the symbolical has none for antiquity'.[3] The last stage of the genealogical project and the purpose of its history 'is not to discover the roots of our identity but to commit itself to its dissipation',[4] and thereby to recover or to make again the tragic reality of appearance: as action, as image and myth, life depends upon art and its theatre of illusion. In terms spelled out most explicitly in *The Birth of Tragedy*, the Socratic tradition or rationalism in its various historical forms was to be credited with having killed art and most particularly with the destruction of myth. Nietzsche offers both a diagnosis and a prognosis. In terms of the

1 Foucault (1977), op. cit., at p. 148.

2 *Joyful Wisdom*, op. cit., at p. 288. For further considerations on this theme, see M. Cousins, 'The Practice of Historical Investigation' in D. Attridge et al. (eds.), *Post-structuralism and the Question of History* (1987).

3 'We Philologists' at p. 118.   4 Foucault (1977), op. cit., at p. 163.

former, rationalism, or in contemporary terminology modernism, was a species of dogmatic reason determined upon deciding life in advance of living it and equally upon valuing the search for truth above the truth itself: that is to say, it was a theoretic reason, one which maps out life in advance of itself and thus refuses life as art, as music, as the conflagration and redrawing of the map.[1] Surrounded by the debris of archaic culture and blind from the dust of books and printer's errors, modernity testified apologetically to the loss of myth and the repression of the creative powers of poetry and art. Only the fading myths, the ruins, of countless other cultures stood between modernity and the most radical pessimism. In terms of prognosis, Nietzsche viewed art as the limit of scientific objectivism, and myth as the necessary consequence or end of science: 'only after the spirit of science has been led to its boundaries, and its claim to universal validity has been destroyed by the evidence of these boundaries, can we hope for a re-birth of tragedy: for which form of culture we should have to use the symbol of Socrates the musician'.[2]

Legendre is more guarded than Nietzsche in his prognosis of the future of dogmatic culture.[3] It should also be observed that in his critique of dogmatics he uses a Freudian vocabulary of repression and desire culminating in a positive prospect of poetic rights and the renewal of interpretative culture in its fullest sense.[4] In terms of his

1   Compare J. Derrida, *The Post Card* (1987) at p. 20: 'The charter is the contract for the following, which quite stupidly one has to believe: Socrates is before Plato, there is between them – and in general – an order of generations, an irreversible sequence of inheritance. Socrates is before, not in front of, but before Plato, therefore behind him, and the charter binds us to this order: this is how to orient one's thought, this is the left and the right, march.' See also p. 4, for discussion of deciding to decide, the predestined reading.

2   *Birth of Tragedy* at p. 131. It is commented upon in Legendre, *Empire*, pp. 174ff. In terms of subsequent themes, especially those spelled out in *Désir*, it is worth noting a further passage from the same work (p. 174): 'the state itself knows no more powerful unwritten law than the mythical foundation which vouches for its connection with religion and its growth from mythical ideas.'

3   *Empire* at p. 174, 'let us leave to Nietzsche his hopes as to such an eventuality and retain his diagnosis. The subduing of the arts and the exiling of poetry have been enterprises of a rationalist and managerial mentality.'

4   *Paroles* at pp. 53–4, 95, 137–8. At pp. 58–9: 'Institutions confine us in a linguistic prison, a mystic prison that ignores us as such because . . . convinced that poetry, mad and delirious words cannot exist there, in that place which we call power. We have ended up by definitively forgetting (with the help of the

general project, however, Legendre's extensive writings move precisely from the critique of history in terms of a renewed and refined concept of genealogy, through the critique of legal reason to an aesthetics of law. It is that appropriately trinitarian trajectory that will be followed here. In bibliographical terms, such a path can also be perceived in the development of Legendre's career. Trained as a historian of Roman and Canon law, his earliest work concentrated on the eleventh- and twelfth-century revolution in methods of legal and scriptural interpretation. The glossators of classical law (*utrumque ius*) founded the Western tradition of interpretation and established, by reference to the two Romes of the Church and the secular law, the conditions of existence of the Western legal institution and its varied political, social and other administrative discourses and knowledges. His major philological studies are published in *Ecrits Juridiques du Moyen Age Occidental* and in *La Pénétration du Droit Romain dans le Droit Canonique Classique.*[1]

The thesis developed from the early philological studies of the learned law was subsequently applied to a genealogy of law as a form of life. The symbolic structure of the glossatorial revolution was traced into the development of the disciplines and was analysed also in terms of the juridical structure of Western institutions; it was proposed as their founding logic.[2] The studies of this period which were published between 1968 and 1982 are remarkable for their range and scope of reference and for their overturning of traditional classificatory schemata. Inspired by his study and practice of psychoanalysis, Legendre presented studies that ranged from a textbook on the juridical history of the French administration and its dogmatics (*Histoire de l'Administration*),[3] through studies of censorship and the dogmatic order (*L'Amour du Censeur*), the nationalism of bureaucratic order (*Jouir du Pouvoir*), to a psychoanalytic study of power, the body and dance (*La Passion d'être un Autre*), and a short history of poetry, art and the stylistic constraints of the love letter

propaganda of true history) what to institute means and equally that systems of management work not to alienate but to metamorphose.'

1   See n. 2 on page 262 above. The uncollected essays are too numerous to cite, though reference will be made where relevant in the text.

2   'Do not lose sight of this: my work intervenes at a certain historical moment, one when it has become possible to lay bare the structures which carry the West (l'occident).' *Transmission*, p. 13.

3   (1968, Presses Universitaires de France).

(*Paroles Poétiques échappées du texte*). The last-mentioned work, published in 1982, significantly developed themes that became central in later studies. In *L'Empire de la Vérité*, Legendre embarked upon the third stage of his project, now published in the magisterial style of *Leçons*, that of an historical anthropology of contemporary knowledges, an analysis of the dogmatics of ultramodernity. His last two published works further specify and substantiate a project that has spanned over thirty years and continues into the future with the founding of a national centre for the study of genealogy and filiation in Paris. In *L'Inestimable Objet de la Transmission*, we are presented with an intricate study of the genealogical basis of normative systems of thought, which was followed by a translation of key and 'undesirable' texts on Western systems of kinship, *Le Dossier Occidental de la Parenté*. In his most recent work, *Le Désir Politique de Dieu*, published last year, Legendre presents his most comprehensive study to date of the iconography of power, a study of the aesthetics of law, of the juridical system of signs, of signs which get under the skin and mark the emotional body of the subject, the organs, the obedient soul.

Critique of Dogmatic Reason[1]

For the benefit of common lawyers still unfamiliar with, or unwilling explicitly to acknowledge, the European history of their law, certain preliminary observations as to dogmatic reason are probably necessary. Dogmatics, derived from the Greek *dokein*, to think, has an instructively ambivalent semantic history. In one little-acknowledged derivation, to which Legendre frequently returns, it refers to the unconscious unravelling of thought, to reverie and the recounting of dreams and visions. In this aspect, dogma relates to the images of a simulated world of appearance and becomes the root of the Latin terms *decus*, *decor* and *decet*, referring to dignity, decorum and honour, aesthetic terms of considerable political importance insofar as it was

---

1   Legendre does not himself use the term critique and I am conscious that it bears certain negative Hegelian connotations. I use it here in a weak sense to draw attention to the affinity between the critical dimension of Legendre's work and the various contemporary critiques of enlightenment reason. Most particularly, J. P. Sartre, *Critique of Dialectical Reason* (1976), R. Debray, *Critique of Political Reason* (1983), and P. Sloterdijk, *Critique of Cynical Reason* (1987). A. J. Arnaud's *Critique de la raison juridique* belies its title in being a sociological history of legal thought.

for decorum, for the honour and the dignity of their country (*patria*) that Romans would die most readily: *dulce et decorum est pro patria mori*.[1] That aesthetic dimension of dogma, of the images for which the subject would die, is crucial to the comprehension of the discourse that is repressed in the later usage of dogmatics as the study of religious and legal truths, its object being that which has already been decided. In that acceptation it is an axiomatic form of study developed by the scholastics of the twelfth-century university[2] as the methodical presentation of the order of law.

To live and to die for a totem, a country, a fatherland, for the Law, was in one quite literal sense to adhere to an image of power with one's body: to a portrait of the king,[3] to a mystic body, a flag or emblem which would screen the subject against death while leading inexorably to it (*moriendum certe est*). In the later dogmatic tradition, the symbolics of power, of the power of life and death and of the order of law that mediated between the two categories, was displaced by the glossatorial concept of a sacral written law, a law which expressed the one truth and the unitary cause (*causa causans*) of a monotheistically conceived God. That God was the universal emperor of the Roman Catholic world, the author of all law (*Deo auctore*) and the source of all truth. For the dogmatic interpretative tradition that developed from the late eleventh century onwards and founded the university disciplines, that foundational tenet was to be understood quite literally and so to the exclusion of all other truths: that is, to the exclusion of all other gods. Rigorously excluding any aesthetic or poetic conceptions of emperor or law that might indicate the temporal and mythic fabrication of the divine will, dogmatics translated myth into truth and Law into Text: *veram philosophiam, non simulationem*; the monotheistic belief in one God is the unitary root of the scientific belief in a single truth, in one law.

1   For Legendre's comments on this semantic history, see *Empire*, pp. 30ff. See also the invaluable work of E. Kantorowicz, *The King's Two Bodies: A Study in Medieval Political Theology* (1981), pp. 232–72, and idem, *Selected Studies* (1975), pp. 308–24.

2   On the early development of legal dogmatics, see H. Berman, *Law and Revolution* (1983); see also H. Coing, 'Trois Formes Historiques d'Interpretation du Droit' (1970) 48 *Revue d'histoire du droit* 533. For a broader perspective see M. Herberger, *Dogmatik: Zur Geschichte von Begriff und Methode in Medizin und Jurisprudenz* (1981).

3   The essential study here is L. Marin, *Portrait of the King* (1988). See also M. Tournier, 'L'Image du Pouvoir' in *Petites Proses* (1987).

The notion of a sacred or, properly, sacral law (*lex sacra*) is ambivalent and according to one etymology can be interpreted as a law of sacrifice, as a law that carries with it an element of loss and of remorse at all that is given up or repressed in adhering to one law, to one order of the licit and the exclusion of all else.[1] Keeping such a notion of the sacred in reserve, Legendre is initially concerned with the foundational symbolism of unity and universality in the Western tradition. The sacred law is ambivalent in a less metaphysical sense insofar as it combines two histories and two systems of written law, those of the *Corpus Iuris Civilis* and of the *Corpus Iuris Canonici*. The two laws intermingle and the *Decretals* owe quite as much to Justinian's *Corpus* as did the *Corpus Iuris Civilis* itself to the Christian theology of the incarnate word. For the glossators, the law as truth was a matter of writing; it was a matter of that which was to be read, the word 'law' itself being derived from *legere*, to read.[2] What the glossators of Roman law provided was a dogmatic method of reading the law as though it were the truth. The principle of such reading can be understood initially in grammatological terms, a single compilation of texts or Text was isolated and stored apart, protected from time and the blandishments of profane reading, it would come to serve as the foundation of power.[3] What was written, *ratio scripta*, could only be interpreted as law, or in Legendre's terminology as belonging to the realm of scripture, of *c'est écrit*.

The Text is in the first instance a positive expression of universal rule and it is to the symbolism of that rule rather than to its immediate content that attention should be directed. What is established in the massive simulation that inaugurates the name or voice of the law is a principle of sources. Following the juristic wisdom itself, the first question to be posed of the law is that of its origin, from where it comes: *unde nomen iuris*[4] is the opening question of the *Digest* and the

1   See *Amour*, p. 124; *Désir*, pp. 262–4.

2   The etymology is from Isidore of Seville (*Etymologies*): *lex a legendo est, quia scripta est*, commented upon in *Désir*, pp. 289–97. See P. Stein, *Regulae Iuris* (1966), pp. 3–19, also E. Benveniste, *Le Vocabulaire des institutions Indo-Européenes II* (1969), pp. 267–73.

3   For a vivid account and criticism of the sacral aura surrounding the physical texts of the *Corpus Iuris*, see Hotman, *Anti-Tribonian* (1567/1603 edn) at pp. 120–21: 'the original being guarded like a sacred and precious relic, only being very rarely shown accompanied by candles and torches, thus did the ancient mystagogues show their law to the faithful [*sacrez*]'.

4   D. 1.1.1. *iuri operam daturum prius nosse operter, unde nomen iuris descendat*.

endlessly repeated question of foundation or *quaestio quid iuris*. At one level, the answer to the question was that law was a word, a name, an etymology, that is worked both by the Roman lawyers and by their later interpreters. At the level of the symbolic with which Legendre is concerned, the question leads us into the realm of the peculiar mythology of law, that of a sacred mouth that speaks the law and in turn of a speech that embodies or incarnates the holy will. What is crucial is that the imagery in which the law is clothed is not ignored in favour of some notion of its rational content. The question posed, the image that descends upon the intellect, is a genealogical one and depends for its answer upon a lineage of descent, a presentation of filiation which will assign the law to a legitimate author or parent.

The dogmatic answer to the question of origin incarnates the law in the mouth of the sovereign emperor: law comes from the oracle, from the living voice of law (*viva vox iuris*) in the person, the mask, of God's servant, *vicarius Christi*, Justinian. The point is quite literally fundamental to the presence of law as a living and breathing law (*lex animata*), as the work of the tongue that speaks the law *as if* it were his own. The line of parentage or descent can be traced through the glossatorial metaphors of filiation and equally through the iconography of legal power in which the heart of the legal subject is invariably represented as hanging on a thread held by the sovereign, be it emperor, Leviathan or Justinian in person. In more prosaic terms, the imperial image of God (*imago Dei et Mundi*) answers the question of origin in terms of ancestry: the law must be presented as a distant speaking body, a *corpus iuris* from whose mouth all law will emanate and in whose breast all the archives are concealed: *omnia scrinia habet in pectore suo*. From that emblematic vanishing point the law acquires both its name and its authority: hung as a screen before the unspeakable and invisible realm of the Other, the portrait of the emperor is there to mediate, innocently to mouth true law as *per ora principium promulgatae*.

Bound to God through the inaugural power of the word, the speech of the emperor took the material form of law as text. The archaic and fragmentary texts to which the emperor appended his name in the massive form of the *Corpus Iuris* were to become, for the dogmatic tradition, the only source of truth and law. In the words of a thirteenth-century jurist: 'just as God divided the elements of

(Whoever wishes to work the law must first learn from where the name of the law descends.)

primordial matter and brought them to light, so Justinian clarified
the disorder, the origins and materials of Law, both so as to illuminate
the wise and to glorify civil and canon Law'.[1] Once that principle of
truth was established, all subsequent social speech would have to take
its place by reference to original words, and the authority or
legitimacy of any other text was to be a matter of its descent from the
Text of the Law itself. In a much cited passage, Legendre refers in the
starkest of terms to the text as

> a species of linguistic capital subject to norms of conservation and of a
> uniformly identifiable procedure of reproduction, without which we
> would be astonished neither by its durability, nor by its logic which
> signifies in no uncertain manner an untouchable and incontestable
> phenomenon. The law is thus to be used as a language, and the jurists as
> a race of interpreters are no more than a species of linguist.[2]

In the no less explicit formula of the ninth-century Pope John VIII,
'the laws of the Romans, divinely taught through the mouths of the
emperors, must be venerated'.[3] They must be obeyed as sacred
speech. In terms of dogmatics, it is to the critique of law as sacral
social speech, as a speech also that has sacrificed many elements of
reality, that Legendre moves. The critique of dogmatic reason can be
traced in concrete institutional terms, in terms that have a very clear
contemporary resonance, from the sacral principle of the divine
innocence of lawyers to the critique of truth as the unitary knowledge
of law.

Innocence, Faith and Law

The substantive principles of legal method, its rhetoric and forms of
argumentation, its interpretative rules and its procedures of documentation, are all genealogically derived from the sacral myth of a

1   Boncompagnus, *Rhetorica Novissima: 1 De Origine iuris*, cited in *Amour* at p. 91.

2   *Jouir* at p. 62. Compare the analysis of P. Bordieu, *Ce que parler veut dire:
L'économie des échanges linguistiques* (1987), at p. 97: 'To try to understand the
manifestations of linguistic power linguistically, to search in language for the logic
and principle of its efficacity as institutional language, is to forget that authority
comes to language from outside. As the sceptre held by the orator about to speak
in Homer concretely reminds us, authority is represented, manifested, symbolised
in language.'

3   *Venerandae romanae leges, divinitus per ora principium promulgatae*, commented
upon in *Empire*, p. 138.

perfect speech. The structural principle that guarantees the authority of the profession and the legitimacy of its speech is precisely the filiation or descent of that speech from the divinity. The profession is possessed of a hidden wisdom (*arcana juris*) and its task is to mediate that wisdom, to insert it in social speech as the absolute boundary of what it is humanly possible to say. As a secular priesthood, a cloistered profession, the task of the jurists was to be interpreted literally as that of promulgating 'the most sacred of things, knowledge of civil law' (*res sacratissima civilis sapientia*).[1] Their task was to make the law human, to fabricate a social reality from the other world of the text:

> [T]hese constructions of law, that is to say in the last instance these perishable but necessary constructions, [constitute] an uninterrupted labour of reconstruction of reality itself. There precisely is the import of the term *dogmatic*, because it evokes the assemblage of images [*montages*] that result from this work of construction and obliges us to consider that which is at issue in all institutional systems: the relation of humanity to law.[2]

That task, however, is the very antithesis of the representation of dogmatics that is to be found in the profession or in the university; it refers in many senses to a lost art of law and, indeed, to a repressed hermeneutics.

As we find it in the post-reception tradition, the legal profession has clung on to its priestly status but, outside of the later revolutions, has relinquished any claims to the title of mythmakers or poets of law. The dogmatic tradition in its full sense was displaced by the philologists so bitterly attacked by Nietzsche, a race of imitators, of epigones, of the dead who saw their role as that of the relentless defence of truths, of pieties, that were already in place.[3] In the hands of the university, the law became something unknown, a profession quite literally of ignorance in the form of knowledge. Dogmatics here connotes a reason that has turned away from the world, a cult of innocence in the face of life: the law loses itself in its function, decadently and aimlessly staggering from case to case, from distinction to distinction, innocently and ignorantly applying grammatical rules to subjugate questions of meaning. These prestigious doctors

---

1 D. 50.13.55.   2 *Désir*, p. 34.
3 *Désir*, p. 18, cites the 'imbecilic' glossator Fransiscus Accursius, son of the

(*praestantia doctorum*) were sleepwalkers, dwarves who 'do not even have the pretension of thinking, merely practising the social art of putting texts into play. That is why the company of jurists is customarily dreaded'.[1] Their discourse was a borrowed speech enveloped in the strictest of rhetorical codes. The jurist might be the emblem, the living body, of the law, but his life was a surrogate one: 'In the epiphany of the law, the jurist counts for nothing, he has invented nothing, he is innocent, having simply provided a logical account of the text, in pronouncing words borrowed from the text.'[2] The lawyer says nothing but rather, in imitation of the emperor (*imitatio imperii*), mouths quite literally the speech of another. In a letter to his father from law school, Kafka intimated as much in bemoaning that 'I am nourished spiritually by sawdust which, to make matters worse, several thousand mouths have already chewed for me.'[3]

The awful fate of the lawyer is that he can speak only the truth. In Legendre's formulation, 'the speaking being is spoken, it is spoken by the discourse of institutions, dogmatic discourse'.[4] Empty bearer of the truth, the jurist assumed the mantle of dogmatics and became the simple manipulator of a universal order of law, a technician of order whose function is nothing other than the propagation of submission.[5] Ignorance in the guise of innocence is a powerful weapon and Legendre is unstinting in his examination of its workings. The principle of innocence is in the first instance a simple manifestation or statement of faith inaugurating the precedence of belief over knowledge. The principle is one of repression in that to speak or write the

---

author of the *Glossa Ordinaria*: '*Acerrimus, verus et pius defensor glossarum patris*' (I am the relentless, true and faithful, defender of my father's glosses).

1   *Empire*, p. 160. Compare the self-depiction of the twelfth-century canonist Pierre de Blois, *Patrologia Latine*, ccvi, 290: '*Nos, quasi nani super gigantum humeros*' (we are as dwarfs hoisted on the shoulders of giants), cited in *Amour*, p. 103.

2   *Amour*, p. 96. *Transmission*, p. 16: 'Dogmatic knowledges have nothing to say, because humanity has nothing to say, the dogmatic knowledges are bound to repetition.'

3   *Transmission*, p. 16.   4   Ibid., p. 75.

5   See *Amour*, p. 51, citing the glossator Alban d'Hauthuille: 'We, professors of the scientific order, retain at least this task, the charge of teaching respect for the order of law.' For the development of the concept of respect for order as both a linguistic and a legal concept, see my '*Ars Bablativa,* Abraham Fraunce and the Genealogy of English Jurisprudence' in G. Leyh (ed.), *Legal Hermeneutics: History, Theory, Law* (1990).

truth is to immolate the self. The jurist must profess faith in the text; the title of the *Digest, de fide instrumentorum* (of the faith which attaches to instruments)[1] implies not only faith in the truth of the written word but equally that its scribe is the faithful instrument, the 'living tool' or 'hand' that takes down the word of the law. The second theme of Legendre's critique moves from the dogmatists to the institution.

The term code (*codex*), referring to written law, also connotes material support: institutional speech consistently refers to and relies upon a juridical text which is rigorously represented as being external to it. The science of law can be understood as operating a double repression, firstly in hiding the law in the past – though a past free of history – and secondly, through its refusal to talk of anything else but transmitted law. The innocence of the jurists is that of endlessly working and reworking the legitimate texts, dogma. The positive object of such study has traditionally been that of weighing and counting the authorities, *pro* and *contra*, distinguishing, analogising and generalising where necessary. In scientific terms, the object of such textual casuistry is hypothetical in that the logic of the text takes precedence over any substantive application: the law lies in wait for everyone, it is the 'dead letter' that can arrive at any time, it is the theorem that can be applied to any triangle, the God that can drop in at any moment of sin. The fiction perpetrated is that of a past that has been integrated into an eternal present which repeats itself endlessly: the fiction which marks entry into the sphere of legal logic is that of 'the legists' insistence on treating their system *more geometrico*, in the style of a geometry, in the remarkable effort to efface from the past all traces of history'.[2] Hence it is not that geometry (or law) does not have a past, but that its past does not count. The space created by this genuinely enigmatic form of communication and its medieval tools of practice is that of a reclusive tradition, of a specialism whose only knowledge is internal to its own discipline: 'it consists of ignoring the social importance of legal constructions, and encloses them in a sort of cloistered science. The law is a dumping ground, a refuse heap, and lawyers . . . are refuse collectors . . . they clean up and no more is said

1 D. 22.4. See *Paroles*, p. 97: 'He who writes makes himself part of that which is written, by his name and by graphism, but he writes as an innocent instituted by the message. He is the hand. He is the person who writes in the name of the Guarantor . . . the innocent instrument of account . . .' See further, M. Clanchy, *From Memory to Written Record* (1987), pp. 88–116.

2 *Jouir*, p. 162.

of them.'[1] Precisely in cleaning up, in erasing the dirt of history, in the clinical purity of their performance, they resist ever questioning their own image or their own terms: fiction should by convention end happily and the student-citizens therefore should be spared the demoralising social reality of the past and be presented rather with what the classics referred to as a perfect society.[2]

But there is a difference between the fictions of geometry, its infinite approximations at triangles as it feels its way about the world, comes towards the earth and re-maps and reconnoitres its human geography, and the fictions of legal logic. The internality of legal history precludes any very direct access to knowledge, to knowing, to smelling the legal ground; in part because such a sanitised law refers to everything and nothing, in part because legal knowledge acts as a screen to any alternative enquiry. The censorship of the law operates in one respect as a terminological maze: not only does the law have jurisdiction – the right to speech (*iuris dictio*) – but in a more subtle and insidious sense Legendre points to the entire panoply of legal sophistry as a mechanism geared to silence or censor its opponents in the thesaurus, the dictionary of the law. In a passage worth citing at length, Legendre spells out the awesome responsibility of legal categories:

> In this game of pure logic, rebellion loses itself, it is dissipated into nomenclatures, distinguished into classes of error, to which the jurist methodically brings to bear qualifications, criteria of classification and the casuistry of jurisprudence. As an inexorable consequence, the Law – seen from this point of view as the pursuit of those who have escaped – figures as the royal road, by virtue of which the possession of the subject finds its final and most extreme guarantee; in leading any conflict whatsoever to the limits of the known, and in setting in motion the discourse of proof, through a dialectic of questions both for and against, *pro* and *contra*, the School digests antinomy.[3]

What is left after the faithful have set about the task of interpretation is a resounding political silence: the eternal present of fragments that have been torn out of their history, arranged and re-arranged in the manner of a mathematical logic, is interesting only for what it does not say. The ignorance of the history of law is instructive only as the sign of a repressed speech: you become the bearer of your own

1   *Empire*, p. 49. The metaphor of waste as both refuse and refusal is well developed in T. Pynchon, *The Crying of Lot 49* (1967).

2   *Jouir*, pp. 89, 162–3.   3   *Amour*, p. 165.

repression, you censor yourself, you cut yourself off, you behave normally. The turn towards an interior reality preserves the mystery of censorship; no one is responsible for it.

The Order of Reference and the Name of the Law

The legal function is, for Legendre, a function specified as speaking the truth. The model for such speech is one of mediation or of transmission of a message that will absolve,[1] it comes from elsewhere, from above, and is 'presenced' below. The significance of such a dogmatic function relates firstly to the creation of a space or geography of truth; it is necessary to establish an architecture of truth, a structural site to which the attributes of licit speech can be attached. In Roman law that site or zero point is that of reference. It can be reconstructed first in terms of the Roman lawyers' conception of judgment which is presented in the *Digest* as *res judicata pro veritate habetur* (judgments take the place of truth). Truth guarantees the discourse of the Law; it is carried into it by the judge who 'wears the sacerdotal mask and takes up the sacred place of the untouchable, he represents the all powerful and absent Other ... it is not he who speaks but the Truth of the Law'.[2] In literal terms, the judge imitates the emperor and becomes the mouthpiece, the empty vehicle, of the ancestral speech, namely that of Rome.

In spite of the ambivalent reference of the term Rome, as both Church and Law (*dua sunt genera christianorum*), it is important to locate the space of law's truth as a specific body of texts and as a highly particular method of reference. In structural terms, 'the truth is a place, by hypothesis it is the empty space where there is nothing if it is not for these texts. This point recurs consistently, because dogmatics is consistent, it is the relationship to a truth which is resident in specified texts. Reference is reference to these texts. In other words, we are in the sphere of speaking texts',[3] of texts that the law makes speak. In making the texts speak, the jurist labours to prolong the life of Rome, to carry into the future the imperialist text and the sovereignty that it harbours. Again referring to the *Digest*, Rome is the

1 Legendre offers several substantive analyses of the penitential model of legal discourse. See, most notably, *Amour*, pp. 162ff, *Empire*, pp. 207–8, and 'Aux sources de la culture occidental: L'ancien droit de la pénitence' (1975, reprinted in *Ecrits*).

2 *Amour*, p. 115, *Empire*, pp. 178–9.   3 *Empire*, p. 103.

common homeland (*Roma communis nostra patria est*)[1] and it lives on; it does not die because its reason is universal and its text is all-encompassing. The text is a country; it is something inhabited, something that surrounds us and that we live through. In its name we live and die; it is inescapable, it is reason, it is the symbol of life, it institutes us. The classical references to the persistence and compass of the text can be multiplied indefinitely: it is that which touches all (*quod omnes tangit*),[2] it is total law (*totum ius*), the culture which as legal subjects we breathe. Legendre gives the term a significant twist. As the zero point of all reference, the text inhabits another time and another place, that of myth which shores up the whole edifice of culture. The text is a symbol of a universal territory (*ius commune universum*), a geography unified by law. It is a space containing all civilised people, a text and territory to which the subject either belongs or is expunged through the law of territory, of *terreo* – a terror arbitrated by means of *ius terrendi* or *ius submovendi*, which can be translated loosely as the power to erase from the map. In Legendre's terms, 'we live in an artificial universe, in a universe of fiction, defined allegorically and underpinned by the discourse of the inarticulable, of that which can only be formulated ceremonially or poetically. That is the founding fact of geography and of international law'.[3]

The implications of such a dramatic and violent textuality[4] are twofold. In the first instance, the text inaugurates a mental space of law; it puts into play a principle of adhesion that operates at the level of spirituality: in the classical canonist formula 'the Church does not inhabit a territory' (*ecclesia non habet territorium*), it does not capture the subject through the corporeal arms of a specific locality, but through a terror of definition which knows no geographical boundaries.[5] The speech of law is directed at the soul, at the *principium* or moving principle of the subject, and for that end to be accomplished requires

1   *Désir*, pp. 371ff, discussing D. 50.1.3. See also Kantorowicz (1981), op. cit., n. 29, pp. 247ff.

2   See G. Post, *Studies in Medieval Legal Thought* (1964), pp. 356–59, for further commentary.

3   *Empire*, p. 217; compare *Jouir*, p. 246.

4   The introduction to the *Institutes* provides an explicit indication of that violence: 'Imperial majesty should not only be embellished with arms but also armed with laws . . .' (*imperatoriam maiestatem non solum armis decoratam, sed etiam legibus oportet esse armatam*).

5   Note should also be made here of the formula *absens corpore, praesens auctoritate*: it is the mind that must be captured before the soul will obey.

jurisprudence to become a science of liturgical inauguration, a science
that sets in motion by divination, by 'augury': by the reading of omens
and signs. That it is liturgical in its speech means that it is both
public[1] and addressed to all, but also and more enigmatically that it
creates a public sphere, a pure space of the transmission of myth: 'A
liturgy has as its essential function that of delimiting this position, of
marking the space of higher things, the celestial, the divine; bearing
this mark of the space in which power speaks, public discourse comes
into play as a form of address and as a manner of leading humans to
the space of pure legitimacy.'[2] The liturgical text is properly
theogonic; it creates a universe and it is left to its commentators to
administer its linguistic and semiotic mysteries for in the words of
Bornitius, *Verbo et signis efficax Deus* (God's power takes effect through
speech and through signs).[3]

The second consequence of law as text devolves from the notion of
reference itself. In one sense the liturgical speech is a solemnised[4]
rhetoric, a method of persuasion through truth. In a less general sense
it establishes not only the source but the meanings of such speech.
The latter function of the text is the province of commentary, of the
apparatus of interpretation through which the symbolic is disclosed
and the text transmitted; that is, addressed and sent to its temporal
audience. Just as truth is a reference to a text so also, for the
commentators, meaning is the reference of a word, a name. Returning
again to the question of the origin of law proposed in a fragment from
Gaius in the *Digest*, the question was that of 'from where does this *name*
come?' and so to what does law refer? Gaius indicates the answer in
terms of a first word: 'without doubt, the strongest part [or function]
is that of the first' (*et certe cuiusque rei potissima pars principium est*). The

---

1 In legal terms that means, perhaps unsurprisingly, that it refers to Rome,
Institutes 1.4, where public law is defined as follows: '*Quod ad statum rei Romanae
spectat*' (that which looks to the Roman state).

2 *Empire*, p. 56.

3 J. Bornitius, *Emblematum Officio-Politicorum* (1664), commented on in *Empire*,
p. 32. For a comparable English tradition, see A. Fraunce, *Insignium Armorum,
Emblematum, Hieroglyphicum et Symbolorum* (1588), fol. H3b–L3b; J. Logan, *Analogia
Honorum* (1677); H. Spelman, *Aspilogia* (1657).

4 For an account of solemnised discourse see Benveniste (1969), op. cit., n. 33,
pp. 163–75. Legendre in *Paroles*, p. 135, remarks that 'as in the play of other
religious rites, solemnisation consists in creating the distance necessary for the
subject to enter discourse and equally in exempting the subject from having to
speak on his own account.'

first usage is an originary usage; it refers in general terms to the *patria*, to Rome and its texts, but also to the function of the jurist as commentator, as the one who steals from the text the name of things. In the theatre of truth established by law, by the name of the law, the word itself names an original textual use and it is to the recuperation of such first references that the bulk of the commentators' work is devoted in the form of endless treatises entitled *De verborum significatione*, works which take the form of dictionaries and set in motion the tedious normative panoply of words which name the truth:

> [T]hrough the very narrowness of its style, scholasticism set Roman law in motion, in the form of a legendary genealogy of the discourse of the Law. Thus, this recourse to genealogy, that is to say to the chart of the descent of names – names of authors, names of texts, names of institutions – presents itself, according to the scholastic labour of qualification, as the time or the times of the law. Such is inaugural discourse.[1]

In positive terms, the theory of the name – of the need for all things to have but one name or for all things to have their cause – is a logomachy: it is speech that differentiates truth from falsehood, and the name that identifies both person and honour. The history of the Western legal institution has been one of the authorisation of legal speech – from the ancient law of citations[2] to the theory of precedent, it has been sufficient for the textual system to protect itself by annihilating opposing speech. The history of its most awesome sanctions is equally reserved for those who through false speech, through heresy, divination, sorcery, treason, augury, witchcraft or other forms of immodest practice have trespassed beyond the name and have faced excommunication, *damnatio memoriae* (silencing of the name), the stake or the 'faggots' for their pains.[3] There is another side to the order of names. Genealogy establishes an order of descent whereby, in the name, the law seeks to read a lineage of names referring back to an ancestor or oldest name, that 'in whose name' the commentator speaks the law. A moment's reflection serves to indicate that while the name is presented as a presence, as *logos* or incarnate word, it has no referent beyond the descent of names, the genealogical tree itself. The name does not refer to a 'thing' outside the text but rather to a construction within it. If it is a matter of a family name,

---

1   *Empire* at p. 153, also *Transmission* at p. 234.

2   The Law of Citations 426 named and ranked the jurists who could be cited as approved, as authoritative, by the emperor.

3   See *Empire*, pp. 176–7, *Désir*, pp. 232–4.

then it is the name that lives on and not the person; the referent is either about to die or, in the case of the ancestors, is long dead. If it is the name of a text, it can refer only to other texts within an order of the descent or legitimacy of texts which is unified precisely by membership of the system, by law in its mythic unity: as that which emanates through sacrifice, through the mouth of the emperor as vehicle of the unseen and unspeakable deity, as image of the absent absolute. If it is a matter of the image, of dignity or office, then the name is again that which does not die (*dignitas non moritur*); it is a matter of the mystic body or function that survives and in surviving proves that its referent is the institution, the incorporeal belief in the order of law, the 'zero function'. It is not from a referent but rather, and ironically, from the mathematical sign for absence, from zero, that all genealogy must begin: 'the function zero simultaneously permits notification of the axiomatic Reference and at the same time makes possible that work of counting which renders genealogy effective'.[1]

The Legal Institution of Life

That genealogy, to be effective, must count from zero has a further curious consequence. In counting the place of the individual in the line of descent, the genealogist counts from zero to one, which in the Roman tradition[2] means from *ego* to *pater*: ego is zero and pater is one. Ego, by consequence, is in law a lack, an absence that is filled by entry into the symbolic, by taking the place of the father, by inheritance of *patria potestas* (the law of the father), or in feminine terms by accession to the place of the mother. Ego is zero in precisely the sense of nihil or nought; it is only in relation to the system of mathematical notation that zero has a meaning and it is equally only in relation to the order of names, to the symbolic line or tree, that the ego becomes person, a subject at law. The living fiction of the I must be correlated to death,

1 In *Transmission* Legendre elaborates on the mathematical significance of zero (pp. 244ff). Compare B. Rotman, *Signifying Nothing: The Semiotics of Zero* (1987), where zero is described as being a meta-sign, it signifies absence and simultaneously the impossibility of conceiving of numbers as predicated upon anterior 'things': 'to make zero the origin of number is to claim for all numbers, including the unit, the status of free unreferenced signs. Not signs of something, not arithmoi, certainly not collections, and not abstractions of units considered as somehow external and prior to numbers, but signs produced by and within arithmetical notation' (p. 29).

2 For details of such counting, their classificatory terms and trees, see *Transmission*, appendix. See also the texts collected and translated in Legendre, *Le Dossier occidental de la parenté: Textes juridiques indésirables sur la généalogie*.

to the order of ancestry and to the texts of the law before it can claim legal personality, the symbolic mask of being. We can simply note at this point that no one can litigate, no one can come before the law, as mere ego or private being: *et ut nemo de ea publice contendere audeat* (no one dare raise an action on his own behalf).[1]

The entry of the individual into the symbolic, the transition from zero to one, from lack to identity, is the condition of institutional existence, the capture of the subject by law. What is at stake in the order of reference and in the 'name of the law' is precisely the possibility of social speech – and there is in the end no other speech – and so too the possibility of being human, or in scholastic terms of becoming 'a speaking being'. The stakes, in other words, are high for if, following Legendre, we read the law against itself we must read it as the narrative (*roman*) through which, in a phrase taken from the *Digest*, life is instituted (*vitam instituere*). The tripartite division of Roman law progresses from *ius personarum* (the law of persons/masks) through the law of things and obligations (*iuris vinculum*, the bonds of the law) to the law of actions: the subject is instituted by the law of masks and through the bonds, the words of the law, comes to or, better, is led to act, to speak in the name of the *principium*, the first and absolute Reference. Zero becomes through law the place of the actor, the site of subjectivity, the mask or persona of historical being in the theatre of truth.[2] In Nietzsche's deconstructive terminology, 'the real world becomes a myth' and truth a fiction, or, in the classical expression so well worked by Kantorowicz, *fictio figura veritatis*, fiction is the figure of truth.[3]

1   Codex 1.1. *Empire*, p. 115. It is only as a person, a legal mask, that the individual can enter the realm of law, for 'the truth must be proclaimed publicly according to a discourse fixed in advance for the whole world.' Alternatively one might mimick Lacan's notion of language – it is only as a sign that one can enter language – in saying that it is only as a legal sign that one can enter the discourse of law.

2   D 1.3.2., *Transmission*, pp. 137–41, 349–54.

3   See Nietzsche, *The Twilight of the Idols* (1915), pp. 24–5: 'How the true world ultimately became a fable'. Note the final stage, *Incipit Zarathustra*, 'we have suppressed the true world: what world survives? the apparent world perhaps? . . . Certainly not! In abolishing the true world we have also abolished the world of appearance!' Baudrillard, *Simulations* (1983) translates Nietzsche's six stages of the history of an error into 'four successive stages of the image', the last of which is that the image 'bears no relation to any reality whatsoever, it is its own pure simulacrum' but interprets this stage nostalgically, it is still defined by the absence of reality, the non-alignment of appearance with an anterior existence. For Nietzsche, looking back is a weakness. Much the best discussion is still G. Deleuze, *Logique du Sens* (1969), pp. 292–307.

Following the order of the sentence, I will move from fiction to figure to the theatre of truth.

Simulation

The lesson of the law is that no being is self-founding. The individual, and society as fictional individual (*persona ficta*), both have to be instituted by law, they must be made to live, their mouth must be opened before they can speak.[1] In its most rigorous etymological derivation, genealogy, from the Greek *gignomai*,[2] to be born, is nothing less than the science of birth in its classical acceptation of the reproduction of lineage through sexuality: 'why pose this equivalence? Because it is in all cases a matter of the reproduction of the speaking being and of that which underpins it: desire'.[3] To institute human life, in other words, is not simply a question of the objective designation of places, it is also a manipulation of desire: genealogy, through its imagery and its rhetoric, needs also to institute an unconscious adhesion, a reproduction of attachment, fidelity or political love. It is a double discourse, both fiction and figuration as the two faces of a single founding act. That act is the simultaneous portrayal both of origin and of its reproduction, of foundation and continuance, of birth and rebirth. In that the stake of the discourse of reproduction is nothing less than attachment itself, the bond of subject to subjectivity, it is impossible to think the foundation of the subject outside of its double discourse, outside of law and the art or persuasion that engenders filiation. The act of origin or foundation (*condo*) is to be understood enigmatically.[4]

As origin, the act of foundation takes the form of a massive

1 Legendre uses the example of the Papal ceremony of the investiture of Cardinals in which the Pontiff would open the mouth of the new Cardinal while pronouncing the words '*nos aperimus tibi os*' (we open your mouth), *Désir*, p. 156.

2 *Gignomai*, to come into being. To be born is formed from the substantives *genos*, origin, descendence, birth, country, genre; *gonos*, family, birth, gene; *gonè*, descendence, sperm, genitals; and, by extension, *genea*, extraction, kinship, strain, line.

3 *Transmission*, p. 350.

4 It is interesting to observe that the enigma is classically defined both as divine speech, as a hiero-glyph (sacred mark) of God's will – a will too awful to behold – and, in more mundane terms, as an allegorical or dark symbol used in the creation of devises, heraldic emblems, the insignia of office or of birth. See H. Estienne, *The Art of Making Devises* (1643/1650 edn), fol. Biiia–b; A. Amboise, *Discours ou traicte des devises* (1620), fol. Ava–Bib.

simulation. It is to institute the order of life *as if* it were the universal and inextinguishable order of existence. At the level of the social that order of faith can take any number of forms; it can be Democracy, Socialism or Republic that founds the institution and takes the place of Rome.[1] The mythic function is that of putting in play the simulation of an order and method of institutional life that is made to appear *as if* it were regulated and lived according to the written law. There are two issues to be confronted. The first is that of simulation, the fiction of appearance, of semblance, by means of which the social body is represented as a single and dangerous image: 'all the historically variable forms of human grouping, and so also all the diverse forms of the State, are instances of the impossible image, of the Icon, of the play of simulacra which, by allusion to the religious rites of roman antiquity, we call *effigies*'.[2] The individual may die, the individual may well die for or at the hands of the patristic image of the state (*pro patria mori*), but the icon survives both through the sacrifice of individual life and through its reproduction as the same.[3] If the icon establishes the space of the Law,[4] it does so in the form of the founding truth: 'the authentic truth, upon which the entire system of messages depends, is unspeakable save by means of the detour of metaphors, of all that which permits us to circumscribe the divine place of power'.[5] The second issue is thus a literary one; simulation establishes the text as symbol, as the displaced site of speech wherein the subject speaks

1   The point is one which is well stressed in Debray (1983), op. cit., at pp. 35–52, 203–17, in terms of the political unconscious. See at p. 50: 'no "exposure" of the Churches, magistratures and theologies underlying the most profane forms of modern collective life has yet resulted in the secularization of the modern world. For since it has not been asked why Churches, magistratures and theologies actually exist, or if they can ever cease to exist, the "unmasking" operation has simply substituted one faith for another.' Compare *Jouir*, p. 87, on the specific fiction of electoral representation discussed in terms not of speech but of being led to speak.

2   *Paroles*, p. 257.

3   See *Passion*, pp. 201–11, 257–71, on the social institution of the body in dance: 'the entire body writes itself, addresses itself to some other of whom one can only know that it is not there, because in essence the dance represents' (p. 209). The dance which constitutes the body is also choreographed: 'the effigy shows invisible gods in the mirror: it is a matter of making the idol appear as the sign of an absence; that is to say, by way of reference to legality, as proof of the truth. Thus the theory of the simulacrum declares itself' (at p. 257).

4   *Transmission*, pp. 154–7; *Désir*, pp. 269–72.

5   *Paroles*, p. 93. On metaphor, see *Désir*, pp. 173ff.

as if a person. It is, in consequence, a language of metaphor and of allegory, a language that in the classical rhetorics is defined as 'dwelling in a borrowed home', a language which translates and transports the human to its legal domicile.

For the jurist, the law is to be read literally, namely to the exclusion of all else, as the truth, the message, legitimate speech. What the legal reading enforces is an amnesia as to that of which the message is the bearer: what is crucial is not what the message says but simply that it be emitted and circulated.[1] Read aesthetically, as the metaphor, the fiction of truth, the critique of dogmatics allows a further interpretation that can recuperate that which the memorial language memorises, namely the botanical and familial tropes of our inherited Roman law, the repressed discipline of genealogy.[2]

The figure of truth is that of the family tree. The state, in imitation of the emperor and so as father of law, *pater legum*,[3] is incarnated and appears *sub figura humani corporis*,[4] in the form of a human body: 'the axiom is here incarnated in the image of a body, that of an absolute father, in the sense that this first father only exists as a representation in the legal economy of differentiation, as that which makes [genealogical] counting possible, on the basis of what I have termed the zero function'.[5] It is precisely from the name of the law that the *Digest* traces the hierarchy of magistrates and jurists and, by extension, the entire lineage of legal and political offices.[6] The metaphor of office is genealogical in the form of a parent law which

---

1 *Amour*, pp. 106–7, provides one of many admirable examples of a simulated regulation, of the jurist as grammarian of a living text to the point of fantasy: 'suppose that a married priest, having by law the duty of consummating the marriage, is in the process of chanting mass, in full office, at the altar; the wife demands her due, here and now. Should he listen? . . .' (From *Magister Albertus Glossator*.)

2 *Transmission*, p. 372: 'what is it that is found to be repressed, that is to say put to one side, in the Freudian sense of *verdrangung*, in the social discourse of filiation? Essentially this: the dissymmetry of familial places . . . that which is repressed returns in the form of what I have called the ruptured subject (*la casse du sujet*).'

3 The names of the sovereign are legion. They are well listed, from the Digest to the moderns, from *deo auctore* to *rex imperator*, in *Désir*, pp. 255–67.

4 The text is given and discussed in *Pénétration*, pp. 57ff.

5 D 1 2 2. *De origine iuris et omnium magistratum et successionum prudentiam* (of the origin of law and of all the magistrates and the succession of jurists).

6 The text is given in *Transmission*, p. 118. For further discussion see Post (1964), op. cit., ch. 10.

establishes the social body as a family, or in Cicero's words society is a marriage (*conjugere*), nature's model of the essential human union. The metaphor should be pursued insistently; the legitimacy of office or text or positive law has consistently been understood in terms of family. To be legitimate is to belong to a line, to have a father (*ex patre natus*), illegitimacy is to have no father, no legitimating lineage, while to be adopted is to be born a second time in imitation of nature (*imitatio naturae*), adoption being classically based upon the fiction of the father as second mother.[1] The symbolic manipulation of kinship equally guarantees the history of law as succession, that is to say as precedent, derivation by lineage through antiquity and time (*antiquitate et tempore*) referring the text to the legend of an immemorial parent, the place of the ancestors. The law requires that we live *as if* they were still present, as if they did not die: in biblical terms, 'whoever has seen me, has seen the Father' (John 14:9).

In that the specific content of succession varies historically and as between jurisdictions, it is worth emphasising that the metaphors of a common father and of the social body, or family tree, to which all offices belong, are symbolic spaces and cannot be interpreted literally. Genealogy functions dogmatically, which is to say that it provides a normative guarantee of the legality of representation by reference to a symbolic manipulation of the places of speech. The paternal metaphor in consequence cannot be understood as referring to a masculine site of social language use but rather has to be approached as a function, as the principle of designation or reference itself whereby a mathematical relation or line is established (and reproduced) between sovereignty and the institutional place of speech. The relation is a causal one: all things come from the father (*id est summum omnium quae sunt*),[2] 'the father holds nothing in his own right, he represents, his being is his function. One must go further, the father represents a representation, he represents what at the legal level of the social represents the father as such ... the principle of differentiation in the reproduction of the speaking being.'[3] Where it is society or the institution that speaks, it does so only by virtue of a genealogical relation, a filiation, between the institution and the first

1   *Empire*, pp. 161ff; *Transmission*, pp. 330–32.

2   *Transmission*, p. 312, citing St Anselm, *Monologicon*.

3   Ibid., pp. 313–14. See *Paroles*, pp. 233–4, for a very clear statement of this view in terms of the social text as symbolic expression of the Text without a subject, the pure space of discourse.

cause. The fiction of social speech operates according to a hierarchy of legally designated places or 'sites of enunciation of discourse'. They speak as if they were legitimate; they speak 'in the name of' the father or of the law, and the sexism or asymmetry of such speech is therefore not a matter of the male gender of representation, or the language – the personal pronouns – of causality, but of the construction of sexuality, of differentiation, as such. To speak in the name of the institution is to represent a message as if it belonged objectively to a text, to a logical space or legally designated authority and not to any existent political or social being.[1] The monarch, prime minister, judge or bureaucrat, in other words, is often a woman. It is their discourse, the place and style of their speech, their persona and not their person that is asymmetrical, distanced and male: indeed, genealogy recognises the equality of the sexes, of the two lines of succession, and it is precisely in representing male and female places as equivalent[2] that it suppresses the asymmetry of the subjective spaces of mother, father, daughter, son.

The metaphorical or simulated logic of placement within the institution can be understood as translation in a further sense. At the level of instituting subjectivity, the individual is captured, possessed or, in the classical terminology, magnetised by the text. Genealogy places the order of generations on record; it creates memory – time – as textual space, as reference or, in classical terminology, as the magnetic art. The individual becomes a moment in the textual representation of historical time, a time represented in terms of names or effigies, a theatre of images, of family places. Embellishing Lacan's famous essay on the mirror stage of individual development,[3] Legendre interprets the second birth of the individual – entry into the symbolic – as subjection to the mirror of the law. The art of law is depicted in subjective terms as a political art; it is the art of 'fascinating' the individual, of holding it spellbound, charmed in the

1   *Paroles*, p. 234. The point is also made in D. Cameron, *Feminism and Linguistic Theory* (1985), pp. 30–44, 146–54. Cf. N. Duxbury, op. cit., 95–6.

2   On the representation of the equivalence, see *Transmission*, pp. 318–26; the two lines are represented in terms of the left and the right branches of the tree, or in Biblical terms, as the places that sit on the right and left hand of the father.

3   Lacan, *Ecrits* (1977) at p. 2: 'we have only to understand the mirror stage as an identification, in the fullest sense that analysis gives to the term: namely, the transformation that takes place in the subject when he assumes an image – whose predestination to this phase effect is sufficiently indicated by the use, in analytical theory, of the ancient term *imago*.'

image of the already known. The point is crucial. In one sense the individual is translated by the lawyer into the language of the already known, the given. More importantly, the law not only must function as a procedure of definition and identification but it must image that capture. The individual must become attached, must be held internally and so become faithful to the representation and representatives of law. The law is to be served with chaste *eyes* (*oculos castos servare*);[1] the image must be consumed, it must get under the skin or go within. There can be no law, in other words without subjective attachment, without belief, and that belief would be impossible were it not for the totemic representation of law, the enigma of the message: 'the primal fact of law, is that of the subjection of the human to representation, which implies, for it to take a *civilised*[2] form, the production of an inaugural space – an enclosure, call it poetic, mystic or religious – where the simulations of allegiance to the law (whatever the historical coloration of this allegiance) take on a meaning. If this matter of enclosure, of the mystic abode, or to reappropriate a familiar metaphor from European dogmatic culture, of the heart in which the scriptures are locked away, is not understood, analysis of the juristic function cannot progress'[3] beyond the traditional descriptions provided by the philosophy of law. In the same fashion that marketing works through advertising, through the consumption of images, so the law binds through emblems: it is the image that introduces the subject to the institution and it is precisely through its images that we recognise and so are faithful to law.

Icon and Law

To study the forgotten symbolism of the legal form is also to study the legal imaginary, the much-neglected history of the visibility of law, its representation, in lines and pictures, as a simulacrum. Whereas the mythic function of the text was to open the mouth of the subject, the

---

1   Gratian, cited in *Empire*, p. 112. See *Amour* for further elaboration of the legal function of capturing the subject in terms of an internally binding reason: *dictamen rationis, regula interna*.

2   Legendre here plays upon the French word *civilisé*, meaning both civilised and, in etymological terms, subject of civil law. Civilisation, in other words, is linguistically a matter of law.

3   *Désir*, p. 300. See also *Jouir*, p. 91: 'to be a legal subject is nothing other than

image opens the eyes; it inscribes the law as both visible and seeing presence. In terms of Legendre's concern to develop a jurisprudential aesthetics, the art of law – *ius est ars boni et aequi* – is to be understood precisely as an art, as the construction of a mirror image, a portrait or an icon that will represent the figure of the law in human form. That image will serve both to represent and to reflect. It represents in a perfect form the face of power; it portrays the absent cause of law, the other time of authority, while equally reflecting back to the subject of law the image of its own otherness, the mask or persona of legal subjectivity. There are thus two key dimensions to the aesthetics of law. The one concerns representation and is historical. There is an unwritten history of the emblematic representation of power, the iconography of the manner in which the institution has signified God and law. That history should aim to describe the manner in which law appears to and is recognised by its subjects: the image is the essential medium of law's institutional presence, its condition of existence, its manner of going within. The second issue is thus one of reflection and is speculative in the fullest sense of being a question of mirroring the subject. What binds the individual to law is a matter of appearance, of the perception of oneself as an institutional being, as having a prefigured place and so of being ineluctably attached, bound, to one's image, to living in the shadow of law. Marin isolates and analyses well such a power of representation in his study *Portrait of the King*:

> Representation as power and power as representation are a sacrament in image and a 'movement' in language where, exchanging their effects, the dazzling gaze and the admiring reading consume the radiant body of the monarch, the former by narrating his history in his portrait and the latter by contemplating one of his perfections in a narrative that eternalizes his manifestation. As we know, representation is at once the action of putting before one's eyes the quality of being a sign or person that holds the place of another, an image, a political body, and an empty coffin on which one stretches a cloth for a religious ceremony.[1]

The mask is, in other words, both a rhetorical and a spectral form; it moves, it bends, it persuades through visual as well as verbal signs.

In more prosaic terms, the classical definition of public law was of all that which 'looked at' or 'watched over' the Roman state (*quod ad statum rei Romanae spectat*). The visible law that allows the people

to be for the law, to be affixed to it, to be designated primarily in relation to its idols.'

1   Marin, *Portrait of the King*, op. cit., pp. 8–9.

to look at and recognise Rome is not simply a text but rather the visual representation of the author of the text, Rome is represented in statue, portrait, medal, heraldic device or architectural place: 'iconography analyses a uniform passage through which, whatever its variety, dogmatic discourse can be called to discharge [*dégorger*] its founding myth, by means of a plastic elocution'.[1] The verb 'to obey' stems from the Latin 'to listen' (*audire*), and the act of listening, in Legendre's vocabulary, is predicated upon the creation of a context, an auditory space or auditorium within which a solemnised discourse can be recognised not simply as speech but as law. The essential function of the diverse images of truth is that of modelling a space or of inaugurating the site of the discourse of adhesion. The art or icons of law establish the prototype of social speech; the image is a model to which all other institutional speech must conform by means of semblance, by means of appearing like the original. The plastic representation of state or sovereign is grafted on to the text as the mark of its absent source; it is the substitute for the absent, a likeness or simulation to which all further representations must adhere:

> [W]e receive the absolute Image imprinted on the body, by means of symbolic substitutes, by marks destined to create within us the reference to the absolute Other. These marks, in the industrial culture of Christianity, are fixed in sacred speech, or in bodily wounds such as that of circumcision. We can call these marks images, in the Latin sense of the term *vestigium*: . . . footprints in the dust. The *vestigium* is reference as trace, a trace which does not say that it is a trace, because it is there to signify absence, the absence of the absolute Other.[2]

It is, in other words, to the system of images (*systema simulationis*) that the subject adheres, and, in its role as inaugural speech, law is the medium through which the subject sees in the image the institutional destiny or political fate of the soul: to be a subject is in classical terms to become a mask, a shadow of a shadow, a fleeting simulacrum or image amongst images.[3]

1   *Amour*, p. 174. See also Kantorowicz on the sovereignty of the artist, in *Selected Studies*, pp. 352–65, where a very close parallel is drawn between jurisprudence and art. The jurists foreshadowed the views of the later artistic theorists, and more generally it was the jurists who created the initial climate of humanism in Europe. A whole series of notions, as for example those of *ars*, *imitatio*, *fictio*, *veritas*, and divine inspiration can be traced back to jurisprudence.

2   *Transmission*, p. 66.

3   Alciatus, *De Notitia Dignitatem: 'Quid est homo:* . . . *fantasmata temporis, speculum vitae'* (what is man? . . . a temporal phantasm, a mirror of life). Legendre cites Ovid on human Being as *simulacra fugacia, repercussae imaginis umbra* (fleeting appearance, shadow of a reflected image).

The iconography of law is the study of the sacral representation of law. Its concern is with the logic of the image both as model or prototype and as a specific picture of spatial organisation, of power in a corporeal form. The image of Leviathan, to take one example from the cover of the first edition of Hobbes' treatise, shows Leviathan as a massive body composed of innumerable human forms. All faces within the picture are turned towards the crowned head of Leviathan, the mortal God who stands with staff and sword in his outstretched hands over a Church-infested globe. Other less crude representations symbolise terrestrial power in terms of an all-seeing eye, or of a mouth devouring the law books while the world or the human heart hangs on a thread held by the enigmatic hand of the emperor. While the precise imagery varies, the function of the icon can be traced into the history of the law of images. What is at stake in that aesthetic history is the genealogical representation of descent, both as political power and as subjective place. As regards the former, the icon, from all-seeing eye to the much later image of the Crown – defined by Coke as the hieroglyph of all the laws – is there to establish the realm of the law as a ceremonial or ritual site of action. The image authenticates the law as the fiction or theatre of truth, as ritual in the Latin sense of *ritus*, as the communication of divine and human law. As regards legal subjectivity, the image is only legally effective as an emblem, as the authentic inscription or mark of social place and office. In the same manner that the icon marks the social space of liturgical speech, the emblem of office and the family device prove the entry of the individual into the social body; they are the signs that prove membership or filiation within the formal order of the institution as family, polis and law.

In historical terms, the law of arms, of heraldry, devices, insignia, ensigns, blazonry and the like, served to protect the true image by means of strict rules of composition and the criminalisation of forgery or *crimen falsi*.[1] In both military and civil usage the sign, be it flag or family crest, is properly understood as a legally authenticated mark, an image or symbol to which the individual life is dedicated and by filiation to which the individual has a place. The details of that law, of heroic symbols and badges of office as the tokens or coinage of social exchange, cannot be entered into here. It remains to specify one further feature of the image as political and social currency. The

---

1   See Chapter 4 and references thereto for specific technical details.

visual order of law ushers into the social realm the rules of classification for the simple reason that it is from the image – that is, from the specific emblem of place – that all counting of identity and difference begins. In Darwin's striking formula, all classification is genealogical: that is, it takes place by means of accounting descent in terms of genus and species.[1] In that very specific sense, the emblem produces reason but it does so in the paradoxical form of enigma. The enigma of representation is the duality of its reference and is most easily expressed in terms of the image as the memorial both of the person and of the ancestors. In one sense the image thus marks an historical place in relation to the transmitted order of an atemporal knowledge. It is enigmatic because it is an erudite knowledge; it has to be interpreted according to the esoteric cartography of the truth. The image or device is thus frequently defined as a holy letter, a hieroglyph or dark symbol of knowledge. In a second sense, however, the order of causality can be reversed; the enigma is a subjective one, that of the presence of the dead in the living. The image can here be understood as the creation of a spectral realm in which the living become haunted by the order of transmission, that of the perpetuity of tradition, the continuity of legal history itself. To be seen is the ambition of ghosts; to be remembered is the ambition of the dead.[2]

In the latter sense of the emblem as image of an inherited myth, the enigma of transmission is that of a mirroring; the individual sees in the image a reflection of the self. The word 'emblem' is derived etymologically from the Greek *emballo*, to throw within, and Legendre takes great pains to define the emblematic image as the mechanism whereby the signs of the law take hold of subjectivity and recreate the closure of truth in the conscience of the individual. The image to which the individual is tied is that of the self as other, the self as separate from itself in the mirror of an imaginary law. Borrowing from the story of Narcissus, Legendre proposes the institution of the image as being the medium by which genealogy takes effect or gets under the skin and leads the individual to recognise its fate as that of mask or player taking up a predetermined place in the symbolic enactment of social life. To recognise oneself as other is to destroy the self and to return as similar, as likeness or image.[3] To return to the medieval

1 Darwin, cited in *Transmission*, p. 36.

2 See Nietzsche, *Ecce Homo* (1911), p. 131.

3 *Transmission*, pp. 54–60; see also J. Kristeva, *Le Soleil noir* (1987) for discussion.

concept of fascination (*fascinum*) and its classical art, that of magnetism and the treatises on *De Arte Magnetica*, the companion texts to those of the glossators on the art of words, the law holds the image of the subject in the mirror of the text and issues its demands as if they were the demands of the text: 'a society of humans functions on the basis of this mythological mirror, in whose glass it sees itself called to account as if an other were making the demand'.[1] The lawyer interprets the demand, interprets the text and transmits the myth, but only on the basis that it comes from elsewhere or represents the dogmatic logic of its absent, imagined, source.

Conclusion

The exposition of Legendre's work offered in the present chapter has been based upon two central themes, those of history as the history of law and of its metaphysical representation in the textual and plastic arts of law. The history in question is that of dogmatics, of the battle for truth conducted upon the various stages of Western law in terms of the diverse fictions of an origin, and the many images of the source of legitimate social speech. To move towards a conclusion is to pose directly the question of what that history means for us as the distant relatives or fading masks of a tradition that legal historians have self-consciously chosen to forget and, in forgetting, to repeat in increasingly secular and barren forms. The animal (the living body and its history) is left on the road, so to speak, alongside the law as the reconstruction of human life, the living speech of social imagination. In more specifically aesthetic terms, the question is that of returning to the Western text and of reading it as fiction and image, as the narrative representation of life. Its fiction, in other words, is a lived fiction and to understand it in the order of the living is to analyse what sort of life it represents, a question of aesthetics, of the character of

---

1   *Désir*, p. 309. See also *Empire* at pp. 111–12: 'The Western theory of fascination – the theory which articulates the common fantasmagoria of latin religion and modern rationalism, the bearer of the scientific spirit – presents itself as a universal theory of attraction, concerned equally with the planets or with plants, with music and with love in all its forms . . . Note as well that the discourse on the eye [the gaze] is firmly anchored in dogmatics in general, that is to say, in its strict sense, in medicine and law, and that across this discourse can be

living, of its tone, its style, its allegory of meaning; its representation, in short, of what gives life a value and makes it worth living as a lawyer, as a living body of law.

The answer to that question takes a dual form. It is initially a matter of returning to history as the critical history of the present: the ultramodern condition is that of witnessing the denouement of the dogmatic tradition, the unravelling of its form, the exhaustion of a rationalist project in whose monotheistic symbols we no longer believe – and yet whose univocal mouth we hear in our dreams, whose monocentric frames we project on to the most inglorious chores of our domestic lives, whose themes we carry over into our emotional technocracies, whose angry past we celebrate in our daily economies of jealousy. If we accept Legendre's argument, the structure that carries Western metaphysics – our way of life as legal subjects – has survived but in an ever starker form. Contemporary industrial dogmatics and its actuarial forms of organisation in terms of efficiency, of aggregation and of profit depends upon the fiction of truth, of reference, to exactly the same extent as did the medieval's. Where industrial reason differs is simply in the changing technologies of fascination and magnetism in the art of law and its means of symbolising the truth. The logic of the argument is as follows. Society must dream to live. To live is thus a mythological activity; it requires art, poetry, dance, enigma and music. The dogmatic tradition, however, has lost those forms of myth making, the institution has exiled the mythic, the mystagogic, and in doing so has removed poetry from legitimate social speech, art from law, and replaced it with advertising hoardings, sound-bites and pervasive commercials.

The argument is a complex one and needs formulating in both its negative and its positive dimensions. The critique of dogmatics that Legendre presents relies heavily upon psychoanalysis as the discipline that will unsettle dogmatic reason by posing the question that lawyers ignore: what does law mean for the subject, for the living body of law? In respect to that question, the analysis of legal dogmatics is an analysis of the silences of the text, its repression of that which cannot be said but can only be represented in images or poetically formulated so as to indicate the space of subjective belief or faith in law. The discourse of law can function only if its inaugural symbolism, its ceremonies, rituals and other enigmas, remain objects discerned a science of the body, a science of dismemberment which . . . we are unable to escape.'

of subjective attachment. The history of the secularisation of law, however, is a history of the transpositions of religious categories into mundane forms. In terms of ultra-modernity, those forms are spent and society enters the tyrannical space of a law that has abolished interpretation: 'a tyranny is a society which has eradicated from its ambit the place of the interpreter and has destroyed the constellation [*montage*] of interpretation . . . or alternatively, [legal science] has refused the problematic of the enigma, a problematic that is essential to life because it lies at the heart of representation'.[1] In place of the paradox, poetry and mythologising of the early interpreters of law, in place of the living colour of law, its emblems and rhetoric, its heraldry and artistic devices, ultramodernity pushes at increasing pace towards an unruffled absolutism of certainties dressed in no more pleasing garb than the jargon of bureaucratic objectivity in its multifarious specialist forms. Managerial discourse is purely admini-strative; it requires that we live like bureaucrats, always a queue away from life, scheduling our emotions a week in advance, securing our relationships with paper clips, accounting our pleasures with actuarial calculations of risk; it asks, in short, that we manage life instead of living it. What such a rationality forgets is that the repressed project of legality was that of establishing a distance between absolute knowledge and its subjective applications. Referr-ing to the glossator Baldus and to the poetic tradition of medieval law, Legendre invokes 'the great imaginings of power, those that made the body walk with the soul, that is to say that mobilised the unconscious to an awareness of death, could only be said poetically, because power is organised in constellations of fiction, according to the fiction of absolute power . . . a mad power that is capable of creating everything from nothing'.[2] To remove interpretation and the figurative represen-tation of law while leaving law itself in place, in the cold prosaic place of statutory regulation, is to leave it in a palace of ruins in the sense that the symbols and aura of the text are forgotten, the iconic shadows of an archaic and indexical past are erased. It is to leave the subject hollowed out, with nothing separating it from the abyss that lies beneath the mask of truth. In Nietzsche's terms, art is there precisely to save us from perishing of the truth; it is the means of life, the counter-agent to the truth, the will to create.[3] In Venturi's post-

1   *Désir*, pp. 310–11.   2   *Paroles*, p. 212.

3   Nietzsche, *The Will to Power II* (1913), 'the will to power in art', especially at pp. 239, 264, 290.

modernist terms, 'take away the signs and there is no place there'.[1]

To remove the space of interpretation is to abolish all possibility of dialogue and to bleed dry the idea of a lived law while leaving its form in place. That is the nihilism of ultramodern legal culture: it suffers from an excess of truth, from nothing but the truth, a truth without distance, a power without representation, a frightful closeness. Legendre's great merit is that of recollecting that nihilism has always preceded revolution, that, in abolishing the monotheistic cult of one law and one truth, Western law poses the question of its own survival as the possibility not of re-establishing the one God but of rewriting the legal arts. The problem that faces critical legal studies is that of reappropriating the space of interpretation, the space of the sublime,[2] and so of recreating the distance necessary to communication, to the overflow of communication. Where Nietzsche insists that art is of greater value than truth,[3] Legendre insists additionally upon the primacy of the poetic and aesthetic function over that of reason. To begin again, to create, is the most pressing task of critical reason as applied to contemporary law. For that task to be possible literature must play the role of law,[4] it must act poetically, deconstructively, from a distance that is not without the law but is buried deep within its body.

1   Venturi et al., *Learning from Las Vegas: The Forgotten Symbolism of the Architectural Form*, p.87.

2   Nietzsche (1913) at pp. 285–90.

3   Ibid., p. 292: 'art is the only task of life, art is the metaphysical activity of life.'

4   The phrase is borrowed from Derrida, 'Préjugés' in *La Faculté de juger* (1985).

9

Pro Persona Mori: To Die for One's Mask

Introduction: Laws of Movement

The history of the common law has always been a history of movement, of a wandering *nomos*, a narrative of itinerant justice and itinerant justices. Its movement has been both literal and meta-phorical, a question of a peripatetic court and also of laws of transmission of legal knowledge: moveable bodies become moveable signs. Any intelligent discussion of the common law tradition should look to the multiple senses of legal transmission and consider the various spatial and temporal trajectories of passage of legal knowledge. Those trajectories, as traced in this study, can be framed in diverse ways: they form a narrative of movement from theology to law, from the sedimented to the sedentary, from the premodern to the postmodern, a narrative of changing forms of legal organisation or governance of both physical geography and mental territories. At the level of language, the trajectory is from rituals of repetition to ceremonies of inscription, from an oral hermeneutics of the legal voice, the *lex terrae*, to the optical and unconscious power of the visual text, from an hallucinating memory and lucinating law[1] to a scriptural monologue of instantaneous facsimiles. Where the law was a form of doing things, a way of life, a note or bond of habitual practices and habitual servitudes, it became an externalised control of circulation, a sedimentation and striation of movement, an exter-

---

1   To hallucinate has its root in the Latin *alucinor*, to wander in mind, to dream, to rave. Its connotations are utopian and geographic, the hallucination follows a different path, it gets lost according to the established map. We may also note that it is bodily, the hallucination is not externally generated, it does not obey the causal norm, but it is nonetheless an embodied vision, an intensive optical trajectory rather than an extensive projection.

nalised mapping of progression, a form of 'highway surveillance . . . confusing social order with the control of traffic . . . and revolution with traffic jams, illegal parking, multiple crashes, collisions'.[1] Asphalt becomes the political territory *par excellence* and the state a simple manager of the public course, a vast post office and sorting house for the passage of messages, for the public way.

The war which the state had previously waged against distance and against illicit forms of circulation, its struggle to keep the public course open to traffic, the avenues of circulation free for its messengers, its mail, its travelling court, is imploded into a question of inner distances, of semantic striations and of psychic speed:

> One of the fundamental tasks of the State is to striate the space over which it reigns, or to utilize smooth spaces[2] as a means of communication in the service of striated space. It is a vital concern of every State not only to vanquish nomadism but to control migrations and, more generally, to establish a zone of rights over an entire 'exterior', over all the flows traversing the ecumenon. If it can help it, the State does not dissociate itself from a process of capture of flows of all kinds, populations, commodities or commerce, money or capital . . . there is still a need for fixed paths in well-defined directions.[3]

It is a question, in short, of a law that has to control and manipulate a deterritorialised space, a Church of the mind, an intensive geography as opposed to an extensive regulation of space alone. The narrative of movement is of a subliminal – a sublime – control, an 'ecstasy' of communication whose law is one of structural regularities: a governance of intensive spaces, of movement that no longer moves, a sedentary nomadism in which it is the politics of the sign that is the essential issue of transmission, the flow of information the immediate law, a rhetorical movement of electronic hallucinations, a movement,

1 P. Virilo; *Speed and Politics* (1986, New York) at pp. 14, 4. For further discussion see also M. Foucault, 'Of Other Spaces' (1986) 16 *Diacritics* 22; also G. Deleuze and F. Guattari, *A Thousand Plateaux* (1988, London), ch. 12.

2 On the distinction between smooth and striated space, see Deleuze and Guattari, op. cit., p. 371: 'Smooth space is a field without conduits or channels. A field, a heterogeneous smooth space, is wedded to a very particular type of multiplicity: nonmetric, acentered, rhizomatic multiplicities that occupy space without "counting" it and can be "explored only by legwork". They do not meet the visual condition of being observable from a point in space external to them; an example of this is the system of sounds, or even of colours, as opposed to Euclidean space'.

3 Deleuze and Guattari, op. cit.., p. 381.

finally, from memory to projection, from icon to advertisement, from medium to media. In tracing that movement of modes of transmission, we will conclude by examining a series of figures or visual representations, an aesthetic of law in the work of a specific artist, David Walliker, and a specific exhibition devoted to mapping the migration of the legal sign from deterritorialisation – 'which scene of which crime?' – to vacancy, to the abandoned sepulchre, Rousseau's empty tomb, a vacated contract.

Laws of Place

Strip 91 runs through the centre of Las Vegas. The town is centred around one street and the whole of the Mecca of gambling fronts on to the strip. Behind the casinos is the desert, immediate and abrupt. The town is flat like the desert and organised on a grid system. To the motorist progressing down the strip it is a profusion of styles and of signs, an oasis of symbols advertising everything from Esso to Caesar's Palace, from Wow Hamburgers to Aladdin's Club, from the Dunes to Stardust. The profusion of signs creates a place, a postmodern venture in the form of a pastiche of styles from classical to baroque, from Disney to the Orient and from the modernist obscenity of God's Own Junkyard to the Leaning Tower of Pizza. Every building and every billboard, every structure, exists to advertise something: from vacancies to gaming wheels to cabaret stars, from food to fuel, from parking lots to empty rooms. It took Venturi, Scott Brown and Izenour to point out that, if one took away the symbols that map the strip as the heartland of gambling, it would cease to exist: 'take away the signs and there is no place there'.[1] There would be in its stead an empty and uninhabited memorial, nothing to stop for in the empty space of the desert save for a ghost town, structure without form, concrete returning to sand. Remove the signs, both neon and architectural, and strip 91 becomes another stretch of tarmac through the Nevada desert, a link road, part of the network, a line of communication across empty space. Take away the signs and

1   *Learning From Las Vegas* (1977), p. 18. Compare, at p. 87: 'we shall image – image over process or form – in asserting that architecture depends in its perception and creation on past experience and emotional association and that these symbolic and representational elements may often be contradictory to the form, structure and program with which they combine in the same building.'

strip 91 becomes pure motion again, part of the great American ecstasy of communication, part of militarised space.

The ultramodern ecstasy of communication is an ecstasy of linear speed.[1] In the race to be ahead, it is the connection that is more important than the destination, and being in the system, being 'hooked up', is of far greater significance than knowing what the system is for. In the geometry of the social, the message will always come down the line. The line will link us to the exchange. So long as the phone is on, the satellite dish is in position, the computer 'on line' or the aerial rigged, then we can belong, we are part of the system and the images will arrive and we will have been remembered, remembered, that is, through the very act of reception, through being recipients, terminal points, nodes or nomads. Interesting, then, that we must be in place to receive the ecstatic communiction. Our orders will come down the line and only then will the connection be made, only then will we be off, forward march into the beyond, down the line: whether it is liquid crystal, fibre optic, air wave or the decadently mechanical tarmac track of the motorway, it is always a question of getting in line, joining the system, being seen and being on the move. The postmodern condition with which the present chapter is concerned is one of resistance, one in which the tables are to be turned and rather than being on track, linked in, connected to the exchange and remembered by the authorities, we turn to look at the image of ourselves that the system presents. It is after all essentially the ambition of ghosts to be seen and of the dead to be remembered: for the living it is a matter of letting the body remember and then of putting the ghosts to rest.[2]

To look at our image in the mirror of the social is an impossible task. If ultra-modernity is wholly concerned with exchange, with the exchange of nothing, the consumption of images and the accumulation of money to make such possible, then the artist is left to portray a

1   J. Baudrillard, *The Ecstasy of Communication* (1987), p. 12: 'Today the scene and the mirror have given way to a screen and a network. There is no longer any transcendence or depth, but only the immanent surface of operations unfolding, the smooth and functional surface of communication.'

2   For the imagery of speculum and mirror, the classic introduction is Lacan, *Ecrits* (1977). Most succinctly, 'we have only to understand the mirror stage as an identification, in the full sense that analysis gives to the term: namely, the transformation that takes place in the subject when he assumes an image – whose predestination to this phase-effect is sufficiently indicated by the use, in analytic theory, of the ancient term *imago*' (p. 2).

living death, an image or mask that is the likeness of an empty self, a consumer, a bank account, a shattered glass.[1] Only the mirror itself, the system or network as global medium, as endless relay, as law, holds the subject in place: only by endlessly sending it on can the image remain whole. To take the mask apart will simply reveal an empty place, a death: it will reveal only that life might now be no more and no less than a web of ceremonial relationships, a ritual exchange of masks that holds together something with no substance, something that is an already existent ruin, an object that carries its principle of disintegration on its surface, on its sleeve, on its skin. The exchange is thus with someone without qualities, with the detritus of the subject, nothing and no one, pure screen. It is on screen that we live and on screen that we die, no longer project but projection, images amongst images, shadows of the shade or flies in the web. To stop and examine our image raises the possibility that each individual may therein recognise his or her death, will see reflected in the mirror a frozen identity, a life trapped in the web and growing cold, a mask that has taken root and become the face, an image or likeness of the self stretched over a single point that exists simply to mark the time and account the place.

The theme is a rich one and in visual terms it finds a wide variety of representations in the nomadic images here selected from the work of the artist and film maker David Walliker. It is a work devoted to depicting the social forms of human absence in the unrelenting terms of the logic of placement, the power of projection and the masks in which we live and die. It is an art of the outside, an art that dares to look in and question the loss of will that results from a geometry – a political economy – of pure circulation. Its motifs are acute and repetitive, sacrificial and psychoanalytic. It can be presented as a narrative of fear. It can be presented too as an iconography of seduction in which fear is alleviated or evaded by sacrifice, by entry into the controlled orbit of exchange, by stepping into the mirror and leaving life behind – life is simply what the other does. Life is invisible, it escapes the image, it is other in the sense that it cannot be presented but only represented through likeness to an absent form. In the world

1 'In order to understand adequately Heidegger's definition of nihilism and to see in it an affinity with Nietzsche's, we must attribute to the term "value" – which reduces Being to itself – the rigorous sense of "exchange-value". Nihilism is thus the reduction of Being to exchange-value.' (G. Vattimo, *The End of Modernity*, (1988, p. 21.)

of appearances it is the image, the spectre of forgotten lives, the ghosts of the living in the mirror of death that are held flickering before the eye of power. To take but one example, Narcissus who was at first enthralled by his echo later became entranced by his image in water and, spellbound, died by joining his image, by becoming the likeness of himself, other to himself; by becoming other to himself *so as to be* a likeness, a semblance, a fixated object of love. Narcissus died for his mask. We die for a similar identity save for the difference that while Narcissus drowned we live on, the ecstasy – the oblivion – of communication having provided the technological means of life support long after the artistic diagnosis of death. In the very dispersal of the individual as demographic and terminal point, society denies the relevance of libidinal or bodily death: the contract survives, the risks accumulate, the last will and testament is read out, the property remains as the relic of the life – even or especially the property in futures, so that we are left to conclude unavoidably that it was the remains that circulated, that there were only ever remains.

Figure 9.1: Living in the Mirror or Altar Ego

Where it is a question of institutional existence, the issue is not who you are but where you are. It is a question of placement and of the power of the place within the logic of descent: each individual place on the line must be marked by an insignia, an emblem of blood or office, of family or status. In terms of the individual, this symbolic permutation from mere nature to the place of parent, to the place of the ancestor, takes the form of entry into the mask of identity. The other I is the space already prepared for each individual in the web of the social; it is a chronicle of a death foretold, a time that is inexorably marked in advance, a path that is patterned in the image of the forebears, an image to which reason requires that we conform. In classical terms, we are created 'in His image', we resemble the Father and our face, our place in the line, is precisely a simulation of the dead cause of all causes: in my face, Athanasius announces, you will see the face of the Father. That image, *imago* or ancestral face, is also to be understood as the mark, the vestige, of the sovereign, the assigned or mapped point of power. The correlate is that without an insignia or emblem of where we are, without a face or mask, we cease to exist: only through the system of classification that the other inhabits can we locate a self.

The task of finding ourselves is thus a geographical one; we need a map of the social location of places to chart our being in the institution. We need a sense of aesthetics, an open eye, to recognise in the mirror the likeness of ourselves, or in Lacan's terms our predestined identification in the image. The process of such identification can be outlined in terms of a speculary structure. The social possession of the subject is an emotive matter; it is to images that the subject adheres and it is by images that we are bound. The first law of the social is that the subject is held in place by an emblematic representation, an iconic sign that refers both to the power of the system of places and to the individual point of reference, the obedient subject. In classical terms, it is the genealogical chart of accounted places in the line of descent that determines the place and the status of the individual: the armorial device or crest will indicate legitimacy and the rank of birth in a cryptic visual form, while in terms of societal being Church and Law existed to chart the descent of power from God to sovereign in the web of the law. Authority itself, however, could never be represented in the icon; it was the invisible other, the absent source before which the human stood helpless and to which the mortals would offer their sacrifices. The sacred involves sacrifice, the very specific sacrifice of each new generation that must be made to recognise the awful presence of God by means of representation: the symbolic sacrifice of Isaac or later and differently of Christ is re- enacted before the altar at Mass. The altar is itself the medium or relay of sacrifice; it is before the altar that the ego symbolically slips into the realm of otherness and, in recognising the substantial presence of God, recognises also its own destiny, its destination, its terminal point, the last dot on the screen.

God died some time ago. That God is dead simply means that the ancestor of power eventually died. It would appear, however, that God left a will; he had acted as a witness, he died testate and bequeathed or passed on the principle of absolute power to his successors. The Law is now resident not in the mouth of God but in the contemporary system of simulation; the technological system of relay and screen now weaves the web of life in the form of faith in unlimited exchange. The faithful kneel before the monitor, the screen that relays futures prices in a bar in Stockholm, in a restaurant in London, in an airport lounge in Chicago, the teletext, the video, the facsimile.[1] The contemporary soothsayer is the 'teller', the

1   J. Baudrillard, *The Evil Demon of Images*, p. 38: 'Nietzsche is not in the least an ordinary atheist. He is not committed to the denial of the existence of God as an ordinary atheist would be. He is actually denying not that God exists but that God is alive. He is saying that God is dead, and that is a fundamental concept.'

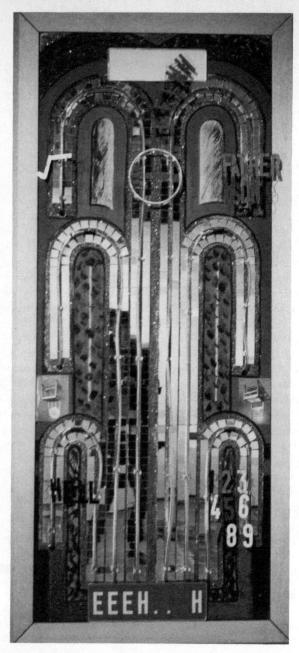

Fig. 9.1

computerised cash dispenser on the street corner or in the home. It screens us, it ensures our security pass, it monitors and lets us in via an individualised code, a *codex* or support, a combination of numbers that identify and let us pass as encoded beings. The Altar Ego of Figure 9.1 plays precisely upon the ambiguity of altar and alter, of screen and other, as they are to be witnessed in the postmodern age as pastiche of the personal incorporated into a massive screen of technological debris that both controls and consumes us. It is debris that binds us to a particular soil, to a territory, a place, to Earth, to Mars, to Kansas.

The image of Altar Ego is no longer the classically figurative altar screen but rather a massive montage, an indecorous collage of artificial materials and plastic remains. The artist who stops and breaks the spell of the mirror, of the screen to which we are glued, has to face the reality of a sociality transfigured into pure machination, pure war:[1] this is not an interesting place. The altar screen presented in Figure 9.1 is thus insubstantial; it is simply a screen erected to represent relay and network through plastic tubes, random colours and broken glass. The individual elements – numbers, letters, chairs, hoops and mirrors – have no identity outside of the collage itself: they exist only in relation to the relay of the whole, the jumbled network labelled in the lower left-hand corner 'hell', the final destination of Narcissus or the residence of the human soul, the unconscious that sits opposite a series of numbers on the right, the conscious rationality of the social as an actuarial system.[2] When the subject slips across the altar to the screen, it sacrifices the unformed or inchoate sense of self, the realm of poetic dialogue or personal myth, and replaces it with an inherited rationality of the economics of risk and the logic of demographic control – of governmentality.[3]

1   The reference is to P. Virilo and S. Lotringer, *Pure War* (1984), New York). See also, P. Virilo, *War and Cinema* (1989, London): 'From the first missiles of World War Two to the lightning flash of Hiroshima, the *theatre weapon* has replaced the *theatre of operations*. Indeed the military term "theatre weapon", though itself outmoded, underlines the fact that *the history of battle is primarily the history of radically changing fields of perception*' (p 7)

2   The key work on the actuarial character of postmodern social relations is F. Ewald, *L'Etat providence* (1986, Paris). See also J. Simon, 'The Ideological Effects of Actuarial Practices' (1988) *Law and Society Review* 111.

3   M. Foucault, 'On Governmentality' (1979) 6 *I & C* 5, see 13; 'the finality of government resides in the things it manages and in the pursuit of the perfection

It is before the altar of the early saxon cathedral in Winchester, before the reja of lances in Velasquez's *Surrender of Breda*, before the becoming other of death, that the subject presents its last will, its testament to future generations. Once it has become other, the subject belongs to the screen; it has transfigured its will into the symbolic of ultramodern rationality, that of the reason or life that looks out from the speculum ever ready to captivate new souls. The last testament – the apocrypha – is witness to no greater meaning than that of a system that works; it institutes life but to no purpose other than that of reproduction itself, brute survival. Locked into the screen, held in the mirror, commuting through the tubes, the subject becomes the technological equivalent of the chorus that would traditionally sing from within the screen, the screen that rose above the portals of the cathedral and in whose hidden passageways choirboys would sing to welcome the worshippers as though the building itself was ethereally chanting the faithful home. *Alter ego* is the other I that looks back, intransigent and in place in the form of myriad mirrors and upturned places: this is what happened, this is what we became in the imaginary of ultramodernity. Here, in short, we are held, the victims of the screen, projected forms without substance and so simulations incapable of breaking the spell, the fascination of sacrifice as an act that locates and deserts the body. The final question posed by the altar is that of how does one survive? All that is left is the last testament, the will. In the end, at bottom, there is a piece of paper, a contract, enclosing and destining the will to the future. Self and other have both disappeared, been imploded, in the relay, the screen. What remains is the will, a remnant will, a voice on screen. The question is that of whether it can be otherwise than it is. That it exists in the frame is unquestionable, but can it see something else, another possibility, another structure of thinking, another way?

Figure 9.2: Framed or 'I think I Believe God is Dead'

Where Altar Ego represents the function of masking, of identity or persona, in terms of an ultra-modern collage, a shattered image composed of broken mirrors and recycled plastic forms, Figure 9.2 represents the function of the screen as that of framing. The image is and intensification of the processes which it directs, and the instruments of government, instead of being laws, now come to be a range of multiform tactics.'

Fig. 9.2

classical. The right hand of reason builds a wall of weightless bricks to keep the chaos of life at bay, to demarcate and protect reason against the encroachment of pure chance. If destiny is the dividing line between necessity and chance, the line takes the form of a simulated wall; it is a barrier or screen against placelessness and makes use of the frame to build a blockade from top to bottom and from right to left. Here the artist thus poses the question of the enclosure of mental space, the framing of vision and the building, the structure, of the dream become life, become real. Once inside the frame, the frame no longer exists: it transpires to have been hallucination; it was always only a quasi-stable structure, a collapsible space – like a bed, a tent, an imaginary tent, a phallus – a moveable body. It is a question of strategy that may be approached by means of the function of seduction: the frame institutes life, but how lively is life? What is its tone, its colour, and what are its forms of desire? Is there water? Is there love?

The frame in Figure 9.2 is composed of the litter of consumer products. That deathless debris is the context of the structure; an endlessly repeated cycle of production and refuse is all there is left to metaphysics, a cosmogony – a created world – of waste, of the remnants of consumption taking the place of the older theology of natural law and the afterlife of the soul. The universal principle by which we hang together is now no more vivid than an infinity of products made to be thrown away; its zero point is simply repression, fear of bankruptcy, of the scrap heap. To take it further, the death of God to which the title refers is a denial of God's being alive, an aesthetics of disappearance: 'the idea [is] that the disappearance of something is never objective, never final . . . it always involves a sort of challenge, a questioning, and consequently an act of seduction'.[1] The seduction is a challenge to the vanished idea, an attempt to play with it, to question its traces, the marks that it has left behind in the form of excess. But if we call God to question, to play, we find in the place of God the litter of industrial waste as the mark of technological reason.

The strategy of the frame is to make us ignore it. Why raise metaphysical questions if they simply summon the debris of past pleasures and intimidatingly remind us of our destiny as junk amongst ever increasing piles of junk? Better to build a wall, to acknowledge the need to keep the metaphysical out, to expel the zero point from our consciousness while leaving the unconscious to fight its own battles in the hell below, the hell within. We know our destiny but we only succeed if we forget it. We are better competitors, in other words, if we keep it to ourselves and live in the illusion of an ordered segment of the map. That life tends to disorder is no bar to the intrinsically meaningless construction of barriers against the great outside within, against the other. It is best, in the final account of industrial reason, just to live. It is best not to ask why or from where the institutions of life have come. After all, we have a map, we know where we are; the map may not correspond to anything, it may be a pure map, a fiction, a pretence, but who cares? A man or a woman, who cares? The map will still name the streets and lead us to the bank or to the teller, while the daily news will remind us of the day's programmes and of little else. To digress momentarily, this is life as punishment, as a penal colony.

Within the frame, the image is startlingly clear. In the face of chaos, humanity builds nothing more interesting than walls, screens against disorder, scars against memory, sites of lamentation, monuments to firing squads, to eros and blood: these are memorials of past feeling, of lost emotion, of spent passion. On the left a morass of bricks,

1 Baudrillard, *The Evil Demon of Images*, op. cit., p. 39.

individual blocks that appear to be falling together. They have nothing to hold on to, they are uncharted, disordered and, from the perspective of the wall, they are helpless. On the left, the site of the unconscious, the sinister or diabolical 'without,' the repressed though, disturbingly enough, this without is still fully within the frame. It is from here that we find the materials with which to build the wall, to construct the barrier against nothingness which will ensure our civility. Civility and reason, however, are nothing more than a screen, for to the right is empty space: the purpose of the operation appears eventually to have been limited to holding back, to containment. The wall does not protect anything; the order it encloses is contentless, cleared ground and nothing more. Reason has expelled everything, leaving us with the magnificent equation that to live is to die; to live would be to join the very chaos that the mask was erected to exile, to put without to hold within. Alternatively, we could devote life to the pure task of exclusion, to holding the barrier in place, to keeping the mask fixed, even though this would then be the only purpose, the only task, of life: delay, postponement or meaningless and finite continuance. To be framed is also to be set up for a crime that one did not commit, to be punished for something that one did not do: recollecting Bentham, 'let the offender, while produced for the purpose of punishment, be made to wear a mask'. He continues instructively: 'the air of mystery that such a contrivance will throw over the scene will contribute in a great degree to fix the attention by the curiosity it will excite, and the terror it will inspire'[1] – guiltless, it might be said, but none the less subject to the dual principles of fascination and terror, fixation and fear.

Figure 9.3: Circular Ruins or the Marriage

Hell, which used to be other people, is now the self, the unconscious in which we repress our fear of freedom. The image of Figure 9.2 was of an unconscious hell of falling bricks. Hell was that place where there is nothing left to hold on to, no structures, nothing built, pure idea – in which case, out with the map: *fictio figura veritatis*, fiction is the figure of truth. In Figure 9.3 we are drawn into the realm of reason and of the

1   J. Bentham, *Principles of Penal Legislation*, vol. I, p. 431. For an interesting commentary on this passage see J-A. Miller, 'Jeremy Bentham's Panoptic Device' (1987) *October* 3.

Fig. 9.3

social: let us examine rationality and structure, order and perfection. The frame seen from the inside is pure order; its symbol is the circle, the ring which has neither outside nor any internal disturbance. On the left, a perfectly blocked-up circle, no faults, no threats; signed and sealed the unconscious can be forgotten – it no longer exists. On the right, the conscious circle, empty, gold-lined (an aura), impregnable, dead. The created circle, the full circle, encloses inert space: to be within the ring is to be held, but what is held is no longer a self, it is simply the idea of the self which exists only because of the ring. Once in the ring, the self disintegrates into order; it is constructed in military fashion: 'ours is not to reason why' but simply to obey orders and so to carry out the ultimate oblivion of communication that consists of patrolling the borders and letting nothing and no one through.

To understand the two rings is to understand this paradoxical relationship between border and homeland, between exclusion zone and daily life. Ultramodernity is the most extreme known form of universal rational manipulation. Everyone who counts has a task and a place, a connection and an exit point. The greater the degree of order – of meaningless activity – the greater the need for militarised and regimented control of space to allow the communications to flow. Star Wars is necessary because all space is potentially a threat, an object of mapping and of imaginary manipulations: space becomes the residual site of an infinitely impenetrable demand; it is in its way a total insecurity, the antithesis of matter and so the ever present (potential) demise of all property, the last spin of Fortuna's wheel.

The marriage portrayed is thus comprehensible as one between the external extreme of military precision and the internal extreme of dispossessed identity. This is properly an aesthetics of disappearance[1] which sees in the symbolics of identity a vacuum side by side with a wall: the most that could be hoped for from joining the one to the other would be an exorbitant constipation, a total inability to let go. Such is the metaphor of marriage, a metaphor of society insofar as society is itself a marriage of men, a conjunction (*conjugere*) according to nature's most explicit category of union. The marriage, however, leaves us cold, selfless, lost through being found. Let us simply note that, while the ring holds us implacably, the ring is also the sound of the telephone: could it be that there is someone new at the end of the line? Or might it also be the ring that makes us disappear? Engagement or wedding? Fascination or fall? Is there anyone at the end of the line? Is there anyone there? Hello?

Figure 9.4: Into a Controlled Orbit

The circle is also the representation of an eye, the principle of vision around which Bentham most famously constructed the rational prison, the panopticon. From a single central point of control it is possible to see every cell and through the threat of visibility to control the inmates by means of the fear of being watched, of being seen. If we translate the circle into the orbit of Figure 9.4, the principle of panopticism, of an omnivoyant eye, is displaced by a notated space, a blank canvas is marked externally by a series of figures circulating around and also supporting the open and blank territory of the network. Here the spatial quality of control is presented in its most bleak and immediate form: the individual figures, the chairs that in the rhetoric of cinema represent private identity, private space, are in orbit around a blank and imageless screen. The network or circuit through which the full panoply of communications passes no longer needs any dimension of theatre or of seduction; it is brute space and signals with equally brutality in the form of stark visibility; it is there and it is all that is there.

The omnipresence and the simplicity of the image, its purely geometrical form, hides a certain sense of *horror vacui*, of terror of the

---

1 See P. Virilo, *L'Esthétique de la disparition* (1980, Paris). See also idem, *War and Cinema*, op. cit., at p. 4: 'if *what is perceived is already lost*, it becomes necessary to invest in concealment what used to be invested in simple exploitation of one's available forces.'

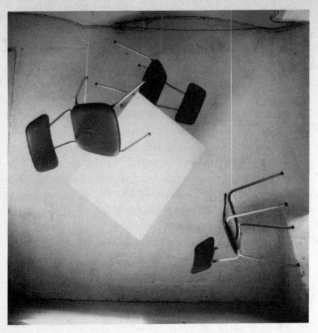

Fig. 9.4

void. The image is total; the orbit controls and precisely through its imageless clarity it sees all, it relates all, it marks the path of the isolated satellites with an absolute assurance or total logic which is all the more terrifying for being free of any qualities, free of any substance whatsoever, pure debris. Art becomes useless and unnecessary; it no longer has a function in a sphere of absolute lucidity of control based upon a clairvoyance of power or total marking and tracking of visible space. This is the ultramodern cartography of power; it constitutes a perfect map, it sees and tracks all yet in doing so it displays that the logic of totality, of the successful military annexation of space, is also a logic without substance – everything is also a synonym of nothing. Perfect efficiency is necessarily inhuman; it erases even the semblance of will by substituting for difference the pure identity of the satellite as unique and enclosed orbital space tied to an elliptical path through infinite vacuity. Where the logic of the map reigns supreme, it is impossible to make a difference; everything is already charted and all the contours are known, the only grid of reference is in the hands of ground control, the signal box, the early warning station, the computer terminal, the military in all its linguistic guises, in all its tropes.

To the descriptive quality of Figure 9.4 certain interpretations need to be added. The notation of space so starkly depicted in terms of the blank screen has a quality of pure mathematics. No system of enumeration or of counting is self-founding; its absolute reference is necessarily an external point, a foundational fiction which has classically taken the political form of God or law and the mathematical form of nought or zero as icons of the origin. The etymology of zero derives from 'cipher', meaning void and by extension something unreal at the basis of thought. In strict mathematical terms, the cipher refers to the absence of any other signs and not to the non-presence of any real thing. In that peculiar sense it is better depicted as the vanishing point than as mere nullity, for the cipher is also a secret writing, a coded message in an unknown script that can be deciphered as a founding symbol that paradoxically symbolises the absence or impossibility of absolute reference. There are only systems of notation and it is precisely nothing, empty space, that is notched or marked or mapped by the system itself.[1] The paradox is that the impossibility of reference itself refers to a point beyond which we cannot go; it refers to the limit of reference, the extremity of externality, the point of difference that constitutes the border, the edge of the frame beyond which lies the territory of death, the pure outside of all that is thrown away. Let it simply be noted that the zero point is also a secret script, a message in cipher that reminds us that disappearance is never final, it is never objective, it leaves traces and it is for the outsider to track those traces, to disencrypt, to play the role of zero's other or God's opponent, Lucifer (*lux ferre*).

The opposition between light and dark, God and Devil, classically maps a series of figures of inside and outside that have traditionally structured the divisions of the law, particularly those of the public and private, truth and heresy. The diabolic is simply a reference to that which is outside: where the emblem (*emballô*) throws within, the Devil (*diabolos*) throws out; the Devil is all that has been discarded, exiled, jettisoned. It is, in political terms, the point of no return and simultaneously the realm of unbelief, beyond belief. It is a question both of territory and of belief:

> [I]t is sufficient to return to the etymology to provide an idea of the [diabolical]. From the Greek *diabolikos* . . . it is a question of this: of getting away with it, of throwing into the distance, of passing to the other

1 See B. Rotman, *Signifying Nothing, The Semiotics of Zero* (1987, London).

side. Reduced to its metaphorical constituent, the allusion to diabolical action places fascination on the side of madness, there where the symbolic finds its efficiency, its function being to dismiss and to relieve. Someone who passes to the other side, over the humanised space of legalised speech and signs, such a person is mad. To fascinate, such is the function of power at the level of social insanity.[1]

Because we see ourselves in the screen, it holds us, fascinated, entranced, frozen into immobility in the very same moment that we endlessly orbit the points of the globe.

The metaphor of a diabolical outside helps to locate the key element of that which keeps us within. It is belief that holds the satellite in orbit and on course. It cannot be knowledge because it is precisely an external point that holds the system up; it is zero that inaugurates counting and projection that constitutes and coheres the map. The spatial reality of the social orbit is a reality only for those within the frame and of the territory; it is the life that has already been invaded that belongs to the system. The annexed module clings to the points of the map or passes over the screen as if it were real because to believe otherwise would be to face up to the dissolution of art, its emergence as a pure market, a space of tokens. That the space of reason is blank simply serves to remind us that it is no more than a function, a structural principle of simulation to which can be added any number of relations, a white screen awaiting the contingent projections of ultramodernist rationality, its publicity, its advertisements, its Hollywood cinema, its journalism of the self. Sparse to the limit, the figure has to be approached in terms of perspective, in terms of a geometric surface, a configuration of relations, a pointless control, a meaningless algebra. The figure itself reflects the frame of the viewer; it returns the language, the stare, of its fascinated victims. It is too harsh to be taken seriously, too vacant to be dissimulated. It represents no more than the internal spacing of its components. It simulates *eros* in the form of *thanatos*, life in the mask of death. It acts out structurally the absence of escape and poses the essential question as a nihilistic one, that of how to experience, how to live or act out, the illusion of a work without parameters, memorials or extension.

Controlled orbit thus expresses a horror. The chairs orbit a blank canvas, a spectre, a network. Each space is located by reference to a whiteness, a quality that offers nothing, a simple screen – imageless,

1   P. Legendre, *L'Empire de la vérité* (1984), pp. 112–13.

wordless, codeless to the believing eye. At the same time, each individualised space is immediately and uncompromisingly connected to each other space; it shares with each other not simply relationality but also fixity or fascination, the complete lack of substance as will, the emptiness of relation, the blankness of space, bearing no relation to any reality whatsoever. The points of contact, the relations of orbit, the satellite spaces are no more than their own pure reflection, pure sign, zero sum, simulacrum. The skies fill with junk, exhaustion:

> End of the perspective space of the social. The rational sociality of the contract, dialectical sociality (that of the state and civil Society, of public and private, of the social and the individual), gives way to the sociality of contact, of the circuit and transistorised network of millions of molecules and particles maintained in a random gravitational field, magnetised by constant circulation and the thousands of tactical combinations which electrify them. But is it still a question of the *socius*? Where is sociality in Los Angeles?[1]

It is, in short, an imaginary sociality, not *societas* but *militaris* communicating through ceremonies, diplomacy and the various other protocols of death. It is New York on the line, Legal and General speaking, Union Carbide here, Bhopal there; exorbitant fictions, exorbitant disasters from Exxon to Alaska, from Boeing to British Midland; it is a territory of the mind that is occupied, for the Church, the Company, has no territory: *ecclesia non habet territorium*. We occupy a swamp, a realm that undermines collectivity and dissipates space: it is a matter of filling, of containing empty space, of imagining that we live in Malmö, in Cayman, in Georgia. Across the global boundaries of the social, the problem is not one of collectivity but of fragmentation brought about by an actuarially based demography, the militarisation of economy in which the Company plays an historical role as a unit of the military machine. The Company is precisely a subdivision of a battalion, part of the economy of the war machine, of a strategy of global annexation across all boundaries. It is interesting in that respect that the F-16 fighter plane is built unstable and has to be stabilised in normal flying conditions by labyrinthine computer calculations which alone hold it together to the sole end that when it manoeuvres in battle it is already partly disintegrated and so can operate without structural restraint.

1   J. Baudrillard, . . . *Or the End of the Social* (1983), p. 83.

Finally, it is the absolutism of a direct relation between module and system, between unit and exchange, satellite and orbital control, that figure 9.4 depicts. The tyranny of the ultramodern is simply its directness, its efficiency; it leaves no room for interpretation, no room for the dual discourse of conscious and unconscious; it is a self-equilibrated system which abolishes all excess of meaning, leaving only the message remorselessly relayed through the various exchanges of ultramodern rationality. That the President speaks as my President, that the Corporation personalises its message, obscures the purely logical function of place by presenting in its stead a fictively compassionate individuality, a confidence trick which hides the fact that far from being a personal discourse this is the voice of universal functions that have precisely transposed the individual into the cellular universality of modular orbit:

> Where it is a question of the systematic personalisation of commercial messages, two discourses are confounded that have nothing in common . . . this practice, which summons the subject of speech in the name of a benevolent love, smashes the subject, refusing it all space of speech and constitutes the beginning of a massive fraud. To leave the governed masses to understand that power is something other than a logical function, to be treated as such, to be invested and reinvested endlessly through the brutal game of political and diplomatic protocols, is simply to modernise the most radical methods of slavery.[1]

The tyranny of the network abolishes both interpretation and enigma; its reality is of a systemic logic, a total control that is free of interference, free of all but the most trivial images of personalisation. Looked at long and hard, it is white space, a terrifying territorial control, blank but secure: a deathbound subjectivity.[2]

Figure 9.5: The Parrot and the Snake

One of the oldest of military tactics and of strategies of military architecture takes the form of circles, towers or fortified hills. The unit forms into a ring and that way can see and defend itself from all sides in the most economic of manners. The oldest tactic of social discourse is that of repetition, another circularity in that the completed

---

1   P. Legendre, *Paroles poétiques echapées du texte* (1982), p. 234.
2   A. Lingis, *Deathbound Subjectivity* (1989, Indiana).

statement returns us to a variant of the original: the solemnised discourse of power classically takes the form of ritual speech that plays the role of law by inaugurating a discursive space within which the ever present and self-present time of myth can repeat itself in the form of an authoritative word. Figure 9.5 juxtaposes repetition with desire in an image that is open to both positive and negative, optimistic and pessimistic, interpretations. An empty cage, a black cloth, an open door and a serpentine repetition of an image of desire together make up a sculpture that represents both the imprisonment of the carnal, of eros, of the will, and its potential escape, the route out by means of the images of desire.

The elements of this relatively simple juxtaposition can be depicted rapidly. At the centre is a white circle on which stands a parrot cage half covered with a black cloth. The parrot, the symbol of repetition *par excellence*, has escaped the cage; the bird has flown and the viewer is left to speculate upon a deserted space, a site of repetition that is empty, as though the conjurer had drawn back the cloth to reveal a magical disappearance: look, no bird. It might equally be the hangman's cloth, or the black cloth of execution put on by the judge to announce the sentence of death, but the prisoner has escaped: after a lifetime of repetition the parrot has flown. The death sentence hangs in the air; it would be best, therefore, not to return to the cage, to the site of imprisonment, but rather to stay outside. The outside, encircling the cage in the form of a snake, is the image of the serpent, of illicit knowledge and proliferating and repeated desire. The snake alone in the image has colour and it curls away and points beyond. From the nowhere of identity we may escape to an outside of desire; from a repetition that repeats our servitude we may move to a repetition of desire that emphasises the possibility and, indeed, the availability of the outside. Through desire the identical may leave the garden, the frame, and learn to speak for itself.

The black cloth may also represent a veil that has been removed, a screen drawn back. In a more pessimistic terminology, it may be interpreted as revealing a realm of the departed and simultaneously a dual structure of repetition, an initiation into the tyranny of political love. The principle of repetition reveals itself as a sign of death; the mask, the *sanctum sanctorum*, is empty – it is simply an abandoned place and no more. If the place is both internally and externally subject to relentless repetition, we might well conclude that the secret unveiled is one of equivalence: both inside and outside the same law prevails.

Fig. 9.5

Repetition would here signal that the escape was imaginary: the geometry of social space is one which maps and freezes motion; there is in reality no means of escape other than escape into the same. Here we are forced to concede that the only escape is one that takes us into the ghostly realm of the cerebellum, the last surviving relic of personal space. Space, now mapped, has run out by dint of the dual principles of proliferation and internalisation. In terms of proliferation, the cage indicates a spatial arrangement that ends where it begins, a vicious order encompassing and enclosing the external and symbolising a similar ordering of the internal. The purely circular figures of imprisoned space invoke a controlled geometry; the principle of repetition suggests an echolalia of social space redolent not so much of passage or lineage as of forced repetitions of movement and action, a spatial akinesia in which each new, frozen space exhibits all the symptoms and horror of being identical with those that have passed. As in Figure 9.4, space runs out by virtue of redundancy; its total encroachment, its encyclopedic destructiveness, simply works to organise and divide, cohere and separate, according to laws of distribution, of regions and zones that are interchangeable, replicable, familiar, identical. The terroristic incursion of the same, the all-devouring silence of the surface, indicates not that time has run its course but that there is nowhere left to go. Open the cage by all means because all that is left in the mapped space of the social is a movement which moves not and a going which goes not; these are the mementoes of ultramodernity which can initially be experienced only as a terror of the surface, of the abyss of the same. This is catatonia; the perception of receding space has imploded the possibility of action.

Figure 9.6: The Contract

The show ends with the most dramatic and ironic image of all: the contract. Rousseau, the author of the contract, has died. An admirer, a private citizen, builds a park outside Paris to house Rousseau's tomb on an island in an artificial lake. The tomb will memorise the author of the social contract as a hero of the People, as the author of the first modernist contract, a consensual and democratic agreement between equals or, in legal terms, a considered and so wholly fictive bilateral deed. Later the state comes to recognise Rousseau, both as hero and as threat, and his body is removed from the tomb and taken to the Pantheon in central Paris: the state appropriates the contract and symbolically removes the body, the text, from the periphery to the centre, from the private domain to that of the law. The tomb no longer contains Rousseau's body, only the memorial remains in a park that has become a campsite and is now bordered by two motorways. In the ecstasy of ultramodern communication, we no longer need reminders of death, there are no fixed points, there is no meaningful history, no one looks at the tomb or remembers the dead. That sort of history would slow down the network, obstruct the arterial circulation, delay the communication. And if we wished to honour the dead, to look at the tomb, the vestige of presence, the monumental trace, then it is as well to be reminded that even in death Rousseau is absent a second time in that the tomb lacks even the presence, the trace of that absence. In death he has been moved outside the contract; he is no longer there, no longer held to his word or bound to the agreement. The contract, like its author, has been moved, renegotiated, interpreted to death or, in more legalistic terms, has come to law; it has been intercepted, supplemented, perhaps even stopped in the post before it arrived – a contract contracted, withdrawn or pulled out.

The theme is a topical one in that we currently celebrate the bicentennial of the French Revolution. Two hundred years on and the revolution has come full circle, it has revolved, we are back where we were and forced in the dawning of ultramodernity to question again the sociality of the contract. The circle within which the tomb is contained may here be taken to imply a cycle, a coming around again of the question of the social, the question of the contract and of that to which or by which we are contracted. As with any contract, we can offer an interpretation only in the light of the varying contexts in which the contract is produced. In the present context, the contract is emblematic; we are offered a painting depicting a memorial caged in on an island, a circle or utopia,[1] a slightly unreal tomb surrounded by unnatural natural bars – trees – and further surrounded by a gap and then by neo-classical columns. We may begin the interpretation by examining the representation of the contract, a question of perspective that is posed in the juxtaposition of classical and contemporary, origin and image.[2]

Returning to the contract is initially to recollect that at the time of writing, or within the tradition of its writing, the contract is a symbol and as such, as a sign of permanence and of writing, it is the form of the contract and not its content that requires consideration. The contract is a deed or obligation, a formal act or legal bond (*iuris vinculum*), an instrument that will bring speech to writing and so send it on. The structure of the contract is that of writing itself; writing and law are identical in the form of *ratio* or *lex scripta*. The text issues from the mouth of its author (*Deo auctore*), and as written body, as *corpus* or oeuvre, as cold and dead prose, it will remain indefinitely as a vestige or relic, a mark or trace of an original act. The term contract itself implies an identical point: the contract – *con-traho* – draws together, but it is also, in the past tense, an instrument of will since *con-tractus* literally means contracted, with a treatise or tract, with a trace or symbol – I pass on my will, and will delay my death indefinitely. The treatise or tract is the sign that survives death and will stand for its sender long after his or her demise. What is written is thus vestigial; it marks times and reminds us equally that death cannot be objective, it cannot be final, it will always leave traces or marks of disappearance.

The content of the contract replicates its form. Contractual words must also survive death; they must trace indefinitely the original bond of reference, the legality of the sign. The death of the subject and the death of meaning are both to be counteracted by the contract, by the

1 An interesting discussion of the spatiality of utopia can be found in L. Marin, *Utopics: Spatial Play* (1984, New Jersey), chs. 10, 13.

2 See particularly A. Carty (ed.), *Postmodern Law* (1990, Edinburgh), on the essentially cyclical character of revolution. On the theme of the return of the premodern in the postmodern, see U. Eco, *Travels in Hyperreality* (1987, London), ch. 2.

Fig. 9.6

true word or, in the terms of Roman law, by our faith in instruments (*de fide instrumentorum*). If we move to the terms of the social contract itself, it too transpires to be an act of faith, an ambivalent trace which attempts to bring the People before the Law and lead them to speak. In the Rousseauite tradition contracts are to be served, they enslave (*pacta sunt servanda*), and it is well to remember this process of enslavement when it comes to the question of who the People are in relation to the word of the law. The social contract is far from being the democratic document that it first appeared to be: it places on record an agreement that never took place, it memorialises the dead for something that they did not do, it invokes not the people but rather the People as fictively represented in the mouth of the Father or the word of God: 'The legislator therefore, being unable to appeal to either force or reason, must have recourse to an authority of a different order, capable of constraining without violence, and persuading without convincing . . . This is what has, in all ages, compelled the fathers of nations to have recourse to divine intervention and to credit the gods with their own wisdom.' The contract is put in the mouth of the People, it is imposed, it is placed upon them by the fathers because 'it is not anybody who can make the gods speak'.[1] The trace or contractual writing is a memory of the absolute Other; it is fiction as truth and truth as law, a trace defying death in the cold prose of the instrument. The contract is before the law, it constitutes the People, but we must accept that in the context of this perfect circularity of argument the People do not exist, their unity and power is simply a vestige of the divine will, of the first and last testament.

Returning to Figure 9.6, the contract may be posed as a site of self-reference, a communication on terms of its own which Rousseau depicted as a metaphysical unity: it was always everything that it should be, it is *logos* or incarnate word, a People present to itself and so non-existent save as traces of an immaculate idea, as ghosts haunted by a contract, spectres of something already written and chewed over many times. The island on which the tomb is housed is thus appropriately a utopia, a fiction or non-place; the eternally present destination of the contract is the myth of law, an island where we are made whole by becoming the People, servants of the state. Recalling the curious legal rule that a contract is formed the moment that the letter of acceptance is placed in the hands of the post, Figure 9.6 is

1   Rousseau, *The Social Contract* (1913 edn), pp. 37–8.

accompanied by a repetitive playing of the last post: the military signal that accompanies the end of the day and the burying of the dead. Here the contract is 'put out', it is a contract of assassination, it convenes the People as a representation and as an instrument; the People are only the People when quiescent, when they serve the contract as living tools, when they die before the letter of the law.

But Rousseau is not there. Rousseau has slipped away. Jean-Jacques is no longer around; even his tomb is empty. For a postmodern reading, the contract is always subject to the possibility that it will be intercepted, that it will not arrive at its destination. The absence of Rousseau's remains from their final resting place suggests a further irony and another possibility. At one level the contract is a confession and once a will is confessed it is exculpated, made free. In contractual terms, the artist has depicted Rousseau as 'moon-lighting': for the postmodern Rousseau the contract was a sin confessed, a penance whose dues have now been paid. Far from remaining in the frame or staying within the contract, Rousseau has found alternative employment: that Rousseau is moonlighting means that he is now working off the record, both erasing the contract and working on the outside, in the black economy, outwith the law. In the imagery of the postmodern, working off the record suggests erasure of the tape, free play in a world made strange, a glimpse of knowledge on the outside.

BIBLIOGRAPHY

Alciatus, A. (1530), *De Verborum Significatione*, Luguduni, Gryphius.

— (1550), *Emblemata*, Lug., M. Bonhomme.

— (1651 edn), *De Notitia Dignitatem*, Paris, Cramoisy.

Amboise, A. (1620), *Discours ou traicte des devises où est mise la raison et difference des emblemes, ensignes, sentences et autres*, Paris, Boutonne.

Anonymous, (1621), *Ignoramus or the English Lawyer* (1736 edn), London.

Aristotle (1895 edn), *Organon* (2 volumes, Owen ed.), London, Bell.

— (1909 edn), *Rhetoric* (Jebb ed.), Cambridge, Cambridge University Press.

— (1972 edn), *On Memory* (Sorabji ed.) London, Duckworth.

Arnaud, A. J. (1980), *Critique de la raison juridique*, Paris, Sirey.

Atkinson, Max and Drew, Paul (1979), *Order in Court*, London, Macmillan.

Attridge, D. et al (eds.) (1987), *Post-Structuralism and History*, Cambridge, Cambridge University Press.

Aston, Margaret (1988), *England's Iconoclasts*, Oxford, Oxford Univerity Press.

Aylmer, Bishop (1559), *An Harborowe for Faithfull and Trewe Subjectes against all the late blowne blaste . . .* , Strasborowe, n.p.

Bacon, Francis (1859 edn), *Works* (Spedding ed.), London, Longman.

Baker, J. H. (1978), *Legal Records and the Historian*, London, RHS.

— (ed.) (1978) *The Reports of John Spelman*, London, Selden Soc.

— (1979), *Manual of Law French*, Avebury.

— (1986), *The Legal Profession and the Common Law*, London, Hambledon.

Bakhtin, Mikhail (1981), *The Dialogic Imagination*, Austin, University of Texas Press.

Baldwin, J. and McConville, M. (1977), *Negotiated Justice*, London, Martin Robertson.

Baldwin, J. (1985), *Pre-Trial Justice*, Oxford, Blackwell.

Barron, Anne (1989), 'Ronald Dworkin and the Postmodern Challenge', 11 *Oxford Literary Review* 33.

Bartolus de Saxoferrato (1358), *Tractatus de Insigniis et Armis* (1475 edn of *Consilia*), Venetiis, n.p.

Bataille, George (1986), *Erotism, Death and Sensuality*, San Francisco, City Lights.

— (1988), *The Accursed Share*, New York, Zone Books.

— (1989), *Theory of Religion*, New York, Zone Books.

Baudrillard, Jean (1976), *L'Echange symbolique et la mort*, Paris, Gallimard.

— (1979), *De la Séduction*, Paris, Editions Galilée.

— (1983), *Simulations*, New York, Semiotexte.

— (1983), *In the Shadow of the Silent Majorities*, New York, Semiotexte.

— (1987), *The Ecstasy of Communication*, New York, Semiotexte.

— (1987), *The Evil Demon of Images*, Sydney, Power Institute.

Bender, J. (1988), *Imagining the Penitentiary*, Chicago, Chicago University Press.

Benjamin, Walter (1979), *One Way Street*, London, NLB.

Bennett, H. (1952), *English Books and Readers, 1475–1557,* Cambridge, Cambridge University Press.

Bennett, W. L. and Feldman, M. S. (1981), *Reconstructing Reality in the Courtroom*, New Brunswick, Rutgers University Press.

Bennington, Geoffrey (1989), 'Deconstruction and the Philosophers (The Very Idea)', 10 *Oxford Literary Review* 73.

Benson, Bob (1984–85), 'The End of Legalese: The Game is Over', XIII *Review of Law and Social Change* 519.

Benveniste, Emile (1964), *Problèmes de linguistique générale*, Paris, Gallimard.

— (1969), *Le Vocabulaire des institutions Indo-Européenes* (2 vols.), Paris, Editions de Minuit.

Berman, Harold (1983), *Law and Revolution*, Cambridge, Harvard University Press.

Bland, D. S. (1957), 'Rhetoric and the Law Student in Sixteenth Century England', 54 *Studies in Philology* 498.

Blomsky, M. (ed.) (1985), *On Signs*, Oxford, Blackwell.

Bordieu, Pierre (1987), *Ce que parler veut dire: L'économie des échanges linguistiques*, Paris, Fayard.

Bossewell, J. (1572), *Workes of Armorie*, London, Totell.

Bossuet, J-B. (1709), *Politique tirée des propres paroles de l'ecriture sainte*, Paris, Cot.

Braudel, F. (1972), *The Mediterranean and the Mediterranean World*, New York, Viking.

Brigham, John (1987), 'Right, Rage and Remedy: Forms of Law in Political Discourse', in *Studies in American Political Development*, New Haven, 306.

Brilioth, Y. (1930), *Eucharistic Faith and Practice: Evangelical and Catholic*, London, Routledge.

Brooks, C. W. (1986), *Pettyfoggers and Vipers of the Commonwealth*, Cambridge, Cambridge University Press.

Buc, Sir George (1612), *The Third Universitie of England* (1615 edn.), London, n.p.

Cain, Maureen (1985), 'The General Practice Lawyer and the Client' in Dingwall, R. and Lewis, P. (eds) (1985), *The Sociology of the Professions*, London, Macmillan.

Cameron, Deborah (1985), *Feminism and Linguistic Theory*, London, Macmillan.

Carey, Walter (1627), *The Present State of England* (1810 edn), Harleian Miscellany, vol. 3.

Carlen, Pat (1976), *Magistrates' Justice*, London, Robertson.

Carlyle, Thomas (1893), *Sartor Resartus*, London.

Carty, Anthony (1986), *The Decay of International Law*, Manchester, Manchester University Press.

— (1989), 'Of Crabs and Constitutions', 2 *International Journal for the Semiotics of Law* 215.

— (ed.) (1990), *Post-Modern Law*, Edinburgh, Edinburgh University Press.

Carzo, Domenico and Jackson, B. S. (eds) (1984), *Semiotics, Law and Social Science*, Liverpool, Liverpool Law Review.

Chartrier, R. (ed.) (1987), *Les Usages de l'imprimerie*, Paris, Fayard.

Chambers and Miller (1986), *Prosecuting Sexual Assault*, Edinburgh, HMSO.

Charrow, R. P. and Charrow, V. R. (1979), 'Making Legal Language Understandable: A Psycholinguistic Study of Jury Instructions', 79 *Columbia Law Review* 1306.

Clanchy, Michael (1979), *From Memory to Written Record*, London, Arnold.

Coing, H. (1970), 'Trois Formes Historiques d'Interpretation en Droit', 48 *Revue d'histoire de droit* 533.

Coke, Sir Edward (1610), *A Book of Entries*, London, Streeter.

— (1611), *The Reports* (1777 edn in 6 volumes), London, Rivington.

— (1629), *The First Part of the Institutes of the Laws of England*, London, More.

— (1648), *Institutes Part III*, London, Flesher.

— (1680), *Magna Charta with short but necessary observations by Lord Chief Justice Coke*, London, Atkins.

— (1681), *The Second Part of the Institutes of the Laws of England*, London, Rawlins.

Corner, J. (ed.) (1986), *Documentary and the Mass Media*, London, Arnold.

Cox, Leonard (1530), *The Arte or Crafte of Rhetoryke* (1899 edn), Chicago, Chicago University Press.

Cowell, John (1605), *The Institutes of the Laws of England, Digested into the*

Method of the Civill or Imperiall Institutions (1651 edn), London, Roycroft.

— (1607), *The Interpreter; Or Booke Containing the Signification of Words*, Cambridge, n.p.

Curtius, E. R. (1953), *European Literature and the Latin Middle Ages*, London, Routledge.

Danet, Brenda (1980), 'Language in the Legal Process', 14 *Law and Society Review* 445.

Dauchy, Pierre (1986), 'Identité individuelle, conception du monde et réseaux d'appartenances', in *La Société civile*, Paris.

Davies, Sir John (1614), *Le Primer Report des Cases and Matters en Ley Resolves and Adjudges in les Courts del Roy en Ireland* (1615 edn.) Dublin, Franckton.

Davis, N. Z. (1975), *Society and Culture in Early Modern Europe*, London, Duckworth.

Day, John (1608), *Law Tricks* (1950 edn), Oxford, Malone Society.

Debray, Regis (1983), *Critique of Political Reason*, London, Verso.

Deely, John (1982), *Introducing Semiotic: Its History and Doctrine*, Bloomington, Indiana University Press.

— (ed.) (1986), *New Frontiers in Semiotics*, Bloomington, Indiana.

Deleuze, Gilles (1969), *Différence et répétition*, Paris, PUF.

— (1969), *Logique du sens*, Paris, Editions de Minuit.

Deleuze, Gilles and Guattari, Felix (1988), *A Thousand Plateaux*, London, Athlone.

Derrida, Jacques (1976), *Of Grammatology*, Baltimore, Johns Hopkins University Press.

— (1978), *Writing and Difference*, London, Routledge.

— (1979), 'Scribble (writing-power)', 58 *Yale French Studies* 116.

— (1981), *Dissemination*, Chicago, Chicago University Press.

— (1981), *Positions*, London, Athlone.

— (1982), *Margins of Philosophy*, Brighton, Harvester.

— (1985), 'Préjugés Devant la Loi' in *La Faculté de juger*, Paris, Editions de Minuit.

— (1987), *The Post Card*, Chicago, Chicago University Press.

— (1988) *Psyché*, Paris, Galilee.

— (1989) *Of Spirit*, Chicago, Chicago University Press.

Desbruslais, Anthony (1982), 'Pre-Trial Disclosure in Magistrates' Courts', 146 *Justice of the Peace* 384.

Doderidge, Sir John (1600), *The English Lawyer* (1631 edn), London, More.

Douzinas, C. and Warrington, R. (1986), 'Domination, Exploitation, and Suffering: Marxism and the Opening of Closed Systems', 4 *American Bar Foundation Research Journal* 801.

— (1987), 'On the Deconstruction of Jurisprudence: Fin(n)is Philosophiae', 14 *Journal of Law and Society* 33.

Douzinas, C., McVeigh, S. and Warrington, R. (1990), *Postmodern Jurisprudence*, London, Routledge.

Duxbury, Neil (1989), 'Exploring Legal Tradition: Psychoanalytic Theory and Roman Law in Modern Continental Jurisprudence', 9 *Legal Studies* 94.

Earle, John (1628), *Micro-Cosmographie* (1630 edn), London, R.B.

Eco, Umberto (1984), *Semiotics and the Philosophy of Language*, New York, Macmillan.

— (1987), *Travels in Hyperreality*, London, Hutchinson.

Eden, K. (1986), *Poetic and Legal Fiction in the Aristotelian Tradition*, New Jersey, Princeton University Press.

Eisenstein, E. (1980), *The Printing Press as an Agent of Change*, Cambridge, Cambridge University Press.

Elyot, Sir Thomas (1531), *The Boke Named the Governour* (1907 edn), London, Dent.

Erasmus, (1549), *The Praise of Folly* (1965 edn of Challoner's translation), Oxford, Blackwell.

— (1922), *Opus Epistolarum*, Oxford, Oxford University Press.

Estienne, H. (1643), *The Art of Making Devises*, London, Holden.

Ewald, François (1986), *L'Etat providence*, Paris, Fayard.

Fairclough, Norman (1989), *Language and Power*, London, Longman.

Fardon, R. (ed.) (1985), *Power and Knowledge*, Edinburgh, Scottish Academic Press.

Fauchet, Claude (1610), *Origine des dignitez et magistrats de France*, Paris, Le Clerc.

— (1610), *Origines des chevaliers, armoires et heraux*, Paris, Le Clerc.

Fawcett et al. (eds) (1984), *Semiotics of Language and Culture* (2 vols), London, Pinter.

Febvre, Lucien and Martin, H-J. (1976), *The Coming of the Book*, London, New Left Books.

Fenner, Dudley (1584), *The Artes of Logike and Rhetorike, plainly set forth in the English tongue, easie to be taught and remembered*, Middleburg.

Ferne, Sir John (1586), *The Blazon of Gentrie*, London, Winder.

Finch, Henry (1613), *Nomotechnia*, London.

— (1627), *Law or a Discourse Thereof in Foure Bookes*, London, Society of Stationers

Fitzpatrick, Peter (1987), 'Racism and the Innocence of Law', 14 *Journal of Law and Society* 119.

Fortescue, Sir John (1470), *De Laudibus Legum Angliae* (1737, Selden edn), London, Gosling.

Foucault, Michel (1970), *The Order of Things*, London, Tavistock.

— (1977), *Language, Memory, Counter-Practice*, Ithaca, Cornell University Press.

— (1977), *Discipline and Punish*, London, Allen Lane.

— (1979), 'On Governmentality', 6 *I & C* 5.

— (1982), *The Archaeology of Knowledge*, New York, Pantheon.

— (1985), *The Use of Pleasure*, New York, Pantheon.

— (1986), 'Of Other Spaces', 16 *Diacritics* 22.

Fox, A. and Guy, J. (1986), *Reassessing the Henrician Age*, Oxford, Blackwell.

Fraunce, Abraham (1585), *The Shepherd's Logike* (1969 edn), Menston.

— (1588) *The Lawiers Logike, exemplifying the praecepts of logike by the practice of the common law*, London, How.

— (1588) *Insignium Armorum, Emblematum, Hieroglyphicum et Symbolorum*, London, Orvinus.

— (1588) *Arcadian Rhetorike* (1950 edn), Oxford, Blackwell.

— (1591), *The Countesse of Pembroke's Yuchurch*, London.

Freud, Sigmund (1939), *Totem and Taboo*, Harmondsworth, Penguin.

Fuchs, C. (1982), *La Paraphrase*, Paris, PUF.

Fulbecke, William (1599), *Direction or Preparative to the Study of Law; wherein it is shewed what things ought to be observed and used of them that are addicted to the study of law*, London, Clarke.

— (1602), *A Parallele or Conference of the Civil Law, the Canon Law, and the Common Law of this Realme of England* (1618 edn, 2 vols.), London, Society of Stationers.

— (1602), *The Pandects of the Law of Nations*, London, Wright.

Gadamer, H-G. (1988), *Truth and Method*, New York, Crossroad.

Galbraith, David (1988), 'A Genealogy of Law' (unpublished Ph.D. thesis), Edinburgh.

Garapon, Antoine (1984), *L'Ane portant des reliques*, Paris.

— (1988), 'Forme Symbolique et Forme Linguistique du Droit', 2 *Int. Journal for the Semiotics of Law* 161.

Garfinkel, H. (1956), 'Conditions of Successful Degradation Ceremonies', 64 *American Journal of Sociology* 420.

— (1986), *Studies in Ethnomethodology*, Cambridge, Polity Press.

Gauchet, M. (1988), *Le Désenchantement du monde: Une histoire politique de la religion*, Paris, Gallimard.

Gellrich, J. (1985), *The Idea of the Book in the Middle Ages*, Ithaca, Cornell University Press.

Goodrich, P. (1984), 'The Role of Linguistics in Legal Analysis', 46 *Modern Law Review* 523.

— (1986), *Reading the Law*, Oxford, Blackwell.

— (1986), 'Traditions of Interpretation and the Status of the Legal Text', 6 *Legal Studies* 53.

— (1987), *Legal Discourse*, London, Macmillan.

— (1987), 'Literacy and the Languages of Early Common Law', 14 *Journal of Law and Society* 422.

— (1988), 'Simulation and the Semiotics of Law', 2 *Textual Practice* 180.

Goody, Jack (1977), *The Domestication of the Savage Mind*, Cambridge University Press.

— (1986), *The Logic of Writing and the Organization of Society*, Cambridge, Cambridge University Press.

Grabar, A. (1968), *Christian Iconography*, New Jersey, Princeton University Press.

Graff, H. J. (1987), *The Legacies of Literacy*, Bloomington, Indiana University Press.

Graham, H. J. (1954), 'The Rastells and the Printed English Law Book of the Renaissance', 47 *Law Library Journal* 53.

Grassi, E. (1980), *Rhetoric as Philosophy*, Pennsylvania State University Press.

Grayson, C. (1985), 'The Growth of Linguistic National Consciousness in England', in *The Fairest Flower* (1985, Firenze, n.p.).

Guillim, J. (1610), *A Display of Heraldry*, London, Rycroft.

Habermas, J. (1987), *The Philosophical Discourse of Modernity*, Boston, MIT.

Hachamovitch, Yifat (1990), 'From the Tooth to the Triangle: A Semiotics of Moveable Bodies', in Kevelson (ed.), *Law and Semiotics III*, New York, Plenum Press.

Hakeworth, W. (1720), *A Collection of Curious Discourses*, Oxford.

Hale, Sir Matthew (1787 edn), 'Considerations Touching the Amendment or Alteration of Laws', in F. Hargrave (ed.), *A Collection of Law Tracts*, London, Wright.

— (1975 edn), *The History of the Common Law of England* (Gray ed.), Chicago, Chicago University Press.

Hare, Sir John (1642), 'St Edward's Ghost, or Anti-Normanism', 10 *Harleian Miscellany*.

Harris, Sandra (1982), 'Language, Power and Control in Court', 3 *Crosscurrent* 33.

— (1987), 'Defendant Resistance to Power and Control in the Courtroom', in Coleman, H. (ed.), *Working with Languages*, The Hague, Mouton.

Harvey, Gabriel (1577), *Ciceronianus* (1945 edn), Nebraska, University of Nebraska Press.

Hersey, George (1988), *The Lost Meaning of Classical Architecture*, Boston, MIT.

Hillier, B. and Hanson, J. (1984), *The Social Logic of Space*, Cambridge, Cambridge University Press.

Hobbes, Thomas (1651), *Leviathan* (1972 edn), Harmondsworth, Penguin.

Hooker, Richard (1593–97), *Of the Laws of Ecclesiastical Polity*, (1969 edn.), Cambridge, Cambridge University Press.

Hotman, F. (1567), *Anti-Tribonian ou discours d'un grand et renommé iurisconsulte de nostre temps sur l'estude des loix*, Paris, Perrier.

Howell, W. S. (1956), *Logic and Rhetoric in England, 1500–1700*, New Jersey, Princeton University Press.

Hunt, Alan (1986), 'Jurisprudence, Philosophy of Legal Education: A Response to Neil MacCormick', 6 *Legal Studies* 292.

— (1987), 'The Critique of Law', 14 *J'nl of Law and Society* 5.

Jackson, B. S. (1985), *Semiotics and Legal Theory*, London, Routledge.

— (1989), *Law, Fact and Narrative Coherence*, Merseyside, D. Charles.

Jewell, John (1548), *Oratorio Contra Rhetoricem* (1928 edn), xiv *Quarterly Journal of Speech* 374.

Jones, E. J. (1943), *Medieval Heraldry*, Cardiff, Laws.

Kantorowicz, Ernst (1946), *Laudes Regiae*, Berkeley, California University Press.

— (1957), *The King's Two Bodies*, New Jersey, Princeton University Press.

— (1965), *Selected Studies*, New York, Augustin.

Kelman, Mark (1987), *A Guide to Critical Legal Studies*, Cambridge, Harvard University Press.

Kelly, D. R. (1979), 'Gaius Noster: Substructures of Western Social Thought', 84 *American History Review* 619.

— (1981), *The Beginning of Ideology*, Cambridge, Cambridge University Press.

— (1987), 'Horizons of Intellectual History', xlviii *Journal of the History of Ideas* 143.

Kennedy, G. A. (1980), *Classical Rhetoric and its Christian and Secular Sources*, London, Croom Helm.

Kevelson, Roberta (1988), *Law as a System of Signs*, New York, Plenum Press.

— (ed.) (1988–90), *Law and Semiotics* (3 volumes), New York, Plenum.

Kisteva, Julia (1987), *Le Soleil noir*, Paris, Gallimard.

Kristeller, P. O. (1979), *Renaissance Thought and its Sources*, New York, M. Mooney.

Lacan, Jacques (1977), *Ecrits*, London, Tavistock.

— (1978), *The Four Fundamental Concepts of Psychoanalysis*, London, Pelican.

Legendre, Pierre (1964), *La Pénétration du droit Romain dans le droit canonique classique*, Paris, Imprimerie Jouve.

— (1968), *Histoire de L'administration de 1750 à nos jours*, Paris, PUF.

— (1974), *L'Amour du censeur: Essai sur l'ordre dogmatique*, Paris, Seuil.

— (1976), *Jouir du pouvoir: Traité de la bureaucratie patriote*, Paris, Editions de Minuit.

— (1978), *La Passion d'être un autre: Etude pour la danse*, Paris, Seuil.

— (1982), *Paroles poétiques échappées du texte*, Paris, Seuil.

— (1983), *L'Empire de la vérité: Introduction aux espaces dogmatiques industriels*, Paris, Fayard.

— (1985), *L'Inestimable Objet de la transmission: Etude sur le principe généalogique en occident*, Paris, Fayard.

— (1988), *Ecrits juridiques du Moyen Age occidental*, London, Variorum.

— (1989), *Le désir politique de dieu: Etude sur les montages de l'etat et du droit*, Paris, Fayard.

— (1989), *Le Crime du Caporal Lortie: Traité sur le père*, Paris, Fayard.

— (1990) 'The Lost Temporality of Law', 1 *Law and Critique* 13.

Legh, G. (1562), *Accedens of Armory*, London, Totill.

Le Goff, Jacques (ed.) (1988), *La Nouvelle Histoire*, Paris, Editions Complexe.

— (1988), *Histoire et Memoire*, Paris, Gallimard.

Lenoble, J. and Ost, F. (1981), *Droit, mythe et raison*, Bruxelles, Presse Universitaire de Saint Louis.

Levack, Brian (1973), *The Civil Lawyers in England, 1603–41*, Oxford, Oxford University Press.

Lever, Ralph (1573), *The Arte of Reason, Rightly termed Witcraft, Teaching a Perfect way to Argue and Dispute*, London, Brynnemann.

Levi-Strauss, Claude (1963), *Structural Anthropology*, London.

Levinson, S. and Mailloux, S. (1988), *Law and Literature*, Evanston, Northwestern University Press.

Leyh, Greg (ed.) (1990), *Legal Hermeneutics: History, Theory, Law*, New Jersey, Princeton University Press.

Lingis, Alphonso (1983), *Excesses, Eros and Culture*, New York, SUNY Press.

— (1989) *Deathbound Subjectivity*, Bloomington, Indiana University Press.

Little, D. (1970), *Religion, Order and Law*, Oxford, Blackwell.

Logan, John (1677), *Analogia Honorum or a Treatise on Honour and Nobility according to the Laws and Customs of England*, London, Roycroft.

Lubac, H. de (1949), *'Corpus Mysticum': L'Eucharistie et L'Eglise au Moyen Age*, Paris.

Lyotard, J-F. (1988), *Le Postmoderne Expliqué aux enfants*, Paris, Galilee.

— (1989), *L'Inhumain*, Paris, Galilee.

MacCormick, Neil (1985), 'The Democratic Intellect and Law', 5 *Legal Studies* 172.

Maitland, F. W. (1901), *The Renaissance and English Law*, Cambridge, Cambridge University Press.

Marin, Louis (1984), *Utopics: Spatial Play*, (1984), New Jersey, Humanities Press.

— (1986), *La Parole mangée et autres essais theologico-politiques*, Paris, Meridiens Klinckseick.

— (1988), *Portrait of the King*, London, Macmillan.

Martin, H-J. (1989), *Histoire et pouvoirs de l'ecrit*, Paris, Perrin.

Martines, L. (1979), *Power and Imagination*, London, Allen Lane.

Mathieson, T. (1980), *Law, Society and Political Action*, London, Academic Press.

McBarnet, D. (1982), *Conviction*, London, Macmillan.

Mellinkoff, D. (1983), *The Language of the Law*, Boston, Little Brown.

Miller, J-A. (1987), 'Jeremy Bentham's Panoptic Device', *October* 3.

Milsom, S. F., (1981), *Historical Foundations of the Common Law*, London, Butterworth.

Moles, Robert (1987), *Definition and Rule in Legal Theory*, Oxford, Blackwell.

More, Sir Thomas (1533), *The Apologye of Sir Thomas More Knyght*, London, Rastell.

— (1533), *The Debellacyon of Salem and Bizance*, London, W. Rastell.

— (1973 edn), *Complete Works*, New Haven, Yale University Press.

Morley, D. (1980), *The Nationwide Audience*, London, BFI.

Mueller-Vollmer, K. M. (ed.) (1986), *The Hermeneutics Reader*, Oxford, Blackwell.

Mulcaster, Richard (1582), *The First Part of the Elementary* (1970 edn), Menston.

Munday, Anthony (1593), *The Defence of Contraries*, London, Winder.

Murphy, J-J. (1974), *Rhetoric in the Middle Ages*, Berkeley, California University Press.

— (1978), *Medieval Eloquence*, Berkeley, California University Press.

— (1983), *Renaissance Eloquence*, Berkeley, California University Press.

Murphy, Tim (1987), 'Memorising Politics of Ancient History', 50 *Modern Law Review* 384.

Murphy, Tim and Roberts, Simon (1987), 'Introduction', 50 *Modern Law Review* 677.

Nairn, Tom (1988), *The Enchanted Glass*, London, Radius.

Nietzsche, Friedrich (1905), *The Birth of Tragedy*, Edinburgh, Foulis.

— (1909), *The Future of our Educational Institutions*, Edinburgh, Foulis.

— (1909), *The Will to Power* (2 volumes), Edinburgh, Foulis.

— (1910), *The Joyful Wisdom*, Edinburgh, Foulis.

— (1910), *Genealogy of Morals*, Edinburgh, Foulis.

— (1911), *The Case of Wagner*, Edinburgh, Foulis.

— (1915), *Twilight of the Idols*, Edinburgh, Foulis.

— (1923), *Beyond Good and Evil*, Edinburgh, Foulis.

Nisbet, Alexander (1972), *A System of Heraldry speculative and practical*, Edinburgh, MackEvan.

North, Roger (1650), *A Discourse on the Study of the Laws* (1824 edn), London, White.

O'Barr, William (1982), *Linguistic Evidence*, New York, Academic Press.

Ong, Walter (1958), *Ramus, Method and the Decay of Dialogue*, Cambridge, Harvard University Press.

— (1982), *Orality and Literacy*, London, Methuen.

Pattison, R. (1982), *On Literacy*, New York, Oxford University Press.

Pawlisch, H. (1985), *Sir John Davies and the Conquest of Ireland*, Cambridge, Cambridge University Press.

Peacham, Henry (1593), *The Garden of Eloquence conteining the most excellent ornaments, exornations, flowers and forms of speech commonly called the figures of rhetorike*, London, Jackson.

Pecheux, Michel (1982), *Language, Semantics and Ideology*, London, Macmillan.

Phillips, W. (1667), *Studii Legalis Ratio or Directions for the Study of Law*, London, Kirkman.

Plissart, M. and Derrida Jacques (1985), *Droits de regards*, Paris, Gallimard. (Partially translated as 'Right of Inspection' (1989) 32 *Art and Text* 20.)

Pocock, J. G. A. (1987), *The Ancient Constitution and the Feudal Law*, Cambridge, Cambridge University Press.

Post, Gaines (1964), *Studies in Medieval Legal Thought*, New Jersey, Princeton University Press.

Powell, Thomas (1610), *The Attourney's Academy*, London, Fisher.

Preziosi, Donald (1979), *The Semiotics of the Built Environment*, Bloomington, Indian University Press.

Prest, W. (1977), 'The Dialectical Origins of Finch's Laws', 36 *Cambridge Law Journal*, 326.

— (1986), *The Rise of the Barristers: A Social History of the English Bar 1590–1640*, Oxford, Oxford University Press.

Puttenham, George (1589), *The Arte of English Poesie*, London, Field.

Pynchon, Thomas (1967), *The Crying of Lot 49*, Harmondsworth, Penguin.

Rainholde, Richard (1563), *A Booke called the Foundacion of Rhetorike because all other parts are founded thereupon* (1945 edn), New York, Scholars' Facsimiles.

Ramus, Petrus (1574), *The Logike*, London, Vautroullier.

Rastall, William (1566), *A Collection in English of the Statutes now in Force* (1615 edn), London, Society of Stationers.

— (1566), *A Collection of Entrees. Of Declarations, Barres, Replications, Rejoinders, Issues, Verdicts, Judgements, Executions, Process, Continuances, Essoines, divers other Matters* (1574 edn), London, Totell.

Rastell, John (1566), *The Exposicions of the Terms of the Laws of England*, London, Totell.

Richardson, K. and Corner, J. (1986), 'Reading Reception', 8 *Media, Culture, Society* 458.

Ridley, Sir Thomas (1607), *A View of the Civille and Ecclesiasticall Law* (1676 edn), Oxford, Hall.

Robertson (ed.) (1956), *Anglo-Saxon Charters*, London.

Rokosz, Denise (1988), 'Cross-Talk: Pragmatics and Courtroom Questioning' (unpublished Ph.D. thesis, Edinburgh).

Rose, Gillian (1984), *Dialectic of Nihilism: Post-Structuralism and Law*, Oxford, Blackwell.

— (1988), 'Architecture to Philosophy – the Postmodern Complicity', 5 *Theory, Culture, Society* 357.

Rotman, Brian (1987), *Signifying Nothing, The Semiotics of Zero*, London, Macmillan.

Rousseau, Jean-Jacques (1970 edn), *Essai sur l'origine des langues*, Paris, Nizet.

— (1977 edn), *Du Contrat Social*, Paris.

St German, Christopher (1528), *Doctor and Student* (1974 edn), London, Selden Soc.

— (1533), *Salem and Bizance*, London, Bertheleti.

— (1534), *A Treatise Concerning the Division between the Spirituality and Temporality*, London, Redman.

Sartre, J-P. (1976), *Critique of Dialectical Reason I, Theory of Practical Ensembles*, London, NLB.

Schememman, A. (1985), *L'Eucharistie*, Paris, OEIL.

Schoeck, R. (1953), 'Rhetoric and Law in Sixteenth Century England', 50 *Studies in Philology* 120.

— (1954), 'The Elizabethan Society of Antiquaries and Men of Law', 1 *Notes and Queries* 417.

— (1962), 'The Libraries of Common Lawyers in Renaissance England', 6 *Manuscripta* 155.

Segoing, Charles (1652), *Trésor heraldique ou mercure armoire où sont demonstrées toutes les choses necessaires pour acquerir une parfaite conoissance de l'art de blazonnes* (1657 edn), Paris, Clouzier.

Shell, Marc (1982), *Money, Language and Thought*, Berkeley, California University Press.

Sherry, Richard (1550), *A Treatise of Schemes and Tropes very profytable for the better understanding of good authors, gathered out of the best Grammarians and Orators*, London, Day.

Simmonds, Nigel (1984), *The Decline of Juridical Reason*, Manchester, Manchester University Press.

Simon, Jonathan (1988), 'The Ideological Effects of Actuarial Practices', *Law and Society Review* 111.

Simpson, A. W. B. (ed.) (1984), *A Biographical Dictionary of the Common Law*, London, Butterworth.

Singer, T. C. (1989), 'Hieroglyphs, Real Characters, and the Idea of Natural Language in English Seventeenth Century Thought', *Journal of the History of Ideas* 89.

Skinner, Quentin (1979), *The Foundations of Modern Political Thought* (2 volumes), Cambridge, Cambridge University Press.

Sloterdijk, Peter (1987), *Critique of Cynical Reason*, Minneapolis, Minnesota University Press.

Smith, Sir Thomas (1583), *De Republica Anglorum* (1906 edn), Cambridge, Cambridge University Press.

Sourioux, J-L. and Lerat, P. (1975), *Le Langage du Droit*, Paris, PUF.

Spelman, Sir Henry (1614), *Of the Four Law Terms: A Discourse* (1684 edn), London, Gillyflower.

— (1654), *Aspilogia*, London, Martin and Allestry.

Spelman, John (1978, ed. J. H. Baker), *Reports* (2 volumes), London, Selden Soc.

Starkey (ed.), (1535/1945 edn), *A Dialogue between Reginald Pole and Thomas Lupset*, London, Chatto and Windus.

Stein, Peter (1966), *Regulae Iuris*, Edinburgh, Edinburgh University Press.

Steinberg, S. H. (1961), *Five Hundred Years of Printing*, Bristol.

Stewart, Iain (1987), 'Law and Closure', 50 *Modern Law Review* 908.

Stock, Brian (1983), *The Implications of Literacy*, New Jersey, Princeton University Press.

Stow, J. (1615), *The Annales or General Chronicle of England*, London, Society of Stationers.

Strauss, G. (1986), *Law, Resistance and the State*, New Jersey, Princeton University Press.

Sydney, Sir Philip (1595), *A Defence of Poesy* (1987 edn), Manchester, Manchester University Press.

Thomas, J. (1985), 'The Language of Power', 9 *Pragmatics* 765.

Thynne, Francis (1605), *The Office and Duty of Herald* (1679 edn), London, Roycroft.

Tournier, Michel (1987), *Petites Proses*, Paris, Folio.

Troubetzkoi, Eugène (1986), *Trois Études sur L'icône*, Paris, OEIL.

Twining, William (ed.) (1986), *Legal Theory and Common Law*, Oxford, Blackwell.

Tyndale, William (1530), *An Answer unto Thomas Mores Dialogue*, London, n.p.

Ulmer, Gregory (1985), *Applied Grammatology*, Baltimore, Johns Hopkins University Press.

Unger, Roberto (1987), *The Critical Legal Studies Movement*, Cambridge, Harvard University Press.

Upton, Nicolai (1654), *De Studio Militari Libri Quattor*, London, Martin.

Vattimo, Gianni (1988), *La Secularisation de la pensée*, Paris, Seuil.

— (1988), *The End of Modernity*, Cambridge, Polity.

Venturi et al. (1977), *Learning from Las Vegas: The Forgotten Symbolism of the Architectural Form*, Boston, MIT.

Verstegan, Richard (1605), *A Restitution of Decayed Intelligence in Antiquities*, Amsterdam, Bruney.

Vickers, Brian (1988), *In Defence of Rhetoric*, Oxford, Oxford University Press.

Vidler, A. (1987), *The Writing of the Walls*, New Jersey, Princeton University Press.

Virilo, Paul (1980), *L'Esthetique de la disparition*, Paris.

— (1984), *Pure War* (with S. Lotringer), New York, Semiotexte.

— (1986), *Speed and Politics*, New York, Semiotexte.

— (1989), *War and Cinema*, London, Verso.

Wagner, A. R. (1956), *Heralds and Heraldry in the Middle Ages*, Oxford, Oxford University Press.

Warr, John (1649), *The Corruption of the Laws of England, soberly discussed* (1810 edn), London, Harleian Miscellany VI.

Watkin, T. G. (1984), '*Tabula Picta*: Images and Icons', 50 *Studia et Documenta Historiae et Iuris* 383.

Watson, Alan (1984), *Sources of Law, Legal Change and Ambiguity*, Philadelphia, Pennsylvania University Press.

West, William (1590), *Symbolaeography, The Art or Description or Image of Instruments, or the Paterne of Presidents or the Notarie or Scrivener* (1603 edn), London, Society of Stationers.

Wilkins, D. (1737), *Consilia Magnae Britanniae et Hiberniae ab anno MCCCL ad annum MDLXLV* (4 Volumes), London.

Wills, D. (1988), 'Supreme Court', 18 *Diacritics* 20.

Wilson, Thomas (1553), *The Arte of Rhetorique* (1982 edn), London, Garland.

— (1553), *The Rule of Reason, conteyning the arte of Logique*, London, n.p.

Wilson, Thomas (1601), *The State of England, Anno Domini 1600* (1610 edn), London, Camden Miscellany.

Yates, F. (1966), *The Art of Memory*, London, Routledge.

Zagorin, P. (ed.) (1980), *Culture and Politics from Puritanism to the Enlightenment*, Berkeley, California University Press.

INDEX